DONNE

POETICAL WORKS

JOHN DONNE

Born, London, 1573
Died, London, 31 March 1631

DONNE

POETICAL WORKS

—

EDITED BY
HERBERT J. C. GRIERSON

Oxford   New York
OXFORD UNIVERSITY PRESS

Oxford University Press, Walton Street, Oxford OX2 6DP

Oxford New York Toronto
Delhi Bombay Calcutta Madras Karachi
Petaling Jaya Singapore Hong Kong Tokyo
Nairobi Dar es Salaam Cape Town
Melbourne Auckland

and associated companies in
Berlin Ibadan

Oxford is a trade mark of Oxford University Press

ISBN 0–19–281113–4

This edition first published 1929 by Oxford University Press
First issued as an Oxford University Press paperback 1971
Reprinted 1977, 1979, 1984, 1985, 1990

Printed and bound in Great Britain by
Biddles Ltd, Guildford and King's Lynn

CONTENTS.

Contents.

LETTERS TO SEVERALL PERSONAGES

AN ANATOMIE OF THE WORLD

Contents.

APPENDIX B.

INTRODUCTION.

Twin brethren dwell within me, twins of strife,
And either fights to free him from the other ;
One grips the earth in savage lust of life,
Clutches the ground and wallows in the mire ;
The other lifts himself and struggles free,
Tearing the chain that binds him to his brother,
Beating the air with wings of vast desire
Toward the far realm of his great ancestry.

GOETHE : *Faust*, ii. 1112–1117.

THE early years of John Donne are invested in the
obscurity common to many authors, for who could
anticipate their greatness ? In Donne's case this obscurity
is intensified firstly by the fact that in his later years he was
not unwilling to cover up his early traces, and secondly by
the difficulty of comprehending contradictions which seem
inherent in all the typical characters of the Renaissance.
'It is above all', says Mr. Lytton Strachey, in a study of
more than one of them, 'the contradictions of the age that
baffle our imagination and perplex our intelligence.
Human beings no doubt would cease to be human beings
unless they were inconsistent ; but the inconsistency of the
Elizabethans exceeds the limits permitted to man. Their
elements fly off from one another wildly . . . wherever we
look it is the same. By what perverse magic were intellectual ingenuity and theological ingenuousness intertwined
in John Donne ? Who has ever explained Bacon ? ' Not
to explain, but rather to make explicit these contradictions
and so to place in clearer perspective the poems composed
in different periods and different moods, but all slumped
together by the first editors, is the object of this preface.

Donne was by birth the member of a very unpopular
minority, looked at askance by the Government of Elizabeth and, since the reign of Mary, by an ever increasing
number of the English people, for as Butler says 'it was
Queen Mary that established the Protestant Religion in

England and not Queen Elizabeth, who could never have
done what she did if her sister's barbarous cruelty had not
prepared the nation to admit of any religion than that
which they saw produced so many horrid inhumanities.'
Donne's family were Catholics, Catholics of the Counter-
Reformation. He came too late to slip into conformity as
many had done before the work of recovering England for
the Church was undertaken by the Jesuits, his own uncle
among them. He was born in 1571 or 1572 the son of
John Donne, a prosperous citizen of London, Warden
in 1574 of the Company of Ironmongers, and of his
wife Elizabeth, daughter of John Heywood the dramatist,
and sister of Jasper Heywood one of the earliest of the
Jesuit missionary priests, but also the granddaughter of
Elizabeth Rastell sister of Sir Thomas More who had
laid down his life for the faith and the spiritual supremacy
of the Pope. Donne's father died in 1576 and the poet and
his brother were educated under private superintendence,
and though the elder matriculated at Oxford in 1584 and
studied there and, it would seem, at Cambridge too, he was
apparently removed before the age at which he would have
been required to subscribe the thirty-nine articles. As late
as 1593, Henry, the younger brother, was imprisoned for
harbouring a priest and died in Newgate. Of the poet's
own life during these early years we know nothing beyond
the fact that he entered at Lincoln's Inn as a law-student
in May 1592, and on coming of age in 1593 entered upon
his full patrimony. Thereafter, as we shall see, his life
comes more into the light.

'I had my first breeding and conversation', he says,
'with men of suppressed and afflicted religion, accustomed
to the despite of death and hungry of an imagined martyrdom.' These early experiences must not be forgotten if we
are to understand Donne's life and work, not particular
incidents and allusions alone, but the inner conflicts of his
tormented soul. Donne was reconciled to the Church of

England and it would be unjust to describe his conversion
as insincere. He was no hypocrite. He never glossed over
his early beliefs or his early irregularities. But if by
' sincere ' more is meant than simply honest; if it implies
a deep conviction of heart and conscience, the discovery
in a new faith of peace and happiness, such happiness as
Crashaw or the Dutch poet Vondel found in reconcilia-
tion with the Catholic Church, then I do not believe
Donne's conversion was sincere, that he ever found his
heart quite at rest, perhaps even his conscience quite
untroubled, in Jacobean Anglicanism. Even as late as 1617
he could write a sonnet which betrays not only some degree
of intellectual scepticism but spiritual unrest:

> Show me, dear Christ, thy spouse so bright and clear

(p. 301). Donne did not show that sonnet to many of his
friends and it was first published from the Westmoreland
manuscript by Sir Edmund Gosse in 1899. It speaks for
itself. Donne would not have become a Protestant in a
Catholic country nor, had circumstances not been too
strong for him, would he have taken orders or become a
controversialist. His nature had not the heroic simplicity
of his great ancestor. His was a poetic temperament,
imaginative, susceptible, impulsive, served by an acute
and subtle intellect, and under the influence of diverse elements in his nature he complied with circumstances more
than once in his life ; but such compliance does not make
for peace of mind.

But it would be a mistake to represent the character and
career of Donne as dominated by the conflict between his
early Catholicism and his later Anglicanism. His nature
was not so simple as that would suggest, nor so devout.
What one seems rather to divine, in attempting to recon-
struct a picture of the young man in these obscure years, is
a reaction on his part against a religious bent imposed by
a devout mother, uncle, and tutors. That would go a long

way to explain the note of extravagance and revolt in his early poems, their exaggerated sensuality, naturalism, and cynicism. The teachers of his youth had endeavoured to impose the temper of the Catholic revival on a mind and temperament that were those of the Italian Renaissance or at least frankly sensuous and daringly witty. And with this may be connected consideration of Donne's sojourn on the continent. It is quite clear that Walton was in error in assigning this journey to so late a date as 1597–8 when we know that Donne was in London and just entering the service of Sir Thomas Egerton. Dr. Jessopp was, to my mind, nearer the truth when he conjectured that Donne, like his college friend Henry Wotton, went abroad after leaving the university and before entering at Lincoln's Inn. Mr. F. P. Wilson's discovery [1] that Donne was born as early as 1571 or the early part of 1572, and not in 1573 as Walton had stated, makes such a journey quite possible. He went to Italy, Walton tells us, intending to proceed to the Holy Land, but disappointed in this hope he turned

[1] See the *Review of English Studies*, vol. iii, no. 11, July 1927. I gather that Mr. Wilson leans to the view that this visit to the continent may have been the first effect of Donne's coming of age and entering on his full paternal inheritance, 19th June 1593. In this case, if one is to give any credence to Walton's statement that there was a residence abroad of 'some years', he would be out of England during the greater part of the years 1593 to 1595. In 1596 he joined the expedition to Cadiz. I find this difficult to reconcile with the impression given by the first three *Satyres* that Donne during the years 1594 and 1595 was in close touch with life in London, as indicated on p. xxv. These, it seems to me, were the years in which he sowed his wild oats and wrote the more audacious of the love poems. To Drummond Ben Jonson 'affirmeth Donne to have written all his best pieces ere he was twenty-five years old.' Donne was twenty-five years old in 1597. It seems to me difficult to push all these experiences and poems into the years 1595 and the early part of 1596; and with the two expeditions Donne's poems begin to show a growing sense of responsibility and ambition. But the subject remains obscure, and my general argument that Donne's more reckless poems are the result of something of a reaction against an early training is not dependent on the earlier date.

aside to Spain. He spent, according to the same authority, some years in the two countries and returned 'perfect in their languages'. In 1623 he tells the Duke of Buckingham that there are more Spanish books, whether of poetry or theology, in his library than of any other language. If, as seems to me possible, Donne was taken abroad with, as the mention of the Holy Land suggests, some idea of his entering the priesthood, then it seems to me that what may have happened is just that at the last he jibbed. He was grown up. The blood was flowing passionately in his veins. He saw perhaps other sides of life in Italy and Spain than that of the Seminaries. He tasted of the sweets of Italian and Spanish poetry. He awoke to the allurements of pleasure and ambition and came home not at all disposed to become a missionary and a martyr as his brother might almost claim to have been, but more of the Inglese Italianato, not a debauchee like Robert Greene nor a defiant sceptic and enemy of Christianity like Marlowe, but a fashionable, brilliant young law-student, avid of pleasure and of worldly advancement, 'not dissolute but very neat: a great visiter of ladies, a great frequenter of plays, a great writer of conceited verses' so Sir Richard Baker recalls him, and another witness adds 'neither was it possible that a vulgar soul should dwell in such promising features'. To this period also belongs the first portrait, the young man holding a sword, eager and intellectual in face rather than beautiful, and his motto already a Spanish one, a lover's motto, 'antes muerto que mudado', 'sooner dead than changed', though in other moods the young man could write :

Change is the nursery
Of music, joy, life and eternity.

Such an early life as I have adumbrated is in harmony with such evidence as we have and with the tenor of the poems of this period, the first three *Satyres* and the more audacious of the *Elegies* and the *Songs and Sonets*, and it

makes them more intelligible and forgivable. The bow
was unbent; the passionate young man was released from
the supervision of too devout guardians, and he had his
fling. Sensual Donne has been called, but it is not quite
the right word. Hot-blooded and passionate he was, with a
passion in which body and soul are sometimes inextricably
blended, again in open conflict, and again conceived in
abstract separation from one another, but sensual in a more
general and deliberate way, without the appeal of passion,
he is not. His poetry has nothing to say of the pleasures of
eating and drinking, like that of his friend Ben Jonson,
and the impression one gathers from poems, records, and
letters is of one indifferent or even ascetic in regard to
such pleasures. Even the most audacious of the _Elegies_,
compared with similar exercises by Carew and others, are
agitated and aerated by a passionate play of wit that makes a
difference, the absence of which, the more frigidly sensuous
tone, marks clearly as _not_ by Donne many poems that
have been attributed to him. It is noteworthy too how little
stress Donne lays on beauty in his love-poems, the aesthetic
element in passion. The feeling for pure beauty was
somewhat defective in his composition. The want of it is
the most definite limitation to the high quality of his poetry.

Not sensual nor sensuous but passionate is the note of the
young Donne and his verse, an intense susceptibility to the
fascination of sex, a fascination that at once allures and
repels, enthralls and awakens a spirit of scornful rebellion.
He ranges through the whole gamut of passion from its
earthliest to its most abstractly detached moods. For there
are different strata in the love poems thrown down together in such confused order by the first editors. At the
one extreme are poems of seduction and illicit love with its
accompaniment of passion and scorn. Such are most of the
Elegies, and in the _Songs and Sonets_ a concentrated out-
burst as _The Apparition_, or so finely woven a web of
thought as _The Extasie_, though the latter, as the poet warms

to his theme, as the wheels of his chariot grow hot with driving, becomes a vindication of the interconnexion and interdependence of soul and body, which was to be a cardinal principle of Donne's religious thought at a later period. One may, if one pleases, descry through these poems a liaison with a married woman, an intrigue with an unmarried girl in *The Perfume*, or one may read them as witty and paradoxical elaborations of general theses suggested by Donne's naturalistic revolt against the insincerities of Petrarchian sonnetteers,—the fickleness of women, his own delight in change, the folly of confining love by rules and relationships, sophisticated justifications of seduction, scorn of women's affected constancy, and of the physical basis of love which no refinements and hyperboles of love-poets can disguise. Some breathe, even if the main theme be the same, a purer and more simply passionate note, the twelfth *Elegy* which seems to tell of a wife passionately loved in secret though over them hung the

> husband's threatening eyes
> That flam'd with the oily sweat of jealousy,

and a large body of the songs as ' I wonder by my troth ', ' For God's sake hold your tongue and let me love ', ' If yet I have not all thy love ', ' Oh do not die', ' Twice or thrice had I loved thee ', 'All kings and all their favourites ', ' I'll tell thee now, dear love, what thou shalt do ', ' Whoever comes to shroud me do not harm ', ' Take heed of loving me ', ' So, so break off this last lamenting kiss '. Some of these may, though I rather doubt it, belong to a later period when Donne was the lover and wooer of Ann More To a later period certainly belongs a small group of songs, and perhaps the sixteenth *Elegy*. The songs are ' Sweetest love, I do not go ', 'As virtuous men pass mildly away ', and *A Valediction : of Weeping*. These were written after his marriage when business of one kind or another called Donne away from his home. They are a beautifully patterned expression of the depth and sweetness of the affection which united the sorely tried couple and contrast strangely with some of the poems with which they stand cheek by jowl.

There remains a group of songs that present somewhat of a problem. They show us Donne in the, rather unusual for him, traditional attitude of the Petrarchian wooer of a fair but obdurate Laura, a lady whom he reproaches, not for fickleness or sensuality or a half-hearted reluctance to yield to love, but for a too impeccable coldness :

> O perverse sex where none is true but shee,
> Who's therefore true because her truth kills mee.

These poems are *Twicknam Garden*, the sombre and powerful *Nocturnall upon St. Lucies Day*, *The Blossome*, *The Primrose*, *The Relique*, and *The Dampe*. None of the *Elegies* is in this key. In them the tone is set, not by Petrarch, but by Ovid.

It would be easier, probably, to accept the explanation which I have already ventured to propound if one might eliminate *The Blossome*, *The Primrose* and *The Dampe*, for in these there is a strain of the more familiar Donne, sardonic and sensual. Apart from these, and perhaps including them, I am disposed to argue that the change of tone in this group of poems represents a difference in the social status of the persons addressed, that he is here, like other poets, adopting the Petrarchian convention to pay compliments to the noble ladies of his acquaintance. The class of women to whom, or on whom, he had composed the *Elegies* and *Songs and Sonets* of a similar kind had been that common object of young lawyers' and courtiers' freer advances and more audacious wit, the wives and daughters of citizens, women of Donne's own rank and station. In the group under consideration, as in the *Letter to the Countesse of Huntingdon* (p. 194), the persons addressed, actual or ideal, more probably the first, are of a higher rank. It may be an accident that the titles of three of them, *Twicknam Garden, A Nocturnall upon St. Lucies Day,* and *The Primrose* suggest a connexion with the Countess of Bedford and Mrs. Magdalen Herbert. The connexion was at least suspected by Donne's contemporaries or by the next generation. 'The Castle of Montgomery', says Aubrey, ' was a most romancy seat. It stands upon a high promontory . . from hence is a most delightful prospect 4 several ways. Southwards without the castle is the Primrose Hill, vid. Donne's Poems, p. 53.' i. e. of the 1635 edition. The title *may* of course have been added by editors familiar only with Donne's later friendships and patronesses. Yet I have a lurking suspicion that *Twicknam Garden* and *St. Lucies Day* were exquisite and passionate compliments to his great lady-patron, Lucy, Countess of Bedford, who occupied Twickenham Park from 1608 to 1617. Nor need even the devout Mrs. Herbert, of whose earlier years we know little, have felt indignant on the receipt of such an impassioned compliment as *The Relique*:

> These miracles we did ; but now alas,
> All measure and all language I should pass,
> Should I tell what a miracle she was.

It is more difficult to imagine her the person addressed in *The Primrose* and *The Dampe.* If a reference to her is ruled out, on the strength of what we know of her from Walton and on general considerations, then these poems may be the product of the years in which Donne began, as a member of Sir Thomas Egerton's household, to move in a more exalted sphere than that which the young law-student had frequented in his more unregenerate days. They are the compliments he paid to ladies like the Countess of Huntingdon and others, charming because passionate compliments with just a touch of more daring suggestion which quite possibly these not too prudish young ladies would not resent. They heard in the theatre and at Court abundance of such frank speech as a later age would not have tolerated. It is after all convention that regulates both the length of a lady's skirt and the kind of compliments one may pay her. Lady Bedford would have been more scandalized at the thought of going through the street in the attire of a Highland regiment than at some freedom of language in a kind of poetry which everyone understood to be purely conventional.

The conflict of moods which the first group of these poems betrays, the war of sense and spirit, the awareness of body and soul as complementary and yet antagonistic, becomes more intelligible against such a background as I have suggested, the revolt against a too strong superimposed bias. Donne's nature had revolted, asserted its claim to life and experience. But experience is bitter as well as sweet— sweet in the mouth but bitter in the belly. Independence humiliates as well as exalts. The emancipated instincts realize their limitations. The spiritual and ascetic impulses reassert their claim when passion has spent itself. Strife and bitterness succeed, finding vent in scornful satire and an exaggeration of sensuality or an equally extravagant and abstract idealism, till the tumult subsides, feeling gathers strength again, and body and soul are merged in the passion of the moment. ' The imagination of a boy is healthy and the mature imagination of a man is healthy; but there is a space of life between in which the soul is in a ferment, the character is undecided, the way of life uncertain, the ambition thick-sighted : thence proceeds mawkishness and all the thousand bitters which these men I speak of necessarily taste of in going over these pages.' So says Keats in the preface to *Endymion.* There were factors and elements in the ferment of Donne's soul which Keats did not know till he was a dying man; and the instinct for beauty was too uncertain in the older poet, too arrogantly controlled by a restless intellect, for him ever to attain to the peace of great imaginative work, though he perhaps comes nearest to it in the beautiful prose of some of the passages in his sermons.

But Donne was no ordinary young man carried by a swing of the pendulum from a too strict education to a life of debauchery and then again to repentance. The movement which these poems reflect in its excesses was one of thought as well as feeling, and the thought remained a central one in all his later development, even if he never succeeded in working it out to a balanced and harmonious conception of life. The dualism of body and soul he re-fused to accept as the absolute one to which medieval thought, influenced by Neo-Platonism, had tended. The body is not simply evil, the spirit good, sense a corrupter and misleader, the soul pure and heavenward aspiring. Man is body and soul, and neither can be complete with-out the other. To separate them absolutely is heresy alike in love and in religion:

> Love 's not so pure and abstract as they use
> To say which have no mistress but the Muse;
> But as all else being elemented too,
> Love sometimes would contemplate, sometimes do.

The same thought in its religious bearing was to recur in many of his poems and letters and sermons:

' A resurrection is a second rising to that state from which anything is formerly fallen. Now though by death the soul do not fall into any such state as that it can complain (for what can that lack which God fills ?), yet by death the soul falls from that for which it was infused and poured into man at first, that is to be the form of that body, the king of that kingdom; and therefore when in the general resurrection the soul returns to that state for which it was created and to which it hath an affection even in the fulness of the joys of Heaven; then when the soul returns to her office, to make up the man, because the whole man hath, therefore the soul hath a resurrection.'

Just so Blake pictures the passionate reunion of soul and body.

But Donne was not yet a preacher penitent for his early excesses. The experience through which he passed in these early years is really a typical though salient instance of the movement of thought and feeling which we call the Renaissance. It is the movement, thrown into sharp relief by the peculiar character of Donne's upbringing, from conceptions of life and morality which made the joys of another world the goal of life and the measure of man's conduct to conceptions in which this world and man's sensible nature are at least constituent elements in the good for which he strives. ' When several centuries had exhausted the enthusiasm for the new religion it was seen that the interests of the world still asserted themselves alongside those of the world beyond . . . the more time elapsed the more men grew weary of having their eyes fixed without relaxation on Heaven. The earth took a larger and larger part in their thoughts.' The movement in Donne's temperament was not a simple reaction from a too strict and pious upbringing to a dissolute life about town. It was the same movement as shows itself, with individual differences, in the life and work of men like Erasmus and Rabelais and Montaigne—the reaction against ascetic ideals. Indeed when one reads the most daring of Donne's sensual and witty extravagances it would be well to recall those of Rabelais and remember that these paradoxical ' ventilations ' of wit and humour and the senses represent the reaction of human nature from a long strain. And when one recalls the Latin poems of Beza and Buchanan one may also remember that the age allowed itself a freedom in wit and poetry which was not always an index to the writer's life.

In Donne's case the result would probably have been, as the tumult of youth and passion and ebullient wit subsided, a life in which not religion but worldly activity and am-

bition were the dominant motives, a strenuous and probably useful career as a public man. The poet might have
been lost to view, as in the career of Thomas Sackville; the
great preacher might never have emerged; and Donne
would have been an ' earthlier happier ' man. But circumstances were not propitious and Donne's temperament
was not as cool as Bacon's. He had hardly put forth on
what promised to be a prosperous voyage before he was
shipwrecked by his own impulsive temperament.

Love and poetry were quite certainly not the sole concern of the years between 1592 and 1596 when Donne was
a student of law at Lincoln's Inn, ' giggling and making
giggle ' with Davies and Hoskins and others, like himself,

Of study and play made strange hermaphrodites.

' In the most unsettled days of his youth ', says Walton, 'his
bed was not able to detain him beyond the hour of four in
the morning; and it was no common business that drew him
out of his chamber till past ten; all which time was employed in study; although he took great liberty after it.'
For these are the years in which Donne wrote the first
three *Satyres*. Several things in them show his familiarity
with the London of 1594–6. Banks's performing horse and
the performing elephant, the ape that would come over the
chain for a mention of the Queen (as later of King James)
but sit still . . for the Pope and the King of Spain, figure
alike in Donne's *Satyres* and the *Epigrams* which Davies
composed in 1594. Donne's second *Satyre* and Davies's
' Gulling Sonnets' were directed against the same person, a
lawyer who had turned poet and published in 1594
Zepheria, a series of sonnets full of legal terms and long,
harsh words, though Donne covertly extends the satire
to include the mean lawyer who makes money by denounc-
ing Catholics. And the picture these *Satyres* present is
just such as Walton indicates. ' Away, thou fondling, motley humourist', he cries to a young gallant, like himself

'a visiter of ladies', but not able to share his graver studies, who has broken in upon him before the hour of ten in the morning:

> Leave me and in this standing wooden chest
> Consorted with these few books let me lie
> In prison and here be coffin'd when I die.
> Here are God's conduits, grave divines; and here
> Nature's Secretary, the philosopher,
> And jolly statesman which teach how to tie
> The sinews of a city's mystic body ;
> Here gathering chroniclers, and by them stand
> Giddy fantastic poets of each land.

The poets we know from a later letter to Buckingham included Spanish poets, and doubtless also Latin, Italian, French and English. Among the chroniclers were Holinshed and Stowe, but also more serious historians as Surius and Sleidan. Nature's Secretary is, of course, Aristotle. Among the divines would be Thomas Aquinas and some of the older theologians, but the majority would be modern controversialists—Spanish, French, Italian and German; and the latest volumes on Donne's shelf in 1594–5 would be the *Disputationes de Controversiis Christianae Religionis* of Cardinal Bellarmine, issued in 1593, for he later showed ' the then Dean of Gloucester ... all the Cardinal's works with many weighty observations under his own hand' (Walton). The trend of his thought on religious controversies, the line of escape by which he made his way to conformity, is indicated in the third of the *Satyres.*

For if, like so many young men of the age—Raleigh, Southampton, Pembroke, Davies—Donne sowed his wild oats, like them also he was ambitious, as ambitious of a public career as Bacon, Wotton, Davies, Hoskins, Gabriel Harvey. But in his way lay a stumbling-block which did not impede them. He was a Catholic, a member of an outlawed and persecuted Church, for whom if he made pubiic avowai of his faith there were only two courses open,

to go abroad and seek service under a Catholic potentate—
the Spanish Court swarmed with young Englishmen
starving on unpaid pensions—or to live the cramped life of
a recusant, obnoxious to spies and fines, at the best cut off
from all hopes of preferment. Donne's poems abound in
thinly veiled allusions to the unhappy lot of his co-
religionists. His position was difficult, the way of escape
which he found is interesting, though easy to misrepresent
by a critic who has no sympathy with or understanding of
the complexities of the human heart. It is very clearly
indicated in the *Satyre* in question. He had studied the
religious controversies of the day. He had been, as I think,
in Catholic countries, whether their Catholicism sat
lightly on them as in France or was of the most intimate
fibre of their minds, as in Spain. 'He is a Catholic', he
says of someone, 'but a French Catholic, and, Sir, French
papistry is but like French velvet—a pretty slack religion
that would soon wear out, and not of the three-piled papistry of Italy and Spain.' He sees that the religion of most
men is largely a matter of accident, the country they were
born in, the religion of their godfathers, or of capricious
choice. A taste for antiquity draws some men to Rome; a
distaste for ceremonies and the fringes of worship drives
others to Geneva. It is a toss up between a ' church in the
lake ' and a ' church upon seven hills ' (*Eighty Sermons*,
1640, p. 769). Yet surely of all things religion should be
the subject of careful consideration and deliberate choice,
to the making of which tradition and reason should both
contribute. But for Donne as for a later poet:

> There lives more faith in honest doubt
>   Believe me than in half the creeds.

>   believe me this
> He's not of none nor worst, that seeks the best.
> To adore or scorn an image, or protest,
> May all be bad; doubt wisely; in strange way
> To stand inquiring right is not to stray;

> To sleep or run wrong is. On a huge hill
> Cragged and steep truth stands, and he that will
> Reach her about must and about must go
> And what the hill's suddenness resists win so.

It was along this line of intellectual inquiry that Donne detached himself from Catholicism rather than by any change of heart. The position he reached is clearly stated in a later letter to his friend Goodyere: ' You know I never fettered nor imprisoned the word religion ; not straitening it Friarly *ad religiones factitias* (as the Romans well call their orders of religion) nor immuring it in a Rome or a Wittenberg or a Geneva. They are all virtual beams of one sun, and wheresoever they find clay hearts they harden them into dust and they entender and mollify waxen.' But the natural inference from such a premise is that one may, and so ought, to conform to the Church of one's King and country. There, had Donne found a secular career, he would probably have left it; but King James and circumstances made him rather, one suspects, against his will a controversialist.

His final decision was probably not made till he entered Egerton's service. Meantime among the young bloods whom his wit entertained in these years of detachment appeared in 1595 his old friend of Oxford days, Henry Wotton, returned from a long tour on the continent, where he had served as one of the secret service collecting information for Anthony Bacon and the Earl of Essex. It was due to Wotton in all probability that Donne was induced to join the band of brilliantly equipped volunteers who sailed with Essex and Raleigh to Cadiz in 1596 and to the Azores, in hope of capturing the Spanish Treasure Fleet, in 1597. He was in the full tide of his witty gallantry. The fifth *Elegy* was written at this juncture, ' Here take my picture '; and so also was the more outrageous twentieth, *Love's War*. One or two of the *Epigrams* were composed during the Cadiz expedition, and the second voyage was the occasion of the first two poems which seem to have made his name known outside the narrower circle permitted to read the amorous songs and elegies. *The Storm* and *The Calm* are verse-epistles addressed to Christopher Brooke, an intimate friend and fellow student at Lincoln's Inn. Witty and vivid, they are characteristically void of any feeling for the beauty or sublimity of nature. Donne was a city and a courtly poet, a poet of circles which appreciated wit; his interest, men and women and the movements of his own mind, the nervous effect of calm and storm at sea.

From these, for volunteers, costly voyages Donne returned probably poorer but with influential friends and the prospect of more remunerative service. The fourth *Satyre*, written in 1597, as the reference to the fall of Amiens shows, lets us see him haunting the Court. The months were spent, it may be, in acting as a Queen's messenger for Cecil to and from France, if the John Donne to whom Sir Edmund Chambers has found references in this capacity be the poet, or in London exchanging letters in verse with various members of the Essex circle—Wotton, Bacon and others. Then in 1598 a door seemed to open to more useful and promising work. Donne was made private secretary to Sir Thomas Egerton, Lord Keeper of the Great Seal. He had served with young Thomas Egerton in the Cadiz expedition, and it was probably he who presented him at his father's house where Donne's learning, languages and other ability ' secured the Lord Keeper's favour. It was a call to put off the gay young man and the too indiscriminate student, diverted from the study of the law ' by the worst voluptuousness, which is an hydroptic, immoderate desire of human learning and languages; beautiful ornaments to great fortunes; but mine needed an occupation and a course, which I thought I had entered well into when I submitted myself to such a service as I thought might have employed these poor advantages which I had '. These words were written after he had forfeited that opportunity, 'there I stumbled,' and they indicate vividly Donne's view of his own life from 1592 to 1598, a life lacking not in energy but in purpose, a life of pleasure, study, adventure, and occasional but not regular service. The despondency which such a life begets is reflected in some of the letters written just before the entry on Egerton's service, e.g. the long letter to Henry Wotton beginning:

Sir,

more than kisses letters mingle souls.

Wotton would seem to have sent him some verses of Bacon in which that despondent suitor bewails the ills of life after the example of Metrodorus in the Greek Anthology:

The world's a bubble and the life of man
Less than a span,

and Donne descants upon the same theme, *vanitas vanitatum*; life in country, city and court are all alike evil; giving a characteristically theological turn to the more simply classical thought of Bacon. The effect of the appointment on Donne's spirits was immediate. He threw himself ardently into the duties of his office, and the fifth *Satyre* was evoked by Egerton's efforts to curtail the exorbitant fees exacted by the Clerk of the Star Chamber from unhappy litigants:

You, Sir, whose righteousness she loves, whom I
By having leave to serve am most richly
For service paid, authoris'd now begin
To know and weed out this enormous sin.

The second of the letters to Wotton, dated 20th July 1598, is in a much gayer, lighter tone than that referred to above, and gives us a glimpse of Donne at Court to which he would have readier admittance as secretary to Egerton. But, on the whole, we have regrettably little detail of his life during these years, till we come to the catastrophe which closed it.

One episode of the period, however, has left a mark on Donne's poems, that is the execution of the Earl of Essex in February 1601. There can, I think, be little doubt that on entering the service of the Lord Keeper Donne had at least conformed to the Church of England. Egerton could hardly have taken a professed Catholic into his confidential service; and after the rupture Donne passionately disclaims, in a letter dated 13th February 1602, 'loving a corrupt religion'. But Donne's sympathies were still a good deal with his Catholic friends as the *Satyre* referred to shows, and is still more clearly shown by the strange and sombre poem he began to compose clandestinely in the summer following the death of Essex. *The Progresse of the Soule, Infinitati Sacrum*, 16 *August* 1601. That Donne never meant to publish this fragment is shown both by his use of the same title for the *Second Anniversary* later and by the direct transference to one of the *Holy Sonnets* of some lines from the poem. It was the expression of the mood of bitter feeling which the execution evoked in many minds. We get a glimpse of it in the satire of a younger contemporary, Sir John Roe, attributed to 1602 (p. 371–5), but which must at least have been finished later:

> What treason is, and what did Essex kill,
> Not true treason, but treason handled ill;
> And which of them stood for their country's good,
> And what might be the cause of so much blood.
> He said she stunk, and men might not have said
> That she was old before that she was dead.

Ben Jonson probably refers to the unpopularity of the Queen in the prologue to *Cynthia's Revels*. Donne's friend Wotton fled the country. Donne's satire in this poem expresses itself in two forms, both traceable to his Catholic upbringing—a satire on heresy and a satire on women. Elizabeth is the arch-heretic, and he will trace the progress of the soul of heresy from the apple which Eve ate

through all the great, bad men it inhabited—Luther,
Mahomet, Calvin—to its present abode in:

> The great soul which here among us now
> Doth dwell, and moves that hand, and tongue, and brow
> Which as the moon the sea, moves us.

He did not get further than to the soul's first emergence in
human form and that the form of a woman:

> keeping some quality
> Of every past shape she knew treachery,
> Rapine, deceit and lust, and ills enow
> To be a woman. Themech she is now
> Sister and wife to Cain, Cain that first did plow.

And there Donne breaks off in a sombre, sceptical contemplation of the fact that it is to bad men we owe some of
the greatest boons conferred on mankind:

> wonder with mee,
> Why plowing, building, ruling and the rest
> Or most of those arts, whence our lives are blest,
> By cursed Cain's race invented be,
> And blest Seth vex us with Astronomie,

i. e. Astrology. It is a strange poem to have been written at
this time by the lover of Ann More and the secretary of
Egerton, and betrays the danger for his career that lurked
in Donne's impulsive, passionate temperament. The
danger was not long in declaring itself. In the December
following the August in which this poem is dated Donne
secretly and hastily married Ann More, daughter of Sir
George More of Losely and niece to Egerton's second wife.
Sir Edmund Gosse has told the story fully and it is unnecessary to resume it in detail—the breaking of the news to the
bride's father in February of the following year, the imprisonment of Donne and his dismissal from the service of
Sir Thomas Egerton, for, before Sir George More had
recovered from his anger on receipt of the news, that fatal
step had been taken, and it was in vain that later his father-

in-law endeavoured to undo the mischief. Egerton expressed his sorrow for what he had done, but declared it was inconsistent with his place and credit to discharge and readmit servants at the request of passionate petitioners. Another report, indeed, states that the Lord Keeper had grown a little jealous of his secretary's ability, but this is probably gossip. In sending his old master a copy of *Pseudo-Martyr* Donne wrote in 1610: ' and for the errors, I cannot despair of your pardon since you have long since pardoned greater faults in me '.

For Donne the consequences were disastrous. He never again until, after long internal strife and the disappointment of other hopes he entered the ministry, found honourable employment which could give him real independence. The years that followed were years of wearing poverty and humiliating dependence. The brilliant young scholar and poet, soldier and secretary, had to eat the bitter bread of charity and patronage. He lived at Pyrford on the charity of his wife's cousin, Francis Wooley, or between Mitcham and London on the allowance made to his wife by her father, for his own patrimony had been dissipated in the years of extravagance. He had to pay with adulatory verse-letters and elegiac extravagances for the favours of the Countess of Bedford, the Earl of Ancrum, Viscount Doncaster, and others. It was to the most elaborate, the most outrageous, and the most brilliant of his *Funerall Elegies*, the *Anniversaries*, on young Elizabeth Drury whom he had never seen, that he owed the friendship of her father, rooms in his spacious mansion in Drury Lane, and the opportunity of travelling in France with comfort and distinction. The worst trials of poverty and sickness seem to have passed by 1609; but the humiliations and disappointments of the suitor and dependent only ended when he finally conquered his scruples and entered the ministry of the Church of England.

The record of these years in writings, private and

intended for publication, form a mirror reflecting vividly
the complexity of his character, his many-sided erudition,
his vigorous and subtle mind. 'Jack Donne' was not dead
and buried in Benedick the married man or the melancholy
suitor and dependent. The audacious wit of the early
poems still found an outlet in his intercourse with the
gallants and courtiers of his acquaintance, the Roes,
Thomas and John, cousins, of whom the one after a wild
career died in Jonson's arms of the plague, the other became the great ambassador to the Mogul and the friend of
the Queen of Bohemia, Henry Goodyere to whom Donne
gave so much unavailing good advice, Thomas Coryat,
John Hoskins, the young men who contributed to Over-
bury's *Characters*, and others. Numerous *jeux d'esprit*,
clever but marred by the bad taste of the time, survive in
manuscript or in badly printed texts. The fourteenth
Elegy, if it be Donne's (and there is no sufficient evidence to
reject it) cannot have been written earlier than 1609, a
year in which he was also composing 'divine poems'. Some
of the Paradoxes and Problems, of which not all have found
their way into print, seem to belong to this period. He had
hardly finished the serious and heavy *Pseudo-Martyr* in
1610 when he assailed the Jesuits, for, whatever his sympathies with old English Catholics, he always hated the Society,
in *Ignatius, his Conclave*, in Latin and English, a wildly
paradoxical pamphlet full of the clever but execrable wit
which polluted politico-religious controversy in those good
Christian days. One will never comprehend or even state
aright the problem of Donne's character if one fails to
recognize that these 'evaporations of wit', as he calls them,
seemed to him quite compatible with more serious pursuits
controversial and devout.

The record of these more serious pursuits in this interval of fourteen years is the *Pseudo-Martyr* (1610); the
Biathanatos; poems in the form of verse-letters to friends
and to noble ladies and other patrons; as well as prose-

letters to the same persons. The first is not a work of interest to the student of Donne's character. His controversial prose has not the poetic quality of his sermons. The close, acute controversial methods of the day did not encourage eloquence. The *Biathanatos*, written in the same crabbed style, has a much greater interest. It was not published till 1644, long after the author's death, but it was sent in MS. from time to time to his friends with the prayer that it should not be published: ' Preserve it for me if I live, and if I die . . . publish it not, but yet burn it not' The treatise is not a defence of suicide as a modern might write such a defence, a grave consideration of the right of a man to commit suicide to escape from inevitable suffering provided his doing so did not entail loss or suffering upon others. Donne was a Christian and could never have raised such a question, for on no duty had the Church since the days of St. Augustine and earlier spoken more clearly, and there is no moral question the answer to which depends so obviously on the belief or disbelief in another world, on a religious sanction for morality. Donne, indeed, raises the question as though that were what he was going to discuss. He wrote the work probably, as Goethe sometimes did, to work off a mood with which he was beset; but the answer which he gives in the end is not one which in itself could dispel the mood in which the question has originated. What that mood was he states very clearly: ' Beza, a man as eminent and illustrious in the full glory and noon of learning, as others were in the dawning and morning, when any the least sparkle was notorious, confesseth of himself that only for the anguish of a scurf which overran his head he had once drowned himself from the miller's bridge in Paris, if his uncle had not by chance come that way. I have often such a sickly inclination; and whether it be because I had my first breeding and conversation with men of a suppressed and afflicted religion, accustomed to the despite of death and hungry of an imagined martyrdom;

or that the common enemy find that door worst locked against him in me, or that there be a perplexity and flexibility in the doctrine itself; or because my conscience assures me that no rebellious grudging at God's gift, nor other sinful concurrence accompanies these thoughts in me, or that a brave scorn or that a faint cowardliness beget it, whensoever any affliction assails me methinks I have the keys of my prison in mine own hand, and no remedy presents itself so soon to my heart as mine own sword. Often meditation of this hath won me to a charitable interpretation of their action who die so; and provoked me a little to watch and exagitate their reasons which pronounce so peremptory judgements upon them.' So speaks the man of the Renaissance in Donne, but the answer is worked out on the lines of a fine question in Christian casuistry, and it is difficult to see what consolation for such a mood is to be extracted from what in the end Donne concludes, namely, that there may be, and have been, cases in which a man may legitimately lay down his life by his own action to serve God and his fellow-men, as Samson did, and the death of Christ on the cross was itself a voluntary surrender of His life, ' for we say the same that this may be done only when the honour of God may be promoted that way and no other'. It is admittedly such a duty, such a high act of virtue, such a promotion of God's honour to expose oneself to almost certain death. Regulus passed sentence upon himself when he returned to Carthage having dissuaded the Romans from peace. The martyrs not only endured, they provoked death. It is permissible, with Job and St. Paul, to wish for death (' I may if I choose suffer myself to be killed by a thief rather than kill him in mortal sin. . . .I may die for another '), to mutilate oneself in certain circumstances, to help those who are in great suffering to die. Donne cites the evidence of an Italian that in England ' men condemned to be hanged are ever accompanied to their execution by their kindred who then hang at their feet to hasten their end; and that when a patient is abandoned by the physicians his nearest kinsman strangles him with a pillow'. Is it inconceivable that there are circumstances in which the last act of all may become a duty, an act of high virtue, a promotion of the honour of God?

Only a few of the verse-letters are actually dated, but it is not difficult to group them with sufficient approximation to their chronological sequence. Of *The Storme* and *The Calme* we have spoken already. The letter which follows, 'Sir, more than kisses', was written before April 1598; and the letter 'Here's no more news' belongs to the same year or to 1599, when in 'Went you to conquer' Donne writes to Wotton, now campaigning with Essex in Ireland. These letters and one or two perhaps of the shorter notes to the Woodwards (e. g. 'If, as mine is, thy life a slumber be') belong to the interval between the Islands Voyage and the date of Donne's marriage. They have a note of the *insouciance* of the young man who wrote the earlier songs and elegies. The rest of those addressed to personal friends, as Sir Henry Goodyere, Rowland Woodward, Henry Wotton departing as an ambassador to Venice, are subsequent to that date and are saturated with the melancholy and almost listless resignation of the prose-letters of these years, the years spent at Pyrford, Mitcham, and London, before in 1608 or 1609 the hopes of a turn of fortune and the favours of the Countess of Bedford brightened Donne's mercurial spirits.

The letters to the Duchess and other noble ladies form a group by themselves. They lack the intimate self-revealing note of those to Goodyere and Wotton and Woodward. They abound in extravagances of metaphysical compliment. Even more than the early extravagances of perverse wit one might regard the excesses of flattery in these letters and the worse funeral elegies as 'an expense of spirit in a waste of shame', but what was a poor man to do who had no profession and to whom a child was born

every year? It is difficult to exempt from this censure even
the much-lauded *Anniversaries,* at least in their entirety.
There are two interwoven strands in these strange poems,
a eulogy of the young Elizabeth Drury, which passes all
limits of decent or convincing hyperbole, even the hyperbole of extravagant grief, and a *de contemptu mundi* passing
in the *Second Anniversarie* into a contemplation of the
glories of heaven the soul's true home, which is the finest
thing in the poem and is developed with the close-packed
eloquence, the passionate feeling quickening the subtle
thought and manifold erudition, the shining felicity of
phrase, the impressive rhetoric of the great passages in the
sermons. It is one of the strangest poems in the language in
its combination of what is execrable with what is magni-
ficent, of the ingenuities of a too subtle and erudite wit
irradiated by a passionate imaginative apprehension of the
spiritual and transcendent, of frigidities and harshness of
imagery and phrasing with felicitous and incandescent
phrases and varied harmonies.

These manifold contradictions encounter us at every
turn in the study of Donne's life and character and work.
No one can trace what Dr. Jessop called his ' steps to the
altar ', as Sir Edmund Gosse's biography has illuminated
them, with entire equanimity or without a sense of the
strange complexity of the human mind which makes compatible with one another sincere religious feeling and
essential moral soundness and the strangest acquiescences
and aberrations of moral judgement and taste. Donne
was a sincerely religious man before he became a divine.
The whole spirit of his work risks being misapprehended
if one think of him as fundamentally insincere, or fail to
recognize that neither the extravagances of his youth, the
ambitious compliances of his later years, nor the sceptical
sense he reveals of the contradictions inherent in theology
and science—of which no man of his day was more acutely
aware—ever effaced the impression of his early religious

upbringing or corrupted the fundamental honesty and
loyalty of his nature. As a son, as a husband, as a friend,
Donne's character whenever it reveals itself is unexception-
able. Nothing could be finer than the tone and spirit of
some of the most intimate of his letters to Goodyere, and no
man had a larger cortege of loyal and devoted friends, from
Goodyere and Wotton and the Brookes and the Woodwards
of his youth to Sir Robert Ker and the Earl of Carlisle and
Bishop King and Izaak Walton in his older age. Yet on
the other hand there are elements in Donne's writings,
not the early poems alone, but in his later writings (even in
his sermons), and there are incidents in his life, not his
early life alone, of which our knowledge is largely conjec-
tural, but in his progress towards the altar, and even in his
clerical career, which are morally and aesthetically jarring
and repellent. It will not do to cut Donne's life across, as
some of his clerical critics would do, and turning away
pained eyes from his early extravagances portray with
unction his later life as a glorious example of the great
penitent. To some of us the early excesses in wit and inde-
cency of his poems are more easily condoned than some of
the compliances of his later life—his fulsome flattery of
noble ladies, his protestations of devotion to the service of
James's abominable favourites, Somerset and Buckingham,
his pluralities and eager touting for preferment. Sir
Edmund Gosse was in error in attributing to him the de-
claration in favour of the nullity of the marriage of Lady
Frances Howard, which was the work of Sir Daniel Donne.
But the error does not materially affect the picture that
he paints of this period of his life. Donne nosed about
the nullity case in a disagreeable manner, willing to help,
while he composed his adulatory *Epithalamion* for the
adulterous marriage that was contemplated, ' honeying
and making love over the nasty sty '. Even after he had
entered the ministry, and had experienced that intensifica-
tion of religious feeling which Sir Edmund Gosse describes

as a conversion, we find him holding pluralities and hunting
for deaneries, though, not to play the *advocatus diaboli* too
strenuously, it is to be remembered that neither Donne nor
others who celebrated the marriage of Somerset knew at
the time all that lay behind it, and Walton shows us Donne
on the bed of sickness in 1623 rejecting a rather scandalous
proposal to increase his income made by the pious Dr.
King. Donne had not the temper of a Milton standing
aloof from the world and hating, as he hated the gates of
Hell, the flattery and corruption of Courts. But it is
equally true to say that he had more of the spirit of charity,
which was too much consumed in Milton by the fury of
political passion and a stern personal pride; so hard is it for
human nature to attain to a mean.

Moreover, if some of Donne's faults indicate certain
radical flaws in his moral taste and susceptibilities, a defective sense of beauty in life and art, others to be fairly
judged must be seen in the light of Plato's statement that
it is impossible to be perfectly virtuous in an evil state. It is
not for our age, when honours and posts are still canvassed
for and purchased, to condemn Donne, a poor man with a
large and ever-growing family, if he sought a livelihood
and a sphere of action by the only avenue along which
these could be obtained, the flattery of the great and
influential, acquiescence in corrupt arrangements, eager
canvassing for every vacancy. It is not Donne but the
Church of England one pities when one contemplates him
begging for preferment from creatures like Somerset and
Buckingham, or kneeling in pious penitence at the feet of
James or Charles because he had been accused of speaking
too freely. The Church of England was, Donne believed,
a true branch of the Catholic Church, the Church Univer-
sal, but it was also a department of the state whose ministers
were bound to do as they were told by James and his
favourites. The only recalcitrants were the Puritans, and
from the Puritans Donne was separated by what was best

as well as what was weakest in his nature, his humanity
and liberality of spirit and his veneration for the Catholic
tradition in faith and worship.

The chief works of these last years were his numerous
sermons, his strange *Essays on Divinity* (published in 1651),
the *Devotions on Emergent Occasions, and Severall steps in
my Sicknes* (1624) and the best of his *Divine Poems.* The
latter do not all belong to this period. A fair number date
from the distressful years which followed his marriage, the
years when, if in trouble, Donne's thoughts turned towards the Church, but, when the warm sun of favour
reappeared reawakening ambition, his interests grew more
secular. The sonnets called *La Corona,* because of the way
they are linked together, were sent to Mrs. Herbert and to
the Earl of Dorset in 1608 or 1609, in which year the
Litanie was also composed. *On the Annuntiation and
Passion* was written on the last day of 1608, as that was
counted, i.e. March 25, 1609. *The Crosse* and the fragment on the *Resurrection* date from about the same time.
Goodfriday is dated 1613, two years before his ordination
and shortly after he had completed the very pagan and
sensuous *Epithalamion* on the marriage of the Princess
Elizabeth. But the finest of these poems are the expression
of his heart under the influence of the death of his wife in
1617 and the sicknesses that preceded his own death. In
these and in his sermons Donne's work recaptures the
peculiar charm of his early love verses at their best, the
unique blend of passionate feeling and rapid subtle thinking,
the strange sense that his verse gives of a certain conflict
between the passionate thought and the varied and often
elaborate pattern into which he moulds its expression,
resulting in a strange blend of harshness and constraint
with reverberating and penetrating harmony. No poems
give more than the *Holy Sonnets* and the three hymns
composed in 1619 and 1623, ' In what torn ship ', ' Since
I am coming ', and ' Wilt thou forgive ', the sense of

conflict of soul, of faith and hope snatched and held desperately, of harmony evoked from harsh combinations as of one who tears his

> pleasures with rough strife
> Thorough the iron gates of life.

The note of these poems is that of the greatest of the sermons. The same spirit is at work in both, the same restless and subtle wit, the same poetic fancy, but in the latter the wit is more subdued, the fancy more sustained by the dominant mood of religious solemnity. As they stand, each sermon is a careful work of art. The sermon as delivered was not the sermon as we have it. The printed sermon is the spoken sermon set down subsequently by the preacher, corrected, polished, expanded at times from one sermon into two. ' At the Haghe, December 16, 1619. I preached upon this text. Since in my sickness at Abrey Hatch in Essex, 1630, revising my short notes of that sermon I digested them into two.'

Donne is the only English poet of the first rank who is also a great orator, it may be as some have claimed a greater orator than poet; but in fact his poetry and his oratory have much in common, for poetry as an art may be said to move between the poles of song or music on the one hand and of eloquence on the other, pure song in which the melody itself is the chief communicant of the feeling, as in Shelley's poetry:

> My soul is an enchanted boat
> Which like a sleeping swan doth float
> Upon the silver waves of thy sweet singing ;
> And thine doth like an angel sit
> Beside the helm conducting it,
> Whilst all the winds with melody are ringing.

That is one extreme, the other is the ordered, polished eloquence to which serious English poetry moved under the influence of Milton whose successors were Dryden,

Pope, Gray, and others of lesser rank, and to which it returned in Tennyson after the explosive and technically somewhat uncertain romantic revival, in the main a lyrical revival. But the poetry of Donne and his most notable followers is neither the one nor the other. It is a poetry of talk vigorous and direct, but poetry because it is ' musicè composita '. His abrupt openings, his vigorous, unconventional, unpolished yet felicitous phrasing, his wit, his imagery homely and erudite—all suggest one who is talking, arguing, expostulating, playing with his thoughts, but neither polishing his eloquence nor surrendering himself to the pure delight of song. But his talk is poetry because it is musically drawn out from line to line in surprisingly varied and elaborate stanzas or paragraphs. And his oratory is of the same kind, not the oratory of the great French preachers or of Burke, carrying one on from point to point in the development of an elaborate, coherent, carefully jointed argument. That was not the method of the preacher in the seventeenth century, of Andrewes or of Donne. A sermon of Donne's is the exposition, word by word, of a text, not what we should call to-day a scientific exposition trying to discover by every available means philological, philosophical, historical, what the words meant for the writer who used them and when he used them, but an exposition erudite, that is based on the tradition of the Fathers and the Schoolmen, fanciful, practical, applying the word to the conscience and faith of his hearers; and the style is that of one holding with his audience a heart-to-heart talk.

An artistic consequence of the method is that the greater flights are not gradually led up to by a *crescendo*, not elaborate perorations as in Burke's speeches. They spring from the thought of the moment, the word or doctrine immediately under consideration, and sometimes there are no such moments. Donne is not a showy preacher on the quest for opportunities to introduce purple passages. Some of the best of his sermons, as that preached before Princess

Elizabeth at Heidelberg, move on a steady level of grave
and sober reflection, just thoughts, happy fancies, weighty
sentences, but no bursts of eloquence. It is when the course
of his reflective exposition brings him to some moving
theme, the occasional mercies of God (*LXXX Sermons*, 2),
death and the resurrection (*LXXX S.*, 22 and 27), prayer,
sin, the Last Judgement, that the preacher rises to moving
imagery and pealing harmonies, and even here it is the
eloquence of one who talks rather than declaims, talks to
himself as well as to his audience. A sermon will open in
the same abrupt way as a poem. A good example is the
fine exordium to the sermon preached at the Cross on the
15th of September, 1622, and printed in the same year.
The text is: ' They fought from Heaven; the stars in their
courses fought against Sisera,' and the preacher opens thus:
' All the words of God are always sweet in themselves,
says David; but sweeter in the mouth, and in the pen of
some of the prophets, and some of the Apostles than of
others, as they differed in their natural gifts, or in their
education: but sweetest of all, where the Holy Ghost hath
been pleased to set the words of God to music, and to convey it in a song; and this text is of that kind.' And so for a
paragraph of two or three pages (in the first quarto) he
sustains the effect of varying cadences and the blowing of
silver trumpets before he settles down to the ' division ' of
his text. Such preaching is more akin both to talk and to
poetry than it is to declamation, even the declamation of
Burke. From one point of view a sermon by Donne has
the appearance of a closely knotted rope, point succeeding
point in a continuous, conversational exposition ; from
another, of a sustained poetical rhapsody, rising and falling
with the inspiration of the moment, always earnest,
passionate, pleading, but ever and again pealing out in
notes of warning or with the music of the spheres. Neither
the argument nor the appeal to the feelings have all the
power they once possessed. Statements are made as indis-

putable which seem to us far from being so ; that called right which our conscience would arraign. But the fancy is still vivid; the feeling still warm; the music of the periods undulled.

Of Donne's last years the adequate and perfect record is Walton's. That gentle and pious biographer made many mistakes as to dates and sequences; his record smooths over wrinkles in the life and character of his hero which a more candid study cannot ignore. Donne's life, like his poetry, is a troubled and tormented one. His passionate youth, his ambitious middle age, his errors of taste, his uncertain treading in the approach to the altar, his acquiescences and adulation of patrons—these things are as undeniable as his fundamental piety, his loyal friendships, his good feeling and good sense, his steady devotion to the more ascetic ideals of the profession he at last embraced. But the nobler qualities were the dominant ones and in the end triumphant, and to do justice to them one cannot do better than cite the words of Walton : ' His fancy was inimitably high, equalled only by his great wit, both being made useful by a commanding judgement. His aspect was cheerful and such as gave a silent testimony of a clear knowing soul and of a conscience at peace with itself. His melting eye showed that he had a soft heart full of noble compassion, of too brave a soul to offer injuries and too much a Christian not to pardon them in others. He did much contemplate . . . the mercies of God, the immortality of the soul, and the joys of heaven; and would often say in a kind of ecstasy, " Blessed be God that he is God, only and divinely like Himself ". He was by nature highly passionate but more apt to reluct at the excesses of it. A great lover of the offices of humanity, and of so merciful a spirit that he never beheld the miseries of mankind without pity and relief.'

That touch of profound melancholy, that sense of detachment which made this strange blend of the voluptuary and the ascetic, ever conscious of life as a thing he could lightly lay aside, was with him to the last, though controlled in its operation by the faith to which he clung. The hymn ' Wilt thou forgive ', composed with ' Since I am coming ' during his great sickness in 1623, was set to music and ' often sung to the organ by the choristers of St. Paul's, in his own hearing, and at his return from his customary devotions in that place he did occasionally say to a friend, ' The words of that hymn have restored me to the same thoughts of joy that possessed my soul in my sickness when I composed it. And Oh ! the power of church-music ! that harmony added to this hymn has raised the affections of my heart and quickened my graces of zeal and gratitude! and I observe that I always return from paying this public duty of prayer and praise to God with an unexpressible tranquillity of mind, and a willingness to leave the world.' All that Walton goes on to tell us of his preparations for death, and of his last hour, recall that this was the author of *Biathanatos*—the refusal to preserve his life by the means which his physician suggested ('cordials and drinking milk twenty days together '), the monument made to his own order representing him in his grave clothes as he would rise on the day of the general resurrection, his putting away of all worldly concerns at a fixed date, the ending: ' and being satisfied with this blessed sight, as his soul ascended, and his last breath departed from him, he closed his own eyes, and then disposed his hands and body into such a posture as required not the least alteration by those that came to shroud him '.

So died one of the strangest and greatest ornaments of the Church of England and of English poetry and prose. Great and strange—Donne is not one of the lesser yet interesting figures whose merits and limitations it is equally easy to appreciate. His is the more difficult case of one whose great virtues and great faults are equally undeniable and inextricably blended. In his life and in his poetry they

are always present to repel and to fascinate ; and one or
other has to gain the upper hand. You must feel the
fascination of Donne as man and poet with all his faults, or
leave him alone. There was nothing in his poetry that
appealed to the taste to which Tennyson ministered,
though Browning felt his fascination to the full. No verse
of his found its way into the *Golden Treasury* for 'Absence,
hear thou my protestation' is not by Donne, nor has it the
essential quality of Donne's poetry in thought or style or
prosody. It is a relic of the poetry inspired by Sidney. The
present Poet Laureate and Sir William Watson feel
nothing but distaste for the frequent ugliness of his imagery
and wit, his prosody ' which is not Milton's but the fore-
runner of Dryden's ', the evil strain in his psychology, the
' pestilential' character of his theological and pseudo-
scientific erudition. To Donne has fallen the unhappy lot,
says Sir William Watson, of being read only by scholars.
But this is not quite true. No English poet of the past has
exercised a stronger influence upon the poetry of the
younger poets of to-day, for their experiments too have
a root in the consciousness that the ugly and the beautiful
are strangely blended in passionate experience, their
prosody is a result of an effort to keep metre in touch, not
alone with music, but with human speech, phrases and
cadences such as men do use, and their poetry seeks to
charge itself, not with experience only, but with the meta-
physic which strives to transcend and to interpret experience. The Poet Laureate and Sir William Watson are
true poets. So is Mr. Yeats, and of Donne he has written:
' that the more precise and learned the thought the greater
the beauty, the passion. The intricacies and subtleties of
his imagination are the length and depth of the furrow
made by his passion. His pedantry and his obscenities—the
rock and the loam of his Eden—but make us the more
certain that one who is but a man like us all has seen God.'

NOTE ON THE TEXT AND CANON OF THIS EDITION.

THE present edition of the poems is based upon the larger edition issued in 1912 by the Oxford University Press. It reproduces the text of that, corrected in some places where either my critics or my own reflection has convinced me I had erred. It contains all the poems which I believe to be genuine with, in an appendix, those which were so early and for so long attributed to Donne that I did not feel justified in omitting them altogether. I have, however, left out a number of poems which have been loosely attached to Donne's name by the old manuscript collectors and by modern editors. The commentary has, of course, been omitted, and the textual notes reduced to a record of the variants of the old editions (1633, 1635, 1639, 1650–4, 1669), with a general indication of the trend of the manuscript evidence. For more detailed information I must refer my readers to the edition of 1912.

I have spoken of my critics. They have been generously appreciative of my endeavour to establish the text and canon of the poems. But I am under a special debt of obligation to one, whose understanding of what I had succeeded in doing and his criticism of my errors, or what he regarded as errors, were alike evidence of his own profound and intelligent study of Donne. I refer to Professor Henry M. Belden, of the University of Missouri. In a long review of my edition in the *Journal of English and Germanic Philology* (xiv, 135–48) he discussed my dealings with the canon and the text of the poems. Accepting generally my corrections of some of the readings of modern editions, mainly reversions on my part to the text of 1633, he challenged some others, and that with such force that in one or two places I have recurred to the earlier text, and I may be allowed to indicate where I have done so and where, on consideration, I have remained ' of the same opinion still '.

Professor Belden quite naturally takes exception to my conjecture in *Satyre* II. 71, where I have hyphened ' Bearing-like Asses ', and so made them the patient Catholic gentry whom Coscus hales into court to pay fines for their recusancy. ' Bearing-like ', he says, ' is preposterously un-English and so far as I know an un-Donnean coinage.' I admit the weight of the first objection, but still maintain that (1) I can see no other way of interpreting the lines, and (2) that the sense which this change does give is exactly what the context requires. 'Bearing-like' is doubtless un-English, but Donne uses the language very freely and he is fond both of compounds with 'like' and of strange compounds generally: 'nymph-like', 'owle-like', 'relique-like', 'elixar-like', 'aire-like', 'gulf-like', 'staff-like', are a few from the poems only, and if none of these is so irregular as my conjecture, it would not be very easy to parallel such compounds as 'self-like', 'self-truth', 'through-vaine', 'through-swum', 'interbring', 'long-animity', 'unsensibleness', &c.

Professor Belden has on the other hand convinced me that I was in error when, in the Letter *To Mr. T. W.* (p. 180) I extended the bracket in ll. 14–15 to include in l. 16 'A monster and a begger', and interpreted 'in Fortunes gifts' as meaning the 'almsman of Fortune'. He has given an interpretation of these difficult lines which to me is convincing: 'I that have ever been (in comparison with the graces which the Muses have conferred on you) a monster in Nature and a beggar in Fortune, am now [i.e. by his marriage] that third and more wretched thing, a fool'.

My critic has likewise convicted me of a notable error in the *Epithalamion made at Lincoln's Inn* (p. 126) when, tempted by Donne's fondness for a pun and especially on the words 'son' and 'sun', I printed

Sonns of these Senators wealths deep oceans

omitting the comma after 'Senators' and so taking 'sonns' as meaning not the sons by the flesh of the senators, but the 'suns' which drank up their wealth by marrying their daughters. I was so overseen as to write 'The sons of wealthy citizens might grow idle and extravagant; they could not be styled patricians'. As Mr. Belden says, 'the sons of senators could not well be styled anything else by so good a Latinist as Donne'. I had in mind the actual rank of citizens in England and forgot the implication of the Latin title Donne had assigned to their fathers. 'This stanza', as he says, 'clearly describes the groom's companions under four heads—first, sons of wealthy citizens; second, courtiers; third, country men; fourth, students of Lincoln's Inn, of which the bridegroom is himself a member.'

Mr. Belden has also challenged my reading of 'eager⟨s⟩ desire' for the ' eager, desires ' of the old texts in the *Farewell to Love* (p. 63, l. 30). Here again I have retained my conjecture because I can give no meaning to the passage except on this view of ' eager ' as a verb. It is quite in keeping with the Aristotelian doctrine and Donne's own mood of mind to speak of man's life as ' only for a minute made to be ', and it is only this reference to the shortness of life, rather than of the act of love, which justifies the words ' desire to raise posterity '. However, the poem is not one of great importance.

Of my dealings with the canon, Mr. Belden has criticized, but in moderate terms, my inclusion of ' Come Fates, I fear you not ' among the poems ascribed to Sir John Roe, a poem ' which in temper, still more in certain peculiarities of rhythm and verse rhetoric seems to me to carry the unmistakable mint-mark of Donne. If all these poems are Roe's we have to reckon with a new poet of satiric power second only to that of Jonson and of Donne himself, though hitherto so little known that his discoverer has to construct an identifying biography for him.' I quote Mr. Belden's words to give them full weight. The poems are here for the reader himself to judge of. I do not quite share this high estimate of ' Sleep next society ', which has more of Jonson in it than of Donne. It is on the external evidence of the manuscripts which I have brought together in the notes and in the introduction, *The Text and Canon of Donne's Poems*, in my fuller edition that I rest my assignation. I cannot separate ' Come Fates ' from its fellows. By an oversight I omitted in the textual notes to point out that in the Harleian MSS., 4064 f. 248, this poem is initialled ' Sr J. R.'.

I agree with Mr. Belden that I made a mistake in even tentatively removing the Letter headed *To the Countesse of Huntingdon* (pp. 194–8) from the canon of Donne's poems. I felt this before had sent off my last proofs, but had not the heart to ask my long-suffering publishers to permit a last reconstruction; and moreover I hoped that the raising of the question might lead to further evidence on one side or the other.

The poem is a difficult one, an enigmatical poem, but it is impossible to think of any one but Donne capable of writing it. It almost seems to me that some lines at the outset have been lost, perhaps a whole paragraph, for the first ten lines do not make a sentence. As they stand they suggest that the poem was written, as Mr. Belden says, ' somewhere in the outskirts of civilization, among savages, and therefore, if it is Donne's, must date from the period of his travels, i.e. before 1600 ', from the Islands Expedition, one imagines. But what aborigines Donne can have known is hard to say. The Azores were ' merely uninhabited ' Linschoten says, when discovered, and the population later consisted of ' Portugalls '. These, however, may have imported Indians from Brazil as labourers, for it seems to be Brazilian Indians of whom Donne is speaking. ' All of them goe naked as well men as women, and have no kind of apparell, and are nothing ashamed: rather it seemeth that they are in the state of innocence touching this behalfe, by the great honestie they doe keepe among themselves; and when any man speaketh with a woman, he turneth his back toward her.' (*Purchas His Pilgrimes. The Seaventh Book. A Treatise of Brasill, written by a Portugall which had long lived there . . . Hakluyt Society,* 1906.) These must be Donne's men as naked as if the news of Adam's Fall had not yet reached them, though they were already suffering from its effects :

> Depriv'd of that free state which they were in,
> And wanting the reward yet bear the sinne.

If I follow the thought of the poem aright, Donne is describing different grades or planes of love—first, the love of those who are still in a state of nature. He is in the middle of this when the poem opens in abrupt fashion :

> That unripe side of earth, &c.

But he recurs to it later :

> What pretty innocence in those days mov'd !
> Man ignorantly walk'd by her he lov'd ;
> Both sigh'd and enterchang'd a speaking eye,
> Both trembled and were sick, both knew not why.

In the plane above these are the Petrarchian lovers, and it is such a lover that Donne must appear to Lady Huntingdon, if she be really the person addressed. But he is not of that company. He scorns their plaintive ways :

> Yet neither will I vexe your eyes to see
> A sighing ode nor cross-arm'd Elegie.

> I come not to call pitty from your heart,
> Like some white-liver'd dotard that would part
> Else from his slipperie soule with a faint groane
> And faithfully (without you smil'd) were gone.

Donne is a bolder lover, who will make a bid for victory, but if defeated will dismiss love from his heart:

> Let others sigh and grieve; one cunning sleight
> Shall freeze my love to Christall in a night.
>   .   .   .   .   .
> The honesties of love with ease I doe,
> But am no porter for a tedious woe (i.e. a tedious wooing).

But there is a higher plane of love than this, and Donne addresses Lady Huntingdon as a Beatrice perfect in herself and the centre and source of a love of which lower loves are the shadow, that is, the reflection.

Whether the poem was actually addressed to Lady Huntingdon we cannot of course tell, for we know nothing of her and little of Donne in his early life. He tells us in a later poem that (p. 179):

> I was your prophet in your younger dayes,
> And now your chaplaine, God in you to praise.

Mr. Belden writes, 'One glimpses the possibility of some early amour . . . half passion and half intrigue, half jealous pride and half intellectual exaltation with some woman of the world above him—perhaps Elizabeth Stanley, more likely another—finding expression in lines which were afterwards allowed to creep about in manuscript until the 1635 edition was being prepared when some one came forward with the suggestion that they had been addressed to Lady Huntingdon in the poet's adventurous youth.' That is one view well stated. I rather incline to believe that the poem is a flight of extravagant compliment and should be read with those of the *Songs and Sonets* which I have ventured to suggest may have been similar compliments addressed to the Countess of Bedford and even to the pious Mrs. Magdalen Herbert. The convention of compliment taking the form of love was well established. But even in such complimentary poems the one thing Donne could not do is to play the wailful Petrarchian lover. He moves between the two poles of a frank, satirically-worded naturalism and a vein of transcendental adoration, as at the close of this poem.

If I have restored this poem to its place in the canon, I have quite definitely withdrawn the *Ode: Of our Sense of Sinne*, which is now rightly included in Professor Moore Smith's edition of the *Poems of Lord Herbert of Cherbury*, Oxford, 1923.

I am glad to have both Professor Belden's and Sir Edmund Chambers' sympathetic acceptance of my suggestion that the Elegie ' Death, be not proud ' (pp. 386–7) may have been composed by Lady Bedford herself. The phrase ' Death, be not proud ' certainly recurs in the tenth of the Holy Sonnets (a favourite with Wordsworth), but Donne may have taken over the noble Lady's happy opening. It is of course *possible* that at her request he wrote this answer to his first effusion.

These are the chief differences between the text and canon of this edition and of that of 1912. I have also collated a manuscript of *The Progresse of the Soule*. *Infinitati Sacrum*, which my friend and former student Mr. Robbie unearthed at the British Museum where it had lain hidden under the name of its transcriber. But · some of the variants which suggest that this was an early version were too long to incorporate. Mr. Percy Simpson in his edition of Ben Jonson's *Conversations with Drummond* (*Ben Jonson.* Edited by C. H. Herford and Percy Simpson, vol. i, p. 158), while not denying the fact, obvious from this poem, that the original intention was to conduct the soul of the apple to a resting place in Queen Elizabeth, argues that Donne may have changed his mind and that this, not intentional misleading, would explain the statement of Jonson to Donne that the final host was to be Calvin. It is of no importance, for the reference to Elizabeth remains.

1929   H. J. C. G.

NOTE ON SIR JOHN ROE.

IT is a strange chance which has bound up with the poems of Donne those of a much less respectable person than certainly Donne became. Sir John Roe's was a name soon forgotten, and it was not till I was busy attempting to fix as far as might be the canon of Donne's poems that his identity became again apparent. It is unnecessary to repeat here an account of the steps by which this was secured, but the reader may reasonably wish to know a little about him since all of his poems that we know of are here printed together.

John Roe, or Rowe, was the eldest son of William Rowe of Higham Hill, near Walthamstowe, in the county of Essex, who was himself the third son of a Lord Mayor of London of that name whose fourth son was the father of the more famous Sir Thomas Roe who went as ambassador to the Court of Jehangir, Mogul emperor of Hindostan, and has left us a vivid narrative of his embassy. A daughter Elizabeth married William Garrett of Dorney, Bucks., whose son George Gerrard or Garrard was an intimate friend of Donne. Indeed the poet seems to have been a friend of the family.

John was born on the 5th of May, 1581. His father died in 1596, leaving him a minor. In 1597 he matriculated at Queen's College, Oxford. How long he stayed there is not known, but it was not probably for long. He chose the career of a soldier and served in Ireland, and probably owes his knighthood to the Earl of Essex, who was somewhat lavish in the bestowal of that honour. He seems to have continued in Ireland when Lord Mountjoy, later Earl of Devonshire, succeeded to Essex's authority, for in 1606 that nobleman recommends him to the English Ambassador in the Low Countries as one wishing to follow the wars and to serve the States, and in the same year thanks him, viz. Sir Ralph Winwood, for his kindness to Roe. By 1608 he was dead, for a list of captains, discharged in Ireland since 1603, contains the following note: ' Born in England and dead in 1608—Sir John Roe '. He died, Ben Jonson told Drummond, in London of the plague, and an epigram by the same poet records his service in Ireland, Holland, and, strangely enough, in Russia. He ' was an infinite spender and used to say that when he had no more to spend he could die '.

It must have been in the years between his service in Ireland

and his campaigns in the Low Countries that Roe spent some time among the wits in London and wrote the poems which after lurking for years in various manuscript collections of miscellaneous poems, frequently with Donne's, found their way into the early editions of Donne's poems. The long *Satyre* ' Sleep, next society ', which was not included among Donne's poems till 1669, is dated in some manuscripts 1602, but must have been written or at least completed later; for, though the death of Essex is fresh in the writer's mind, James has succeeded to the throne :

> How since her death, with Sumpter horse the Scot
> Hath rid, who, at his coming up, had not
> A Sumpter-dog.

An Elegie to Mrs. Boulstred, ' Shall I goe force an Elegie', is dated the same year, and the three verse-letters, two to Ben Jonson and one to his cousin Thomas Roe, were apparently written in 1603. The occasion of the first, ' The State and mens affairs', to which Jonson alluded in his conversations with Drummond, was the performance of Daniel's Masque, *The Vision of the Twelve Goddesses*, January 8th 1603. Jonson and Roe, possibly in their cups, had behaved so noisily that they were turned out by the Lord Chamberlain. Roe refers to the Masque :

> But ; that they that allow
> But one God, should have religions enow
> For the Queen's Masque, and their husbands, far more
>   Then all the Gentiles knew or Atlas bore !
> Well let all passe, and trust him who nor cracks
> The bruised reed, nor quencheth smoking flaxe.

Roe had imbibed a large measure of Jonson's self-righteousness. So for a moment he emerges to our sight and then disappears into the ' dark backward and abysm of time '.

THE
PRINTER
TO THE
UNDERSTANDERS.

FOr this time I must speake only to you, at another, *Readers* may perchance serve my turne; and I thinke this a way very free from exception, in hope that very few will have a minde to confesse themselves ignorant.

If you looke for an Epistle, as you have before ordinary publications, I am sory that I must deceive you; but you will not lay it to my charge, when you shall consider that this is not ordinary, for if I should say it were the best in this kinde, that ever this Kingdome hath yet seene; he that would doubt of it must goe out of the Kingdome to enforme himselfe, for the best judgments, within it, take it for granted.

You may imagine (if it please you) that I could endeare it unto you, by saying, that importunity drew it on; that had it not beene presented here, it would have come to us from beyond the Seas; (which perhaps is true enough,) That my charge and paines in procuring of it hath beene such, and such. I could adde hereto, a promise of more correctnesse, or enlargement in the next Edition, if you shall in the meane time content you with this. But these things are so common, as that I should profane this Peece by applying them to it; A Peece which who so takes not as he findes it, in what manner soever, he is unworthy of it, sith a scattered limbe of this Author, hath more amiable-

The Printer &c. *1633–49:* om. *1650–69, which substitute Dedication* To the &c. (*p.* 4)

nesse

nesse in it, in the eye of a discerner, then a whole body of
some other; Or, (to expresse him best by himselfe)

*In the
Storme.*

> —*A hand, or eye,*
> By Hilyard *drawne, is worth a history*
> *By a worse Painter made;*—

If any man (thinking I speake this to enflame him for the
vent of the Impression) be of another opinion, I shall as
willingly spare his money as his judgement.   I cannot lose
so much by him as hee will by himselfe.   For I shall
satisfie my selfe with the conscience of well doing, in
making so much good common.

Howsoever it may appeare to you, it shall suffice mee to
enforme you, that it hath the best warrant that can bee,
publique authority, and private friends.

There is one thing more wherein I will make you of
my counsell, and that is, That whereas it hath pleased
some, who had studyed and did admire him, to offer to the
memory of the Author, not long after his decease, I have
thought I should do you service in presenting them unto
you now;   onely whereas, had I placed them in the
beginning, they might have serv'd for so many Encomiums
of the Author (as is usuall in other workes, where perhaps
there is need of it, to prepare men to digest such stuffe as
follows after,) you shall here finde them in the end, for
whosoever reades the rest so farre, shall perceive that there
is no occasion to use them to that purpose;   yet there they
are, as an attestation for their sakes that knew not so much
before, to let them see how much honour was attributed
to this worthy man, by those that are capable to give it.
Farewell.

The Printer to the Vnderstanders. *1635–69:* The Printer to the
Reader. *1633.*   24 here *1635–69: om. 163?*

Hexastichon

Hexastichon Bibliopolae.

I See in his last preach'd, and printed Booke,
His Picture in a sheet; in *Pauls* I looke,
And see his Statue in a sheete of stone,
And sure his body in the grave hath one:
Those sheetes present him dead, these if you buy,
You have him living to Eternity.

JO. MAR.

Hexastichon ad Bibliopolam.

Incerti.

*I*N *thy Impression of* Donnes *Poems rare,*
For his Eternitie thou hast ta'ne care:
'Twas well, and pious; And for ever may
He live: Yet shew I thee a better way;
Print but his Sermons, and if those we buy,
He, We, and Thou shall live t' Eternity.

Hexastichon Bibliopolae. *1633–69*
Hexastichon ad Bibliopolam. *1635–69*

Incerti] *In one copy of 1633 a seventeenth-century hand adds*
R. B. *See p. 355 : probably* Richard Busby.

Dedication

To the Right Honourable

William Lord *Craven* Baron of

Hamsted-Marsham.

My Lord,

MAny of these Poems have, for severall impressions, wandred up and down trusting (as well they might) upon the Authors reputation; neither do they now complain of any injury but what may proceed either from the kindnesse of the Printer, or the curtesie of the Reader; the one by adding something too much, lest any spark of this sacred fire might perish undiscerned, the other by putting such an estimation upon the wit & fancy they find here, that they are content to use it as their own: as if a man should dig out the stones of a royall Amphitheatre to build a stage for a countrey show. Amongst all the monsters this unlucky age has teemed with, I finde none so prodigious, as the Poets of these later times, wherein men as if they would level understandings too as well as estates, acknowledging no inequality of parts and Judgements, pretend as indifferently to the chaire of wit as to the Pulpit, & conceive themselves no lesse inspired with the spirit of Poetry then with that of Religion: so it is not onely the noise of Drums and Trumpets which have drowned the Muses harmony, or the feare that the Churches ruine wil destroy their Priests likewise, that now frights them from this Countrey, where they have been so ingenuously received, but these rude pretenders to excellencies they unjustly own who profanely rushing into *Minervaes* Temple, with noysome Ayres blast the lawrell wch thunder cannot hurt.

To the &c. *1650–69*

In this sad condition these learned sisters are fled over to
beg your *L*ᵖˢ. protection, who have been so certain a
patron both to arts and armes, and who in this generall
confusion have so intirely preserved your Honour, that
in your Lordship we may still read a most perfect character
of what *England* was in all her pompe and greatnesse, so
that although these poems were formerly written upon
severall occasions, and to severall persons, they now unite
themselves, and are become one pyramid to set your Lord-
ships statue upon, where you may stand like Armed *Apollo*
the defendor of the Muses, encouraging the Poets now
alive to celebrate your great Acts by affording your countenance to his poems that wanted onely so noble a subject.

My Lord,

Your most humble servant

JOHN DONNE.

To John Donne.

DOnne, *the delight of Phoebus, and each Muse,*
Who, to thy one, all other braines refuse;
Whose every work, of thy most early wit,
    Came forth example, and remaines so, yet:
Longer a knowing, then most wits doe live;
    And which no affection praise enough can give!
To it, thy language, letters, arts, best life,
    Which might with halfe mankind maintain a strife;
All which I meant to praise, and, yet, I would;
    But leave, because I cannot as I should!

B. JONS.

To John Donne. *16 50–69, following the* Hexastichon ad Bibliopolam: here corrected from Jonson's *Works,* 1616.

To

To Lucy, Countesse of Bedford,
with M. Donnes Satyres.

L*Vcy*, you brightnesse of our Spheare, who are
    Life of the *Muses* day, their morning Starre!
If works (not th'Authors) their own grace should look,
Whose poems would not wish to be your book?
But these, desir'd by you, the makers ends
Crown with their own. Rare Poems ask rare friends.
Yet, *Satyres*, since the most of mankind bee
Their unavoided subject, fewest see:
For none ere took that pleasure in sins sense,
But, when they heard it tax'd, took more offence.
They, then, that living where the matter is bred,
Dare for these Poems, yet, both ask, and read,
And like them too; must needfully, though few,
Be of the best: and 'mongst those, best are you;
Lucy, you brightnesse of our Spheare, who are
The *Muses* evening, as their morning-Starre.

B. Jon.

To John Donne.

W^{Ho} shall doubt, *Donne*, where I a *Poet* bee,
    When I dare send my *Epigrammes* to thee?
That so alone canst judge, so'alone do'st make:
And, in thy censures, evenly, dost take
As free simplicity, to dis-avow,
As thou hast best authority, t'allow.
Read all I send: and, if I finde but one
Mark'd by thy hand, and with the better stone,
My title's seal'd. Those that for claps doe write,
Let pui'nees, porters, players praise delight,
And, till they burst, their backs, like asses load:
A man should seek great glory, and not broad.

B. Jon.

To Lucy &c. To John Donne &c. *1650–69, in sheets added 1650:*
here corrected from Jonson's *Works* 1616, e. g. 14 those, best *1616:*
those best *1650–69*

SONGS

SONGS

AND

SONETS.

The good-morrow.

I Wonder by my troth, what thou, and I
Did, till we lov'd? were we not wean'd till then?
But suck'd on countrey pleasures, childishly?
Or snorted we in the seaven sleepers den?
T'was so; But this, all pleasures fancies bee.   5
If ever any beauty I did see,
Which I desir'd, and got, t'was but a dreame of thee.

And now good morrow to our waking soules,
Which watch not one another out of feare;
For love, all love of other sights controules,   10
And makes one little roome, an every where.
Let sea-discoverers to new worlds have gone,
Let Maps to other, worlds on worlds have showne,
Let us possesse one world, each hath one, and is one.

My face in thine eye, thine in mine appeares,   15
And true plain hearts doe in the faces rest,
Where can we finde two better hemispheares
Without sharpe North, without declining West?

SONGS AND SONETS. *1635–69: no division into sections, 1633*
 The good-morrow.   3 countrey pleasures, childishly?] childish
pleasures seelily? *1669 and many MSS.*   4 snorted] slumbred *1669
and some MSS.*   5 this,] as *1669*   10 For] But *many MSS.*
14 one world] our world *many MSS.*   17 better *1633 and some
MSS.: fitter 1635–69 and rest of MSS.*

What

What ever dyes, was not mixt equally;
If our two loves be one, or, thou and I   20
Love so alike, that none doe slacken, none can die.

Song.

GOe, and catche a falling starre,
    Get with child a mandrake roote,
Tell me, where all past yeares are,
    Or who cleft the Divels foot,
Teach me to heare Mermaides singing,   5
    Or to keep off envies stinging,
                And finde
                What winde
Serves to advance an honest minde.

If thou beest borne to strange sights,   10
    Things invisible to see,
Ride ten thousand daies and nights,
    Till age snow white haires on thee,
Thou, when thou retorn'st, wilt tell mee
All strange wonders that befell thee,   15
                And sweare
                No where
Lives a woman true, and faire.

If thou findst one, let mee know,
    Such a Pilgrimage were sweet;   20
Yet doe not, I would not goe,
    Though at next doore wee might meet,

19 was not] is not *1669*   20–1 or, thou and I . . . can die. *1633
and some MSS.:*
                both thou and I
    Love just alike in all, none of these loves can die. *1635–69:*
                or thou and I
    Love just alike in all, none of these loves can die. *some MSS.*
    Song.   3 past yeares] times past *1669*   11 to see] go see *1669:*
see *most MSS.*

                                                Though

Though shee were true, when you met her,
And last, till you write your letter,
   Yet shee   25
   Will bee
Falfe, ere I come, to two, or three.

Womans constancy.

NOw thou hast lov'd me one whole day,
 To morrow when thou leav'st, what wilt thou say?
Wilt thou then Antedate some new made vow?
   Or say that now
We are not just those persons, which we were? 5
Or, that oathes made in reverentiall feare
Of Love, and his wrath, any may forsweare?
Or, as true deaths, true maryages untie,
So lovers contracts, images of those,
Binde but till sleep, deaths image, them unloose? 10
   Or, your owne end to Justifie,
For having purpos'd change, and falsehood; you
Can have no way but falsehood to be true?
Vaine lunatique, against these scapes I could
   Dispute, and conquer, if I would, 15
   Which I abstaine to doe,
For by to morrow, I may thinke so too.

The undertaking.

I Have done one braver thing
 Then all the *Worthies* did,
And yet a braver thence doth spring,
 Which is, to keepe that hid.

27 False, . . . three] False, ere she come to two or three. *1669*
Womans constancy. 8 Or, *1633, 1669:* For, *1635-54* (*ll.* 8-10
in brackets)
 The undertaking.] Platonique Love. *some MSS.*

It were but madnes now t'impart   5
 The skill of specular stone,
When he which can have learn'd the art
 To cut it, can finde none.

So, if I now should utter this,
 Others (because no more   10
Such stuffe to worke upon, there is,)
 Would love but as before.

But he who lovelinesse within
 Hath found, all outward loathes,
For he who colour loves, and skinne,   15
 Loves but their oldest clothes.

If, as I have, you also doe
 Vertue'attir'd in woman see,
And dare love that, and say so too,
 And forget the Hee and Shee;   20

And if this love, though placed so,
 From prophane men you hide,
Which will no faith on this bestow,
 Or, if they doe, deride:

Then you have done a braver thing   25
 Then all the *Worthies* did;
And a braver thence will spring,
 Which is, to keepe that hid.

The Sunne Rising.

BUsie old foole, unruly Sunne,
  Why dost thou thus,
Through windowes, and through curtaines call on us?
Must to thy motions lovers seasons run?

18 Vertue'attir'd in *1633 and most MSS.:* Vertue in *1635–69 and
one MS.*
The Sunne Rising. 3 call] look *1669*

            Sawcy

Sawcy pedantique wretch, goe chide   5
Late schoole boyes, and sowre prentices,
Goe tell Court-huntsmen, that the King will ride,
Call countrey ants to harvest offices;
Love, all alike, no season knowes, nor clyme,
Nor houres, dayes, moneths, which are the rags of time.

Thy beames, so reverend, and strong   11
Why shouldst thou thinke?
I could eclipse and cloud them with a winke,
But that I would not lose her sight so long:
If her eyes have not blinded thine,   15
Looke, and to morrow late, tell mee,
Whether both the'India's of spice and Myne
Be where thou leftst them, or lie here with mee.
Aske for those Kings whom thou saw'st yesterday,
And thou shalt heare, All here in one bed lay.   20

She'is all States, and all Princes, I,
Nothing else is.
Princes doe but play us; compar'd to this,
All honor's mimique; All wealth alchimie.
Thou sunne art halfe as happy'as wee,   25
In that the world's contracted thus;
Thine age askes ease, and since thy duties bee
To warme the world, that's done in warming us.
Shine here to us, and thou art every where;
This bed thy center is, these walls, thy spheare.   30

6 and] or *1669*   sowre] slowe *some MSS.*   11–14 Thy beames,
. . . so long: *1633 and all MSS.:*
Thy beames so reverend, and strong
Dost thou not thinke
I could eclipse and cloude them with a winke,
But that I would not lose her sight so long? *1635–69*
18 leftst *1633:* left *1635–69*   26 thus; *Ed:* thus. *1633–69*

The

The Indifferent.

I Can love both faire and browne,
 Her whom abundance melts, and her whom want betraies,
Her who loves lonenesse best, and her who maskes and
  plaies,
Her whom the country form'd, and whom the town,
Her who beleeves, and her who tries,   5
Her who still weepes with spungie eyes,
And her who is dry corke, and never cries;
I can love her, and her, and you and you,
I can love any, so she be not true.

Will no other vice content you?   10
Wil it not serve your turn to do, as did your mothers?
Or have you all old vices spent, and now would finde out
  others?
Or doth a feare, that men are true, torment you?
Oh we are not, be not you so,
Let mee, and doe you, twenty know.   15
Rob mee, but binde me not, and let me goe.
Must I, who came to travaile thorow you,
Grow your fixt subject, because you are true?

Venus heard me sigh this song,
And by Loves sweetest Part, Variety, she swore, 20
She heard not this till now; and that it should be so no
  more.
She went, examin'd, and return'd ere long,
And said, alas, Some two or three
Poore Heretiques in love there bee,
Which thinke to stablish dangerous constancie. 25
But I have told them, since you will be true,
You shall be true to them, who are false to you.

 The Indifferent. 3 lonenesse] lovers *1669* maskes] sports
1669 12 spent] worn *1669* 19 sigh] sing *1669* 20 sweetest
Part,] sweetest sweet, *1669*

Loves

Loves Vsury.

FOr every houre that thou wilt spare mee now,
      I will allow,
Usurious God of Love, twenty to thee,
When with my browne, my gray haires equall bee;
Till then, Love, let my body raigne, and let   5
Mee travell, sojourne, snatch, plot, have, forget,
Resume my last yeares relict: thinke that yet
      We'had never met.

Let mee thinke any rivalls letter mine,
      And at next nine   10
Keepe midnights promise; mistake by the way
The maid, and tell the Lady of that delay;
Onely let mee love none, no, not the sport;
From country grasse, to comfitures of Court,
Or cities quelque choses, let report   15
      My minde transport.

This bargaine's good; if when I'am old, I bee
      Inflam'd by thee,
If thine owne honour, or my shame, or paine,
Thou covet most, at that age thou shalt gaine.   20
Doe thy will then, then subject and degree,
And fruit of love, Love I submit to thee,
Spare mee till then, I'll beare it, though she bee
      One that loves mee.

Loves Vsury.   5 raigne, *1633 and most MSS.:* range, *1635–69*
6 snatch, *1633, 1669:* match, *1635–54*   15 let report *1633, 1669,
and most MSS.:* let not report *1635–54 and two MSS.*   19 or
paine *1633, 1669 and most MSS.:* and paine *1635–54*   22 fruit]
fruites *some MSS.*

The

The Canonization.

FOr Godsake hold your tongue, and let me love,
   Or chide my palsie, or my gout,
My five gray haires, or ruin'd fortune flout,
    With wealth your state, your minde with Arts improve,
      Take you a course, get you a place,   5
      Observe his honour, or his grace,
Or the Kings reall, or his stamped face
   Contemplate, what you will, approve,
   So you will let me love.

Alas, alas, who's injur'd by my love?   10
   What merchants ships have my sighs drown'd?
Who saies my teares have overflow'd his ground?
    When did my colds a forward spring remove?
      When did the heats which my veines fill
      Adde one more to the plaguie Bill?   15
Soldiers finde warres, and Lawyers finde out still
   Litigious men, which quarrels move,
   Though she and I do love.

Call us what you will, wee are made such by love;
   Call her one, mee another flye,   20
We'are Tapers too, and at our owne cost die,
    And wee in us finde the'Eagle and the Dove.
      The Phœnix ridle hath more wit
      By us, we two being one, are it.
So to one neutrall thing both sexes fit,   25
   Wee dye and rise the same, and prove
   Mysterious by this love.

Wee can dye by it, if not live by love,
   And if unfit for tombes and hearse
Our legend bee, it will be fit for verse;   30
    And if no peece of Chronicle wee prove,

The Canonization.   15 more, *1633–54:* man *1669 and most MSS.*
25 So *1650–69:* So, *1633–39*   fit,] fit. *1633–69*   30 legend]
legends *1633*

We'll

We'll build in sonnets pretty roomes;
  As well a well wrought urne becomes
The greatest ashes, as halfe-acre tombes,
  And by these hymnes, all shall approve   35
  Us *Canoniz'd* for Love:

And thus invoke us; You whom reverend love
  Made one anothers hermitage;
You, to whom love was peace, that now is rage;
  Who did the whole worlds soule contract, and drove 40
    Into the glasses of your eyes
    So made such mirrors, and such spies,
That they did all to you epitomize,
  Countries, Townes, Courts: Beg from above
  A patterne of your love!   45

The triple Foole.

I Am two fooles, I know,
For loving, and for saying so
  In whining Poëtry;
But where's that wiseman, that would not be I,
  If she would not deny?   5
Then as th'earths inward narrow crooked lanes
Do purge sea waters fretfull salt away,
  I thought, if I could draw my paines,
Through Rimes vexation, I should them allay,
Griefe brought to numbers cannot be so fierce,   10
For, he tames it, that fetters it in verse.

But when I have done so,
Some man, his art and voice to show,
  Doth Set and sing my paine,
And, by delighting many, frees againe   15
  Griefe, which verse did restraine.

40 contract] extract *all MSS.*   45 your *1669 and most MSS.:*
our *1633–54*   love! *Ed:* love. *1633–69*
  The triple Foole.   11 For, he tames it] He tames it much *one MS.*

To

To Love, and Griefe tribute of Verse belongs,
But not of such as pleases when'tis read,
   Both are increased by such songs:
For both their triumphs so are published,   20
And I, which was two fooles, do so grow three;
Who are a little wise, the best fooles bee.

Lovers infinitenesse.

IF yet I have not all thy love,
  Deare, I shall never have it all,
I cannot breath one other sigh, to move;
Nor can intreat one other teare to fall.
And all my treasure, which should purchase thee,   5
Sighs, teares, and oathes, and letters I have spent,
Yet no more can be due to mee,
Then at the bargaine made was ment,
If then thy gift of love were partiall,
That some to mee, some should to others fall,   10
  Deare, I shall never have Thee All.

Or if then thou gavest mee all,
All was but All, which thou hadst then,
But if in thy heart, since, there be or shall,
New love created bee, by other men,   15
Which have their stocks intire, and can in teares,
In sighs, in oathes, and letters outbid mee,
This new love may beget new feares,
For, this love was not vowed by thee.
And yet it was, thy gift being generall,   20
The ground, thy heart is mine, what ever shall
  Grow there, deare, I should have it all.

  Lovers infinitenesse.   *Query* Loves infinitenesse. 11 Thee
1633: It *1635–69*   19 thee. *1639–69:* thee, *1633–35*   21 is
1633, 1669: was *1635–54*

Yet

Yet I would not have all yet,
Hee that hath all can have no more,
And since my love doth every day admit   25
New growth, thou shouldst have new rewards in store;
Thou canst not every day give me thy heart,
If thou canst give it, then thou never gavest it:
Loves riddles are, that though thy heart depart,
It stayes at home, and thou with losing savest it: 30
But wee will have a way more liberall,
Then changing hearts, to joyne them, so wee shall
 Be one, and one anothers All.

Song.

SWeetest love, I do not goe,
 For wearinesse of thee,
Nor in hope the world can show
 A fitter Love for mee;
  But since that I   5
Must dye at last, 'tis best,
To use my selfe in jest
  Thus by fain'd deaths to dye;

25–6 And since my heart doth every day beget New love, &c. *one MS.*
29–30 Except mine come when thine doth part
   And in such giving it, thou savest it: *two MSS.*
   Perchance mine comes, when thine doth parte,
   And by such losing it, &c. *one MS.*
31 have] find *two MSS.*
 Song.   *In one group of MSS. this with* Send home my long
stray'd eyes *and* The Bait *are given as* Songs which were made to
certain ayres which were made before 1–4 *In most MSS. these lines
are written as two long lines, and so with ll.* 9–12, 17–20, 25–28, 33–36
5–8 But since . . . dye; *1633 and many MSS.*
     At the last must part 'tis best,
     Thus to use my selfe in jest
      By fained deaths to dye; *1635–54:*
     Must dye a. last, 'tis best,
     Thus to use my self in jest
      By fained death to dye; *1669*

Yesternight

Yesternight the Sunne went hence,
  And yet is here to day,   10
He hath no desire nor sense,
  Nor halfe so short a way:
    Then feare not mee,
But beleeve that I shall make
Speedier journeyes, since I take   15
  More wings and spurres then hee.

O how feeble is mans power,
  That if good fortune fall,
Cannot adde another houre,
  Nor a lost houre recall!   20
    But come bad chance,
And wee joyne to'it our strength,
And wee teach it art and length,
  It selfe o'r us to'advance.

When thou sigh'st, thou sigh'st not winde,   25
  But sigh'st my soule away,
When thou weep'st, unkindly kinde,
  My lifes blood doth decay.
    It cannot bee
That thou lov'st mee, as thou say'st,   30
If in thine my life thou waste,
  Thou art the best of mee.

Let not thy divining heart
  Forethinke me any ill,
Destiny may take thy part,   35
  And may thy feares fulfill;
    But thinke that wee
Are but turn'd aside to sleepe;
They who one another keepe
  Alive, ne'r parted bee.   40

25 not wind *1633:* no wind *1635–69*
generally: That *1635–54:* Which *1669*
make *1639–54*

32 Thou *1633 and MSS.*
36 may *1633–35, 1669:*

The

The Legacie.

WHen I dyed last, and, Deare, I dye
    As often as from thee I goe,
  Though it be but an houre agoe,
And Lovers houres be full eternity,
I can remember yet, that I   5
  Something did say, and something did bestow;
Though I be dead, which sent mee, I should be
Mine owne executor and Legacie.

I heard mee say, Tell her anon,
    That my selfe, (that is you, not I,)   10
  Did kill me, and when I felt mee dye,
I bid mee send my heart, when I was gone,
But I alas could there finde none,
    When I had ripp'd me,'and search'd where hearts did
      lye;
It kill'd mee againe, that I who still was true,   15
In life, in my last Will should cozen you.

Yet I found something like a heart,
    But colours it, and corners had,
    It was not good, it was not bad,
It was intire to none, and few had part.   20
As good as could be made by art
    It seem'd; and therefore for our losses sad,
I meant to send this heart in stead of mine,
But oh, no man could hold it, for twas thine.

The Legacie.   7 sent *1633, 1669:* meant *1635–54*   10 that is
1635–69: that's *1633: brackets from some MSS.*   14 When . . .
did *1633 and some MSS.:* When I had ripp'd, and search'd where
hearts should *1635–69 and other MSS.*   22 seem'd; *Ed:* seem'd,
1633–69   23 this *1633:* that *1635–69*

A Feaver

A Feaver.

OH doe not die, for I shall hate
All women so, when thou art gone,
That thee I shall not celebrate,
   When I remember, thou wast one.

But yet thou canst not die, I know;   5
   To leave this world behinde, is death,
But when thou from this world wilt goe,
   The whole world vapors with thy breath.

Or if, when thou, the worlds soule, goest,
   It stay, tis but thy carkasse then,   10
The fairest woman, but thy ghost,
   But corrupt wormes, the worthyest men.

O wrangling schooles, that search what fire
   Shall burne this world, had none the wit
Unto this knowledge to aspire,   15
   That this her feaver might be it?

And yet she cannot wast by this,
   Nor long beare this torturing wrong,
For much corruption needfull is
   To fuell such a feaver long.   20

These burning fits but meteors bee,
   Whose matter in thee is soone spent.
Thy beauty,'and all parts, which are thee,
   Are unchangeable firmament.

Yet t'was of my minde, seising thee,   25
   Though it in thee cannot persever.
For I had rather owner bee
   Of thee one houre, then all else ever.

A Feaver.   16 might] must *one MS.*   18 beare] endure *1669*
19 For much *1633 and most MSS.:* For more *1635–69*

Aire

Aire and Angels.

Twice or thrice had I loved thee,
   Before I knew thy face or name,
So in a voice, so in a shapelesse flame,
Angells affect us oft, and worship'd bee;
   Still when, to where thou wert, I came,   5
Some lovely glorious nothing I did see.
   But since my soule, whose child love is,
Takes limmes of flesh, and else could nothing doe,
   More subtile then the parent is,
Love must not be, but take a body too,   10
   And therefore what thou wert, and who,
     I bid Love aske, and now
That it assume thy body, I allow,
And fixe it selfe in thy lip, eye, and brow.

Whilst thus to ballast love, I thought,   15
And so more steddily to have gone,
With wares which would sinke admiration,
I saw, I had loves pinnace overfraught,
   Ev'ry thy haire for love to worke upon
Is much too much, some fitter must be sought;   20
   For, nor in nothing, nor in things
Extreme, and scatt'ring bright, can love inhere;
   Then as an Angell, face, and wings
Of aire, not pure as it, yet pure doth weare,
   So thy love may be my loves spheare;
     Just such disparitie   25
As is twixt Aire and Angells puritie,
'Twixt womens love, and mens will ever bee.

Aire and Angels.   14 lip, eye,] lips, eyes, *1669*   19
Ev'ry thy *1633–39 and most MSS.:* Thy every *1650–69*   27 Aire
1633–54 and all MSS.: Airs *1669*

Break

Breake of day.

'TIs true, 'tis day; what though it be?
　O wilt thou therefore rise from me?
Why should we rise, because 'tis light?
Did we lie downe, because 'twas night?
Love which in spight of darknesse brought us hether,　5
Should in despight of light keepe us together.

Light hath no tongue, but is all eye;
If it could speake as well as spie,
This were the worst, that it could say,
That being well, I faine would stay,　　　　10
And that I lov'd my heart and honor so,
That I would not from him, that had them, goe.

Must businesse thee from hence remove?
Oh, that's the worst disease of love,
The poore, the foule, the false, love can　　15
Admit, but not the busied man.
He which hath businesse, and makes love, doth doe
Such wrong, as when a maryed man doth wooe.

The Anniversarie.

ALL Kings, and all their favorites,
　All glory of honors, beauties, wits,
The Sun it selfe, which makes times, as they passe,
Is elder by a yeare, now, then it was
When thou and I first one another saw:　　5
All other things, to their destruction draw,
　Only our love hath no decay;
This, no to morrow hath, nor yesterday,
Running it never runs from us away,
But truly keepes his first, last, everlasting day.　　10

Breake of day.　　5 in spight] in dispight *1650–54 and many
MSS.*　　6 in despight] in spight *1635–39*
The Anniversarie.　　3 times, as they passe, *1633, 1669, MSS.:
times, as these pass, 1635–54*

Two

Two graves must hide thine and my coarse,
  If one might, death were no divorce·
Alas, as well as other Princes, wee,
(Who Prince enough in one another bee,)
Must leave at last in death, these eyes, and eares,   15
Oft fed with true oathes, and with sweet salt teares;
  But soules where nothing dwells but love
(All other thoughts being inmates) then shall prove
This, or a love increased there above,
When bodies to their graves, soules from their graves re-
    move.   20

And then wee shall be throughly blest,
  But wee no more, then all the rest;
Here upon earth, we'are Kings, and none but wee
Can be such Kings, nor of such subjects bee;
Who is so safe as wee? where none can doe   25
Treason to us, except one of us two.
  True and false feares let us refraine,
Let us love nobly, and live, and adde againe
Yeares and yeares unto yeares, till we attaine
To write threescore: this is the second of our raigne. 30

A Valediction: of my name, in the window.

I.

MY name engrav'd herein,
Doth contribute my firmnesse to this glasse,
  Which, ever since that charme, hath beene
  As hard, as that which grav'd it, was;
Thine eye will give it price enough, to mock   5
    The diamonds of either rock.

II.

II.

'Tis much that Glasse should bee
As all confessing, and through-shine as I,
    'Tis more, that it shewes thee to thee,
    And cleare reflects thee to thine eye.   10
But all such rules, loves magique can undoe,
    Here you see mee, and I am you.

III.

As no one point, nor dash,
Which are but accessaries to this name,
    The showers and tempests can outwash,   15
    So shall all times finde mee the same;
You this intirenesse better may fulfill,
    Who have the patterne with you still.

IIII.

Or if too hard and deepe
This learning be, for a scratch'd name to teach,   20
    It, as a given deaths head keepe,
    Lovers mortalitie to preach,
Or thinke this ragged bony name to bee
    My ruinous Anatomie.

V.

Then, as all my soules bee,   25
Emparadis'd in you, (in whom alone
    I understand, and grow and see,)
    The rafters of my body, bone
Being still with you, the Muscle, Sinew, and Veine,
    Which tile this house, will come againe: 30

---

14 accessaries *1633–69:* accessary *most MSS.*   30 againe:]
againe. *1633–69*

VI.

VI.

Till my returne, repaire
And recompact my scattered body so.
As all the vertuous powers which are
Fix'd in the starres, are said to flow
Into such characters, as graved bee   35
When these starres have supremacie:

VII.

So since this name was cut
When love and griefe their exaltation had,
No doore 'gainst this names influence shut;
As much more loving, as more sad,   40
'Twill make thee; and thou shouldst, till I returne,
Since I die daily, daily mourne.

VIII.

When thy inconsiderate hand
Flings ope this casement, with my trembling name,
To looke on one, whose wit or land,   45
New battry to thy heart may frame,
Then thinke this name alive, and that thou thus
In it offendst my Genius.

IX.

And when thy melted maid,
Corrupted by thy Lover's gold, and page,   50
His letter at thy pillow'hath laid,
Disputed it, and tam'd thy rage,
And thou begin'st to thaw towards him, for this,
May my name step in, and hide his.

32 so. *1633–35:* so, *1639–69*   34 flow *Ed:* flow, *1633–69*
36 these *1633:* those *1635–69*   44 ope *1633–69:* out *most MSS.*

                                                                    X.

X.

And if this treason goe   55
To an overt act, and that thou write againe;
   In superscribing, this name flow
   Into thy fancy, from the pane.
So, in forgetting thou remembrest right,
     And unaware to mee shalt write.   60

XI.

But glasse, and lines must bee,
No meanes our firme substantiall love to keepe;
   Neere death inflicts this lethargie,
   And this I murmure in my sleepe;
Impute this idle talke, to that I goe,   65
     For dying men talke often so.

Twicknam garden.

BLasted with sighs, and surrounded with teares,
  Hither I come to seeke the spring,
   And at mine eyes, and at mine eares,
Receive such balmes, as else cure every thing;
   But O, selfe traytor, I do bring   5
The spider love, which transubstantiates all,
   And can convert Manna to gall,
And that this place may thoroughly be thought
   True Paradise, I have the serpent brought.

'Twere wholsomer for mee, that winter did   10
  Benight the glory of this place,
   And that a grave frost did forbid
These trees to laugh, and mocke mee to my face;
   But that I may not this disgrace

55 goe] growe *some MSS.*   57 this] my *1669*   60 unaware]
unawares *several MSS.*   64 this] thus *1635–69*
   Twicknam garden. Twicknam Garden. (*as pronounced*) *some MSS.*
4 balms . . . cure *1633:* balm . . . cures *1635–69 and many MSS.*

Indure

Indure, nor yet leave loving, Love let mee   15
  Some senslesse peece of this place bee;
Make me a mandrake, so I may groane here,
  Or a stone fountaine weeping out my yeare.

Hither with christall vyals, lovers come,
  And take my teares, which are loves wine,   20
And try your mistresse Teares at home,
  For all are false, that tast not just like mine;
  Alas, hearts do not in eyes shine,
Nor can you more judge womans thoughts by teares,
  Then by her shadow, what she weares.   25
O perverse sexe, where none is true but shee,
  Who's therefore true, because her truth kills mee.

A Valediction : of the booke.

I'Ll tell thee now (deare Love) what thou shalt doe
  To anger destiny, as she doth us,
How I shall stay, though she Esloygne me thus,
And how posterity shall know it too;
    How thine may out-endure   5
    Sybills glory, and obscure
    Her who from Pindar could allure,
  And her, through whose helpe *Lucan* is not lame,
And her, whose booke (they say) *Homer* did finde, and
    name.

Study our manuscripts, those Myriades   10
  Of letters, which have past twixt thee and mee,
  Thence write our Annals, and in them will bee
To all whom loves subliming fire invades,

15 nor yet leave loving, *1633:* nor leave this garden, *1635–69
and most MSS.*   17 groane *several MSS.:* grow *1633–69 and
some MSS.*   18 my yeare, *1633, 1669:* the yeare. *1635–54*
24 womans *several MSS.:* womens *1633–69 and some MSS.*

Rule

        Rule and example found;
        There, the faith of any ground   15
        No schismatique will dare to wound,
    That sees, how Love this grace to us affords,
To make, to keep, to use, to be these his Records.

This Booke, as long-liv'd as the elements,
    Or as the worlds forme, this all-graved tome   20
    In cypher writ, or new made Idiome,
Wee for loves clergie only'are instruments:
        When this booke is made thus,
        Should againe the ravenous
        Vandals and Goths inundate us,   25
    Learning were safe; in this our Universe
Schooles might learne Sciences, Spheares Musick, Angels
            Verse.

Here Loves Divines, (since all Divinity
    Is love or wonder) may finde all they seeke,
    Whether abstract spirituall love they like,   30
Their Soules exhal'd with what they do not see,
        Or, loth so to amuze
        Faiths infirmitie, they chuse
        Something which they may see and use;
    For, though minde be the heaven, where love doth
            sit,   35
Beauty a convenient type may be to figure it.

Here more then in their bookes may Lawyers finde,
    Both by what titles Mistresses are ours,
    And how prerogative these states devours,
Transferr'd from Love himselfe, to womankinde,   40

    A Valediction: of *&c.*   25 and Goths inundate us, *several
MSS.:* and the Goths invade us, *1633–54:* and Goths invade us,
1669   33 infirmitie,] infirmities, *1669, some MSS.*   39 these
states] those rites *some MSS.*

                                                            Who

Who though from heart, and eyes,
They exact great subsidies,
Forsake him who on them relies,
And for the cause, honour, or conscience give,
Chimeraes, vaine as they, or their prerogative.　　45

Here Statesmen, (or of them, they which can reade,)
May of their occupation finde the grounds:
Love and their art alike it deadly wounds,
If to conşider what 'tis, one proceed,
In both they doe excell　　50
Who the present governe well,
Whose weaknesse none doth, or dares tell;
In this thy booke, such will their nothing see,
As in the Bible some can finde out Alchimy.

Thus vent thy thoughts; abroad I'll studie thee,　　55
As he removes farre off, that great heights takes;
How great love is, presence best tryall makes,
But absence tryes how long this love will bee;
To take a latitude
Sun, or starres, are fitliest view'd　　60
At their brightest, but to conclude
Of longitudes, what other way have wee,
But to marke when, and where the darke eclipses bee?

Communitie.

GOod wee must love, and must hate ill,
For ill is ill, and good good still,
But there are things indifferent,
Which wee may neither hate, nor love,
But one, and then another prove,　　5
As wee shall finde our fancy bent.

53 their nothing *1635–54 and most MSS. (but the MSS. waver between* their *and* there)*:* there something *1633, 1669*
　Communitie.　3 there *1635–69 and some MSS.:* these *1633 and other MSS.*

If

If then at first wise Nature had
Made women either good or bad,
   Then some wee might hate, and some chuse,
But since shee did them so create,   10
That we may neither love, nor hate,
   Onely this rests, All, all may use.

If they were good it would be seene,
Good is as visible as greene,
   And to all eyes it selfe betrayes: 15
If they were bad, they could not last,
Bad doth it selfe, and others wast,
   So, they deserve nor blame, nor praise.

But they are ours as fruits are ours,
He that but tasts, he that devours,   20
   And he that leaves all, doth as well:
Chang'd loves are but chang'd sorts of meat,
And when hee hath the kernell eate,
   Who doth not fling away the shell?

Loves growth.

I Scarce beleeve my love to be so pure
   As I had thought it was,
     Because it doth endure
Vicissitude, and season, as the grasse;
Me thinkes I lyed all winter, when I swore,   5
My love was infinite, if spring make'it more.

But if this medicine, love, which cures all sorrow
With more, not onely bee no quintessence,
But mixt of all stuffes, paining soule, or sense,
And of the Sunne his working vigour borrow,   10

Loves growth.   9 paining *1633 and some MSS.:* vexing *1635–69*
and other MSS.   10 working *1633 and some MSS.:* active *1635–69*
and some MSS.

Love's

Love's not so pure, and abstract, as they use
To say, which have no Mistresse but their Muse,
But as all else, being elemented too,
Love sometimes would contemplate, sometimes do.

And yet no greater, but more eminent,   15
  Love by the spring is growne;
  As, in the firmament,
Starres by the Sunne are not inlarg'd, but showne.
Gentle love deeds, as blossomes on a bough,
From loves awakened root do bud out now.   20

If, as in water stir'd more circles bee
Produc'd by one, love such additions take,
Those like so many spheares, but one heaven make,
For, they are all concentrique unto thee;
And though each spring doe adde to love new heate, 25
As princes doe in times of action get
New taxes, and remit them not in peace,
No winter shall abate the springs encrease.

Loves exchange.

Love, any devill else but you,
  Would for a given Soule give something too.
At Court your fellowes every day,
Give th'art of Riming, Huntsmanship, or Play,
For them which were their owne before;   5
Onely I have nothing which gave more,
But am, alas, by being lowly, lower.

I aske no dispensation now
To falsifie a teare, or sigh, or vow,

18–19 Starres . . . showne. Gentle love *Ed:* Starres . . . showne,
Gentle love *1633–69:*
   Stars are not by the sunne enlarg'd; but showne
   Greater; Loves deeds *one MS.*
28 the *1633 and some MSS.:* this *1635–69 and some MSS.*

I do

I do not sue from thee to draw   10
A *non obstante* on natures law,
These are prerogatives, they inhere
In thee and thine; none should forsweare
Except that hee *Loves* minion were.

Give mee thy weaknesse, make mee blinde,   15
Both wayes, as thou and thine, in eies and minde;
Love, let me never know that this
Is love, or, that love childish is;
Let me not know that others know
That she knowes my paines, least that so   20
A tender shame make me mine owne new woe.

If thou give nothing, yet thou'art just,
Because I would not thy first motions trust;
Small townes which stand stiffe, till great shot
Enforce them, by warres law *condition* not.   25
Such in loves warfare is my case,
I may not article for grace,
Having put Love at last to shew this face.

This face, by which he could command
And change the Idolatrie of any land,   30
This face, which wheresoe'r it comes,
Can call vow'd men from cloisters, dead from tombes,
And melt both Poles at once, and store
Deserts with cities, and make more
Mynes in the earth, then Quarries were before.   35

For this, Love is enrag'd with mee,
Yet kills not.   If I must example bee
To future Rebells; If th'unborne
Must learne, by my being cut up, and torne:
Kill, and dissect me, Love; for this   40
Torture against thine owne end is,
Rack't carcasses make ill Anatomies.

Loves exchange.   20 paines] paine *some MSS*.   36 For this,
Ed: For, this *1633–69*

Confined

Confined Love.

SOme man unworthy to be possessor
Of old or new love, himselfe being false or weake,
  Thought his paine and shame would be lesser,
If on womankind he might his anger wreake,
        And thence a law did grow,   5
        One might but one man know;
        But are other creatures so?

  Are Sunne, Moone, or Starres by law forbidden,
To smile where they list, or lend away their light?
  Are birds divorc'd, or are they chidden   10
If they leave their mate, or lie abroad a night?
        Beasts doe no joyntures lose
        Though they new lovers choose,
        But we are made worse then those.

  Who e'r rigg'd faire ship to lie in harbors,   15
And not to seeke new lands, or not to deale withall?
  Or built faire houses, set trees, and arbors,
Only to lock up, or else to let them fall?
        Good is not good, unlesse
        A thousand it possesse,   20
        But doth wast with greedinesse.

The Dreame.

DEare love, for nothing lesse then thee
  Would I have broke this happy dreame,
        It was a theame
For reason, much too strong for phantasie,
Therefore thou wakd'st me wisely; yet   5
My Dreame thou brok'st not, but continued'st it,

Confined Love.   3 lesser] the lesser *some MSS.*   11 a night
(*i.e.* a-night) *1633–54:* all night *1669*   withall *1633:* with all
1635–69
  The Dreame.   7 so truth, *1633 and some MSS.:* so true,
1635–69 and other MSS.

Thou

Thou art so truth, that thoughts of thee suffice,
To make dreames truths; and fables histories;
Enter these armes, for since thou thoughtst it best,
Not to dreame all my dreame, let's act the rest.　　10

As lightning, or a Tapers light,
Thine eyes, and not thy noise wak'd mee;
　　　　Yet I thought thee
(For thou lovest truth) an Angell, at first sight,
But when I saw thou sawest my heart,　　　　15
And knew'st my thoughts, beyond an Angels art,
When thou knew'st what I dreamt, when thou knew'st
Excesse of joy would wake me, and cam'st then,　[when
I must confesse, it could not chuse but bee
Prophane, to thinke thee any thing but thee.　　20

Comming and staying show'd thee, thee,
But rising makes me doubt, that now,
　　　　Thou art not thou.
That love is weake, where feare's as strong as hee;
'Tis not all spirit, pure, and brave,　　　　25
If mixture it of *Feare, Shame, Honor*, have.
Perchance as torches which must ready bee,
Men light and put out, so thou deal'st with mee,
Thou cam'st to kindle, goest to come;　Then I
Will dreame that hope againe, but else would die.　30

A Valediction : of weeping.

LEt me powre forth
My teares before thy face, whil'st I stay here,
For thy face coines them, and thy stampe they beare,
And by this Mintage they are something worth,

10 act] doe *most MSS.*　　14 (Thou lovest truth) but an Angell,
some MSS.　　19 must] doe *most MSS.*　　20 Prophane,] Profaness
some MSS.　　24 feare's as strong *1633–54 and some MSS.*: feares
are strong, *1669 and some MSS.*　　29 Then I] Thus I *most MSS.*

For

For thus they bee 5
Pregnant of thee;
Fruits of much griefe they are, emblemes of more,
When a teare falls, that thou falst which it bore,
So thou and I are nothing then, when on a divers shore.

On a round ball 10
A workeman that hath copies by, can lay
An Europe, Afrique, and an Asia,
And quickly make that, which was nothing, *All*,
So doth each teare,
Which thee doth weare, 15
A globe, yea world by that impression grow,
Till thy teares mixt with mine doe overflow
This world, by waters sent from thee, my heaven dissolved so.

O more then Moone,
Draw not up seas to drowne me in thy spheare, 20
Weepe me not dead, in thine armes, but forbeare
To teach the sea, what it may doe too soone;
Let not the winde
Example finde,
To doe me more harme, then it purposeth; 25
Since thou and I sigh one anothers breath,
Who e'r sighes most, is cruellest, and hasts the others death.

Loves Alchymie.

SOme that have deeper digg'd loves Myne then I,
Say, where his centrique happinesse doth lie:
I have lov'd, and got, and told,
But should I love, get, tell, till I were old,
I should not finde that hidden mysterie; 5
Oh, 'tis imposture all:

A Valediction: of &c. 8 falst *1633–69:* falls *MSS.*
Loves Alchymie. *1633–69:* Mummye. *MSS.*

And

And as no chymique yet th'Elixar got,
    But glorifies his pregnant pot,
    If by the way to him befall
Some odoriferous thing, or medicinall,   10
    So, lovers dreame a rich and long delight,
    But get a winter-seeming summers night.

Our ease, our thrift, our honor, and our day,
Shall we, for this vaine Bubles shadow pay?
        Ends love in this, that my man,   15
Can be as happy'as I can; If he can
Endure the short scorne of a Bridegroomes play?
        That loving wretch that sweares,
'Tis not the bodies marry, but the mindes,
        Which he in her Angelique findes,   20
        Would sweare as justly, that he heares,
In that dayes rude hoarse minstralsey, the spheares.
    Hope not for minde in women; at their best
    Sweetnesse and wit, they'are but *Mummy,* possest.

The Flea.

MArke but this flea, and marke in this,
  How little that which thou deny'st me is;
It suck'd me first, and now sucks thee,
And in this flea, our two bloods mingled bee;
Thou know'st that this cannot be said   5
A sinne, nor shame, nor losse of maidenhead,
    Yet this enjoyes before it wooe,
    And pamper'd swells with one blood made of two,
    And this, alas, is more then wee would doe.

15 my *1633–69 and MSS.:* any *ene MS., 1855, and Grolier*
The Flea. 3 It suckt mee first *1633–54 and some MSS.:* Mee it
suck'd first *1669 and other MSS.* 5 Thou know'st that, *&c.*] Confess
it. This cannot be said *1669 and several MSS.* 6 nor shame, nor
losse] or shame, or loss *1669 and several MSS.* 9 would] could
1669

                                            Oh

Oh stay, three lives in one flea spare,　　　　　10
Where wee almost, yea more then maryed are,
This flea is you and I, and this
Our mariage.bed, and mariage temple is;
Though parents grudge, and you, w'are met,
And cloysterd in these living walls of Jet.　　　15
　　Though use make you apt to kill mee,
　　Let not to that, selfe murder added bee,
　　And sacrilege, three sinnes in killing three.

Cruell and sodaine, hast thou since
Purpled thy naile, in blood of innocence?　　　20
Wherein could this flea guilty bee,
Except in that drop which it suckt from thee?
Yet thou triumph'st, and saist that thou
Find'st not thy selfe, nor mee the weaker now;
　　'Tis true, then learne how false, feares bee;　　25
　　Just so much honor, when thou yeeld'st to mee,
　　Will wast, as this flea's death tooke life from thee.

The Curse.

WHo ever guesses, thinks, or dreames he knowes
　　Who is my mistris, wither by this curse;
　　His only, and only his purse
　　May some dull heart to love dispose,
And shee yeeld then to all that are his foes;　　　5
　　May he be scorn'd by one, whom all else scorne,
　　Forsweare to others, what to her he'hath sworne,
　　With feare of missing, shame of getting, torne:

---

11 yea] nay, *1669 and several MSS.*　　　16 you] thee *some MSS.*
21 Wherein] In what *several MSS.*
　　The Curse.　　3 His only, and only his purse] Him, only for his
purse *1669*　　4 heart] whore *1669*　　5 And shee yeeld then to] And
then yield unto *1669*

Madnesse

Madnesse his sorrow, gout his cramp, may hee
Make, by but thinking, who hath made him such: 10
  And may he feele no touch
  Of conscience, but of fame, and bee
Anguish'd, not that 'twas sinne, but that 'twas shee:
 In early and long scarcenesse may he rot,
 For land which had been his, if he had not   15
 Himselfe incestuously an heire begot:

May he dreame Treason, and beleeve, that hee
Meant to performe it, and confesse, and die,
  And no record tell why:
  His sonnes, which none of his may bee,   20
Inherite nothing but his infamie:
 Or may he so long Parasites have fed,
 That he would faine be theirs, whom he hath bred,
 And at the last be circumcis'd for bread:

The venom of all stepdames, gamsters gall,   25
What Tyrans, and their subjects interwish,
  What Plants, Mynes, Beasts, Foule, Fish,
  Can contribute, all ill which all
Prophets, or Poets spake; And all which shall
 Be annex'd in schedules unto this by mee,   30
 Fall on that man; For if it be a shee
 Nature before hand hath out-cursed mee.

---

9 cramp,] cramps, *1669 and most MSS.*   12 fame,] shame;
some MSS.   14–16 In early and long scarcenesse . . . an heire begot.
1633 and some MSS.:
  Or may he for her vertue reverence
  One that hates him onely for impotence,
  And equall Traitors be she and his sense.
1635–69 and other MSS.   27 Mynes, *most MSS.*: Myne, *1633–69
and some MSS.*

The

The Message.

SEnd home my long strayd eyes to mee,
Which (Oh) too long have dwelt on thee;
Yet since there they have learn'd such ill,
    Such forc'd fashions,
    And false passions,   5
        That they be
        Made by thee
Fit for no good sight, keep them still.

Send home my harmlesse heart againe,
Which no unworthy thought could staine;   10
But if it be taught by thine
    To make jestings
    Of protestings,
        And crosse both
        Word and oath,   15
Keepe it, for then 'tis none of mine.

Yet send me back my heart and eyes,
That I may know, and see thy lyes,
And may laugh and joy, when thou
    Art in anguish   20
    And dost languish
        For some one
        That will none,
Or prove as false as thou art now.

A nocturnall upon S. Lucies day,
Being the shortest day.

TIs the yeares midnight, and it is the dayes,
  Lucies, who scarce seaven houres herself unmaskes,
The Sunne is spent, and now his flasks
Send forth light squibs, no constant rayes;

The Message.   11 But *1635–69:* Which *1633 and some MSS.*
14 crosse *all MSS.:* breake *1633–69*

                    The

The worlds whole sap is sunke: 5
The generall balme th'hydroptique earth hath drunk,
Whither, as to the beds-feet, life is shrunke,
Dead and enterr'd; yet all these seeme to laugh,
Compar'd with mee, who am their Epitaph.

Study me then, you who shall lovers bee   10
At the next world, that is, at the next Spring:
   For I am every dead thing,
   In whom love wrought new Alchimie.
     For his art did expresse
A quintessence even from nothingnesse,   15
From dull privations, and leane emptinesse:
He ruin'd mee, and I am re-begot
Of absence, darknesse, death; things which are not.

All others, from all things, draw all that's good,
Life, soule, forme, spirit, whence they beeing have;   20
   I, by loves limbecke, am the grave
   Of all, that's nothing. Oft a flood
     Have wee two wept, and so
Drownd the whole world, us two; oft did we grow
To be two Chaosses, when we did show   25
Care to ought else; and often absences
Withdrew our soules, and made us carcasses.

But I am by her death, (which word wrongs her)
Of the first nothing, the Elixer grown;
   Were I a man, that I were one,   30
   I needs must know; I should preferre,
     If I were any beast,
Some ends, some means; Yea plants, yea stones detest,
And love; All, all some properties invest;
If I an ordinary nothing were,   35
As shadow, a light, and body must be here.

  A nocturnall &c.   12 every] a very *1635–69*   16 emptinesse:
1719. emptinesse *1633–54.* emptinesse, *1669*

                            But

But I am None; nor will my Sunne renew.
You lovers, for whose sake, the lesser Sunne
 At this time to the Goat is runne
  To fetch new lust, and give it you,   40
   Enjoy your summer all;
Since shee enjoyes her long nights festivall,
Let mee prepare towards her, and let mee call
This houre her Vigill, and her Eve, since this
Both the yeares, and the dayes deep midnight is. 45

Witchcraft by a picture.

I Fixe mine eye on thine, and there
 Pitty my picture burning in thine eye,
My picture drown'd in a transparent teare,
 When I looke lower I espie;
  Hadst thou the wicked skill   5
By pictures made and mard, to kill,
How many wayes mightst thou performe thy will?

But now I have drunke thy sweet salt teares,
 And though thou poure more I'll depart;
My picture vanish'd, vanish feares,   10
 That I can be endamag'd by that art;
  Though thou retaine of mee
One picture more, yet that will bee,
Being in thine owne heart, from all malice free.

The Baite.

COme live with mee, and bee my love,
 And we will some new pleasures prove
Of golden sands, and christall brookes,
With silken lines, and silver hookes.

   Witchcraft &c. 11 that] thy *some MSS.*
      D   There

There will the river whispering runne   5
Warm'd by thy eyes, more then the Sunne.
And there the'inamor'd fish will stay,
Begging themselves they may betray.

When thou wilt swimme in that live bath,
Each fish, which every channell hath,   10
Will amorously to thee swimme,
Gladder to catch thee, then thou him.

If thou, to be so seene, beest loath,
By Sunne, or Moone, thou darknest both,
And if my selfe have leave to see,   15
I need not their light, having thee.

Let others freeze with angling reeds,
And cut their legges, with shells and weeds,
Or treacherously poore fish beset,
With strangling snare, or windowie net: 20

Let coarse bold hands, from slimy nest
The bedded fish in banks out-wrest,
Or curious traitors, sleavesilke flies
Bewitch poore fishes wandring eyes.

For thee, thou needst no such deceit,   25
For thou thy selfe art thine owne bait;
That fish, that is not catch'd thereby,
Alas, is wiser farre then I.

The Baite.   7 inamor'd] enamelled *Walton*   11 Most
amorously to thee will swim *Walton*   15 my selfe] mine eyes
Walton: my heart *some MSS.*   20 snare,] snares, *Walton*   23 Or
1633–69: Let *Walton*   24 To witch poor wandring fishes eyes.
Walton   25 thou needst] there needs *some MSS.*   28 Is wiser far,
alas *Walton*

The

The Apparition.

WHen by thy scorne, O murdresse I am dead,
　　And that thou thinkst thee free
From all solicitation from mee,
Then shall my ghost come to thy bed,
And thee, fain'd vestall, in worse armes shall see;　　5
Then thy sicke taper will begin to winke,
And he, whose thou art then, being tyr'd before,
Will, if thou stirre, or pinch to wake him, thinke
　　　Thou call'st for more,
And in false sleepe will from thee shrinke,　　10
And then poore Aspen wretch, neglected thou
Bath'd in a cold quicksilver sweat wilt lye
　　　A veryer ghost then I;
What I will say, I will not tell thee now,
Lest that preserve thee'; and since my love is spent,　　15
I'had rather thou shouldst painfully repent,
Then by my threatnings rest still innocent.

The broken heart.

HE is starke mad, who ever sayes,
　　That he hath beene in love an houre,
Yet not that love so soone decayes,
　　But that it can tenne in lesse space devour;
Who will beleeve mee, if I sweare　　5
That I have had the plague a yeare?
　　Who would not laugh at mee, if I should say,
　　I saw a flaske of *powder burne a day?*

Ah, what a trifle is a heart,
　　If once into loves hands it come!　　10
All other griefes allow a part
　　To other griefes, and aske themselves but some;

The broken heart.　　8 flaske *1633 and most MSS.:* flash *1635–69
and some MSS.*

They

They come to us, but us Love draws,
Hee swallows us, and never chawes:
    By him, as by chain'd shot, whole rankes doe dye,   15
    He is the tyran Pike, our hearts the Frye.

If 'twere not so, what did become
    Of my heart, when I first saw thee?
I brought a heart into the roome,
    But from the roome, I carried none with mee: 20
If it had gone to thee, I know
Mine would have taught thine heart to show
    More pitty unto mee: but Love, alas,
    At one first blow did shiver it as glasse.

Yet nothing can to nothing fall,   25
    Nor any place be empty quite,
Therefore I thinke my breast hath all
    Those peeces still, though they be not unite;
And now as broken glasses show
A hundred lesser faces, so   30
    My ragges of heart can like, wish, and adore,
    But after one such love, can love no more.

A Valediction : forbidding mourning.

AS virtuous men passe mildly away,
    And whisper to their soules, to goe,
Whilst some of their sad friends doe say,
    The breath goes now, and some say, no:

So let us melt, and make no noise,   5
    No teare-floods, nor sigh-tempests move,
T'were prophanation of our joyes
    To tell the layetie our love.

    17 did] could *many MSS.*   24 first] fierce *some MSS.*   30
hundred] thousand *many MSS.*
    A Valediction: forbidding *&c.*   6 No wind-sighs or tear-floods
us move, *Walton's Life of Donne*   8 layetie our love. *1633–69 and
some MSS.:* layetie of our love. *many MSS.*

                               Moving

Moving of th'earth brings harmes and feares,
 Men reckon what it did and meant,   10
But trepidation of the spheares,
 Though greater farre, is innocent.

Dull sublunary lovers love
 (Whose soule is sense) cannot admit
Absence, because it doth remove   15
 Those things which elemented it.

But we by a love, so much refin'd,
 That our selves know not what it is,
Inter-assured of the mind,
 Care lesse, eyes, lips, and hands to misse.   20

Our two soules therefore, which are one,
 Though I must goe, endure not yet
A breach, but an expansion,
 Like gold to ayery thinnesse beate.

If they be two, they are two so   25
 As stiffe twin compasses are two,
Thy soule the fixt foot, makes no show
 To move, but doth, if the'other doe.

And though it in the center sit,
 Yet when the other far doth rome,   30
It leanes, and hearkens after it,
 And growes erect, as that comes home.

Such wilt thou be to mee, who must
 Like th'other foot, obliquely runne;
Thy firmnes makes my circle just,   35
 And makes me end, where I begunne.

9 Moving . . . brings] Movings . . . cause *Walton* 10 it] they *Walton* 18 our selves] our souls *Walton* 20 Care not *Walton* lips, and hands *1669 and all MSS.*: lips, hands *1633*: hands, eyes, or lips *Walton* 30 the other] my other *Walton* 31 It] Thine *Walton* 32 that] mine *Walton* 35 makes] drawes *one MS.* circle] circles *1639–54* 36 makes me] me to *Walton*

The

The Extasie.

WHere, like a pillow on a bed,
    A Pregnant banke swel'd up, to rest
The violets reclining head,
    Sat we two, one anothers best.
Our hands were firmely cimented   5
    With a fast balme, which thence did spring,
Our eye-beames twisted, and did thred
    Our eyes, upon one double string;
So to'entergraft our hands, as yet
    Was all the meanes to make us one,   10
And pictures in our eyes to get
    Was all our propagation.
As 'twixt two equal Armies, Fate
    Suspends uncertaine victorie,
Our soules, (which to advance their state,   15
    Were gone out,) hung 'twixt her, and mee.
And whil'st our soules negotiate there,
    Wee like sepulchrall statues lay;
All day, the same our postures were,
    And wee said nothing, all the day.   20
If any, so by love refin'd,
    That he soules language understood,
And by good love were growen all minde,
    Within convenient distance stood,
He (though he knew not which soule spake,   25
    Because both meant, both spake the same)
Might thence a new concoction take,
    And part farre purer then he came.

The Extasie.   3 reclining *1633–54:* declining *1669*   6 With
1633 and most MSS.: By *1635–69*   9 to'entergraft *1633 and best
MSS.:* to engraft *1635–69 and some MS.*   11 in *1633–69:* on *many
MSS.*   15 their] our *1635–69 and two MSS.*   25 knew *1635–69 and
most MSS.:* knowes *1633*

This

This Extasie doth unperplex
    (We said) and tell us what we love, 30
Wee see by this, it was not sexe,
    Wee see, we saw not what did move:
But as all severall soules containe
    Mixture of things, they know not what,
Love, these mixt soules doth mixe againe, 35
    And makes both one, each this and that.
A single violet transplant,
    The strength, the colour, and the size,
(All which before was poore, and scant,)
    Redoubles still, and multiplies. 40
When love, with one another so
    Interinanimates two soules,
That abler soule, which thence doth flow,
    Defects of lonelinesse controules.
Wee then, who are this new soule, know, 45
    Of what we are compos'd, and made,
For, th'Atomies of which we grow,
    Are soules, whom no change can invade.
But O alas, so long, so farre
    Our bodies why doe wee forbeare? 50
They'are ours, though they'are not wee, Wee are
    The intelligences, they the spheare.
We owe them thankes, because they thus,
    Did us, to us, at first convay,
Yeelded their forces, sense, to us, 55
    Nor are drosse to us, but allay.
On man heavens influence workes not so,
    But that it first imprints the ayre,
Soe soule into the soule may flow,
    Though it to body first repaire. 60

42 Interinanimates *most MSS.:* Interanimates *1633–69 and some MSS.* 51 though they are not *all MSS.:* though not *1633–69* 52 spheare. *all MSS.:* spheares. *1633–69* 55 forces, sense, *all MSS.:* senses force *1633–69* 59 Soe *most MSS.:* For *1633–69 and one MS group*

                                                             As

As our blood labours to beget
  Spirits, as like soules as it can,
Because such fingers need to knit
  That subtile knot, which makes us man:
So must pure lovers soules descend   65
  T'affections, and to faculties,
Which sense may reach and apprehend,
  Else a great Prince in prison lies.
To'our bodies turne wee then, that so
  Weake men on love reveal'd may looke;   70
Loves mysteries in soules doe grow,
  But yet the body is his booke.
And if some lover, such as wee,
  Have heard this dialogue of one,
Let him still marke us, he shall see   75
  Small change, when we'are to bodies gone.

Loves Deitie.

I Long to talke with some old lovers ghost,
  Who dyed before the god of Love was borne:
I cannot thinke that hee, who then lov'd most,
  Sunke so low, as to love one which did scorne.
But since this god produc'd a destinie,   5
And that vice-nature, custome, lets it be;
  I must love her, that loves not mee.

Sure, they which made him god, meant not so much,
  Nor he, in his young godhead practis'd it;
But when an even flame two hearts did touch,   10
  His office was indulgently to fit
Actives to passives.   Correspondencie
Only his subject was; It cannot bee
  Love, till I love her, that loves mee.

76 gone. *1633 and most MSS.:* growne. *1635–69*
Loves Deitie.   14 Love, if I love, who loves not me. *1635–54*

                                                      But

But every moderne god will now extend   15
  His vast prerogative, as far as Jove.
To rage, to lust, to write to, to commend,
  All is the purlewe of the God of Love.
Oh were wee wak'ned by this Tyrannie
To ungod this child againe, it could not bee   20
  I should love her, who loves not mee.

Rebell and Atheist too, why murmure I,
  As though I felt the worst that love could doe?
Love might make me leave loving, or might trie
  A deeper plague, to make her love me too,   25
Which, since she loves before, I'am loth to see;
Falshood is worse then hate; and that must bee,
  If shee whom I love, should love mee.

Loves diet.

TO what a combersome unwieldinesse
  And burdenous corpulence my love had growne,
  But that I did, to make it lesse,
  And keepe it in proportion,
Give it a diet, made it feed upon   5
That which love worst endures, *discretion.*

Above one sigh a day I'allow'd him not,
Of which my fortune, and my faults had part;
  And if sometimes by stealth he got
  A she sigh from my mistresse heart,   10
And thought to feast on that, I let him see
'Twas neither very sound, nor meant to mee.

If he wroung from mee'a teare, I brin'd it so
With scorne or shame, that him it nourish'd not;
  If he suck'd hers, I let him know   15
  'Twas not a teare, which hee had got,

21 That I should love, who loves not me. *many MSS.* 24 might
make *most MSS.:* may make 1633–69

His

His drinke was counterfeit, as was his meat;
For, eyes which rowle towards all, weepe not, but sweat.

What ever he would dictate, I writ that,
But burnt my letters; When she writ to me,   20
　　And that that favour made him fat,
　　　I said, if any title bee
Convey'd by this, Ah, what doth it availe,
To be the fortieth name in an entaile?

Thus I reclaim'd my buzard love, to flye   25
At what, and when, and how, and where I chuse;
　　Now negligent of sport I lye,
　　　And now as other Fawkners use,
I spring a mistresse, sweare, write, sigh and weepe:
And the game kill'd, or lost, goe talke, and sleepe.   30

The Will.

BEfore I sigh my last gaspe, let me breath,
　Great love, some Legacies; Here I bequeath
　　Mine eyes to *Argus*, if mine eyes can see,
　　If they be blinde, then Love, I give them thee;
　　My tongue to Fame; to'Embassadours mine eares;   5
　　　To women or the sea, my teares.
　　Thou, Love, hast taught mee heretofore
　　By making mee serve her who'had twenty more,
That I should give to none, but such, as had too much
　　before.

　　Loves diet.   19 Whatever . . . that, *1633–39, 1669:* Whate'er
might him distast I still writ that, *1650–54*   20 But burnt my
letters; When she writ to me, *1633:* But burnt her letters when she
writ to me, *1635:* But burnt her letters when she writ to me; *1639–54:*
But burnt my letters which she writ to me; *1669*   21 that that
1633: if that *1635–69*   25 reclaim'd *1635–69 and most MSS.:*
redeem'd *1633*   30 and *1633 and most MSS.:* or *1635–69*

　　　　　　　　　　　　　　　　　　　My

My constancie I to the planets give; 10
My truth to them, who at the Court doe live;
Mine ingenuity and opennesse,
To Jesuites; to Buffones my pensivenesse;
My silence to'any, who abroad hath beene;
    My mony to a Capuchin. 15
Thou Love taught'st me, by appointing mee
To love there, where no love receiv'd can be,
Onely to give to such as have an incapacitie.

My faith I give to Roman Catholiques;
All my good works unto the Schismaticks 20
Of Amsterdam; my best civility
And Courtship, to an Universitie;
My modesty I give to souldiers bare;
    My patience let gamesters share.
Thou Love taughtst mee, by making mee 25
Love her that holds my love disparity,
Onely to give to those that count my gifts indignity.

I give my reputation to those
Which were my friends; Mine industrie to foes;
To Schoolemen I bequeath my doubtfulnesse; 30
My sicknesse to Physitians, or excesse;
To Nature, all that I in Ryme have writ;
    And to my company my wit.
Thou Love, by making mee adore
Her, who begot this love in mee before, 35
Taughtst me to make, as though I gave, when I did but
    restore.

To him for whom the passing bell next tolls,
I give my physick bookes; my writen rowles
Of Morall counsels, I to Bedlam give;
My brazen medals, unto them which live 40

The Will. 19–27 *omitted in many MSS.* 36 did *1633 and MSS.:*
do *1635–69*

                                             In

In want of bread; To them which passe among
      All forrainers, mine English tongue.
Thou, Love, by making mee love one
Who thinkes her friendship a fit portion
For yonger lovers, dost my gifts thus disproportion.   45

Therefore I'll give no more; But I'll undoe
The world by dying; because love dies too.
Then all your beauties will bee no more worth
Then gold in Mines, where none doth draw it forth;
And all your graces no more use shall have   50
      Then a Sun dyall in a grave.
Thou Love taughtst mee, by making mee
Love her, who doth neglect both mee and thee,
To'invent, and practise this one way, to'annihilate all three.

The Funerall.

WHo ever comes to shroud me, do not harme
            Nor question much
That subtile wreath of haire, which crowns my arme;
The mystery, the signe you must not touch,
            For 'tis my outward Soule,   5
Viceroy to that, which then to heaven being gone,
            Will leave this to controule,
And keepe these limbes, her Provinces, from dissolution.

For if the sinewie thread my braine lets fall
            Through every part,   10
Can tye those parts, and make mee one of all;
These haires which upward grew, and strength and art
            Have from a better braine,

The Funerall.   6 then to *all MSS.:* unto *1633–69*   12 These
most MSS.: Those *1633–69*

                                                  Can

Can better do'it; Except she meant that I
    By this should know my pain,   15
As prisoners then are manacled, when they'are condemn'd
    to die.

What ere shee meant by'it, bury it with me,
    For since I am
Loves martyr, it might breed idolatrie,
If into others hands these Reliques came;   20
    As 'twas humility
To afford to it all that a Soule can doe,
    So,'tis some bravery,
That since you would save none of mee, I bury some of
    you.

The Blossome.

LIttle think'st thou, poore flower,
    Whom I have watch'd sixe or seaven dayes,
And seene thy birth, and seene what every houre
Gave to thy growth, thee to this height to raise,
And now dost laugh and triumph on this bough,   5
    Little think'st thou
That it will freeze anon, and that I shall
To morrow finde thee falne, or not at all.

    Little think'st thou poore heart
    That labour'st yet to nestle thee,
And think'st by hovering here to get a part   10
In a forbidden or forbidding tree,
And hop'st her stiffenesse by long siege to bow:
    Little think'st thou,
That thou to morrow, ere that Sunne doth wake,   15
Must with this Sunne, and mee a journey take.

17 with me, *1635–69 and MSS.:* by me, *1633*   24 save *most
MSS.:* have *1633–69 and some MSS.*
    The Blossome.   10 labour'st *one MS. group:* labourest *1635–69:*
labours *1633*

                                           But

But thou which lov'st to bee
Subtile to plague thy selfe, wilt say,
Alas, if you must goe, what's that to mee?
Here lyes my businesse, and here I will stay:　　　20
You goe to friends, whose love and meanes present
　　　　　　Various content
To your eyes, eares, and tongue, and every part.
If then your body goe, what need you a heart?

Well then, stay here; but know,　　　25
When thou hast stayd and done thy most;
A naked thinking heart, that makes no show,
Is to a woman, but a kinde of Ghost;
How shall shee know my heart; or having none,
　　　　　　Know thee for one?　　　30
Practise may make her know some other part,
But take my word, shee doth not know a Heart.

Meet mee at London, then,
Twenty dayes hence, and thou shalt see
Mee fresher, and more fat, by being with men,　　　35
Then if I had staid still with her and thee.
For Gods sake, if you can, be you so too:
　　　　　　I would give you
There, to another friend, whom wee shall finde
As glad to have my body, as my minde.　　　40

*The Primrose, being at Mountgomery Castle, upon
the hill, on which it is situate.*

VPon this Primrose hill,
　　Where, if Heav'n would distill
A shoure of raine, each severall drop might goe
To his owne primrose, and grow Manna so;

23 tongue *most MSS.:* tast *1633–69*　　24 need you a heart? *most
MSS.:* need your heart? *1633–69*　　38 I would *most MSS.:* I will
1633–69

And

And where their forme, and their infinitie   5
    Make a terrestriall Galaxie,
    As the small starres doe in the skie:
I walke to finde a true Love; and I see
That 'tis not a mere woman, that is shee,
But must, or more, or lesse then woman bee.   10

    Yet know I not, which flower
    I wish; a sixe, or foure;
For should my true-Love lesse then woman bee,
She were scarce any thing; and then, should she
Be more then woman, shee would get above   15
    All thought of sexe, and thinke to move
    My heart to study her, and not to love;
Both these were monsters; Since there must reside
Falshood in woman, I could more abide,
She were by art, then Nature falsify'd.   20

    Live Primrose then, and thrive
    With thy true number five;
And women, whom this flower doth represent,
With this mysterious number be content;
Ten is the farthest number; if halfe ten   25
    Belonge unto each woman, then
    Each woman may take halfe us men;
Or if this will not serve their turne, Since all
Numbers are odde, or even, and they fall
First into this, five, women may take us all.   30

The Relique.

WHen my grave is broke up againe
    Some second ghest to entertaine,
    (For graves have learn'd that woman-head
    To be to more then one a Bed)

The Primrose.   17 and not] and *om. 1635–39 and some MSS.*
26 Belonge *all the MSS.:* Belongs *1633–69*   30 this, *Ed:* this
1633 and most MSS.: om. 1635–69

And

And he that digs it, spies   5
A bracelet of bright haire about the bone,
    Will he not let'us alone,
And thinke that there a loving couple lies,
Who thought that this device might be some way
To make their soules, at the last busie day,   10
Meet at this grave, and make a little stay?

    If this fall in a time, or land,
    Where mis-devotion doth command,
    Then, he that digges us up, will bring
    Us, to the Bishop, and the King,   15
        To make us Reliques; then
Thou shalt be a Mary Magdalen, and I
    A something else thereby;
All women shall adore us, and some men;
And since at such time, miracles are sought,   20
I would have that age by this paper taught
What miracles wee harmelesse lovers wrought.

    First, we lov'd well and faithfully,
    Yet knew not what wee lov'd, nor why,
    Difference of sex no more wee knew,   25
    Then our Guardian Angells doe;
        Comming and going, wee
Perchance might kisse, but not between those meales;
    Our hands ne'r toucht the seales,
Which nature, injur'd by late law, sets free: 30
These miracles wee did; but now alas,
All measure, and all language, I should passe,
Should I tell what a miracle shee was.

The Relique.   20 time] times *some MSS.*   25–26 Difference
. . . doe, *1633:*
            Difference of Sex we never knew,
            No more then Guardian Angells do, *1635–69:*
            Difference of Sex we never knew,
            More then our Guardian Angells do. *many MSS.*

                                                          The

The Dampe.

WHen I am dead, and Doctors know not why,
    And my friends curiositie
Will have me cut up to survay each part,
When they shall finde your Picture in my heart,
        You thinke a sodaine dampe of love   5
        Will through all their senses move,
And worke on them as mee, and so preferre
Your murder, to the name of Massacre.

Poore victories! But if you dare be brave,
            And pleasure in your conquest have,   10
First kill th'enormous Gyant, your *Disdaine*,
And let th'enchantresse *Honor*, next be slaine,
        And like a Goth and Vandall rize,
        Deface Records, and Histories
Of your owne arts and triumphs over men,   15
And without such advantage kill me then.

For I could muster up as well as you
            My Gyants, and my Witches too,
Which are vast *Constancy*, and *Secretnesse*,
But these I neyther looke for, nor professe;   20
        Kill mee as Woman, let mee die
        As a meere man; doe you but try
Your passive valor, and you shall finde than,
In that you'have odds enough of any man.

The Dissolution.

SHee'is dead; And all which die
    To their first Elements resolve;
And wee were mutuall Elements to us,
    And made of one another.

The Dampe.   10 conquest] conquests *one MS.*   24 In that *1633
and some MSS.:* Naked *1635–69 and other MSS.*

My

My body then doth hers involve,   5
And those things whereof I consist, hereby
In me abundant grow, and burdenous,
        And nourish not, but smother.
My fire of Passion, sighes of ayre,
Water of teares, and earthly sad despaire,   10
        Which my materialls bee,
But neere worne out by loves securitie,
Shee, to my losse, doth by her death repaire,
        And I might live long wretched so
But that my fire doth with my fuell grow.   15
        Now as those Active Kings
    Whose foraine conquest treasure brings,
Receive more, and spend more, and soonest breake:
This (which I am amaz'd that I can speake)
        This death, hath with my store   20
        My use encreas'd.
And so my soule more earnestly releas'd,
Will outstrip hers; As bullets flowen before
A latter bullet may o'rtake, the pouder being more.

A Jeat Ring sent.

THou art not so black, as my heart,
    Nor halfe so brittle, as her heart, thou art;
What would'st thou say? shall both our properties by thee
        bee spoke,
Nothing more endlesse, nothing sooner broke?

        Marriage rings are not of this stuffe;   5
    Oh, why should ought lesse precious, or lesse tough
Figure our loves? Except in thy name thou have bid it say,
    I'am cheap, and nought but fashion, fling me'away.

The Dissolution.   10 earthly *1633:* earthy *1635-69*   12
neere *1635-69:* ne'r *1633*   24 latter] later *1669*

                                                    Yet

Yet stay with mee since thou art come,
Circle this fingers top, which did'st her thombe. 10
Be justly proud, and gladly safe, that thou dost dwell with
     me,
She that, Oh, broke her faith, would soon breake thee.

Negative love.

I Never stoop'd so low, as they
  Which on an eye, cheeke, lip, can prey,
    Seldome to them, which soare no higher
    Then vertue or the minde to'admire,
For sense, and understanding may 5
  Know, what gives fuell to their fire:
My love, though silly, is more brave,
  For may I misse, when ere I crave,
  If I know yet, what I would have.

If that be simply perfectest 10
Which can by no way be exprest
  But *Negatives*, my love is so.
  To All, which all love, I say no.
If any who deciphers best,
  What we know not, our selves, can know, 15
Let him teach mee that nothing; This
As yet my ease, and comfort is,
Though I speed not, I cannot misse.

The Prohibition.

Take heed of loving mee,
At least remember, I forbade it thee;
Not that I shall repaire my'unthrifty wast
Of Breath and Blood, upon thy sighes, and teares,

By

By being to thee then what to me thou wast;   5
But, so great Joy, our life at once outweares,
Then, least thy love, by my death, frustrate bee,
If thou love mee, take heed of loving mee.

Take heed of hating mee,
Or too much triumph in the Victorie.   10
Not that I shall be mine owne officer,
And hate with hate againe retaliate;
But thou wilt lose the stile of conquerour,
If I, thy conquest, perish by thy hate.
Then, least my being nothing lessen thee,   15
If thou hate mee, take heed of hating mee.

Yet, love and hate mee too,
So, these extreames shall neithers office doe;
Love mee, that I may die the gentler way;
Hate mee, because thy love'is too great for mee;   20
Or let these two, themselves, not me decay;
So shall I, live, thy Stage, not triumph bee;
Lest thou thy love and hate and mee undoe,
To let mee live, O love and hate mee too.

   The Prohibition.   *In one MS. first two verses headed* J. D., *last
verse* T. R.: *in one group of MSS. the last stanza is omitted*   5 By
. . . wast; *Ed:* By . . . wast, *1635–69 and most MSS.*: By being to mee
then that which thou wast; *1633: om. in some good MSS.*   18
neithers *MSS.*: ne'r their *1633–69*   22 I, live, *Ed:* I live *1633–69*
23–4   Lest thou thy love and hate and mee undoe
         To let mee live, Oh (of *in some copies*) *love and hate mee too. 1633:*
         Then lest thou thy love hate, and mee thou undoe
         O let me live, yet love and hate me too. 1635–54 and most MSS.
         (*MSS. omitting first* thou *and some with* Oh *for* yet):
         Lest thou thy love, and hate, and me thou undo,
         O let me live, yet love and hate me too. 1669

                                                              The

The Expiration.

SO, so, breake off this last lamenting kisse,
Which sucks two soules, and vapors Both away,
Turne thou ghost that way, and let mee turne this,
    And let our selves benight our happiest day,
We ask'd none leave to love; nor will we owe
    Any, so cheape a death, as saying, Goe;

Goe; and if that word have not quite kil'd thee,
    Ease mee with death, by bidding mee goe too.
Or, if it have, let my word worke on mee,
    And a just office on a murderer doe.   10
Except it be too late, to kill me so,
    Being double dead, going, and bidding, goe.

The Computation.

FOr the first twenty yeares, since yesterday,
    I scarce beleev'd, thou could'st be gone away,
For forty more, I fed on favours past,
    And forty'on hopes, that thou would'st, they might last.
Teares drown'd one hundred, and sighes blew out two, 5
    A thousand, I did neither thinke, nor doe,
    Or not divide, all being one thought of you;
    Or in a thousand more, forgot that too.
Yet call not this long life; But thinke that I
Am, by being dead, Immortall; Can ghosts die?   10

The Paradox.

NO Lover saith, I love, nor any other
    Can judge a perfect Lover;
Hee thinkes that else none can, nor will agree
    That any loves but hee:

The Expiration.   5 ask'd *most MSS.:* aske *1633–69 and some
MSS.*   9 Or, *1635–69:* Oh, *1633*
    The Computation.   1 the *1633:* my *1635–69*   8 forgot] forget
1669 and some MSS.
    The Paradox.   3 nor *most MSS.:* or *1633–69*

                                        I cannot

I cannot say I lov'd, for who can say   5
    Hee was kill'd yesterday?
Love with excesse of heat, more yong then old,
    Death kills with too much cold;
Wee dye but once, and who lov'd last did die,
    Hee that saith twice, doth lye: 10
For though hee seeme to move, and stirre a while,
    It doth the sense beguile.
Such life is like the light which bideth yet
    When the lights life is set,
Or like the heat, which fire in solid matter   15
    Leaves behinde, two houres after.
Once I lov'd and dy'd; and am now become
    Mine Epitaph and Tombe.
Here dead men speake their last, and so do I;
    Love-slaine, loe, here I lye.   20

Farewell to love.

W Hilst yet to prove,
I thought there was some Deitie in love
    So did I reverence, and gave
Worship, as Atheists at their dying houre
Call, what they cannot name, an unknowne power,   5
    As ignorantly did I crave:
        Thus when
Things not yet knowne are coveted by men,
    Our desires give them fashion, and so
As they waxe lesser, fall, as they sise, grow.   10

      But, from late faire
His highnesse sitting in a golden Chaire,
    Is not lesse cared for after three dayes
By children, then the thing which lovers so

14 lights life *some MSS.:* lifes light *1633–69 and some MSS.*
20 lye. *some MSS.:* dye. *1633–69 and some MSS.*
    Farewell to love.   10 sise, *1635–69:* rise *one MS.*   highnesse]
hignesse *1633*

                    Blindly

Blindly admire, and with such worship wooe;   15
   Being had, enjoying it decayes:
      And thence,
What before pleas'd them all, takes but one sense,
   And that so lamely, as it leaves behinde
A kinde of sorrowing dulnesse to the minde.   20

      Ah cannot wee,
As well as Cocks and Lyons jocund be,
   After such pleasures? Unlesse wise
Nature decreed (since each such Act, they say,
Diminisheth the length of life a day)   25
   This, as shee would man should despise
      The sport;
Because that other curse of being short,
   And onely for a minute made to be,
⟨Eagers desire⟩ to raise posterity.   30

      Since so, my minde
Shall not desire what no man else can finde,
   I'll no more dote and runne
To pursue things which had indammag'd me.
And when I come where moving beauties be,   35
   As men doe when the summers Sunne
      Growes great,
Though I admire their greatnesse, shun their heat;
   Each place can afford shadowes. If all faile,
'Tis but applying worme-seed to the Taile.   40

A Lecture upon the Shadow.

STand still, and I will read to thee
  A Lecture, Love, in loves philosophy.
    These three houres that we have spent,
    Walking here, Two shadowes went

29–30 be, ⟨Eagers desire⟩ *Ed:* be Eager, desires *1635–69*
   A Lecture *&c.*   4 Walking *1635–69 and some MSS.:* In walking *some MSS.*

Along

Along with us, which we our selves produc'd;   5
But, now the Sunne is just above our head,
 We doe those shadowes tread;
 And to brave clearnesse all things are reduc'd.
So whilst our infant loves did grow,
Disguises did, and shadowes, flow,   10
 From us, and our cares; but, now 'tis not so.

That love hath not attain'd the high'st degree,
Which is still diligent lest others see.

Except our loves at this noone stay,
We shall new shadowes make the other way.   15
 As the first were made to blinde
 Others; these which come behinde
Will worke upon our selves, and blind our eyes.
If our loves faint, and westwardly decline;
 To me thou, falsly, thine,   20
 And I to thee mine actions shall disguise.
The morning shadowes weare away,
But these grow longer all the day,
But oh, loves day is short, if love decay.

Love is a growing, or full constant light;   25
And his first minute, after noone, is night.

Sonnet. The Token.

SEnd me some token, that my hope may live,
 Or that my easelesse thoughts may sleep and rest;
Send me some honey to make sweet my hive,
 That in my passion I may hope the best.

12 high'st] least *many MSS.*   14 loves *1635–69 and some MSS.:*
love *some MSS.*   19 If our loves faint *1635–69 and some MSS.:*
If once love faint, *some MSS.*   26 first *all MSS.:* short *1635–69*
 Sonnet. The Token.   1 token *MSS.:* Tokens *1650–69*   4
passion *MS.:* passions *1650–69*

           I beg

I beg noe ribbond wrought with thine owne hands,   5
    To knit our loves in the fantastick straine
Of new-toucht youth; nor Ring to shew the stands
    Of our affection, that as that's round and plaine,
So should our loves meet in simplicity;
    No, nor the Coralls which thy wrist infold,   10
Lac'd up together in congruity,
    To shew our thoughts should rest in the same hold;
No, nor thy picture, though most gracious,
    And most desir'd, because best like the best;
Nor witty Lines, which are most copious,   15
    Within the Writings which thou hast addrest.

Send me nor this, nor that, t'increase my store,
But swear thou thinkst I love thee, and no more.

⟨*Selfe Love.*⟩

HE that cannot chuse but love,
    And strives against it still,
Never shall my fancy move;
    For he loves 'gaynst his will;
Nor he which is all his own,   5
    And can att pleasure chuse,
When I am caught he can be gone,
    And when he list refuse.
Nor he that loves none but faire,
    For such by all are sought;   10
Nor he that can for foul ones care,
    For his Judgement then is nought:
Nor he that hath wit, for he
    Will make me his jest or slave;
Nor a fool, for when others . . . .,   15

5 noe *MSS.:* nor *1650–69*   14 desir'd because . . . best; *MSS.:*
desired 'cause 'tis like thee best; *1650–54:* desired 'cause 'tis like the
best; *1669*   17 store, *MSS.:* score, *1650–69*

He

He can neither . . . . . .
Nor he that still his Mistresse payes,
For she is thrall'd therefore:
Nor he that payes not, for he sayes
Within, shee's worth no more.
Is there then no kinde of men
Whom I may freely prove?
I will vent that humour then
In mine owne selfe love.

⟨Selfe Love.⟩   17 payes, *MSS.:* prays, *1650–69*

The end of the Songs and Sonets.

EPIGRAMS.

EPIGRAMS.

Hero and Leander.

BOth rob'd of aire, we both lye in one ground,
Both whom one fire had burnt, one water drownd.

Pyramus and Thisbe.

TWo, by themselves, each other, love and feare
Slaine, cruell friends, by parting have joyn'd here.

Niobe.

BY childrens births, and death, I am become
So dry, that I am now mine owne sad tombe.

A burnt ship.

OUt of a fired ship, which, by no way
But drowning, could be rescued from the flame,
Some men leap'd forth, and ever as they came
Neere the foes ships, did by their shot decay;
So all were lost, which in the ship were found,
   They in the sea being burnt, they in the burnt ship
      drown'd.

Fall of a wall.

VNder an undermin'd, and shot-bruis'd wall
A too-bold Captaine perish'd by the fall,
Whose brave misfortune, happiest men envi'd,
That had a towne for tombe, his bones to hide.

Niobe. 2 mine owne sad tombe. *1633–69:* made mine owne
tombe. *some good MSS.*

                                              A tame

A lame begger.

I Am unable, yonder begger cries,
  To stand, or move; if he say true, hee *lies.*

Cales and *Guyana.*

I F you from spoyle of th'old worlds farthest end
  To the new world your kindled valors bend,
What brave examples then do prove it trew
That one things end doth still beginne a new.

Sir *John Wingefield.*

B Eyond th'old Pillers many have travailed
  Towards the Suns cradle, and his throne, and bed:
A fitter Piller our Earle did bestow
In that late Island; for he well did know
Farther then Wingefield no man dares to goe.

A selfe accuser.

Y Our mistris, that you follow whores, still taxeth you:
  'Tis strange that she should thus confesse it, though'it
    be true.

A licentious person.

T Hy sinnes and haires may no man equall call,
  For, as thy sinnes increase, thy haires doe fall.

Antiquary.

I F in his Studie he hath so much care
  To'hang all old strange things, let his wife beware.

A lame begger. *1633–69:* Zoppo. *some MSS.*
  Sir Iohn Wingefield.   2 throne] grave *one MS.*   4 late] Lady
one MS.
  A licentious person.   1 Thy] His *and so throughout, MS.*
  Antiquary. *1633–69:* Hammon. *MS.*   1 he hath so much
1633–69: he have such *some MSS.:* Hamon hath such *several MSS.*

Disinherited.

Disinherited.

THy father all from thee, by his last Will,
Gave to the poore; Thou hast good title still.

Phryne.

THy flattering picture, *Phryne*, is like thee,
Onely in this, that you both painted be.

An obscure writer.

PHilo, with twelve yeares study, hath beene griev'd
To be understood; when will hee be beleev'd?

Klockius.

KLockius so deeply hath sworne, ne'r more to come
In bawdie house, that hee dares not goe home.

Raderus.

WHy this man gelded *Martiall* I muse,
Except himselfe alone his tricks would use,
As *Katherine*, for the Courts sake, put downe Stewes.

Mercurius Gallo-Belgicus.

LIke *Esops* fellow-slaves, O *Mercury*,
Which could do all things, thy faith is; and I
Like *Esops* selfe, which nothing; I confesse
I should have had more faith, if thou hadst lesse;
Thy credit lost thy credit: 'Tis sinne to doe,
In this case, as thou wouldst be done unto,
To beleeve all: Change thy name: thou art like
Mercury in stealing, but lyest like a *Greeke*.

Klockius. 1 *Klockius*] Rawlings *MS.* 2 In bawdie] in a
bawdie *MS.*
Raderus. *1633–69:* Martial: castrat*us. one MS.*

Ralphius.

Ralphius.

COmpassion in the world againe is bred:
   Ralphius is sick, the broker keeps his bed.

The Lier.

THou in the fields walkst out thy supping howers,
   And yet thou swear'st thou hast supp'd like a king:
Like Nebuchadnezar perchance with grass and flowers,
   A sallet worse then Spanish dieting.

The Lier.   2 supp'd like] supp'd and like *one MS*.   3 grass]
hearbes *one MS*.

ELEGIES.

ELEGIES.

ELEGIE I.

Jealosie.

FOnd woman, which would'st have thy husband die,
  And yet complain'st of his great jealousie;
If swolne with poyson, hee lay in'his last bed,
His body with a sere-barke covered,
Drawing his breath, as thick and short, as can   5
The nimblest crocheting Musitian,
Ready with loathsome vomiting to spue
His Soule out of one hell, into a new,
Made deafe with his poore kindreds howling cries,
Begging with few feign'd teares, great legacies,   10
Thou would'st not weepe, but jolly,'and frolicke bee,
As a slave, which to morrow should be free;
Yet weep'st thou, when thou seest him hungerly
Swallow his owne death, hearts-bane jealousie.
O give him many thanks, he'is courteous,   15
That in suspecting kindly warneth us.
Wee must not, as wee us'd, flout openly,
In scoffing ridles, his deformitie;
Nor at his boord together being satt,
With words, nor touch, scarce lookes adulterate.   20
Nor when he swolne, and pamper'd with great fare,
Sits downe, and snorts, cag'd in his basket chaire,
Must wee usurpe his owne bed any more,
Nor kisse and play in his house, as before.

Elegie I.   4 sere-barke *1633–54 and most MSS.:* sere-cloth *1669
and some MSS.:* sore barke *several MSS.*   16 us. *1633–35:* us,
1639–69   21 great *1633–54 and most MSS.:* high *1669 and some
MSS.*

                                                    Now

Now I see many dangers; for that is   25
His realme, his castle, and his diocesse.
But if, as envious men, which would revile
Their Prince, or coyne his gold, themselves exile
Into another countrie,'and doe it there,
Wee play'in another house, what should we feare?   30
There we will scorne his houshold policies,
His seely plots, and pensionary spies,
As the inhabitants of Thames right side
Do Londons Major; or Germans, the Popes pride.

ELEGIE II.

The Anagram.

MArry, and love thy *Flavia*, for, shee
Hath all things, whereby others beautious bee,
For, though her eyes be small, her mouth is great,
Though they be Ivory, yet her teeth be jeat,
Though they be dimme, yet she is light enough,   5
And though her harsh haire fall, her skinne is rough;
What though her cheeks be yellow, her haire's red,
Give her thine, and she hath a maydenhead.
These things are beauties elements, where these
Meet in one, that one must, as perfect, please.   10
If red and white and each good quality
Be in thy wench, ne'r aske where it doth lye.
In buying things perfum'd, we aske; if there
Be muske and amber in it, but not where.
Though all her parts be not in th'usuall place,   15
She'hath yet an Anagram of a good face.
If we might put the letters but one way,
In the leane dearth of words, what could wee say?

25 that *all MSS.:* it *1633–69*   30 We into some third place
retired were *some MSS.*
    Elegie II. 6 is rough *1633, 1669, and MSS.:* is tough *1635–54*
18 the *1633:* that *1635–69*   words] letters *some MSS.*

When

When by the Gamut some Musitions make
A perfect song, others will undertake,   20
By the same Gamut chang'd, to equall it.
Things simply good, can never be unfit.
She's faire as any, if all be like her,
And if none bee, then she is singular.
All love is wonder; if wee justly doe   25
Account her wonderfull, why not lovely too?
Love built on beauty, soone as beauty, dies,
Chuse this face, chang'd by no deformities.
Women are all like Angels; the faire be
Like those which fell to worse; but such as shee,   30
Like to good Angels, nothing can impaire:
'Tis lesse griefe to be foule, then to'have beene faire.
For one nights revels, silke and gold we chuse,
But, in long journeyes, cloth, and leather use.
Beauty is barren oft; best husbands say,   35
There is best land, where there is foulest way.
Oh what a soveraigne Plaister will shee bee,
If thy past sinnes have taught thee jealousie!
Here needs no spies, nor eunuches; her commit
Safe to thy foes; yea, to a Marmosit.   40
When Belgiaes citties, the round countries drowne,
That durty foulenesse guards, and armes the towne:
So doth her face guard her; and so, for thee,
Which, forc'd by businesse, absent oft must bee,
Shee, whose face, like clouds, turnes the day to night, 45
Who, mightier then the sea, makes Moores seem white,
Who, though seaven yeares, she in the Stews had laid,
A Nunnery durst receive, and thinke a maid,
And though in childbeds labour she did lie,

41–2 When Belgiaes . . . towne: *1633–54*: Like Belgia's cities when
the Country is drown'd, That . . . towns; *1669*: Like Belgia's cities
the round country drowns, That . . . towns, *Chambers*: *MSS. agree
with 1633–54, but before* countries *read variously* round, lowe, foul
49 childbeds *1633–54 and some MSS.*: childbirths *1669 and most MSS.*

Midwifes would sweare,'twere but a tympanie,　　50
Whom, if shee accuse her selfe, I credit lesse
Then witches, which impossibles confesse,
Whom Dildoes, Bedstaves, and her Velvet Glasse
Would be as loath to touch as Joseph was:
One like none, and lik'd of none, fittest were,　　55
For, things in fashion every man will weare.

ELEGIE III.

Change.

ALthough thy hand and faith, and good workes too,
Have seal'd thy love which nothing should undoe,
Yea though thou fall backe, that apostasie
Confirme thy love; yet much, much I feare thee.
Women are like the Arts, forc'd unto none,　　5
Open to'all searchers, unpriz'd, if unknowne.
If I have caught a bird, and let him flie,
Another fouler using these meanes, as I,
May catch the same bird; and, as these things bee,
Women are made for men, not him, nor mee.　　10
Foxes and goats; all beasts change when they please,
Shall women, more hot, wily, wild then these,
Be bound to one man, and did Nature then
Idly make them apter to'endure then men?
They'are our clogges, not their owne; if a man bee　　15
Chain'd to a galley, yet the galley'is free;
Who hath a plow-land, casts all his seed corne there,
And yet allowes his ground more corne should beare;
Though Danuby into the sea must flow,
The sea receives the Rhene, Volga, and Po.　　20
By nature, which gave it, this liberty
Thou lov'st, but Oh! canst thou love it and mee?

53-4 om. 1633-54
Elegie III.　5 forc'd unto none] forbid to none *one MS.*　8 these
1633-54 and some MSS.: those *1669 and most MSS.*

Likenesse

Likenesse glues love: and if that thou so doe,
To make us like and love, must I change too?
More then thy hate, I hate'it, rather let mee   25
Allow her change, then change as oft as shee,
And soe not teach, but force my'opinion
To love not any one, nor every one.
To live in one land, is captivitie,
To runne all countries, a wild roguery;   30
Waters stincke soone, if in one place they bide,
And in the vast sea are more putrifi'd:
But when they kisse one banke, and leaving this
Never looke backe, but the next banke doe kisse,
Then are they purest; Change'is the nursery   35
Of musicke, joy, life, and eternity.

ELEGIE IV.

The Perfume.

ONce, and but once found in thy company,
  All thy suppos'd escapes are laid on mee;
And as a thiefe at barre, is question'd there
By all the men, that have beene rob'd that yeare,
So am I, (by this traiterous meanes surpriz'd)   5
By thy Hydroptique father catechiz'd.
Though he had wont to search with glazed eyes,
As though he came to kill a Cockatrice,
Though hee hath oft sworne, that hee would remove
Thy beauties beautie, and food of our love,   10
Hope of his goods, if I with thee were seene,
Yet close and secret, as our soules, we'have beene.

. 23 and . . . doe,] then if so thou do, *most MSS.*   24 like *i.e.* **alike**
as in some MSS.   32 more putrifi'd *1633–39:* more purifi'd *1650–*
54: worse purifi'd *1669:* worse putrifi'd *most MSS.:* worst putrifi'd
some MSS.
    Elegie IV.   4 By] For *one MS.*   7–8 *1635–69 and MSS. generally:*
om. 1633 and some MSS.

Though

Though thy immortall mother which doth lye
Still buried in her bed, yet will not dye,
Takes this advantage to sleepe out day-light,   15
And watch thy entries, and returnes all night,
And, when she takes thy hand, and would seeme kind,
Doth search what rings, and armelets she can finde,
And kissing notes the colour of thy face,
And fearing least thou'art swolne, doth thee embrace; 20
To trie if thou long, doth name strange meates,
And notes thy palenesse, blushing, sighs, and sweats;
And politiquely will to thee confesse
The sinnes of her owne youths ranke lustinesse;
Yet love these Sorceries did remove, and move   25
Thee to gull thine owne mother for my love.
Thy little brethren, which like Faiery Sprights
Oft skipt into our chamber, those sweet nights,
And kist, and ingled on thy fathers knee,
Were brib'd next day, to tell what they did see: 30
The grim eight-foot-high iron-bound serving-man,
That oft names God in oathes, and onely than,
He that to barre the first gate, doth as wide
As the great Rhodian Colossus stride,
Which, if in hell no other paines there were,   35
Makes mee feare hell, because he must be there:
Though by thy father he were hir'd to this,
Could never witnesse any touch or kisse.
But Oh, too common ill, I brought with mee
That, which betray'd mee to my enemie: 40
A loud perfume, which at my entrance cryed
Even at thy fathers nose, so were wee spied.
When, like a tyran King, that in his bed
Smelt gunpowder, the pale wretch shivered.
Had it beene some bad smell, he would have thought 45

21 To trie &c. *1633 and some MSS.:* And to trie &c. *1635–69
and most MSS.* 22 blushing *1633–54 and some MSS.:* blushes *1669:*
blushings *most MSS.* 37 to *1633–69:* for *MSS.*

That

That his owne feet, or breath, that smell had wrought.
But as wee in our Ile emprisoned,
Where cattell onely,'and diverse dogs are bred,
The pretious Vnicornes, strange monsters call,
So thought he good, strange, that had none at all.   50
I taught my silkes, their whistling to forbeare,
Even my opprest shoes, dumbe and speechlesse were,
Onely, thou bitter sweet, whom I had laid
Next mee, mee traiterously hast betraid,
And unsuspected hast invisibly   55
At once fled unto him, and staid with mee.
Base excrement of earth, which dost confound
Sense, from distinguishing the sicke from sound;
By thee the seely Amorous sucks his death
By drawing in a leprous harlots breath;   60
By thee, the greatest staine to mans estate
Falls on us, to be call'd effeminate;
Though you be much lov'd in the Princes hall,
There, things that seeme, exceed substantiall;
Gods, when yee fum'd on altars, were pleas'd well,   65
Because you'were burnt, not that they lik'd your smell;
You'are loathsome all, being taken simply alone,
Shall wee love ill things joyn'd, and hate each one?
If you were good, your good doth soone decay;
And you are rare, that takes the good away.   70
All my perfumes, I give most willingly
To'embalme thy fathers corse; What? will hee die?

ELEGIE V.

His Picture.

HEre take my Picture; though I bid farewell,
      Thine, in my heart, where my soule dwels, shall dwell.
'Tis like me now, but I dead,'twill be more
When wee are shadowes both, then 'twas before.

                                        When

When weather-beaten I come backe; my hand,   5
Perhaps with rude oares torne, or Sun beams tann'd,
My face and brest of hairecloth, and my head
With cares rash sodaine stormes, being o'rspread,
My body'a sack of bones, broken within,
And powders blew staines scatter'd on my skinne;   10
If rivall fooles taxe thee to'have lov'd a man,
So foule, and course, as, Oh, I may seeme than,
This shall say what I was: and thou shalt say,
Doe his hurts reach mee? doth my worth decay?
Or doe they reach his judging minde, that hee   15
Should now love lesse, what hee did love to see?
That which in him was faire and delicate,
Was but the milke, which in loves childish state
Did nurse it: who now is growne strong enough
To feed on that, which to disused tasts seemes tough.   20

ELEGIE VI.

OH, let mee not serve so, as those men serve
Whom honours smoakes at once fatten and sterve;
Poorely enrich't with great mens words or lookes;
Nor so write my name in thy loving bookes
As those Idolatrous flatterers, which still   5
Their Princes stiles, with many Realmes fulfill
Whence they no tribute have, and where no sway.
Such services I offer as shall pay
Themselves, I hate dead names: Oh then let mee
Favorite in Ordinary, or no favorite bee.   10
When my Soule was in her owne body sheath'd,

Elegie V. 8 With cares rash sodaine stormes, being o'rspread,
1633 and some MSS.: With cares rash sodaine horiness o'erspread,
one good MS.: With cares harsh sodaine horinesse o'rspread, *1635–69:*
see 1912 edition   20 disused *Ed:* disus'd *1633–39 and MSS.:*
weake *1650–69*
    Elegie VI.   2 fatten] flatter *1669 and some MSS.*

Nor

Nor yet by oathes betroth'd, nor kisses breath'd
Into my Purgatory, faithlesse thee,
Thy heart seem'd waxe, and steele thy constancie:
So carelesse flowers strow'd on the waters face,   15
The curled whirlepooles suck, smack, and embrace,
Yet drowne them; so, the tapers beamie eye
Amorously twinkling, beckens the giddie flie,
Yet burnes his wings; and such the devill is,
Scarce visiting them, who are intirely his.   20
When I behold a streame, which, from the spring,
Doth with doubtfull melodious murmuring,
Or in a speechlesse slumber, calmely ride
Her wedded channels bosome, and then chide
And bend her browes, and swell if any bough   25
Do but stoop downe, or kisse her upmost brow;
Yet, if her often gnawing kisses winne
The traiterous banke to gape, and let her in,
She rusheth violently, and doth divorce
Her from her native, and her long-kept course,   30
And rores, and braves it, and in gallant scorne,
In flattering eddies promising retorne,
She flouts the channell, who thenceforth is drie;
Then say I; that is shee, and this am I.
Yet let not thy deepe bitternesse beget   35
Carelesse despaire in mee, for that will whet
My minde to scorne; and Oh, love dull'd with paine
Was ne'r so wise, nor well arm'd as disdaine.
Then with new eyes I shall survay thee,'and spie
Death in thy cheekes, and darknesse in thine eye.   40
Though hope bred faith and love; thus taught, I shall
As nations do from Rome, from thy love fall.
My hate shall outgrow thine, and utterly

24 then *1633 and some MSS.:* there *1635–69 and some MSS.*
26 upmost *1633 and most MSS.:* utmost *1635–69*   28 banke
some MSS.: banks *1633–69*   33 the *1633:* her *1635–69*   who
1633 and MSS.: which *1635–69*

I will

I will renounce thy dalliance: and when I
Am the Recusant, in that resolute state,   45
What hurts it mee to be'excommunicate?

ELEGIE VII.

NAtures lay Ideot, I taught thee to love,
And in that sophistrie, Oh, thou dost prove
Too subtile: Foole, thou didst not understand
The mystique language of the eye nor hand:
Nor couldst thou judge the difference of the aire   5
Of sighes, and say, this lies, this sounds despaire:
Nor by the'eyes water call a maladie
Desperately hot, or changing feaverously.
I had not taught thee then, the Alphabet
Of flowers, how they devisefully being set   10
And bound up, might with speechlesse secrecie
Deliver arrands mutely, and mutually.
Remember since all thy words us'd to bee
To every suitor; *I, if my friends agree;*
Since, household charmes, thy husbands name to teach, 15
Were all the love trickes, that thy wit could reach;
And since, an houres discourse could scarce have made
One answer in thee, and that ill arraid
In broken proverbs, and torne sentences.
Thou art not by so many duties his,   20
That from the worlds Common having sever'd thee,
Inlaid thee, neither to be seene, nor see,
As mine: who have with amorous delicacies
Refin'd thee'into a blis-full Paradise.
Thy graces and good words my creatures bee;   25
I planted knowledge and lifes tree in thee,
Which Oh, shall strangers taste? Must I alas

Elegie VII.   7 call *1633 and most MSS.:* know *1635–69:* cast
Chambers and Grosart following one MS.   12 arrands] errands
1635–69   25 words *1633–54 and some MSS.:* works *1669 and some*
MSS.

Frame

Frame and enamell Plate, and drinke in Glasse?
Chafe waxe for others seales? breake a colts force
And leave him then, beeing made a ready horse?   30

ELEGIE VIII.
The Comparison.

AS the sweet sweat of Roses in a Still,
  As that which from chaf'd muskats pores doth trill,
As the Almighty Balme of th'early East,
Such are the sweat drops of my Mistris breast,
And on her ⟨brow⟩ her skin such lustre sets,   5
They seeme no sweat drops, but pearle coronets.
Ranke sweaty froth thy Mistresse's brow defiles,
Like spermatique issue of ripe menstruous boiles,
Or like the skumme, which, by needs lawlesse law
Enforc'd, Sanserra's starved men did draw   10
From parboild shooes, and bootes, and all the rest
Which were with any soveraigne fatnes blest,
And like vile lying stones in saffrond tinne,
Or warts, or wheales, they hang upon her skinne.
Round as the world's her head, on every side,   15
Like to the fatall Ball which fell on Ide,
Or that whereof God had such jealousie,
As, for the ravishing thereof we die.
Thy *head* is like a rough-hewne statue of jeat,
Where marks for eyes, nose, mouth, are yet scarce set; 20
Like the first Chaos, or flat seeming face
Of Cynthia, when th'earths shadowes her embrace.
Like Proserpines white beauty-keeping chest,
Or Joves best fortunes urne, is her faire brest.

Elegie VIII.   5 ⟨brow⟩ *Ed:* necke *1633–69 and MSS.*   6
coronets. *1633–69 and most MSS.:* carcanets. *some MSS.*   8 boiles,
in MSS. generally spelt as pronounced, biles *or* byles   13 vile lying
stones *1635–54 and MSS.:* vile stones lying *1633, 1669*   14 they
hang *MSS.:* it hangs *1633–69*

Thine's

Thine's like worme eaten trunkes, cloth'd in seals skin, 25
Or grave, that's dust without, and stinke within.
And like that slender stalke, at whose end stands
The wood-bine quivering, are her armes and hands.
Like rough bark'd elmboughes, or the russet skin
Of men late scurg'd for madnes, or for sinne,   30
Like Sun-parch'd quarters on the citie gate,
Such is thy tann'd skins lamentable state.
And like a bunch of ragged carrets stand
The short swolne fingers of thy gouty hand.
Then like the Chymicks masculine equall fire,   35
Which in the Lymbecks warme wombe doth inspire
Into th'earths worthlesse durt a soule of gold,
Such cherishing heat her best lov'd part doth hold.
Thine's like the dread mouth of a fired gunne,
Or like hot liquid metalls newly runne   40
Into clay moulds, or like to that Ætna
Where round about the grasse is burnt away.
Are not your kisses then as filthy, and more,
As a worme sucking an invenom'd sore?
Doth not thy fearefull hand in feeling quake,   45
As one which gath'ring flowers, still feares a snake?
Is not your last act harsh, and violent,
As when a Plough a stony ground doth rent?
So kisse good Turtles, so devoutly nice
Are Priests in handling reverent sacrifice,   50
And such in searching wounds the Surgeon is
As wee, when wee embrace, or touch, or kisse.
Leave her, and I will leave comparing thus,
She, and comparisons are odious.

26 dust *1633–69:* durt *most MSS.*   34 thy gouty hand.*1635–69*
and most MSS.: her gouty hand; *1633:* thy mistress hand; *1669*
48 when] where *1633*   51 such *MSS.:* nice *1633–69*

ELEGIE

ELEGIE IX.

The Autumnall.

NO *Spring*, nor *Summer* Beauty hath such grace,
 As I have seen in one *Autumnall* face.
Yong *Beauties* force our love, and that's a *Rape*,
 This doth but *counsaile*, yet you cannot scape.
If t'were a *shame* to love, here t'were no *shame*,   5
 Affection here takes *Reverences* name.
Were her first yeares the *Golden Age*; That's true,
 But now shee's *gold* oft tried, and ever new.
That was her torrid and inflaming time,
 This is her tolerable *Tropique clyme*.   10
Faire eyes, who askes more heate then comes from hence,
 He in a fever wishes pestilence.
Call not these wrinkles, *graves*; If *graves* they were,
 They were *Loves graves*; for else he is no where.
Yet lies not Love *dead* here, but here doth sit   15
 Vow'd to this trench, like an *Anachorit*.
And here, till hers, which must be his *death*, come,
 He doth not digge a *Grave*, but build a *Tombe*.
Here dwells he, though he sojourne ev'ry where,
 In *Progresse*, yet his standing house is here.   20
Here, where still *Evening* is; not *noone*, nor *night*;
 Where no *voluptuousnesse*, yet all *delight*.
In all her words, unto all hearers fit,
 You may at *Revels*, you at *Counsaile*, sit.
This is loves timber, youth his under-wood;   25
 There he, as wine in *June*, enrages blood,
Which then comes seasonabliest, when our tast
 And appetite to other things, is past.

Elegie IX. 3 our love, *1633 and some MSS.:* our Loves. *1669:*
your love, *1635–54 and most MSS.* 6 *Affection* . . . takes *most
MSS.:* Affections . . . take *1633–69* 8 shee's *1635–69 and MSS.:*
they're *1633* 10 tolerable *1633 and some MSS.:* habitable *1635–
69 and most MSS.* 22 Where] Where's *some MSS.*

Xerxes

Xerxes strange *Lydian* love, the *Platane* tree,
　　Was lov'd for age, none being so large as shee,　　30
Or else because, being yong, nature did blesse
　　Her youth with ages glory, *Barrennesse.*
If we love things long sought, *Age* is a thing
　　Which we are fifty yeares in compassing.
If transitory things, which soone decay,　　35
　　Age must be lovelyest at the latest day.
But name not *Winter-faces,* whose skin's slacke;
　　Lanke, as an unthrifts purse; but a soules sacke;
Whose *Eyes* seeke light within, for all here's shade;
　　Whose *mouthes* are holes, rather worne out, then made; 40
Whose every tooth to a severall place is gone,
　　To vexe their soules at *Resurrection;*
Name not these living *Deaths-heads* unto mee,
　　For these, not *Ancient,* but *Antique* be.
I hate extreames; yet I had rather stay　　45
　　With *Tombs,* then *Cradles,* to weare out a day.
Since such loves naturall lation is, may still
　　My love descend, and journey downe the hill,
Not panting after growing beauties, so,
　　I shall ebbe out with them, who home-ward goe.　　50

ELEGIE X.

The Dreame.

IMage of her whom I love, more then she,
　Whose faire impression in my faithfull heart,
Makes mee her *Medall,* and makes her love mee,
　　As Kings do coynes, to which their stamps impart

30 large *1633:* old *1635–69*　　44 *Ancient,* ... *Antique 1633,
1669, and best MSS.:* Ancients, ... Antiques *1635–54 and some MSS.:*
ancient . . . antiques, *many MSS.*　be. *Ed:* be; *1633*　46 a] the *1669*
47 naturall lation *most MSS.:* motion naturall *1633:* naturall station
1635–69　　50 ebbe out *1633:* ebbe on *1635–69 and all MSS.*

The

The value: goe, and take my heart from hence,   5
    Which now is growne too great and good for me:
Honours oppresse weake spirits, and our sense
    Strong objects dull; the more, the lesse wee see.
When you are gone, and *Reason* gone with you,
    Then *Fantasie* is Queene and Soule, and all;   10
She can present joyes meaner then you do;
    Convenient, and more proportionall.
So, if I dreame I have you, I have you,
    For, all our joyes are but fantasticall.
And so I scape the paine, for paine is true;   15
    And sleepe which locks up sense, doth lock out all.
After a such fruition I shall wake,
    And, but the waking, nothing shall repent;
And shall to love more thankfull Sonnets make,
    Then if more *honour, teares,* and *paines* were spent. 20
But dearest heart, and dearer image stay;
    Alas, true joyes at best are *dreame* enough;
Though you stay here you passe too fast away:
    For even at first lifes *Taper* is a snuffe.
Fill'd with her love, may I be rather grown   25
Mad with much *heart,* then *ideott* with none.

ELEGIE XI.

The Bracelet.

*Vpon the losse of his Mistresses Chaine, for which
he made satisfaction.*

NOt that in colour it was like thy haire,
    For Armelets of that thou maist let me weare:
Nor that thy hand it oft embrac'd and kist,
For so it had that good, which oft I mist:

Elegie XI. 2 For . . . weare:] Armelets of that thou maist still let
me weare: *1669*

Nor

Nor for that silly old moralitie, 5
That as these linkes were knit, our love should bee:
Mourne I that I thy seavenfold chaine have lost;
Nor for the luck sake; but the bitter cost.
O, shall twelve righteous Angels, which as yet
No leaven of vile soder did admit; 10
Nor yet by any way have straid or gone
From the first state of their Creation;
Angels, which heaven commanded to provide
All things to me, and be my faithfull guide;
To gaine new friends, t'appease great enemies; 15
To comfort my soule, when I lie or rise;
Shall these twelve innocents, by thy severe
Sentence (dread judge) my sins great burden beare?
Shall they be damn'd, and in the furnace throwne,
And punisht for offences not their owne? 20
They save not me, they doe not ease my paines,
When in that hell they'are burnt and tyed in chains.
Were they but Crownes of France, I cared not,
For, most of these, their naturall Countreys rot
I think possesseth, they come here to us, 25
So pale, so lame, so leane, so ruinous;
And howsoe'r French Kings most Christian be,
Their Crownes are circumcis'd most Jewishly.
Or were they Spanish Stamps, still travelling,
That are become as Catholique as their King, 30
Those unlickt beare-whelps, unfil'd pistolets
That (more than Canon shot) availes or lets;
Which negligently left unrounded, looke
Like many angled figures, in the booke
Of some great Conjurer that would enforce 35

6 were knit, *1635–69:* are tyde *most MSS.* 11 way *1635–69:*
taynt *some MSS.:* fault *most MSS.* 15 great] old *1669* 16 rise;
Ed: rise. *1635–69* 24 their naturall Countreys *some MSS.:* their
Countreys naturall *1635–54:* their naturall Countrey *1669 and most*
MSS.

Nature

Nature, as these doe justice, from her course;
Which, as the soule quickens head, feet and heart,
As streames, like veines, run through th'earth's every
    part,
Visit all Countries, and have slily made
Gorgeous *France*, ruin'd, ragged and decay'd;   40
Scotland, which knew no State, proud in one day:
And mangled seventeen-headed *Belgia*.
Or were it such gold as that wherewithall
Almighty *Chymiques* from each minerall,
Having by subtle fire a soule out-pull'd;   45
Are dirtely and desperately gull'd:
I would not spit to quench the fire they'are in,
For, they are guilty of much hainous Sin.
But, shall my harmlesse angels perish? Shall
I lose my guard, my ease, my food, my all?   50
Much hope which they should nourish will be dead,
Much of my able youth, and lustyhead
Will vanish; if thou love let them alone,
For thou will love me lesse when they are gone;
And be content that some lowd squeaking Cryer   55
Well-pleas'd with one leane thred-bare groat, for hire,
May like a devill roare through every street;
And gall the finders conscience, if they meet.
Or let mee creepe to some dread Conjurer,
That with phantastique scheames fils full much paper; 60
Which hath divided heaven in tenements,
And with whores, theeves, and murderers stuft his rents,
So full, that though hee passe them all in sinne,
He leaves himselfe no roome to enter in.
But if, when all his art and time is spent,   65
Hee say 'twill ne'r be found; yet be content;

40 ruin'd, ragged and decay'd; *1669 and MSS.*, *but end stop varies:*
ruin'd: ragged and decay'd *1635:* ruin'd: ragged and decay'd, *1639–*
54   60 scheames *most MSS.:* scenes *1635–69 and some MSS.*
66 yet *1635–69:* Oh *most MSS.*

Receive

Receive from him that doome ungrudgingly,
Because he is the mouth of destiny.
    Thou say'st (alas) the gold doth still remaine,
Though it be chang'd, and put into a chaine;   70
So in the first falne angels, resteth still
Wisdome and knowledge; but,'tis turn'd to ill:
As these should doe good works; and should provide
Necessities; but now must nurse thy pride.
And they are still bad angels; Mine are none;   75
For, forme gives being, and their forme is gone:
Pitty these Angels; yet their dignities
Passe Vertues, Powers, and Principalities.
    But, thou art resolute; Thy will be done!
Yet with such anguish, as her onely sonne   80
The Mother in the hungry grave doth lay,
Vnto the fire these Martyrs I betray.
Good soules, (for you give life to every thing)
Good Angels, (for good messages you bring)
Destin'd you might have beene to such an one,   85
As would have lov'd and worship'd you alone:
One that would suffer hunger, nakednesse,
Yea death, ere he would make your number lesse.
But, I am guilty of your sad decay;
May your few fellowes longer with me stay.   90
    But ô thou wretched finder whom I hate
So, that I almost pitty thy estate:
Gold being the heaviest metal amongst all,
May my most heavy curse upon thee fall:
Here fetter'd, manacled, and hang'd in chains,   95
First mayst thou bee; then chaind to hellish paines;
Or be with forraine gold brib'd to betray
Thy Countrey, and faile both of that and thy pay.
May the next thing thou stoop'st to reach, containe
Poyson, whose nimble fume rot thy moist braine;   100

77 Angels; yet *most MSS.:* Angels yet; *1635–69 and one good MS.*
98 that *MSS.:* it *1635–69*

Or

Or libels, or some interdicted thing,
Which negligently kept, thy ruine bring.
Lust-bred diseases rot thee; and dwell with thee
Itching desire, and no abilitie.
May all the evils that gold ever wrought;   105
All mischiefes that all devils ever thought;
Want after plenty; poore and gouty age;
The plagues of travellers; love; marriage
Afflict thee, and at thy lives last moment,
May thy swolne sinnes themselves to thee present.   110
    But, I forgive; repent thee honest man:
Gold is Restorative, restore it then:
But if from it thou beest loath to depart,
Because 'tis cordiall, would twere at thy heart.

ELEGIE XII.

His parting from her.

SInce she must go, and I must mourn, come Night,
Environ me with darknesse, whilst I write:
Shadow that hell unto me, which alone
I am to suffer when my Love is gone.
Alas the darkest Magick cannot do it,   5
Thou and greate Hell to boot are shadows to it.
Should *Cinthia* quit thee, *Venus*, and each starre,
It would not forme one thought dark as mine are.
I could lend thee obscureness now, and say,

104 Itching] Itchy *MSS.*   105 evils that gold ever *1635–69:* hurt
that ever gold hath *MSS.*   106 mischiefes *all MSS.*: mischiefe
1635–69   108 love; marriage *1635–54:* love and marriage *1669
and MSS.*   113 But if from it . . . depart, *1635–54:* But if that
from it . . . part, *1669:* Or if with it . . . depart *most MSS.*

    Elegie XII. 4 Love] soule *1635–54*   5–44 *omit 1635–54*   6
Thou and greate Hell *MSS.*: And that great Hell *1669*   to boot
are] are nought but *some MSS.*   9 thee] one *MS.*: them *1669 and
most MSS.*

                                                                        Out

Out of my self, There should be no more Day,   10
Such is already my felt want of sight,
Did not the fires within me force a light.
Oh Love, that fire and darkness should be mixt,
Or to thy Triumphs soe strange torments fixt?
Is't because thou thy self art blind, that wee   15
Thy Martyrs must no more each other see?
Or tak'st thou pride to break us on the wheel,
And view old Chaos in the Pains we feel?
Or have we left undone some mutual Right,
Through holy fear, that merits thy despight?   20
No, no. The falt was mine, impute it to me,
Or rather to conspiring destinie,
Which (since I lov'd for forme before) decreed,
That I should suffer when I lov'd indeed:
And therefore now, sooner then I can say,   25
I saw the golden fruit, 'tis rapt away.
Or as I had watcht one drop in a vast stream,
And I left wealthy only in a dream.
Yet Love, thou'rt blinder then thy self in this,
To vex my Dove-like friend for my amiss: 30
And, where my own sad truth may expiate
Thy wrath, to make her fortune run my fate:
So blinded Justice doth, when Favorites fall,
Strike them, their house, their friends, their followers all.
Was't not enough that thou didst dart thy fires   35
Into our blouds, inflaming our desires,
And made'st us sigh and glow, and pant, and burn,
And then thy self into our flame did'st turn?

11 felt want *MSS:* self-want *1669*   12 fires *most MSS.:* fire *1669*
17 the *MSS.:* thy 1669   20 Through holy fear, that merits thy
despight *MSS.:* That thus with parting thou seek'st us to spight? *1669*
21 was] is *1669*   23 Which . . . decreed] Which (since I lov'd)
for me before decreed, *1669 and some MSS.*   27 a vast *MSS.:* the
vast *1669*   31 sad *1669:* glad *MSS.*   34 followers *MSS.:* favourites *1669*   37 glow *MSS.:* blow *1669*   38 flame *MSS.:* flames
1669

Was't

Was't not enough, that thou didst hazard us
To paths in love so dark, so dangerous: 40
And those so ambush'd round with houshold spies,
And over all, thy husbands towring eyes
That flam'd with oylie sweat of jealousie:
Yet went we not still on with Constancie?
Have we not kept our guards, like spie on spie?   45
Had correspondence whilst the foe stood by?
Stoln (more to sweeten them) our many blisses
Of meetings, conference, embracements, kisses?
Shadow'd with negligence our most respects?
Varied our language through all dialects,   50
Of becks, winks, looks, and often under-boards
Spoak dialogues with our feet far from our words?
Have we prov'd all these secrets of our Art,
Yea, thy pale inwards, and thy panting heart?
And, after all this passed Purgatory,   55
Must sad divorce make us the vulgar story?
First let our eyes be rivited quite through
Our turning brains, and both our lips grow to:
Let our armes clasp like Ivy, and our fear
Freese us together, that we may stick here,   60
Till Fortune, that would rive us, with the deed
Strain her eyes open, and it make them bleed:
For Love it cannot be, whom hitherto
I have accus'd, should such a mischief doe.
Oh Fortune, thou'rt not worth my least exclame,   65
And plague enough thou hast in thy own shame.

40 so dangerous *MSS.:* and dangerous *1669*   42 towring *1669:*
MSS. vary   43 That flam'd with oylie *MSS.:* Inflam'd with
th'ouglie *1669*   44 with *MSS.:* in *1669*   45 Have we not kept
our guards, *MSS.:* Have we for this kept guards, *1669*   49 most
1635–69, MSS.: best *1669*   53 these secrets *MSS.:* the secrets *1635–*
69   54 Yea . . . panting heart?] *1635–69:* Yea thy pale colours
inward as thy heart? *most MSS.*   57–66 *om. 1635–54 and some MSS.*
61 would rive us, with *MSS.:* would ruine us with *1669*   66 shame.
MSS.: name. *1669*

Do

Do thy great worst, my friend and I have armes,
Though not against thy strokes, against thy harmes.
Rend us in sunder, thou canst not divide
Our bodies so, but that our souls are ty'd,   70
And we can love by letters still and gifts,
And thoughts and dreams; Love never wanteth shifts.
I will not look upon the quickning Sun,
But straight her beauty to my sense shall run;
The ayre shall note her soft, the fire most pure;   75
Water suggest her clear, and the earth sure.
Time shall not lose our passages; the Spring
How fresh our love was in the beginning;
The Summer how it ripened in the eare;
And Autumn, what our golden harvests were.   80
The Winter I'll not think on to spite thee,
But count it a lost season, so shall shee.
And dearest Friend, since we must part, drown night
With hope of Day, burthens well born are light.
Though cold and darkness longer hang somewhere,   85
Yet *Phoebus* equally lights all the Sphere.
And what he cannot in like Portions pay,
The world enjoyes in Mass, and so we may.
Be then ever your self, and let no woe
Win on your health, your youth, your beauty: so   90
Declare your self base fortunes Enemy,
No less by your contempt then constancy:
That I may grow enamoured on your mind,
When my own thoughts I there reflected find.
For this to th'comfort of my Dear I vow,   95

67 armes, *1635–69 and MSS.:* charmes, *Grosart and Chambers*
79 ripened in the eare; *MSS.:* ripened in the yeare; *1635:* inripened
the yeare; *1639–69*   83–94 *omit 1635–54 and some MSS.*   87 he
... Portions] we ... Portion *1669:* he can't in like proportion
Grosart   92 by your contempt then constancy] be your contempt
then her inconstancy: *1669*   94 there reflected *MSS.:* here neglected
1669   95 For *MSS.:* And *1635–69*

My Deeds shall still be what my words are now;
The Poles shall move to teach me ere I start;
And when I change my Love, I'll change my heart;
Nay, if I wax but cold in my desire,
Think, heaven hath motion lost, and the world, fire: 100
Much more I could, but many words have made
That, oft, suspected which men would perswade;
Take therefore all in this: I love so true,
As I will never look for less in you.

ELEGIE XIII.

Julia.

HArke newes, ô envy, thou shalt heare descry'd
My *Julia*; who as yet was ne'r envy'd.
To vomit gall in slander, swell her vaines
With calumny, that hell it selfe disdaines,
Is her continuall practice; does her best,   5
To teare opinion even out of the brest
Of dearest friends, and (which is worse than vilde)
Sticks jealousie in wedlock; her owne childe
Scapes not the showres of envie, To repeate
The monstrous fashions, how, were, alive, to eate   10
Deare reputation. Would to God she were
But halfe so loath to act vice, as to heare
My milde reproofe. Liv'd *Mantuan* now againe,
That fœmall Mastix, to limme with his penne
This she *Chymera*, that hath eyes of fire,   15
Burning with anger, anger feeds desire,
Tongued like the night-crow, whose ill boding cries
Give out for nothing but new injuries,

96 my words are now;] my deeds are now; *1635–69 and some
MSS.:* my thoughts are now; *one MS.*   102 would *1635–54 and
MSS.:* most 1669
    Elegie XIII. 7 vilde *Ed:* vile *1635–69:* vilde *is the regular spelling
of this word in the Donne MSS.*

Her

Her breath like to the juice in *Tenarus*
That blasts the springs, though ne'r so prosperous,　20
Her hands, I know not how, us'd more to spill
The food of others, then her selfe to fill.
But oh her minde, that *Orcus*, which includes
Legions of mischiefs, countlesse multitudes
Of formlesse curses, projects unmade up,　25
Abuses yet unfashion'd, thoughts corrupt,
Mishapen Cavils, palpable untroths,
Inevitable errours, self-accusing oaths:
These, like those Atoms swarming in the Sunne,
Throng in her bosome for creation.　30
I blush to give her halfe her due; yet say,
No poyson's halfe so bad as *Julia.*

ELEGIE XIV.

A Tale of a Citizen and his Wife.

I Sing no harme good sooth to any wight,
　To Lord or foole, Cuckold, begger or knight,
To peace-teaching Lawyer, Proctor, or brave
Reformed or reduced Captaine, Knave,
Officer, Jugler, or Justice of peace,　5
Juror or Judge; I touch no fat sowes grease,
I am no Libeller, nor will be any,
But (like a true man) say there are too many.
I feare not *ore tenus*; for my tale,
Nor Count nor Counsellour will redd or pale.　10
A Citizen and his wife the other day
Both riding on one horse, upon the way
I overtooke, the wench a pretty peate,

24 mischiefs *MS.:* mischiefe, *1635–69*　　28 oaths:] loathes:
1635–69 and one MS.
　Elegie XIV. 10 will redd or pale. *1669, MSS.:* will looke redd or
pale. *1635–54*

　　　　　　　　　　　　　　　　　　　　　　And

And (by her eye) well fitting for the feate.
I saw the lecherous Citizen turne backe 15
His head, and on his wifes lip steale a smacke,
Whence apprehending that the man was kinde,
Riding before, to kisse his wife behinde,
To get acquaintance with him I began
To sort discourse fit for so fine a man: 20
I ask'd the number of the Plaguy Bill,
Ask'd if the Custome Farmers held out still,
Of the Virginian plot, and whether Ward
The traffique of the I⟨n⟩land seas had marr'd,
Whether the Brittaine *Burse* did fill apace, 25
And likely were to give th'Exchange disgrace;
Of new-built *Algate*, and the *More-field* crosses,
Of store of Bankerouts, and poore Merchants losses
I urged him to speake; But he (as mute
As an old Courtier worne to his last suite) 30
Replies with onely yeas and nayes; At last
(To fit his element) my theame I cast
On Tradesmens gaines; that set his tongue agoing:
Alas, good sir (quoth he) *There is no doing*
In Court nor City now; she smil'd and I, 35
And (in my conscience) both gave him the lie
In one met thought: but he went on apace,
And at the present time with such a face
He rail'd, as fray'd me; for he gave no praise,
To any but my Lord of *Essex* dayes; 40
Call'd those the age of action; true (quoth Hee)
There's now as great an itch of bravery,
And heat of taking up, but cold lay downe,
For, put to push of pay, away they runne;
Our onely City trades of hope now are 45
Bawd, Tavern-keeper, Whore and Scrivener;

24 I⟨n⟩land *Ed:* Iland *1635–54:* Midland *1669:* Island *Chambers and Grolier*   41 those ... (quoth Hee) *1669, MSS.:* that ... (quoth I) *1635–54*

The

The much of Privileg'd kingsmen, and the store
Of fresh protections make the rest all poore;
In the first state of their Creation,
Though many stoutly stand, yet proves not one   50
A righteous pay-master. Thus ranne he on
In a continued rage: so void of reason
Seem'd his harsh talke, I sweat for feare of treason.
And (troth) how could I lesse? when in the prayer
For the protection of the wise Lord Major,   55
And his wise brethrens worships, when one prayeth,
He swore that none could say Amen with faith.
To get him off from what I glowed to heare,
(In happy time) an Angel did appeare,
The bright Signe of a lov'd and wel-try'd Inne,   60
Where many Citizens with their wives have bin
Well us'd and often; here I pray'd him stay,
To take some due refreshment by the way.
Looke how hee look'd that hid the gold (his hope)
And at's returne found nothing but a Rope,   65
So he on me, refus'd and made away,
Though willing she pleaded a weary day:
I found my misse, struck hands, and praid him tell
(To hold acquaintance still) where he did dwell;
He barely nam'd the street, promis'd the Wine,   70
But his kinde wife gave me the very Signe.

ELEGIE XV.

The Expostulation.

TO make the doubt cleare, that no woman's true,
 Was it my fate to prove it strong in you?
Thought I, but one had breathed purest aire,
 And must she needs be false because she's faire?

47 kingsmen, and the store *1669, MSS.:* kinsmen, and store *1635-54*
61 have bin *MSS.:* had beene, *1635-69*   65 at's *1669:* at *1635-54*
67 day: *1669, MSS.:* stay. *1635-39:* stay: *1650-54*

Is

Is it your beauties marke, or of your youth,   5
    Or your perfection, not to study truth?
Or thinke you heaven is deafe, or hath no eyes?
    Or those it hath, smile at your perjuries?
Are vowes so cheape with women, or the matter
    Whereof they are made, that they are writ in water,   10
And blowne away with winde? Or doth their breath
    (Both hot and cold at once) make life and death?
Who could have thought so many accents sweet
    Form'd into words, so many sighs should meete
As from our hearts, so many oathes, and teares   15
    Sprinkled among, (all sweeter by our feares
And the divine impression of stolne kisses,
    That seal'd the rest) should now prove empty blisses?
Did you draw bonds to forfet? signe to breake?
    Or must we reade you quite from what you speake,   20
And finde the truth out the wrong way? or must
    Hee first desire you false, would wish you just?
O I prophane, though most of women be
    This kinde of beast, my thought shall except thee;
My dearest love, though froward jealousie,   25
    With circumstance might urge thy'inconstancie,
Sooner I'll thinke the Sunne will cease to cheare
    The teeming earth, and *that* forget to beare,
Sooner that rivers will runne back, or Thames
    With ribs of Ice in June would bind his streames,   30
Or Nature, by whose strength the world endures,
    Would change her course, before you alter yours.
But O that treacherous breast to whom weake you
    Did trust our Counsells, and wee both may rue,
Having his falshood found too late, 'twas hee   35
    That made me *cast* you guilty, and you me,

Elegie XV. 8 smile] winke *Jonson's Underwoods*   12 (Both hot
and cold at once) *MS.:* Both . . . at once, *Und:* (Both . . . cold) at
once *1633–69*   24 This kinde of beast,] The common Monster,
Und   my thought *1633:* my thoughts *1635–69*

Whilst

Whilst he, black wretch, betray'd each simple word
   Wee spake, unto the cunning of a third.
Curst may hee be, that so our love hath slaine,
   And wander on the earth, wretched as *Cain*,   40
Wretched as hee, and not deserve least pitty;
   In plaguing him, let misery be witty;
Let all eyes shunne him, and hee shunne each eye,
   Till hee be noysome as his infamie;
May he without remorse deny God thrice,   45
   And not be trusted more on his Soules price;
And after all selfe torment, when hee dyes,
   May Wolves teare out his heart, Vultures his eyes,
Swine eate his bowels, and his falser tongue
   That utter'd all, be to some Raven flung,   50
And let his carrion coarse be a longer feast
   To the Kings dogges, then any other beast.
Now have I curst, let us our love revive;
   In mee the flame was never more alive;
I could beginne againe to court and praise,   55
   And in that pleasure lengthen the short dayes
Of my lifes lease; like Painters that do take
   Delight, not in made worke, but whiles they make;
I could renew those times, when first I saw
   Love in your eyes, that gave my tongue the law   60
To like what you lik'd; and at maskes and playes
   Commend the selfe same Actors, the same wayes;
Aske how you did, and often with intent
   Of being officious, be impertinent;
All which were such soft pastimes, as in these   65
   Love was as subtilly catch'd, as a disease;
But being got it is a treasure sweet,
   Which to defend is harder then to get:
And ought not be prophan'd on either part,
   For though 'tis got by *chance*, 'tis kept by *art*.   70

     58 worke, *1633–39, most MSS.:* works, *1650–69, Und*

ELEGIE

ELEGIE XVI.

On his Mistris.

B Y our first strange and fatall interview,
By all desires which thereof did ensue,
By our long starving hopes, by that remorse
Which my words masculine perswasive force
Begot in thee, and by the memory   5
Of hurts, which spies and rivals threatned me,
I calmly beg: But by thy fathers wrath,
By all paines, which want and divorcement hath,
I conjure thee, and all the oathes which I
And thou have sworne to seale joynt constancy,   10
Here I unsweare, and overswear them thus,
Thou shalt not love by wayes so dangerous.
Temper, ô faire Love, loves impetuous rage,
Be my true Mistris still, not my faign'd Page;
I'll goe, and, by thy kinde leave, leave behinde   15
Thee, onely worthy to nurse in my minde,
Thirst to come backe; ô if thou die before,
My soule from other lands to thee shall soare.
Thy (else Almighty) beautie cannot move
Rage from the Seas, nor thy love teach them love,   20
Nor tame wilde Boreas harshnesse; Thou hast reade
How roughly hee in peeces shivered
Faire Orithea, whom he swore he lov'd.
Fall ill or good, 'tis madnesse to have prov'd
Dangers unurg'd; Feed on this flattery,   25
That absent Lovers one in th'other be.
Dissemble nothing, not a boy, nor change
Thy bodies habite, nor mindes; bee not strange

Elegie XVI.   3 starving] striving *1669:* starvling *some MSS.*
7 fathers *1635–69:* Parents *most MSS.*   12 wayes *1635–54:* means
1669 and most MSS.   18 My soule . . . to thee] From other lands
my soule towards thee *most MSS.*   28 mindes; *some MSS.:* minde,
1635–69 and other MSS.

To thy selfe onely;   All will spie in thy face
A blushing womanly discovering grace;   30
Richly cloath'd Apes, are call'd Apes, and as soone
Ecclips'd as bright we call the Moone the Moone.
Men of France, changeable Camelions,
Spittles of diseases, shops of fashions,
Loves fuellers, and the rightest company   35
Of Players, which upon the worlds stage be,
Will quickly know thee, and no lesse, alas!
Th'indifferent Italian, as we passe
His warme land, well content to thinke thee Page,
Will hunt thee with such lust, and hideous rage,   40
As *Lots* faire guests were vext. But none of these
Nor spungy hydroptique Dutch shall thee displease,
If thou stay here. O stay here, for, for thee
England is onely a worthy Gallerie,
To walke in expectation, till from thence   45
Our greatest King call thee to his presence.
When I am gone, dreame me some happinesse,
Nor let thy lookes our long hid love confesse,
Nor praise, nor dispraise me, nor blesse nor curse
Openly loves force, nor in bed fright thy Nurse   50
With midnights startings, crying out, oh, oh
Nurse, ô my love is slaine, I saw him goe
O'r the white Alpes alone; I saw him I,
Assail'd, fight, taken, stabb'd, bleed, fall, and die.
Augure me better chançe, except dread *Jove*   55
Thinke it enough for me to'have had thy love.

37 Will quickly know thee, and know thee, and alas! *some good*
MSS.   40 hunt *1635–69:* haunt *most MSS.*   49 me, nor blesse]
me; Blesse *most MSS.*

ELEGIE

ELEGIE XVII.

⟨*Variety.*⟩

THe heavens rejoyce in motion, why should I
   Abjure my so much lov'd variety,
And not with many youth and love divide?
Pleasure is none, if not diversifi'd:
The sun that sitting in the chaire of light   5
Sheds flame into what else so ever doth seem bright,
Is not contented at one Signe to Inne,
But ends his year and with a new beginnes.
All things doe willingly in change delight,
The fruitfull mother of our appetite: 10
Rivers the clearer and more pleasing are,
Where their fair spreading streames run wide and farr;
And a dead lake that no strange bark doth greet,
Corrupts it self and what doth live in it.
Let no man tell me such a one is faire,   15
And worthy all alone my love to share.
Nature in her hath done the liberall part
Of a kinde Mistresse, and imploy'd her art
To make her loveable, and I aver
Him not humane that would turn back from her: 20
I love her well, and would, if need were, dye
To doe her service. But followes it that I
Must serve her onely, when I may have choice
Of other beauties, and in change rejoice?
The law is hard, and shall not have my voice.   25
The last I saw in all extreames is faire,
And holds me in the Sun-beames of her haire;
Her nymph-like features such agreements have

Elegie XVII. 6 what else is not so *MS.*   12 fair-spreading
1650–69: broad silver *MS.*   14 it self and *1650–69:* it self, kills
MS.   16 And only worthy to be past compare; *MS.*   20 would
turn back from *1650–69:* could not fancy *MS.*   24 Of other beauties,
and in change rejoice? *MS.:* om. *1650–69*   25–36 *omitted in MS.*

That

That I could venture with her to the grave:
Another's brown, I like her not the worse, 30
Her tongue is soft and takes me with discourse.
Others, for that they well descended are,
Do in my love obtain as large a share;
And though they be not fair, 'tis much with mee
To win their love onely for their degree. 35
And though I faile of my required ends,
The attempt is glorious and it self commends.
How happy were our Syres in ancient times,
Who held plurality of loves no crime!
With them it was accounted charity 40
To stirre up race of all indifferently;
Kindreds were not exempted from the bands:
Which with the Persian still in usage stands.
Women were then no sooner asked then won,
And what they did was honest and well done. 45
But since this title honour hath been us'd,
Our weake credulity hath been abus'd;
The golden laws of nature are repeald,
Which our first Fathers in such reverence held;
Our liberty's revers'd, our Charter's gone, 50
And we're made servants to opinion,
A monster in no certain shape attir'd,
And whose originall is much desir'd,
Formlesse at first, but growing on it fashions,
And doth prescribe manners and laws to nations. 55
Here love receiv'd immedicable harmes,
And was dispoiled of his daring armes.
A greater want then is his daring eyes,
He lost those awfull wings with which he flies;
His sinewy bow, and those immortall darts 60
Wherewith he'is wont to bruise resisting hearts.
Onely some few strong in themselves and free

43 Persian *1650–54:* Persians *1669,* MS.   51 we're] we *1650–69*
58 is *1650–69:* of MS.   61 bruise *1650–69:* wound MS.

Retain

Retain the seeds of antient liberty,
Following that part of Love although deprest,
And make a throne for him within their brest,   65
In spight of modern censures him avowing
Their Soveraigne, all service him allowing.
Amongst which troop although I am the least,
Yet equall in perfection with the best,
I glory in subjection of his hand,   70
Nor ever did decline his least command:
For in whatever forme the message came
My heart did open and receive the same.
But time will in his course a point discry
When I this loved service must deny,   75
For our allegiance temporary is,
With firmer age returnes our liberties.
What time in years and judgement we repos'd,
Shall not so easily be to change dispos'd,
Nor to the art of severall eyes obeying;   80
But beauty with true worth securely weighing,
Which being found assembled in some one,
Wee'l love her ever, and love her alone.

ELEGIE XVIII.
Loves Progress.

WHo ever loves, if he do not propose
     The right true end of love, he's one that goes
To sea for nothing but to make him sick:
Love is a bear-whelp born, if we o're lick
Our love, and force it new strange shapes to take,   5
We erre, and of a lump a monster make.

63 seeds of antient] seed of pristine *MS.*   70 of his *1650–69:*
under's *MS.*   71 Nor ... decline *1650–69:* Never declining from
MS.   72–7 *omitted in one MS.*   73 same.] flame. *MS.*   81 securely
1650–69: unpartially *MS.*   82 being *1650–69:* having *MS.*   83
Wee'l love her ever, *Ed:* Wee'l leave her ever, *1650–69 and one MS.:*
Would love for ever *another MS.*

                                                            Were

Were not a Calf a monster that were grown
Face'd like a man, though better then his own?
Perfection is in unitie: preferr
One woman first, and then one thing in her.   10
I, when I value gold, may think upon
The ductilness, the application,
The wholsomness, the ingenuitie,
From rust, from soil, from fire ever free:
But if I love it, 'tis because 'tis made   15
By our new nature (Use) the soul of trade.
　　All these in women we might think upon
(If women had them) and yet love but one.
Can men more injure women then to say
They love them for that, by which they're not they? 20
Makes virtue woman? must I cool my bloud
Till I both be, and find one wise and good?
May barren Angels love so. But if we
Make love to woman; virtue is not she:
As beauty'is not nor wealth: He that strayes thus   25
From her to hers, is more adulterous,
Then if he took her maid. Search every spheare
And firmament, our *Cupid* is not there:
He's an infernal god and under ground,
With *Pluto* dwells, where gold and fire abound: 30
Men to such Gods, their sacrificing Coles
Did not in Altars lay, but pits and holes.
Although we see Celestial bodies move
Above the earth, the earth we Till and love:
So we her ayres contemplate, words and heart,   35
And virtues; but we love the Centrique part.
　　Nor is the soul more worthy, or more fit
For love, then this, as infinite as it.
But in attaining this desired place
How much they erre; that set out at the face?   40

Elegie XVIII.　14 ever *1669:* for ever *some MSS.*　32 in *MSS.:*
on *1669*　40 erre *1661–69:* stray *most MSS.*

The

The hair a Forest is of Ambushes,
Of springes, snares, fetters and manacles:
The brow becalms us when 'tis smooth and plain,
And when 'tis wrinckled, shipwracks us again.
Smooth, 'tis a Paradice, where we would have   45
Immortal stay, and wrinkled 'tis our grave.
The Nose (like to the first Meridian) runs
Not 'twixt an East and West, but 'twixt two suns;
It leaves a Cheek, a rosie Hemisphere
On either side, and then directs us where   50
Upon the Islands fortunate we fall,
(Not faynte *Canaries*, but *Ambrosiall*)
Her swelling lips; To which when wee are come,
We anchor there, and think our selves at home,
For they seem all: there Syrens songs, and there   55
Wise Delphick Oracles do fill the ear;
There in a Creek where chosen pearls do swell,
The Remora, her cleaving tongue doth dwell.
These, and the glorious Promontory, her Chin
Ore past; and the streight *Hellespont* betweene   60
The *Sestos* and *Abydos* of her breasts,
(Not of two Lovers, but two Loves the neasts)
Succeeds a boundless sea, but yet thine eye
Some Island moles may scattered there descry;
And Sailing towards her *India*, in that way   65
Shall at her fair Atlantick Navell stay;
Though thence the Current be thy Pilot made,
Yet ere thou be where thou wouldst be embay'd,
Thou shalt upon another Forest set,
Where many Shipwrack, and no further get.   70

47 first Meridian *1661 and MSS.:* sweet Meridian *1669*   52-3
(Not . . . *Ambrosiall*) . . . lips *&c. 1661 and MSS.:* Not . . . Ambrosiall. Unto her swelling lips when we are come, *1669*   55 For they
seem all: there *1669 and most MSS.:* For they sing all their
1661 and some MSS.   60 Ore past; . . . betweene *1661 and MSS.:*
Being past the Straits of *Hellespont* between *1669*   63 yet] that
some MSS.   70 many *1669:* some doe *most MSS.*

F   When

When thou art there, consider what this chace
Mispent by thy beginning at the face.
   Rather set out below; practice my Art,
Some Symetry the foot hath with that part
Which thou dost seek, and is thy Map for that   75
Lovely enough to stop, but not stay at:
Least subject to disguise and change it is;
Men say the Devil never can change his.
It is the Emblem that hath figured
Firmness; 'tis the first part that comes to bed.   80
Civilitie we see refin'd: the kiss
Which at the face began, transplanted is,
Since to the hand, since to the Imperial knee,
Now at the Papal foot delights to be:
If Kings think that the nearer way, and do   85
Rise from the foot, Lovers may do so too;
For as free Spheres move faster far then can
Birds, whom the air resists, so may that man
Which goes this empty and Ætherial way,
Then if at beauties elements he stay.   90
Rich Nature hath in women wisely made
Two purses, and their mouths aversely laid:
They then, which to the lower tribute owe,
That way which that Exchequer looks, must go:
He which doth not, his error is as great,   95
As who by Clyster gave the Stomack meat.

ELEGIE XIX.
Going to Bed.

COme, Madam, come, all rest my powers defie,
  Until I labour, I in labour lie.
The foe oft-times having the foe in sight,
Is tir'd with standing though he never fight.

81–2 Civilitie, we see, refin'd the kisse Which at the face begonne, transplanted is *scme MSS.*   96 Clyster gave *some MSS.:* glister gives *1669*

Off

Off with that girdle, like heavens Zone glittering,   5
But a far fairer world incompassing.
Unpin that spangled breastplate which you wear,
That th'eyes of busie fooles may be stopt there.
Unlace your self, for that harmonious chyme,
Tells me from you, that now it is bed time.   10
Off with that happy busk, which I envie,
That still can be, and still can stand so nigh.
Your gown going off, such beautious state reveals,
As when from flowry meads th'hills shadow steales.
Off with that wyerie Coronet and shew   15
The haiery Diademe which on you doth grow:
Now off with those shooes, and then safely tread
In this loves hallow'd temple, this soft bed.
In such white robes, heaven's Angels us'd to be
Receavd by men; Thou Angel bringst with thee   20
A heaven like Mahomets Paradise; and though
Ill spirits walk in white, we easly know,
By this these Angels from an evil sprite,
Those set our hairs, but these our flesh upright.

   Licence my roaving hands, and let them go,   25
Before, behind, between, above, below.
O my America! my new-found-land,
My kingdome, safeliest when with one man man'd,
My Myne of precious stones, My Emperie,
How blest am I in this discovering thee!   30
To enter in these bonds, is to be free;
Then where my hand is set, my seal shall be.

Elegie XIX. 5 glittering] glistering *MSS.* 8 That I may
see my shrine that shines so fair. *some MSS.* 10 it is *1669:* 'tis your
MSS. 11 which] whom *MSS.* 14 from *MSS.:* through *1669*
17 safely *most MSS.:* softly *1669 and some MSS.* 20 Receavd by
men; Thou *all MSS.:* Reveal'd to men; thou *1669* 22 Ill *1669
and most MSS.:* All *some MSS.* spirits *1669 and most MSS.:* angels
some MSS. 28 kingdome, *MSS.:* Kingdom's *1669* safeliest *MSS.:*
safest, *1669* 30 this *most MSS.:* thus *1669 and some MSS.*

Full

Full nakedness! All joyes are due to thee,
As souls unbodied, bodies uncloth'd must be,
To taste whole joyes. Gems which you women use   35
Are like Atlanta's balls, cast in mens views,
That when a fools eye lighteth on a Gem,
His earthly soul may covet theirs, not them.
Like pictures, or like books gay coverings made
For lay-men, are all women thus array'd;   40
Themselves are mystick books, which only wee
(Whom their imputed grace will dignifie)
Must see reveal'd. Then since that I may know;
As liberally, as to a Midwife, shew
Thy self: cast all, yea, this white lynnen hence,   45
There is no pennance due to innocence.
    To teach thee, I am naked first; why than
What needst thou have more covering then a man.

ELEGIE XX.
Loves Warre.

TILL I have peace with thee, warr other men,
    And when I have peace, can I leave thee then?
All other Warrs are scrupulous; Only thou
O fayr free Citty, maist thyselfe allowe
To any one: In Flanders, who can tell   5
Whether the Master presse; or men rebell?
Only we know, that which all Ideots say,
They beare most blows which come to part the fray.
France in her lunatique giddiness did hate
Ever our men, yea and our God of late;   1c
Yet she relyes upon our Angels well,
Which nere returne; no more then they which fell.

36 like *1669:* as *MSS.* balls, *MSS.:* ball: *1669*   38 covet *most
MSS.:* court *1669 and some MSS.* theirs, *most MSS.:* that, *1669
and some MSS.*   41 Themselves . . . only wee] Themselves are
only mystick books, which we, *1669*   43 see] be *some MSS.*   44 a
all *MSS.:* thy *1669*   46 pennance due to innocence. *1669 and
some MSS.:* pennance, much less innocence; *most MSS.*

                                                        Sick

Sick Ireland is with a strange warr possest
Like to an Ague; now raging, now at rest;
Which time will cure: yet it must doe her good   15
If she were purg'd, and her head vayne let blood.
And Midas joyes our Spanish journeys give,
We touch all gold, but find no food to live.
And I should be in the hott parching clyme,
To dust and ashes turn'd before my time.   20
To mew me in a Ship, is to inthrall
Mee in a prison, that weare like to fall;
Or in a Cloyster; save that there men dwell
In a calme heaven, here in a swaggering hell.
Long voyages are long consumptions,   25
And ships are carts for executions.
Yea they are Deaths; Is't not all one to flye
Into an other World, as t'is to dye?
Here let mee warr; in these armes lett mee lye;
Here lett mee parlee, batter, bleede, and dye.   30
Thyne armes imprison me, and myne armes thee;
Thy hart thy ransome is; take myne for mee.
Other men war that they their rest may gayne;
But wee will rest that wee may fight agayne.
Those warrs the ignorant, these th'experienc'd love, 35
There wee are always under, here above.
There Engins farr off breed a just true feare,
Neere thrusts, pikes, stabs, yea bullets hurt not here.
There lyes are wrongs; here safe uprightly lye;
There men kill men, we'will make one by and by.   40
Thou nothing; I not halfe so much shall do
In these Warrs, as they may which from us two
Shall spring. Thousands wee see which travaile not
To warrs; But stay swords, armes, and shott
To make at home; And shall not I do then   45
More glorious service, staying to make men?

Elegie XX. 19 the *most MSS.*: that *some MSS.*

HEROICALL

HEROICALL EPISTLE.

Sapho to *Philænis.*

WHere is that holy fire, which *Verse* is said
   To have? is that inchanting force decai'd?
Verse that drawes *Natures* workes, from *Natures* law,
   Thee, her best worke, to her worke cannot draw.
Have my teares quench'd my old *Poetique* fire;   5
   Why quench'd they not as well, that of *desire?*
Thoughts, my mindes creatures, often are with thee,
   But I, their maker, want their libertie.
Onely thine image, in my heart, doth sit,
   But that is waxe, and fires environ it.   10
My fires have driven, thine have drawne it hence;
   And I am rob'd of *Picture, Heart,* and *Sense.*
Dwells with me still mine irksome *Memory,*
   Which, both to keepe, and lose, grieves equally.
That tells me'how faire thou art: Thou art so faire,   15
   As, *gods,* when *gods* to thee I doe compare,
Are grac'd thereby; And to make blinde men see,
   What things *gods* are, I say they'are like to thee.
For, if we justly call each silly *man*
   A *litle world,* What shall we call thee than?   20
Thou art not soft, and cleare, and strait, and faire,
   As *Down,* as *Stars, Cedars,* and *Lillies* are,
But thy right hand, and cheek, and eye, only
   Are like thy other hand, and cheek, and eye.
Such was my *Phao* awhile, but shall be never,   25
   As thou, wast, art, and, oh, maist be ever.

 Heroicall Epistle.] *In 1635 this was placed with some other miscella-*
neous and dubious poems among the Letters *to severall* Personages, *where*
it appeared in all subsequent editions. I transferred it in 1912 to
the neighbourhood of the Elegies *and gave it the title which seems to*
describe the genre to which it belongs. In some MSS. ll. 31–54 are
omitted.

Here

Here lovers sweare in their *Idolatrie*,
   That I am such; but *Griefe* discolors me.
And yet I grieve the lesse, least *Griefe* remove
   My beauty, and make me'unworthy of thy love.   30
Plaies some soft boy with thee, oh there wants yet
   A mutuall feeling which should sweeten it.
His chinne, a thorny hairy unevennesse
   Doth threaten, and some daily change possesse.
Thy body is a naturall *Paradise*,   35
   In whose selfe, unmanur'd, all pleasure lies,
Nor needs *perfection*; why shouldst thou than
   Admit the tillage of a harsh rough man?
Men leave behinde them that which their sin showes,
   And are as theeves trac'd, which rob when it snows. 40
But of our dallyance no more signes there are,
   Then *fishes* leave in streames, or *Birds* in aire.
And betweene us all sweetnesse may be had;
   All, all that *Nature* yields, or *Art* can adde.
My two lips, eyes, thighs, differ from thy two,   45
   But so, as thine from one another doe;
And, oh, no more; the likenesse being such,
   Why should they not alike in all parts touch?
Hand to strange hand, lippe to lippe none denies;
   Why should they brest to brest, or thighs to thighs?   50
Likenesse begets such strange selfe flatterie,
   That touching my selfe, all seemes done to thee.
My selfe I embrace, and mine owne hands I kisse,
   And amorously thanke my selfe for this.
Me, in my glasse, I call thee; But, alas,   55
   When I would kisse, teares dimme mine *eyes*, and
     glasse.
O cure this loving madnesse, and restore
   Me to mee; thee, my *halfe*, my *all*, my *more.*

33 thorny hairy *1633–69:* thorney-hairy *one MS.:* thorny, hairy,
modern edd.   58 me to mee; thee, *1635–69 and MSS.:* me to mee;
shee, *1633:* me to thee, thee *Chambers*

So

So may thy cheekes red outweare scarlet dye,
   And their white, whitenesse of the *Galaxy*,   60
So may thy mighty, amazing beauty move
   Envy'in all *women*, and in all *men*, *love*,
And so be *change*, and *sicknesse*, farre from thee,
   As thou by comming neere, keep'st them from me.

    59–60 So may thy cheekes outweare all scarlet dye
            May blisse and thee be one eternallye *one MS*.
61 mighty, amazing] almighty amazing *one MS*.

EPITHALAMIONS,

EPITHALAMIONS,

OR

MARRIAGE SONGS.

An Epithalamion, Or mariage Song on the Lady Elizabeth,
and Count Palatine *being married on St.* Valentines *day.*

I.

Haile Bishop Valentine, whose day this is,
　　All the Aire is thy Diocis,
　　And all the chirping Choristers
And other birds are thy Parishioners,
　　　　Thou marryest every yeare　　　　　　5
The Lirique Larke, and the grave whispering Dove,
The Sparrow that neglects his life for love,
The household Bird, with the red stomacher,
　　　　Thou mak'st the black bird speed as soone,
As doth the Goldfinch, or the Halcyon;　　　　10
The husband cocke lookes out, and straight is sped,
And meets his wife, which brings her feather-bed.
This day more cheerfully then ever shine,
This day, which might enflame thy self, Old Valentine.

II.

Till now, Thou warmd'st with multiplying loves　15
　　　Two larkes, two sparrowes, or two Doves,
　　　　All that is nothing unto this,
For thou this day couplest two Phœnixes;
　　　　Thou mak'st a Taper see
What the sunne never saw, and what the Arke　　20
(Which was of foules, and beasts, the cage, and park,)
Did not containe, one bed containes, through Thee,
　　　Two Phœnixes, whose joyned breasts
Are unto one another mutuall nests,

　　　　　　　　　　　　　　　Where

Where motion kindles such fires, as shall give   25
Yong Phœnixes, and yet the old shall live.
Whose love and courage never shall decline,
But make the whole year through, thy day, O Valentine.

III.

Up then faire Phœnix Bride, frustrate the Sunne,
     Thy selfe from thine affection   30
     Takest warmth enough, and from thine eye
All lesser birds will take their Jollitie.
     Up, up, faire Bride, and call,
Thy starres, from out their severall boxes, take
Thy Rubies, Pearles, and Diamonds forth, and make   35
Thy selfe a constellation, of them All,
     And by their blazing, signifie,
That a Great Princess falls, but doth not die;
Bee thou a new starre, that to us portends
Ends of much wonder; And be Thou those ends.   40
Since thou dost this day in new glory shine,
May all men date Records, from this thy Valentine.

IIII.

Come forth, come forth, and as one glorious flame
     Meeting Another, growes the same,
     So meet thy Fredericke, and so   45
To an unseparable union growe.
     Since separation
Falls not on such things as are infinite,
Nor things which are but one, can disunite,
You'are twice inseparable, great, and one;   50
     Goe then to where the Bishop staies,
To make you one, his way, which divers waies
Must be effected; and when all is past,
And that you'are one, by hearts and hands made fast,

An Epithalamion, &c.   37 their blazing *1633–69 and some MSS.:*
this blazing *most MSS.*   46 growe. *most MSS.:* goe, *1633–69*

                   You

You two have one way left, your selves to'entwine, 55
Besides this Bishops knot, or Bishop Valentine.

V.

But oh, what ailes the Sunne, that here he staies,
　　Longer to day, then other daies?
　　Staies he new light from these to get?
And finding here such store, is loth to set? 60
　　　And why doe you two walke,
So slowly pac'd in this procession?
Is all your care but to be look'd upon,
And be to others spectacle, and talke?
　　The feast, with gluttonous delaies, 65
Is eaten, and too long their meat they praise,
The masquers come too late, and'I thinke, will stay,
Like Fairies, till the Cock crow them away.
Alas, did not Antiquity assigne
A night, as well as day, to thee, O Valentine? 70

VI.

They did, and night is come; and yet wee see
　　Formalities retarding thee.
　　What meane these Ladies, which (as though
They were to take a clock in peeces,) goe
　　So nicely about the Bride; 75
A Bride, before a good night could be said,
Should vanish from her cloathes, into her bed,
As Soules from bodies steale, and are not spy'd.
　　But now she is laid; What though shee bee?
Yet there are more delayes, For, where is hc? 80
He comes, and passes through Spheare after Spheare,
First her sheetes, then her Armes, then any where.

56 Bishops knot, or Bishop Valentine. *MSS.:* Bishops knot, O Bishop
Valentine. *1633–54:* Bishops knot of Bishop Valentine. *1669:* Bishops
knot, of Bishop Valentine. *Chambers*　　60 store, *1633 and most
MSS.:* starres, *1635–69*　　67 come too late, *1633:* come late,
1635–69　　70 O Valentine?] old Valentine? *1669*

Let not this day, then, but this night be thine,
Thy day was but the eve to this, O Valentine.

VII.

Here lyes a shee Sunne, and a hee Moone here,   85
    She gives the best light to his Spheare,
    Or each is both, and all, and so
They unto one another nothing owe,
    And yet they doe, but are
So just and rich in that coyne which they pay,   90
That neither would, nor needs forbeare, nor stay;
Neither desires to be spar'd, nor to spare,
    They quickly pay their debt, and then
Take no acquittances, but pay again;
They pay, they give, they lend, and so let fall   95
No such occasion to be liberall.
More truth, more courage in these two do shine,
Then all thy turtles have, and sparrows, Valentine.

VIII.

And by this act of these two Phenixes
    Nature againe restored is,   100
    For since these two are two no more,
Ther's but one Phenix still, as was before.
    Rest now at last, and wee
As Satyres watch the Sunnes uprise, will stay
Waiting, when your eyes opened, let out day,   105
Onely desir'd, because your face wee see;
    Others neare you shall whispering speake,
And wagers lay, at which side day will breake,
And win by'observing, then, whose hand it is
That opens first a curtaine, hers or his;   110
This will be tryed to morrow after nine,
Till which houre, wee thy day enlarge, O Valentine.

85 *here, 1633–39 and most MSS.:* there, *1650–69 and some MSS.*
94 acquittances, *1635–69:* acquittance, *1633*

ECCLOGVE.

ECCLOGVE.

1613. *December* 26.

Allophanes *finding* Idios *in the country in Christmas time, reprehends his absence from court, at the mariage Of the Earle of Sommerset;* Idios *gives an account of his purpose therein, and of his absence thence.*

Allophanes.

Vnseasonable man, statue of ice,
　　What could to countries solitude entice
Thee, in this yeares cold and decrepit time?
　　Natures instinct drawes to the warmer clime
Even small birds, who by that courage dare,　　　　　5
　　In numerous fleets, saile through their Sea, the aire.
What delicacie can in fields appeare,
　　Whil'st Flora'herselfe doth a freeze jerkin weare?
Whil'st windes do all the trees and hedges strip
　　Of leafes, to furnish roddes enough to whip　　　10
Thy madnesse from thee; and all springs by frost
　　Have taken cold, and their sweet murmures lost;
If thou thy faults or fortunes would'st lament
　　With just solemnity, do it in Lent;
At Court the spring already advanced is,　　　　　15
　　The Sunne stayes longer up; and yet not his
The glory is, farre other, other fires.
　　First, zeale to Prince and State; then loves desires
Burne in one brest, and like heavens two great lights,
　　The first doth governe dayes, the other nights.　　20
And then that early light, which did appeare
　　Before the Sunne and Moone created were,
The Princes favour is defus'd o'r all,
　　From which all Fortunes, Names, and Natures fall;

ECCLOGVE. *&c.* his absence thence. *1633:* his Actions there. *1635–69 and most MSS.:* his absence then, *some MSS.* 5 small *1633 and MSS.:* smaller *1635–69* 12 murmures *1633–59:* murmure *MSS.*

Then

Then from those wombes of starres, the Brides bright eyes,
   At every glance, a constellation flyes,   26
And sowes the Court with starres, and doth prevent
   In light and power, the all-ey'd firmament;
First her eyes kindle other Ladies eyes,
   Then from their beames their jewels lusters rise,   3ᴑ
And from their jewels torches do take fire,
   And all is warmth, and light, and good desire;
Most other Courts, alas, are like to hell,
   Where in darke plotts, fire without light doth dwell:
Or but like Stoves, for lust and envy get   35
   Continuall, but artificiall heat;
Here zeale and love growne one, all clouds disgest,
   And make our Court an everlasting East.
And can'st thou be from thence?

Idios.   No, I am there.
   As heaven, to men dispos'd, is every where,   40
So are those Courts, whose Princes animate,
   Not onely all their house, but all their State.
Let no man thinke, because he is full, he hath all,
   Kings (as their patterne, God) are liberall
Not onely in fulnesse, but capacitie,   45
   Enlarging narrow men, to feele and see,
And comprehend the blessings they bestow.
   So, reclus'd hermits often times do know
More of heavens glory, then a worldling can.
   As man is of the world, the heart of man,   50
Is an epitome of Gods great booke
   Of creatures, and man need no farther looke;
So is the Country of Courts, where sweet peace doth,
   As their one common soule, give life to both,
I am not then from Court.

34 plotts, *1635–54 and most MSS.:* places, *1633, 1669, and one MS.*
39 there. *MS.:* there *1633–69*   55 I am ... Court. *1633 and most*
MSS.: And am I then from Court? *1635–69*

                                      Allophanes.

Allophanes.   Dreamer, thou art.   55
  Think'st thou fantastique that thou hast a part
In the East-Indian fleet, because thou hast
  A little spice, or Amber in thy taste?
Because thou art not frozen, art thou warme?
  Seest thou all good because thou seest no harme?   60
The earth doth in her inward bowels hold
  Stuffe well dispos'd, and which would faine be gold,
But never shall, except it chance to lye,
  So upward, that heaven gild it with his eye;
As, for divine things, faith comes from above,   65
  So, for best civil use, all tinctures move
From higher powers; From God religion springs,
  Wisdome, and honour from the use of Kings.
Then unbeguile thy selfe, and know with mee,
  That Angels, though on earth employd they bee,   70
Are still in heav'n, so is hee still at home
  That doth, abroad, to honest actions come.
Chide thy selfe then, O foole, which yesterday
  Might'st have read more then all thy books bewray;
Hast thou a history, which doth present   75
  A Court, where all affections do assent
Unto the Kings, and that, that Kings are just?
  And where it is no levity to trust?
Where there is no ambition, but to'obey,
  Where men need whisper nothing, and yet may;   80
Where the Kings favours are so plac'd, that all
  Finde that the King therein is liberall
To them, in him, because his favours bend
  To vertue, to the which they all pretend?
Thou hast no such; yet here was this, and more,   85
  An earnest lover, wise then, and before.
Our little Cupid hath sued Livery,
  And is no more in his minority,

57 East-Indian *all MSS.*: Indian *1633–69*   61 inward *all MSS.*:
Inner *1633–69*   75 present] represent *one MS. group*

                                                     Hee

Hee is admitted now into that brest
  Where the Kings Counsells and his secrets rest.   90
What hast thou lost, O ignorant man?

Idios.   I knew
  All this, and onely therefore I withdrew.
To know and feele all this, and not to have
  Words to expresse it, makes a man a grave
Of his owne thoughts; I would not therefore stay   95
  At a great feast, having no Grace to say.
And yet I scap'd not here; for being come
  Full of the common joy, I utter'd some;
Reade then this nuptiall song, which was not made
  Either the Court or mens hearts to invade,   100
But since I'am dead, and buried, I could frame
  No Epitaph, which might advance my fame
So much as this poore song, which testifies
  I did unto that day some sacrifice.

EPITHALAMION.

I.

The time of the Mariage.

THou art repriv'd old yeare, thou shalt not die,   105
  Though thou upon thy death bed lye, .
    And should'st within five dayes expire,
Yet thou art rescu'd by a mightier fire,
    Then thy old Soule, the Sunne,
When he doth in his largest circle runne.   110
The passage of the West or East would thaw,
And open wide their easie liquid jawe
To all our ships, could a Promethean art
Either unto the Northerne Pole impart
The fire of these inflaming eyes, or of this loving
    heart.   115
                         II.

II.

Equality of persons.

But undiscerning Muse, which heart, which eyes,
 In this new couple, dost thou prize,
  When his eye as inflaming is
As hers, and her heart loves as well as his?
 Be tryed by beauty, and than   120
The bridegroome is a maid, and not a man.
If by that manly courage they be tryed,
 Which scornes unjust opinion; then the bride
Becomes a man. Should chance or envies Art
Divide these two, whom nature scarce did part? 125
Since both have both th'enflaming eyes, and both the loving
  heart.

III.

Raysing of the Bridegroome.

Though it be some divorce to thinke of you
 Singly, so much one are you two,
  Yet let me here contemplate thee,
First, cheerfull Bridegroome, and first let mee see, 130
 How thou prevent'st the Sunne,
And his red foming horses dost outrunne,
How, having laid downe in thy Soveraignes brest
 All businesses, from thence to reinvest
Them, when these triumphs cease, thou forward art 135
To shew to her, who doth the like impart,
The fire of thy inflaming eyes, and of thy loving heart.

EPITHALAMION. 126 both th'enflaming eyes, *MSS.:* th'enflaming eye, *1633:* the enflaming eye, *1635–69* 128 Singly, *most
MSS.:* Single, *1633–69* 129 Yet let *some MSS.:* Let *1633–69*

IIII.

IIII.
Raising of the Bride.

But now, to Thee, faire Bride, it is some wrong,
  To thinke thou wert in Bed so long,
   Since Soone thou lyest downe first, tis fit   140
Thou in first rising should'st allow for it.
   Pouder thy Radiant haire,
  Which if without such ashes thou would'st weare,
Thou, which to all which come to looke upon,
Art meant for Phœbus, would'st be Phaëton.   145
For our ease, give thine eyes th'unusual part
Of joy, a Teare; so quencht, thou maist impart,
To us that come, thy inflaming eyes, to him, thy loving
  heart.

V.
Her Apparrelling.

Thus thou descend'st to our infirmitie,
  Who can the Sun in water see.   150
   Soe dost thou, when in silke and gold,
Thou cloudst thy selfe; since wee which doe behold,
   Are dust, and wormes, 'tis just
Our objects be the fruits of wormes and dust;
Let every Jewell be a glorious starre,   155
Yet starres are not so pure, as their spheares are.
And though thou stoope, to'appeare to us in part,
Still in that Picture thou intirely art,
Which thy inflaming eyes have made within his loving
  heart.

VI.
Going to the Chappell.

Now from your Easts you issue forth, and wee,   160
  As men which through a Cipres see
   The rising sun, doe thinke it two,

---

 145 Art *some MSS.:* Are *1633 and some MSS.:* Wert *1635–69
and one MS.*

                 Soe,

Soe, as you goe to Church, doe thinke of you,
    But that vaile being gone,
By the Church rites you are from thenceforth one.   165
The Church Triumphant made this match before,
And now the Militant doth strive no more;
Then, reverend Priest, who Gods Recorder art,
Doe, from his Dictates, to these two impart
All blessings, which are seene, or thought, by Angels eye
    or heart.   170

VII.

The Benediction.

Blest payre of Swans, Oh may you interbring
    Daily new joyes, and never sing,
      Live, till all grounds of wishes faile,
Till honor, yea till wisedome grow so stale,
      That, new great heights to trie,   175
It must serve your ambition, to die;
Raise heires, and may here, to the worlds end, live
Heires from this King, to take thankes, you, to give,
Nature and grace doe all, and nothing Art.
May never age, or error overthwart   180
With any West, these radiant eyes, with any North, this
    heart.

VIII.

Feasts and Revells.

But you are over-blest. Plenty this day
    Injures; it causeth time to stay;
      The tables groane, as though this feast
Would, as the flood, destroy all fowle and beast.   185
      And were the doctrine new
That the earth mov'd, this day would make it true;
For every part to dance and revell goes.
They tread the ayre, and fal not where they rose.

178 you,] yours, *some MSS.*

Though

Though six houres since, the Sunne to bed did part,   190
The masks and banquets will not yet impart
A sunset to these weary eyes, A Center to this heart.

IX.

The Brides going to bed.

What mean'st thou Bride, this companie to keep?
    To sit up, till thou faine wouldst sleep?
      Thou maist not, when thou art laid, doe so.   195
Thy selfe must to him a new banquet grow,
      And you must entertaine
And doe all this daies dances o'r againe.
Know that if Sun and Moone together doe
Rise in one point, they doe not set so too;   200
Therefore thou maist, faire Bride, to bed depart,
Thou art not gone, being gone; where e'r thou art,
Thou leav'st in him thy watchfull eyes, in him thy loving
    heart.

X.

The Bridegroomes comming.

As he that sees a starre fall, runs apace,
    And findes a gellie in the place,   205
      So doth the Bridegroome hast as much,
Being told this starre is falne, and findes her such.
      And as friends may looke strange,
By a new fashion, or apparrells change,
Their soules, though long acquainted they had beene,   210
These clothes, their bodies, never yet had seene;
Therefore at first shee modestly might start,
But must forthwith surrender every part,
As freely, as each to each before, gave either eye or
    heart.

XI.

XI.
The good-night.

Now, as in Tullias tombe, one lampe burnt cleare,   215
    Unchang'd for fifteene hundred yeare,
    May these love-lamps we here enshrine,
In warmth, light, lasting, equall the divine.
      Fire ever doth aspire,
And makes all like it selfe, turnes all to fire,   220
But ends in ashes, which these cannot doe,
For none of these is fuell, but fire too.
This is joyes bonfire, then, where loves strong Arts
Make of so noble individuall parts   224
One fire of foure inflaming eyes, and of two loving hearts.
   Idios.

As I have brought this song, that I may doe
    A perfect sacrifice, I'll burne it too.
   Allophanes.

No S^r. This paper I have justly got,
    For, in burnt incense, the perfume is not
His only that presents it, but of all;   230
    What ever celebrates this Festivall
Is common, since the joy thereof is so.
    Nor may your selfe be Priest: But let me goe,
Backe to the Court, and I will lay'it upon
    Such Altars, as prize your devotion.   235

Epithalamion made at Lincolnes Inne.

THe Sun-beames in the East are spred,
    Leave, leave, faire Bride, your solitary bed,
No more shall you returne to it alone,
It nourseth sadnesse, and your bodies print,
Like to a grave, the yielding downe doth dint;   5
    You and your other you meet there anon;
    Put forth, put forth that warme balme-breathing thigh,

Epithalamion &c. *1633–69*   Epithalamion on a Citizen. *some MSS.*
                       Which

Which when next time you in these sheets wil smother,
 There it must meet another,   9
  Which never was, but must be, oft, more nigh;
Come glad from thence, goe gladder then you came,
To day put on perfection, and a womans name.

Daughters of London, you which bee
Our Golden Mines, and furnish'd Treasurie,
 You which are Angels, yet still bring with you 15
Thousands of Angels on your mariage daies,
Help with your presence and devise to praise
 These rites, which also unto you grow due;
 Conceitedly dresse her, and be assign'd,
By you, fit place for every flower and jewell, 20
 Make her for love fit fewell
  As gay as Flora, and as rich as Inde;
So may shee faire, rich, glad, and in nothing lame,
To day put on perfection, and a womans name.

And you frolique Patricians,   25
Sonnes of these Senators, wealths deep oceans,
 Ye painted courtiers, barrels of others wits,
Yee country men, who but your beasts love none,
Yee of those fellowships whereof hee's one,
 Of study and play made strange Hermaphrodits, 30
 Here shine; This Bridegroom to the Temple bring.
Loe, in yon path which store of straw'd flowers graceth,
 The sober virgin paceth;
  Except my sight faile, 'tis no other thing;
Weep not nor blush, here is no griefe nor shame, 35
To day put on perfection, and a womans name.

23 faire, rich, glad, and in *some MSS.:* faire and rich, in *1633–69
and some MSS.* 26 Sonnes of these Senatours, wealths deep
oceans *Westm. MS.:* Some of these Senators wealths deep oceans,
1633 and one group of MSS.: Sonnes of those Senatours, wealths deepe
oceans, *1635–69 and some MSS.*

Thy two-leav'd gates faire Temple unfold,
And these two in thy sacred bosome hold,
  Till, mystically joyn'd, but one they bee;
Then may thy leane and hunger-starved wombe   40
Long time expect their bodies and their tombe,
  Long after their owne parents fatten thee.
All elder claimes, and all cold barrennesse,
All yeelding to new loves bee far for ever,
    Which might these two dissever,   45
      All wayes all th'other may each one possesse;
For, the best Bride, best worthy of praise and fame,
To day puts on perfection, and a womans name.

Oh winter dayes bring much delight,
Not for themselves, but for they soon bring night;   50
  Other sweets wait thee then these diverse meats,
Other disports then dancing jollities,
Other love tricks then glancing with the eyes,
  But that the Sun still in our halfe Spheare sweates;
    Hee flies in winter, but he now stands still.   55
Yet shadowes turne; Noone point he hath attain'd,
    His steeds nill bee restrain'd,
    But gallop lively downe the Westerne hill;
Thou shalt, when he hath runne the worlds half frame,
To night put on perfection, and a womans name.   60

The amorous evening starre is rose,
Why then should not our amorous starre inclose
  Her selfe in her wish'd bed? Release your strings
Musicians, and dancers take some truce

<hr>

46 All wayes *Westm. MS.:* Alwaies, *1633:* Alwayes, *1635–69*
49 Oh winter dayes *Westm. and other MSS.:* Winter dayes *1633–69
and some MSS.*   55 still. *Westm. MS.:* still, *1633–69*   57 nill *Westm.
MS.:* will *1633–69 and rest of MSS.; one MS. inserts* not.   59 runne
the worlds halfe frame, *Westm. and other MSS.:* runne the Heavens
halfe frame, *1635–69:* come the worlds half frame, *1633 and some
MSS.*

With

With these your pleasing labours, for great use   65
    As much wearinesse as perfection brings;
       You, and not only you, but all toyl'd beasts
Rest duly; at night all their toyles are dispensed;
But in their beds commenced
       Are other labours, and more dainty feasts;   70
She goes a maid, who, least she turne the same,
To night puts on perfection, and a womans name.

Thy virgins girdle now untie,
And in thy nuptiall bed (loves altar) lye
    A pleasing sacrifice; now dispossesse   75
Thee of these chaines and robes which were put on
T'adorne the day, not thee; for thou, alone,
    Like vertue'and truth, art best in nakednesse;
       This bed is onely to virginitie
A grave, but, to a better state, a cradle;   80
Till now thou wast but able
    To be what now thou art; then that by thee
No more be said, *I may bee,* but, *I am,*
To night put on perfection, and a womans name.

Even like a faithfull man content,   85
That this life for a better should be spent,
    So, shee a mothers rich stile doth preferre,
And at the Bridegroomes wish'd approach doth lye,
Like an appointed lambe, when tenderly
    The priest comes on his knees t'embowell her;   90
       Now sleep or watch with more joy; and O light
Of heaven, to morrow rise thou hot, and early;
This Sun will love so dearely
    Her rest, that long, long we shall want her sight;
Wonders are wrought, for shee which had no maime,   95
To night puts on perfection, and a womans name.

95 maime, *1633 and Westm. MS.:* name, *1635–69 and most MSS.*

SATYRES

SATYRES.

Satyre I.

AWay thou fondling motley humorist,
Leave mee, and in this standing woodden chest,
Consorted with these few bookes, let me lye
In prison, and here be coffin'd, when I dye;
Here are Gods conduits, grave Divines; and here   5
Natures Secretary, the Philosopher;
And jolly Statesmen, which teach how to tie
The sinewes of a cities mistique bodie;
Here gathering Chroniclers, and by them stand
Giddie fantastique Poëts of each land.   10
Shall I leave all this constant company,
And follow headlong, wild uncertaine thee?
First sweare by thy best love in earnest
(If thou which lov'st all, canst love any best)
Thou wilt not leave mee in the middle street,   15
Though some more spruce companion thou dost meet,
Not though a Captaine do come in thy way
Bright parcell gilt, with forty dead mens pay,
Not though a briske perfum'd piert Courtier
Deigne with a nod, thy courtesie to answer.   20
Nor come a velvet Justice with a long
Great traine of blew coats, twelve, or fourteen strong,
Wilt thou grin or fawne on him, or prepare
A speech to Court his beautious sonne and heire!
For better or worse take mee, or leave mee: 25
To take, and leave mee is adultery.
Oh monstrous, superstitious puritan,

Satyre I.   1 fondling *1633 and some MSS.:* changeling *1635–69
and most MSS.*   7 jolly *1633 and most MSS.:* wily *1635–69*   13
love in earnest] love, here, in earnest *1635–69*   19 Not *1633–69 and
some MSS.:* Nor *most MSS.*   23 Wilt] Shalt *many MSS.*   25 or
worse] and worse *some MSS.*

Of

Of refin'd manners, yet ceremoniall man,
That when thou meet'st one, with enquiring eyes
Dost search, and like a needy broker prize   30
The silke, and gold he weares, and to that rate
So high or low, dost raise thy formall hat:
That wilt consort none, untill thou have knowne
What lands hee hath in hope, or of his owne,
As though all thy companions should make thee   35
Jointures, and marry thy deare company.
Why should'st thou (that dost not onely approve,
But in ranke itchie lust, desire, and love
The nakednesse and barenesse to enjoy,
Of thy plumpe muddy whore, or prostitute boy)   40
Hate vertue, though shee be naked, and bare?
At birth, and death, our bodies naked are;
And till our Soules be unapparrelled
Of bodies, they from blisse are banished.
Mans first blest state was naked, when by sinne   45
Hee lost that, yet hee was cloath'd but in beasts skin,
And in this course attire, which I now weare,
With God, and with the Muses I conferre.
But since thou like a contrite penitent,
Charitably warn'd of thy sinnes, dost repent   50
These vanities, and giddinesses, loe
I shut my chamber doore, and come, lets goe.
But sooner may a cheape whore, who hath beene
Worne by as many severall men in sinne,
As are black feathers, or musk-colour hose,   55
Name her childs right true father, 'mongst all those:
Sooner may one guesse, who shall beare away
The Infanta of London, Heire to an India;

32 raise] vaile *some MSS.*   39 barenesse *most MSS.:* barrennesse
1633–69 and some MSS.   45 first blest] first best *some MSS.*
58 The Infanta . . . India; *Ed:* The Infanta . . . India, *some MSS.:*
The infant . . . India, *1633–54 and MSS. generally:* The Infantry of
London, hence to India: *1669*

                                                          And

And sooner may a gulling weather Spie
By drawing forth heavens Scheme tell certainly   60
What fashioned hats, or ruffes, or`suits next yeare
Our subtile-witted antique youths will weare;
Then thou, when thou depart'st from mee, canst show
Whither, why, when, or with whom thou wouldst go.
But how shall I be pardon'd my offence   65
That thus have sinn'd against my conscience?
Now we are in the street; He first of all
Improvidently proud, creepes to the wall,
And so imprisoned, and hem'd in by mee
Sells for a little state his libertie;   70
Yet though he cannot skip forth now to greet
Every fine silken painted foole we meet,
He them to him with amorous smiles allures,
And grins, smacks, shrugs, and such an itch endures,
As prentises, or schoole-boyes which doe know   75
Of some gay sport abroad, yet dare not goe.
And as fidlers stop lowest, at highest sound,
So to the most brave, stoops hee nigh'st the ground.
But to a grave man, he doth move no more
Then the wise politique horse would heretofore,   80
Or thou O Elephant or Ape wilt doe,
When any names the King of Spaine to you.
Now leaps he upright, Joggs me, & cryes, Do you see
Yonder well favoured youth? Which? Oh, 'tis hee
That dances so divinely; Oh, said I,   85
Stand still, must you dance here for company?
Hee droopt, wee went, till one (which did excell
Th'Indians, in drinking his Tobacco well)
Met us; they talk'd; I whispered, let'us goe,

60 Scheme *1635–69 and most MSS.:* Sceanes *1633 and some MSS.*
62 subtile-witted *MS.:* subtile wittied *1633–54 and some MSS.:* supple-
witted *most MSS.:* giddy-headed *1669*   63 depart'st from mee]
depart'st from hence *many MSS.*   78 stoops *1635–69 and most MSS.:*
stoopt *1633 and some MSS.*   81–2 om. *1633*

'T may

'T may be you smell him not, truely I doe;　　　　90
He heares not mee, but, on the other side
A many-coloured Peacock having spide,
Leaves him and mee; I for my lost sheep stay;
He followes, overtakes, goes on the way,
Saying, him whom I last left, all repute　　　　95
For his device, in hansoming a sute,
To judge of lace, pinke, panes, print, cut, and pleite,
Of all the Court, to have the best conceit;
Our dull Comedians want him, let him goe;
But Oh, God strengthen thee, why stoop'st thou so?　100
Why? he hath travayld; Long? No; but to me
(Which understand none,) he doth seeme to be
Perfect French, and Italian; I replyed,
So is the Poxe; He answered not, but spy'd
More men of sort, of parts, and qualities;　　　105
At last his Love he in a windowe spies,
And like light dew exhal'd, he flings from mee
Violently ravish'd to his lechery.
Many were there, he could command no more;
Hee quarrell'd, fought, bled; and turn'd out of dore　110
　　Directly came to mee hanging the head,
　　And constantly a while must keepe his bed.

Satyre II.

SIr; though (I thanke God for it) I do hate
Perfectly all this towne, yet there's one state
In all ill things so excellently best,
That hate, toward them, breeds pitty towards the rest.
Though Poëtry indeed be such a sinne　　　　5

95 all repute *1635–69 and MSS. generally:* s'all repute *1633 and
one MS.*　　108 lechery. *1635–69 and MSS.:* liberty; *1633*
　　Satyre II.　　　　　　　*there is one*
2–3　　　All this towne perfectly yet in every state
　　　　In all ill things so excellently best
　　　There are some found so villainously best, *one early MS.*

As

As I thinke That brings dearths, and Spaniards in,
Though like the Pestilence and old fashion'd love,
Ridlingly it catch men; and doth remove
Never, till it be sterv'd out; yet their state
Is poore, disarm'd, like Papists, not worth hate.   10
One, (like a wretch, which at Barre judg'd as dead,
Yet prompts him which stands next, and cannot reade,
And saves his life) gives ideot actors meanes
(Starving himselfe) to live by his labor'd sceanes;
As in some Organ, Puppits dance above   15
And bellows pant below, which them do move.
One would move Love by rithmes; but witchcrafts charms
Bring not now their old feares, nor their old harmes:
Rammes, and slings now are seely battery,
Pistolets are the best Artillerie.   20
And they who write to Lords, rewards to get,
Are they not like singers at doores for meat?
And they who write, because all write, have still
That excuse for writing, and for writing ill;
But hee is worst, who (beggarly) doth chaw   25
Others wits fruits, and in his ravenous maw
Rankly digested, doth those things out-spue,
As his owne things; and they are his owne, 'tis true,
For if one eate my meate, though it be knowne
The meate was mine, th'excrement is his owne: 30
But these do mee no harme, nor they which use
To out-doe Dildoes, and out-usure Jewes;
To out-drinke the sea, to out-sweare the Letanie;
Who with sinnes all kindes as familiar bee

6 dearths, *most MSS.:* dearth, *1633–69*   8 Ridlingly it *1633–69*
and some MSS.: It riddlinglie *rest of MSS.*   15 Organ *1633–54:* Organs
1669 and most MSS.   17 rithmes; *1633–69:* rimes; *most MSS.*
22 singers at doores] Boyes singing at dore (*or* dores) *many MSS.*
24 excuse] scuse *MSS.*   33 Letanie; *Ed:* Letanie, *1669 and all
MSS.:* ——— *1633: simply omit,* 1635–39*:* gallant, he *1650–54.*   34
sinnes all kindes *1635–69 and most MSS.:* sinnes of all kindes *1633
and some MSS.*

As

As Confessors; and for whose sinfull sake,   35
Schoolemen new tenements in hell must make:
Whose strange sinnes, Canonists could hardly tell
In which Commandements large receit they dwell.
But these punish themselves; the insolence
Of Coscus onely breeds my just offence,   40
Whom time (which rots all, and makes botches poxe,
And plodding on, must make a calfe an oxe)
Hath made a Lawyer, which was (alas) of late
But a scarce Poët; jollier of this state,
Then are new benefic'd ministers, he throwes   45
Like nets, or lime-twigs, wheresoever he goes,
His title of Barrister, on every wench,
And wooes in language of the Pleas, and Bench:
A motion, Lady; Speake Coscus; I have beene
In love, ever since *tricesimo* of the Queene,   50
Continuall claimes I have made, injunctions got
To stay my rivals suit, that hee should not
Proceed; spare mee; In Hillary terme I went,
You said, If I return'd next size in Lent,
I should be in remitter of your grace;   55
In th'interim my letters should take place
Of affidavits: words, words, which would teare
The tender labyrinth of a soft maids eare,
More, more, then ten Sclavonians scolding, more
Then when winds in our ruin'd Abbeyes rore.   60
When sicke with Poëtrie, and possest with muse
Thou wast, and mad, I hop'd; but men which chuse
Law practise for meere gaine, bold soule, repute
Worse then imbrothel'd strumpets prostitute.
Now like an owlelike watchman, hee must walke   65
His hand still at a bill, now he must talke
Idly, like prisoners, which whole months will sweare

40 just] great *most MSS*.   44 a scarce *most MSS.:* scarce a *1633–69 and some MSS*.   54 next size *1633–69 and some MSS.:* this size *rest of MSS.*

That

That onely suretiship hath brought them there,
And to every suitor lye in every thing,
Like a Kings favourite, yea like a King;   70
Like a wedge in a blocke, wring to the barre,
Bearing-like Asses; and more shamelesse farre
Then carted whores, lye, to the grave Judge; for
Bastardy abounds not in Kings titles, nor
Symonie and Sodomy in Churchmens lives,   75
As these things do in him; by these he thrives.
Shortly (as the sea) hee will compasse all our land;
From Scots, to Wight; from Mount, to Dover strand.
And spying heires melting with luxurie,
Satan will not joy at their sinnes, as hee.   80
For as a thrifty wench scrapes kitching-stuffe,
And barrelling the droppings, and the snuffe,
Of wasting candles, which in thirty yeare
(Relique-like kept) perchance buyes wedding geare;
Peecemeale he gets lands, and spends as much time   85
Wringing each Acre, as men pulling prime.
In parchments then, large as his fields, hee drawes
Assurances, bigge, as gloss'd civill lawes,
So huge, that men (in our times forwardnesse)
Are Fathers of the Church for writing lesse.   90
These hee writes not; nor for these written payes,
Therefore spares no length; as in those first dayes
When Luther was profest, He did desire
Short *Pater nosters*, saying as a Fryer
Each day his beads, but having left those lawes,   95
Addes to Christs prayer, the Power and glory clause.

69–70 *These lines represented by dashes, 1633*   70 yea *all MSS.:* or *1635–69*   72 Bearing-like Asses; *Ed:* Bearing like Asses, *1633–69 and MSS.*   74–5 *These lines represented by dashes, 1633* 77 our land;] our land, *most MSS.:* the land; *1633–69 and one MS.* 79 luxurie, *1633–69 and many MSS.:* Gluttony *many MSS.*   84 Relique-like *most MSS.:* Reliquely *1633–69 and some MSS.*   87 parchments *MSS.:* parchment *1633–69 and some MSS.*

But

But when he sells or changes land, he'impaires
His writings, and (unwatch'd) leaves out, *ses heires*,
As slily as any Commenter goes by
Hard words, or sense; or in Divinity   100
As controverters, in vouch'd Texts, leave out
Shrewd words, which might against them cleare the doubt.
Where are those spred woods which cloth'd hertofore
Those bought lands? not built, nor burnt within dore.
Where's th'old landlords troops, and almes? In great hais
Carthusian fasts, and fulsome Bachanalls   106
Equally I hate; meanes blesse; in rich mens homes
I bid kill some beasts, but no Hecatombs,
None starve, none surfet so; But (Oh) we allow,
Good workes as good, but out of fashion now,   110
Like old rich wardrops; but my words none drawes
Within the vast reach of th'huge statute lawes.

Satyre III.

K Inde pitty chokes my spleene; brave scorn forbids
   Those teares to issue which swell my eye-lids;
I must not laugh, nor weepe sinnes, and be wise,
Can railing then cure these worne maladies?
Is not our Mistresse faire Religion,   5
As worthy of all our Soules devotion,
As vertue was to the first blinded age?
Are not heavens joyes as valiant to asswage
Lusts, as earths honour was to them? Alas,
As wee do them in meanes, shall they surpasse   10

105 Where's &c. *Ed:* Where's th'old landlords troops, and almes,
great hals? *1633 and some MSS.:* Where the old landlords troops, and
almes? In hals *1635–69 and some MSS.:* Where the old landlords
troopes and almes? In great halls *most MSS.*   107 Equally I
hate;] Equallie hate, *one MS.* meanes bless; *1633 and most MSS.:*
Meane's blest. *1635–69 and some MSS.*   112 statute lawes. *1633–
54 and all MSS.:* statutes jawes. *1669*
    Satyre III. 7 to *1635–69 and most MSS.:* in *1633 and some MSS.*

Us in the end, and shall thy fathers spirit
Meete blinde Philosophers in heaven, whose merit
Of strict life may be imputed faith, and heare
Thee, whom hee taught so easie wayes and neare
To follow, damn'd? O if thou dar'st, feare this;   15
This feare great courage, and high valour is.
Dar'st thou ayd mutinous Dutch, and dar'st thou lay
Thee in ships woodden Sepulchers, a prey
To leaders rage, to stormes, to shot, to dearth?
Dar'st thou dive seas, and dungeons of the earth?   20
Hast thou couragious fire to thaw the ice
Of frozen North discoveries? and thrise
Colder then Salamanders, like divine
Children in th'oven, fires of Spaine, and the line,
Whose countries limbecks to our bodies bee,   25
Canst thou for gaine beare? and must every hee
Which cryes not, Goddesse, to thy Mistresse, draw,
Or eate thy poysonous words? courage of straw!
O desperate coward, wilt thou seeme bold, and
To thy foes and his (who made thee to stand   30
Sentinell in his worlds garrison) thus yeeld,
And for forbidden warres, leave th'appointed field?
Know thy foes: The foule Devill (whom thou
Strivest to please,) for hate, not love, would allow
Thee faine, his whole Realme to be quit; and as   35
The worlds all parts wither away and passe,

31 Sentinell] Souldier *many MSS.*
33–4   Know thy foes; the foule Devell whom thou
        Strivest to please *&c.*
MSS. generally (but with varying punctuation and sometimes foe):
        Know thy foe, the foule devill h'is, whom thou
        Strivest to please: for hate, not love, would allow
                1633 and some MSS.:
        Know thy foes: The foule devill, he, whom thou
        Striv'st to please, for hate, not love, would allow
            1635–69 (he, ... please, *bracketed, 1669*)
35 quit *1633–69 and some MSS.:* ridd *other MSS.*

So the worlds selfe, thy other lov'd foe, is
In her decrepit wayne, and thou loving this,
Dost love a withered and worne strumpet; last,
Flesh (it selfes death) and joyes which flesh can taste,   40
Thou lovest; and thy faire goodly soule, which doth
Give this flesh power to taste joy, thou dost loath.
Seeke true religion. O where? Mirreus
Thinking her unhous'd here, and fled from us,
Seekes her at Rome, there, because hee doth know   45
That shee was there a thousand yeares agoe,
He loves her ragges so, as wee here obey
The statecloth where the Prince sate yesterday.
Crantz to such brave Loves will not be inthrall'd,
But loves her onely, who at Geneva is call'd   50
Religion, plaine, simple, sullen, yong,
Contemptuous, yet unhansome; As among
Lecherous humors, there is one that judges
No wenches wholsome, but course country drudges.
Graius stayes still at home here, and because   55
Some Preachers, vile ambitious bauds, and lawes
Still new like fashions, bid him thinke that shee
Which dwels with us, is onely perfect, hee
Imbraceth her, whom his Godfathers will
Tender to him, being tender, as Wards still   60
Take such wives as their Guardians offer, or
Pay valewes. Carelesse Phrygius doth abhorre
All, because all cannot be good, as one
Knowing some women whores, dares marry none.
Graccus loves all as one, and thinkes that so   65
As women do in divers countries goe
In divers habits, yet are still one kinde,
So doth, so is Religion; and this blind-

40 (it selfes death) *1635–69 and most MSS.:* (it selfe death) *1633
and some MSS.*   47 her *MSS.:* the *1633–69*   49 Crantz *one
MS.:* Crants *1633–54 and some MSS.:* Grants *1669 and some MSS.:*
Crates *one MS.*   57 bid *or* bidd *MSS.:* bids *1633–69*

nesse

nesse too much light breeds; but unmoved thou
Of force must one, and forc'd but one allow;   70
And the right; aske thy father which is shee,
Let him aske his; though truth and falshood bee
Neare twins, yet truth a little elder is;
Be busie to seeke her, beleeve mee this,
Hee's not of none, nor worst, that seekes the best.   75
To adore, or scorne an image, or protest,
May all be bad; doubt wisely; in strange way
To stand inquiring right, is not to stray;
To sleepe, or runne wrong, is. On a huge hill,
Cragged, and steep, Truth stands, and hee that will   80
Reach her, about must, and about must goe;
And what the hills suddennes resists, winne so;
Yet strive so, that before age, deaths twilight,
Thy Soule rest, for none can worke in that night.
To will, implyes delay, therefore now doe: 85
Hard deeds, the bodies paines; hard knowledge too
The mindes indeavours reach, and mysteries
Are like the Sunne, dazling, yet plaine to all eyes.
Keepe the truth which thou hast found; men do not
  stand
In so ill case here, that God hath with his hand   90
Sign'd Kings blanck-charters to kill whom they hate,
Nor are they Vicars, but hangmen to Fate.
Foole and wretch, wilt thou let thy Soule be tyed
To mans lawes, by which she shall not be tryed
At the last day? Oh, will it then boot thee   95

70 must . . . but *in reverse order one MS.*   78 stray;] staye; *some
MS.*   79 huge] high *some MS.*   80 Cragged, 1669: Cragg'd,
1633–54: Ragged *most MSS.: Ruggued *some MSS.*   84 Soule
1633–69 and some MSS.: minde *rest of MSS.*   85 doe: Ed: doe
1633, Chambers and Grolier: doe. 1635–69   86 too some MSS.: spelt
to 1633–69 and many MSS.   90 here om. 1633–69   94 mans
1633–69 and most MSS.: mens some MSS.: not om. 1635–54   95
Oh, will it then boot thee Ed: Will . . boot thee 1633 and some MSS.:
Or . . . boot thee 1635–69: Oh will it then serve thee *many MSS.*

To

To say a Philip, or a Gregory,
A Harry, or a Martin taught thee this?
Is not this excuse for mere contraries,
Equally strong? cannot both sides say so?
That thou mayest rightly obey power, her bounds
    know;   100
Those past, her nature, and name is chang'd; to be
Then humble to her is idolatrie.
As streames are, Power is; those blest flowers that dwell
At the rough streames calme head, thrive and do well,
But having left their roots, and themselves given   105
To the streames tyrannous rage, alas, are driven
Through mills, and rockes, and woods, and at last, almost
Consum'd in going, in the sea are lost:
So perish Soules, which more chuse mens unjust
Power from God claym'd, then God himselfe to trust. 110

Satyre IIII.

WEll; I may now receive, and die; My sinne
    Indeed is great, but I have beene in
A Purgatorie, such as fear'd hell is
A recreation to, and scarse map of this. .
My minde, neither with prides itch nor yet hath been 5

---

97 thee] me *1669*   99 strong? *Ed:* strong *1633:* strong; *1635–69*
101 is] are *1669*   chang'd;] chang'd *1633*   to be *Ed:* to be, *1633–69*
102 idolatrie.] idolatrie; *1633* ᐧ 103 is;] is, *1633*   104 do well
1633–69 and some MSS.: prove well *most MSS.*   106 alas,] alas
1633   107 mills, and rockes, *1633 and some MSS.:* Mils, rocks,
1635–69 and rest of MSS.

Satyre IIII. *Described in one MS. as* Mr *Dunn's first Satire, and
in another, a good MS., dated* 1594; *but the reference to the capture
of Amiens (l.* 114) *suggests* 1597 *or later*   2 but I *1633 and most
MSS.:* but yet I *1635–69 and some MSS.*   4 A recreacion to, and
scarse *one MS.:* A recreation, and scant *1633–69 and other MSS.*
5 neither *1633–69:* nor *some MSS. and Chambers, who wrongly attributes to* 1635–39

Poyson'd

Poyson'd with love to see, or to bee seene,
I had no suit there, nor new suite to shew,
Yet went to Court; But as Glaze which did goe
To'a Masse in jest, catch'd, was faine to disburse
The hundred markes, which is the Statutes curse;   10
Before he scapt, So'it pleas'd my destinie
(Guilty of my sin of going,) to thinke me
As prone to all ill, and of good as forget-
full, as proud, as lustfull, and as much in debt,
As vaine, as witlesse, and as false as they   15
Which dwell at Court, for once going that way.
Therefore I suffered this; Towards me did runne
A thing more strange, then on Niles slime, the Sunne
E'r bred; or all which into Noahs Arke came;
A thing, which would have pos'd Adam to name;   20
Stranger then seaven Antiquaries studies,
Then Africks Monsters, Guianaes rarities.
Stranger then strangers; One, who for a Dane,
In the Danes Massacre had sure beene slaine,
If he had liv'd then; And without helpe dies,   25
When next the Prentises 'gainst Strangers rise.
One, whom the watch at noone lets scarce goe by,
One, to whom, the examining Justice sure would cry,
Sir, by your priesthood tell me what you are.
His cloths were strange, though coarse; and black, though
    bare;   30
Sleevelesse his jerkin was, and it had beene

---

8 Glaze *1633 and some MSS.:* Glare *1635–69 and rest of MSS.*
9 To'a mass *most MSS.:* To Masse *1633–69 and some MSS.* 10–11
curse; . . . scapt, *1633–39:* curse, . . . scapt, *1650–69* 12 of going,
1633, 1669, and most MSS.: in going, *1635–54 and some MSS.* 14
as lustfull,] as *om. 1635–69 and many MSS.* 16 at Court, *most
MSS.:* in Court, *1633–69* 18 Niles] Nilus *many MSS.* 19
bred; *MS.:* bred, *1633–69* came; *MS.:* came: *1633–69* 20
name; *MS.:* name, *1633:* name: *1635–69* 22 rarities. *MS.:* rarities,
1633–69 23 then strangers; *1633–69 and most MSS.:* then
strangest. *some MSS.*

Velvet,

Velvet, but 'twas now (so much ground was seene)
Become Tufftaffatie; and our children shall
See it plaine Rashe awhile, then nought at all.
This thing hath travail'd, and saith, speakes all tongues 35
And only knoweth what to all States belongs.
Made of th'Accents, and best phrase of all these,
He speakes no language; If strange meats displease,
Art can deceive, or hunger force my tast,
But Pedants motley tongue, souldiers bumbast,   40
Mountebankes drugtongue, nor the termes of law
Are strong enough preparatives, to draw
Me to beare this: yet I must be content
With his tongue, in his tongue call'd complement:
In which he can win widdowes, and pay scores,   45
Make men speake treason, cosen subtlest whores,
Out-flatter favorites, or outlie either
Jovius, or Surius, or both together.
He names mee, and comes to mee; I whisper, God!
How have I sinn'd, that thy wraths furious rod,   50
This fellow chuseth me? He saith, Sir,
I love your judgement; Whom doe you prefer,
For the best linguist? And I seelily.
Said, that I thought Calepines Dictionarie;
Nay, but of men, most sweet Sir; Beza then,   55
Some other Jesuites, and two reverend men
Of our two Academies, I named; There
He stopt mee, and said; Nay, your Apostles were
Good pretty linguists, and so Panurge was;
Yet a poore gentleman, all these may passe   60

32 ground] the ground *one MS.*   35 saith, *1633–54 and MSS.:*
faith, *1669, Chambers and Grolier*   37 th'Accents,] the antient,
MS.   38 no language; *some MSS.:* one language; *1633–69 and
MSS. generally*   47 or] and *many MSS.*   48 Surius,] Sleydon
some MSS.   51 chuseth] chaseth *MS.*   56 Some other *one MS.:*
Some *1633–69 and most MSS.:* two other *one MS.*   59 Panurge]
Panurgus *1669 (omitting and) and some MSS.*

                                                    By

By travaile. Then, as if he would have sold
His tongue, he prais'd it, and such wonders told
That I was faine to say, If you'had liv'd, Sir,
Time enough to have beene Interpreter
To Babells bricklayers, sure the Tower had stood.   65
He adds, If of court life you knew the good,
You would leave lonenesse. I said, not alone
My lonenesse is, but Spartanes fashion,
To teach by painting drunkards, doth not last
Now; Aretines pictures have made few chast;   70
No more can Princes courts, though there be few
Better pictures of vice, teach me vertue;
He, like to a high stretcht lute string squeakt, O Sir,
'Tis sweet to talke of Kings. At Westminster,
Said I, The man that keepes the Abbey tombes,   75
And for his price doth with who ever comes,
Of all our Harries, and our Edwards talke,
From King to King and all their kin can walke:
Your eares shall heare nought, but Kings; your eyes meet
Kings only; The way to it, is Kingstreet.   80
He smack'd, and cry'd, He's base, Mechanique, coarse,
So are all your Englishmen in their discourse.
Are not your Frenchmen neate? Mine? as you see,
I have but one Frenchman, looke, hee followes mee.
Certes they are neatly cloth'd; I, of this minde am,   85
Your only wearing is your Grogaram.
Not so Sir, I have more. Under this pitch
He would not flie; I chaff'd him; But as Itch
Scratch'd into smart, and as blunt iron ground

62 wonders *1635–69 and most MSS.:* words *1633 and some MSS.*
67 lonenesse. *1635–69 and most MSS.:* lonelinesse; *1633 and some*
MSS.   68 lonenesse *1635–69 and most MSS.:* lonelinesse *1633 and*
some MSS.   69 last *1633, 1669, and most MSS.:* taste *1635–54 and*
some MSS.   83 Mine? *1635–54 and MSS.:* Fine, *1633:* Mine, *1669*
84 Frenchman, *Ed:* frenchman, *1633 and most MSS.:* Sir, *1635–69 and*
one MS.   86 your Grogaram *1633–69 and some MSS.:* this Grogaram *most MSS.*   89 ground *Ed:* grown'd *1633:* grownd *1635–69*

Into

Into an edge, hurts worse: So, I (foole) found,   99
Crossing hurt mee; To fit my sullennesse,
He to another key, his stile doth addresse,
And askes, what newes? I tell him of new playes.
He takes my hand, and as a Still, which staies
A Sembriefe, 'twixt each drop, he nigardly,   95
As loth to enrich mee, so tells many a lye.
More then ten Hollensheads, or Halls, or Stowes,
Of triviall houshold trash he knowes; He knowes
When the Queene frown'd, or smil'd, and he knowes what
A subtle States-man may gather of that;   100
He knowes who loves; whom; and who by poyson
Hasts to an Offices reversion;
He knowes who'hath sold his land, and now doth beg
A licence, old iron, bootes, shooes, and egge-
shels to transport; Shortly boyes shall not play   105
At span-counter, or blow-point, but they pay
Toll to some Courtier; And wiser then all us,
He knowes what Ladie is not painted; Thus
He with home-meats tries me; I belch, spue, spit,
Looke pale, and sickly, like a Patient; Yet   110
He thrusts on more; And as if he'd undertooke
To say Gallo-Belgicus without booke
Speakes of all States, and deeds, that have been since
The Spaniards came, to the losse of Amyens.
Like a bigge wife, at sight of loathed meat,   115
Readie to travaile: So I sigh, and sweat
To heare this Makeron talke: In vaine; for yet,

.

98 trash he knowes; He knowes *some MSS.:* trash; He knowes; He
knowes *1633:* trash. He knowes; He knowes *1635–39:* trash, He
knowes; He knowes *1650–69*   104 and *1633–69 and some MSS.:* or
most MSS.   106 At blow-point or span-counter *most MSS.*   they
pay *MSS.:* shall pay *1633–69*   108 what *1633–69 and some MSS.:*
which *most MSS.*   109 tries *1633 and most MSS.:* cloyes *1635–69*
111 as if he'd undertooke *most MSS.:* as if he'undertooke *1633:* as
he'had undertooke *1635–69*   117 talke: In vaine; for *MSS.:* talke in
vaine: For *1633:* talke, in vaine: For *1635–69*

Either

Either my humour, or his owne to fit,
He like a priviledg'd spie, whom nothing can
Discredit, Libells now 'gainst each great man.   120
He names a price for every office paid;
He saith, our warres thrive ill, because delai'd;
That offices are entail'd, and that there are
Perpetuities of them, lasting as farre
As the last day; And that great officers,   125
Doe with the Pirates share, and Dunkirkers.
Who wasts in meat, in clothes, in horse, he notes;
Who loves whores, who boyes, and who goats.
I more amas'd then Circes prisoners, when
They felt themselves turne beasts, felt my selfe then   130
Becomming Traytor, and mee thought I saw
One of our Giant Statutes ope his jaw
To sucke me in, for hearing him. I found
That as burnt venome Leachers do grow sound
By giving others their soares, I might growe   135
Guilty, and he free: Therefore I did shew
All signes of loathing; But since I am in,
I must pay mine, and my forefathers sinne
To the last farthing; Therefore to my power
Toughly and stubbornly I beare this crosse; But the'houre
Of mercy now was come; He tries to bring   141
Me to pay a fine to scape his torturing,
And saies, Sir, can you spare me; I said, willingly;
Nay, Sir, can you spare me a crowne? Thankfully I
Gave it, as Ransome; But as fidlers, still,   145
Though they be paid to be gone, yet needs will
Thrust one more jigge upon you; so did hee
With his long complementall thankes vexe me.
But he is gone, thankes to his needy want,
And the prerogative of my Crowne: Scant   150
His thankes were ended, when I, (which did see

134–6 (That . . . free:) *represented by dashes in 1633*   134
venome *1635–54:* venomous *1669:* venomd *many MSS.*

Ail

All the court fill'd with more strange things then hee)
Ran from thence with such or more hast, then one
Who feares more actions, doth make from prison.
At home in wholesome solitarinesse   155
My precious soule began, the wretchednesse
Of suiters at court to mourne, and a trance
Like his, who dreamt he saw hell, did advance
It selfe on mee; Such men as he saw there,
I saw at court, and worse, and more; Low feare   160
Becomes the guiltie, not the accuser; Then,
Shall I, nones slave, of high borne, or rais'd men
Feare frownes? And, my Mistresse Truth, betray thee
To th'huffing braggart, puft Nobility?
No, no, Thou which since yesterday hast beene   165
Almost about the whole world, hast thou seene,
O Sunne, in all thy journey, Vanitie,
Such as swells the bladder of our court? I
Thinke he which made your waxen garden, and
Transported it from Italy to stand   170
With us, at London, flouts our Presence, for
Just such gay painted things, which no sappe, nor
Tast have in them, ours are; And naturall
Some of the stocks are, their fruits, bastard all.
'Tis ten a clock and past; All whom the Mues,   175
Baloune, Tennis, Dyet, or the stewes,
Had all the morning held, now the second
Time made ready, that day, in flocks, are found
In the Presence, and I, (God pardon mee.)
As fresh, and sweet their Apparrells be, as bee   180

154 make *most MSS.:* haste *1633–69 (from previous line):*   156
precious *1633:* piteous *1635–69 and most MSS.*   159 on mee;] o're
mee; *1635–69*   164 th'huffing braggart, *1669 and most MSS.:*
huffing, braggart, *1633–54 and some MSS.*   169 your *1633–69 and
some MSS.:* yon *or the other MSS.*   170 Transported *1633–69 and
some MSS.:* Transplanted *most MSS.*   171 our Presence, *1633
and some MSS.:* our Court here, *most MSS.:* our Courtiers, *1635–69*

                                                        The

The fields they sold to buy them; For a King
Those hose are, cry the flatterers; And bring
Them next weeke to the Theatre to sell;
Wants reach all states; Me seemes they doe as well
At stage, as court; All are players; who e'r lookes   185
(For themselves dare not goe) o'r Cheapside books,
Shall finde their wardrops Inventory. Now,
The Ladies come; As Pirats, which doe know
That there came weak ships fraught with Cutchannel,
The men board them; and praise, as they thinke, well, 190
Their beauties; they the mens wits; Both are bought.
Why good wits ne'r weare scarlet gownes, I thought
This cause, These men, mens wits for speeches buy,
And women buy all reds which scarlets die.
He call'd her beauty limetwigs, her haire net;   195
She feares her drugs ill laid, her haire loose set.
Would not Heraclitus laugh to see Macrine,
From hat to shooe, himselfe at doore refine,
As if the Presence were a Moschite, and lift
His skirts and hose, and call his clothes to shrift,   200
Making them confesse not only mortall
Great staines and holes in them; but veniall
Feathers and dust, wherewith they fornicate:
And then by *Durers* rules survay the state
Of his each limbe, and with strings the odds trye   205
Of his neck to his legge, and wast to thighe.
So in immaculate clothes, and Symetrie
Perfect as circles, with such nicetie
As a young Preacher at his first time goes
To preach, he enters, and a Lady which owes   210

187 wardrops *1633:* wardrobes *1635–69*   188 doe know *1633–
69 and some MSS.:* did know *other MSS.*   194 scarlets] scarlett
some MSS.   199 As if the Presence . . . Moschite, *1633–69:* As
the Presence . . . Moschite, *(or* Meschite,*) most MSS.:* As the Queenes
Presence . . . Meschite, *one MS.*   204 survay *1633–69 and some
MSS.:* survayes *other MSS.*   205 trye *Ed:* tryes *1633–69 and MSS.*
206 to thighe. *Ed:* to thighes. *1633–69 and MSS.*

Him

Him not so much as good will, he arrests,
And unto her protests protests protests,
So much as at Rome would serve to have throwne
Ten Cardinalls into the Inquisition;
And whisperd by Jesu, so often, that A   215
Pursevant would have ravish'd him away
For saying of our Ladies psalter; But'tis fit
That they each other plague, they merit it.
But here comes Glorius that will plague them both,
Who, in the other extreme, only doth   220
Call a rough carelessenesse, good fashion;
Whose cloak his spurres teare; whom he spits on
He cares not, His ill words doe no harme
To him; he rusheth in, as if arme, arme,
He meant to crie; And though his face be as ill   225
As theirs which in old hangings whip Christ, still
He strives to looke worse, he keepes all in awe;
Jeasts like a licenc'd foole, commands like law.
Tyr'd, now I leave this place, and but pleas'd so
As men which from gaoles to'execution goe,   230
Goe through the great chamber (why is it hung
With the seaven deadly sinnes?). Being among
Those Askaparts, men big enough to throw
Charing Crosse for a barre, men that doe know
No token of worth, but Queenes man, and fine   235
Living, barrells of beefe, flaggons of wine;
I shooke like a spyed Spie. Preachers which are
Seas of Wit and Arts, you can, then dare,
Drowne the sinnes of this place, for, for mee

---

211 he arrests *1633–69 and some MSS.:* straight arrests, *other MSS.*
216 Topcliffe would have ravish'd him quite away *some MSS.*
217 of *om. some good MSS.*   226 still *1635–69 and most MSS.:* yet
still *1633*   230 men which from *all MSS.:* men from *1633–69*
238 Seas of Wit and Arts, *several MSS.:* Seas of Wits and Arts,
1633 and some MSS.: Seas of witt and art, *two MSS.:* Great seas of
witt and art, *two MSS.*

Which

Which am but a scarce brooke, it enough shall bee   240
To wash the staines away; Although I yet
With *Macchabees* modestie, the knowne merit
Of my worke lessen: yet some wise man shall,
I hope, esteeme my writs Canonicall.

Satyre V.

THou shalt not laugh in this leafe, Muſe, nor they
   Whom any pitty warmes; He which did lay
Rules to make Courtiers, (hee being understood
May make good Courtiers, but who Courtiers good?)
Frees from the sting of jests all who in extreme   5
Are wreched or wicked: of these two a theame
Charity and liberty give me. What is hee
Who Officers rage, and Suiters misery
Can write, and jest? If all things be in all,
As I thinke, since all, which were, are, and shall   10
Bee, be made of the same elements:
Each thing, each thing implyes or represents.
Then man is a world; in which, Officers
Are the vast ravishing seas; and Suiters,
Springs; now full, now shallow, now drye; which, to   15
That which drownes them, run: These selfe reasons do
Prove the world a man, in which, officers
Are the devouring stomacke, and Suiters
The excrements, which they voyd. All men are dust;
How much worse are Suiters, who to mens lust   20
Are made preyes? O worse then dust, or wormes meat,

240 Which] Who *MSS.*   am but a scarce brooke, *1633 and some
MSS.:* am but a scant brooke, *1635–69:* am a scant brooke, *some good
MSS.:* am a shallow brooke, *some MSS.*   241 the] their *many MSS.*
Although] though *1633 and MSS.*   242 knowne *om. many MSS.*
243 wise man] wise men *1650–69 and some MSS.*
   Satyre V.   12 implyes *1635–69:* spelt employes *1633 and some
MSS.*   14 ravishing *1633–69:* ravenous *one MS.:* ravening *some
MSS.*

For

For they do eate you now, whose selves wormes shall eate.
They are the mills which grinde you, yet you are
The winde which drives them; and a wastfull warre
Is fought against you, and you fight it; they   25
Adulterate lawe, and you prepare their way
Like wittals; th'issue your owne ruine is.
Greatest and fairest Empresse, know you this?
Alas, no more then Thames calme head doth know
Whose meades her armes drowne, or whose corne o'rflow:
You Sir, whose righteousnes she loves, whom I   31
By having leave to serve, am most richly
For service paid, authoriz'd, now beginne
To know and weed out this enormous sinne.
O Age of rusty iron! Some better wit   35
Call it some worse name, if ought equall it;
The iron Age *that* was, when justice was sold; now
Injustice is sold dearer farre. Allow
All demands, fees, and duties, gamsters, anon
The mony which you sweat, and sweare for, is gon   40
Into other hands: So controverted lands
Scape, like Angelica, the strivers hands.
If Law be in the Judges heart, and hee
Have no heart to resist letter, or fee,
Where wilt thou appeale? powre of the Courts below   45
Flow from the first maine head, and these can throw
Thee, if they sucke thee in, to misery,
To fetters, halters; But if the injury
Steele thee to dare complaine, Alas, thou go'st
Against the stream, when upwards: when thou art most   50
Heavy and most faint; and in these labours they,
'Gainst whom thou should'st complaine, will in the way
Become great seas, o'r which, when thou shalt bee
Forc'd to make golden bridges, thou shalt see
That all thy gold was drown'd in them before;   55
All things follow their like, only who have may have more.

50 when upwards: *1633–54 and all MSS.:* upwards, *1669*

Judges

Judges are Gods; he who made and said them so,
Meant not that men should be forc'd to them to goe,
By meanes of Angels; When supplications
We send to God, to Dominations,   60
Powers, Cherubins, and all heavens Courts, if wee
Should pay fees as here, Daily bread would be
Scarce to Kings; so 'tis. Would it not anger
A Stoicke, a coward, yea a Martyr,
To see a Pursivant come in, and call   65
All his cloathes, Copes, Bookes, Primers; and all
His Plate, Challices; and mistake them away,
And aske a fee for comming? Oh, ne'r may
Faire lawes white reverend name be strumpeted,
To warrant thefts: she is established   70
Recorder to Destiny, on earth, and shee
Speakes Fates words, and but tells us who must bee
Rich, who poore, who in chaires, who in jayles:
Shee is all faire, but yet hath foule long nailes,
With which she scracheth Suiters; In bodies   75
Of men, so in law, nailes are th'extremities,
So Officers stretch to more then Law can doe,
As our nailes reach what no else part comes to.
Why barest thou to yon Officer? Foole, Hath hee
Got those goods, for which erst men bar'd to thee?   80
Foole, twice, thrice, thou hast bought wrong, and now
      hungerly
Beg'st right; But that dole comes not till these dye.
Thou had'st much, and lawes Urim and Thummim trie
Thou wouldst for more; and for all hast paper
Enough to cloath all the great Carricks Pepper.   85

61 Courts, *1635–69 and most MSS.:* Court, *1633 and some MSS.*
68 aske *1669 and most MSS.:* lack *1633–54, one MS.*   72 Speakes
Fates words, and but tells us *&c. two good MSS.:* Speakes Fates
words, and tells who must bee *1633–69*   76 th'extremities, *MSS.:*
extremities, *1633:* extremities. *1635–69*   80 which erst men bar'd
1635–69 and some MSS.: which men bared *1633 and some MSS.*

Sell that, and by that thou much more shalt leese,
Then Haman, when he sold his Antiquities.
O wretch that thy fortunes should moralize
Esops fables, and make tales, prophesies.
Thou'art the swimming dog whom shadows cosened,   90
And div'st, neare drowning, for what's vanished.

Vpon Mr. Thomas Coryats Crudities.

OH to what height will love of greatnesse drive
    Thy leavened spirit, *Sesqui-superlative?*
Venice vast lake thou hadst seen, and would seek than
Some vaster thing, and found'st a Curtizan.
That inland Sea having discovered well,   5
A Cellar gulfe, where one might saile to hell
From Heydelberg, thou longdst to see: And thou
This Booke, greater then all, producest now.
Infinite worke, which doth so far extend,
That none can study it to any end.   10
'Tis no one thing, it is not fruit nor roote;
Nor poorely limited with head or foot.
If man be therefore man, because he can
Reason, and laugh, thy booke doth halfe make man.
One halfe being made, thy modestie was such,   15
That thou on th'other half wouldst never touch.
When wilt thou be at full, great Lunatique?
Not till thou exceed the world? Canst thou be like

87 Haman, *1633:* Hammon, *1635–69: MSS. generally vary be-*
tween Haman *and* Hammond   *when 1633, 1669, and most MSS.:*
if 1635–54, some MSS.   91. And *1633:* Which *1635–69:* Whoe *one*
MS.   div'st, *1633–54 and some MSS.:* div'st *1669:* div'dst *some*
good MSS.: div'd, *other MSS.*   what's vanished. *one MS.:* what
vanished. *1633–54 and rest of MSS.:* what vanisheth. *1669*
    Vpon Mr. *&c. 1649, where it was placed with* The Token *at the*
end of the Funerall Elegies: *appeared originally in* Coryats Crudities
(1611) with heading Incipit Joannes Donne.   2 leavened *1911:*
learned *1649–69 and mod. edd.*

                                              A prosperous

A prosperous nose-borne wenne, which sometimes growes
To be farre greater then the Mother-nose? 20
Goe then; and as to thee, when thou didst go,
Munster did Townes, and *Gesner* Authors show,
Mount now to *Gallo-belgicus;* appear
As deepe a States-man, as a Gazettier.
Homely and familiarly, when thou com'st back, 25
Talke of *Will. Conquerour*, and *Prester Jack.*
Go bashfull man, lest here thou blush to looke
Vpon the progresse of thy glorious booke,
To which both Indies sacrifices send;
The West sent gold, which thou didst freely spend, 30
(Meaning to see't no more) upon the presse.
The East sends hither her deliciousnesse;
And thy leaves must imbrace what comes from thence,
The Myrrhe, the Pepper, and the Frankincense.
This magnifies thy leaves; but if they stoope 35
To neighbour wares, when Merchants do unhoope
Voluminous barrels; if thy leaves do then
Convey these wares in parcels unto men;
If for vast Tons of Currans, and of Figs,
Of Medicinall and Aromatique twigs, 40
Thy leaves a better method do provide,
Divide to pounds, and ounces sub-divide;
If they stoope lower yet, and vent our wares,
Home-*manufactures*, to thick popular Faires,
If *omni-praegnant* there, upon warme stalls, 45
They hatch all wares for which the buyer calls;
Then thus thy leaves we justly may commend,
That they all kinde of matter comprehend.
Thus thou, by means which th'Ancients never took,
A Pandect makest, and Vniversall Booke. 50
The bravest Heroes, for publike good,
Scattered in divers Lands their limbs and blood.
Worst malefactors, to whom men are prize,
Do publike good, cut in Anatomies;

So

So will thy booke in peeces; for a Lord   55
Which casts at Portescues, and all the board,
Provide whole books; each leafe enough will be
For friends to passe time, and keep company.
Can all carouse up thee? no, thou must fit
Measures; and fill out for the half-pint wit: 60
Some shall wrap pils, and save a friends life so,
Some shall stop muskets, and so kill a foe.
Thou shalt not ease the Criticks of next age
So much, at once their hunger to asswage:
Nor shall wit-pirats hope to finde thee lye   65
All in one bottome, in one Librarie.
Some Leaves may paste strings there in other books,
And so one may, which on another looks,
Pilfer, alas, a little wit from you;
But hardly* much; and yet I think this true;   [*] I meane from one 70
As *Sibyls* was, your booke is mysticall,   page which
For every peece is as much worth as all.   shall paste strings in a
Therefore mine impotency I confesse,   booke.[1]
The healths which my braine bears must be far lesse:
Thy Gyant-wit'orethrowes me, I am gone;   75
And rather then read all, I would reade none.

                      J.D.

In eundem Macaronicon.

Quot, dos haec, **Linguists** *perfetti, Disticha* fairont,
Tot cuerdos **States-men,** *hic* livre fara *tuus.*
Es *sat* a my l'honneur estre hic inteso; Car **I leabe**
L'honra, de personne nestre creduto, *tibi.*
                    Explicit Joannes Donne.

[1] I meane &c. side-note in *1611*
In eundem &c. *1611, concluding the above*

LETTERS

LETTERS

TO SEVERALL PERSONAGES.

THE STORME.
To Mr. *Christopher Brooke.*

THou which art I, ('tis nothing to be soe)
   Thou which art still thy selfe, by these shalt know
Part of our passage; And, a hand, or eye
By *Hilliard* drawne, is worth an history,
By a worse painter made; and (without pride)   5
When by thy judgment they are dignifi'd,
My lines are such: 'Tis the preheminence
Of friendship onely to'impute excellence.
England to whom we'owe, what we be, and have,
Sad that her sonnes did seeke a forraine grave   10
(For, Fates, or Fortunes drifts none can soothsay,
Honour and misery have one face and way.)
From out her pregnant intrailes sigh'd a winde
Which at th'ayres middle marble roome did finde
Such strong resistance, that it selfe it threw   15
Downeward againe; and so when it did view
How in the port, our fleet deare time did leese,
Withering like prisoners, which lye but for fees,
Mildly it kist our sailes, and, fresh and sweet,
As to a stomack sterv'd, whose insides meete,   20
Meate comes, it came; and swole our sailes, when wee
So joyd, as *Sara*'her swelling joy'd to see.
But 'twas but so kinde, as our countrimen,
Which bring friends one dayes way, and leave them then.

The Storme. To Mr. Christopher Brooke. *1633* (*1635–69 add*
from the Iland voyage with the Earle of Essex)   2 these *1633 and
most MSS.:* this *1635–69*

Then

Then like two mighty Kings, which dwelling farre   25
Asunder, meet against a third to warre,
The South and West winds joyn'd, and, as they blew,
Waves like a rowling trench before them threw.
Sooner then you read this line, did the gale,
Like shot, not fear'd till felt, our sailes assaile;   30
And what at first was call'd a gust, the same
Hath now a stormes, anon a tempests name.
Jonas, I pitty thee, and curse those men,
Who when the storm rag'd most, did wake thee then;
Sleepe is paines easiest salve, and doth fullfill   35
All offices of death, except to kill.
But when I wakt, I saw, that I saw not;
I, and the Sunne, which should teach mee'had forgot
East, West, Day, Night, and I could onely say,
If'the world had lasted, now it had beene day.   40
Thousands our noyses were, yet wee'mongst all
Could none by his right name, but thunder call:
Lightning was all our light, and it rain'd more
Then if the Sunne had drunke the sea before.
Some coffin'd in their cabbins lye,'equally   45
Griev'd that they are not dead, and yet must dye;
And as sin-burd'ned soules from graves will creepe,
At the last day, some forth their cabbins peepe:
And tremblingly'aske what newes, and doe heare so,
Like jealous husbands, what they would not know.   50
Some sitting on the hatches, would seeme there,
With hideous gazing to feare away feare.
Then note they the ships sicknesses, the Mast
Shak'd with this ague, and the Hold and Wast
With a salt dropsie clog'd, and all our tacklings   55

38 I, and the Sunne, *1633–69 and most MSS.:* yea, and the Sunne,
one MS.   40 lasted, now *1633, 1669:* lasted, yet *1635–54:* Lasted
yet, *one MS.*   47 graves *1669 and most MSS.:* grave *1633–54*
49 tremblingly *1633 and most MSS.:* trembling *1635–69 and some
MSS.*   50 Like *1633 and MSS.:* As *1635–69*

Snapping,

Snapping, like too-high-stretched treble strings.
And from our totterd sailes, ragges drop downe so,
As from one hang'd in chaines, a yeare agoe.
Even our Ordinance plac'd for our defence,
Strive to breake loose, and scape away from thence.   60
Pumping hath tir'd our men, and what's the gaine?
Seas into seas throwne, we suck in againe;
Hearing hath deaf'd our saylers; and if they
Knew how to heare, there's none knowes what to say.
Compar'd to these stormes, death is but a qualme,   65
Hell somewhat lightsome, and the'Bermuda calme.
Darknesse, lights elder brother, his birth-right
Claims o'r this world, and to heaven hath chas'd light.
All things are one, and that one none can be,
Since all formes, uniforme deformity   70
Doth cover, so that wee, except God say
Another *Fiat*, shall have no more day.
So violent, yet long these furies bee,
That though thine absence sterve me,'I wish not thee.

THE CALME.

OUr storme is past, and that storms tyrannous rage,
A stupid calme, but nothing it, doth swage.
The fable is inverted, and farre more
A blocke afflicts, now, then a storke before.
Stormes chafe, and soone we'are out themselves, or us;   5
In calmes, Heaven laughs to see us languish thus.

56 too-high-stretched *1633 and most MSS.* (*MS. spelling generally*
to and stretcht): too-too-high-stretch'd *1635–54:* to too-high-
stretch'd *1669*   59 Even our Ordinance *1633 and MSS.:* Yea
even our Ordinance *1635–69*   60 Strive *1633 and MSS.:* Strives
1635–69   66 and the'Bermuda *1633 and most MSS.:* and the
Bermudas *some MSS.:* the Bermudas *1635–54:* the Bermuda's *1669*
67 elder *most MSS.:* eldest *1633–69 and some MSS.*   68 Claims
1635–69 and MSS.: Claim'd *1633*   this *1633 and most MSS.:*
the *1635–69 and some MSS.*

As

As steady'as I can wish, that my thoughts were,
Smooth as thy mistresse glasse, or what shines there,
The sea is now. And, as the Iles which wee
Seeke, when wee can move, our ships rooted bee.   10
As water did in stormes, now pitch runs out:
As lead, when a fir'd Church becomes one spout.
And all our beauty, and our trimme, decayes,
Like courts removing, or like ended playes.
The fighting place now seamens ragges supply;   15
And all the tackling is a frippery.
No use of lanthornes; and in one place lay
Feathers and dust, to day and yesterday.
Earths hollownesses, which the worlds lungs are,
Have no more winde then the upper valt of aire.   20
We can nor lost friends, nor sought foes recover,
But meteorlike, save that wee move not, hover.
Onely the Calenture together drawes
Deare friends, which meet dead in great fishes jawes:
And on the hatches as on Altars lyes   25
Each one, his owne Priest, and owne Sacrifice.
Who live, that miracle do multiply
Where walkers in hot Ovens, doe not dye.
If in despite of these, wee swimme, that hath
No more refreshing, then our brimstone Bath,   30
But from the sea, into the ship we turne,
Like parboyl'd wretches, on the coales to burne.
Like *Bajazet* encag'd, the shepheards scoffe,
Or like slacke sinew'd *Sampson*, his haire off,
Languish our ships. Now, as a Miriade   35
Of Ants, durst th'Emperours lov'd snake invade,

The Calme. *1633–69*   7 can wish, that my *1633 and most MSS.:*
could wish, that my *one MS.:* could wish my *1635–69*   9 the Iles
1633–69: these isles *one MS. group:* those Iles *most MSS.*   21 lost]
lefte *many MSS.*   24 jawes: *1633 and most MSS.:* mawes, *1635–69
and some MSS.*   30 our *1633 and most MSS.:* a *1635–69 and some
MSS.*

The

The crawling Gallies, Sea-goales, finny chips,
Might brave our Pinnaces, now bed-ridde ships.
Whether a rotten state, and hope of gaine,
Or to disuse mee from the queasie paine   40
Of being belov'd, and loving, or the thirst
Of honour, or faire death, out pusht mee first,
I lose my end: for here as well as I
A desperate may live, and a coward die.
Stagge, dogge, and all which from, or towards flies,   45
Is paid with life, or pray, or doing dyes.
Fate grudges us all, and doth subtly lay
A scourge,'gainst which wee all forget to pray,
He that at sea prayes for more winde, as well
Under the poles may begge cold, heat in hell.   50
What are wee then? How little more alas
Is man now, then before he was? he was
Nothing; for us, wee are for nothing fit;
Chance, or our selves still disproportion it.
Wee have no power, no will, no sense; I lye,   55
I should not then thus feele this miserie.

To Sʳ *Henry Wotton.*

SIr, more then kisses, letters mingle Soules;
For, thus friends absent speake. This ease controules
The tediousnesse of my life: But for these
I could ideate nothing, which could please,
But I should wither in one day, and passe   5
To'a bottle'of Hay, that am a locke of Grasse.

37 Sea-goales, (*or* gayles &*c.*) *1633, 1669, and most MSS.:* Sea-
gulls, *1635–54*   38 our Pinnaces, now *1635–54 and two MSS.:*
our venices, now *1633 and rest of MSS.*   48 forget] forgot *1669
and many MSS.*   52–3 he was? he was Nothing; for us, wee are for
nothing fit; *1633 and some MSS.:* he was, he was? Nothing; for us,
wee are for nothing fit; *1635–54:* he was, he was? Nothing for us, we
are for nothing fit; *1669 and most MSS.*

Life is a voyage, and in our lifes wayes
Countries, Courts, Towns are Rockes, or Remoraes;
They breake or stop all ships, yet our state's such,
That though then pitch they staine worse, wee must touch.
If in the furnace of the even line,   11
Or under th'adverse icy poles thou pine,
Thou know'st two temperate Regions girded in,
Dwell there: But Oh, what refuge canst thou winne
Parch'd in the Court, and in the country frozen?   15
Shall cities, built of both extremes, be chosen?
Can dung and garlike be'a perfume? or can
A Scorpion and Torpedo cure a man?
Cities are worst of all three; of all three
(O knottie riddle) each is worst equally.   20
Cities are Sepulchers; they who dwell there
Are carcases, as if no such there were.
And Courts are Theaters, where some men play
Princes, some slaves, all to one end, and of one clay.
The Country is a desert, where no good,   25
Gain'd (as habits, not borne,) is understood.
There men become beasts, and prone to more evils;
In cities blockes, and in a lewd court, devills.

  To Sr Henry Wotton.   7 lifes *1633:* lives *1635–69*   11 even *1669
and MSS.:* raging *1633–54*   12 poles *most MSS.:* pole *1633–69 and
some MSS.*   17 dung and garlike *1633 and most MSS.:* dung, or
garlike *1635–69 and some MSS.*   18 and Torpedo *best MSS.:* or
Torpedo *1633–69 and some MSS.*   22 no such *1633 and most MSS.:*
none such *1635–69*   there were. *1635–69 and most MSS.:* they were.
1633 and one MS.: then were *one MS.*   24 and of one clay. *1633
and MSS. generally:* of one clay. *1635–39:* of one day. *1650–54*
25–6   The Country is a desert, where no good,
    Gain'd, as habits, not borne, is understood.   *1633, 1669, and
most MSS.*
    The Country is a desert, where the good,
    Gain'd inhabits not, borne, is not understood. *1635–54 and
some MSS.*
27 more *1633 and some MSS.:* meere *most MSS.:* all *1635–69*

                 As

As in the first Chaos confusedly
Each elements qualities were in the'other three;   30
So pride, lust, covetize, being severall
To these three places, yet all are in all,
And mingled thus, their issue incestuous.
Falshood is denizon'd. Virtue is barbarous.
Let no man say there, Virtues flintie wall   35
Shall locke vice in mee, I'll do none, but know all.
Men are spunges, which to poure out, receive.
Who know false play, rather then lose, deceive.
For in best understandings, sinne beganne,
Angels sinn'd first, then Devills, and then man.   40
Onely perchance beasts sinne not; wretched wee
Are beasts in all, but white integritie.
I thinke if men, which in these places live
Durst looke for themselves, and themselves retrive,
They would like strangers greet themselves, seeing than 45
Utopian youth, growne old Italian.
  Be thou thine owne home, and in thy selfe dwell;
Inne any where, continuance maketh hell.
And seeing the snaile, which every where doth rome,
Carrying his owne house still, still is at home,   50
Follow (for he is easie pac'd) this snaile,
Bee thine owne Palace, or the world's thy gaile.
And in the worlds sea, do not like corke sleepe
Upon the waters face; nor in the deepe
Sinke like a lead without a line: but as   55
Fishes glide, leaving no print where they passe,
Nor making sound; so closely thy course goe,
Let men dispute, whether thou breathe, or no.
Onely'in this one thing, be no Galenist: To make
Courts hot ambitions wholesome, do not take   60

  35 there] then *one good MS.*   44 for themselves, *most MSS.:* in themselves, *1633–69:* into themselves, themselves retrive, *some MSS* 47 Be thou *1633:* Be then *1635–69 and MSS.*   52 gaile. *1635–69:* goale; *1633*

A dramme

A dramme of Countries dulnesse; do not adde
Correctives, but as chymiques, purge the bad.
But, Sir, I advise not you, I rather doe
Say o'er those lessons, which I learn'd of you:
Whom, free from German schismes, and lightnesse   65
Of France, and faire Italies faithlesnesse,
Having from these suck'd all they had of worth,
And brought home that faith, which you carried forth,
I throughly love. But if my selfe, I'have wonne
To know my rules, I have, and you have   70

DONNE:

To Sʳ *Henry Goodyere.*

WHo makes the Past, a patterne for next yeare,
    Turnes no new leafe, but still the same things reads,
Seene things, he sees againe, heard things doth heare,
    And makes his life, but like a paire of beads.

A Palace, when 'tis that, which it should be,   5
    Leaves growing, and stands such, or else decayes:
But hee which dwels there, is not so; for hee
    Strives to urge upward, and his fortune raise;

So had your body'her morning, hath her noone,
    And shall not better; her next change is night: 10
But her faire larger guest, to'whom Sun and Moone
    Are sparkes, and short liv'd, claimes another right.

The noble Soule by age growes lustier,
    Her appetite, and her digestion mend,
Wee must not sterve, nor hope to pamper her   15
    With womens milke, and pappe unto the end.

Provide you manlyer dyet; you have seene
    All libraries, which are Schools, Camps, and Courts;
But aske your Garners if you have not beene
    In harvests, too indulgent to your sports.   20

65 German *1633 and all MSS.:* Germanies *1635–69*
    To Sir Henry Goodyere.   1 Past] Last *1669*   20 harvests,
1633–54 and most MSS.: harvest, *1669 and some MSS.*

Would

Would you redeeme it? then your selfe transplant
   A while from hence. Perchance outlandish ground
Beares no more wit, then ours, but yet more scant
   Are those diversions there, which here abound.

To be a stranger hath that benefit,   25
   Wee can beginnings, but not habits choke.
Goe; whither? Hence; you get, if you forget;
   New faults, till they prescribe in us, are smoake.

Our soule, whose country'is heaven, and God her father,
   Into this world, corruptions sinke, is sent,   30
Yet, so much in her travaile she doth gather,
   That she returnes home, wiser then she went;

It payes you well, if it teach you to spare,
   And make you,'asham'd, to make your hawks praise,
      yours,
Which when herselfe she lessens in the aire,   35
   You then first say, that high enough she toures.

However, keepe the lively tast you hold
   Of God, love him as now, but feare him more,
And in your afternoones thinke what you told
   And promis'd him, at morning prayer before.   40

Let falshood like a discord anger you,
   Else be not froward. But why doe I touch
Things, of which none is in your practise new,
   And Tables, or fruit-trenchers teach as much;

But thus I make you keepe your promise Sir,   45
   Riding I had you, though you still staid there,
And in these thoughts, although you never stirre,
   You came with mee to Micham, and are here.

28 in us, *1633 and most MSS.*: to us, *1635–69*   34 you,'asham'd,
Ed: you'asham'd, *1633–69:* you asham'd *mod. edd.*   44 Tables
1633–54 and one MS.: Fables *1669 and most MSS.*

To Mr *Rowland Woodward.*

Like one who'in her third widdowhood doth professe
  Her selfe a Nunne, tyed to retirednesse,
So'affects my muse now, a chast fallownesse;

Since shee to few, yet to too many'hath showne
How love-song weeds, and Satyrique thornes are growne   5
Where seeds of better Arts, were early sown.

Though to use, and love Poëtrie, to mee,
Betroth'd to no'one Art, be no'adulterie;
Omissions of good, ill, as ill deeds bee.

For though to us it seeme,'and be light and thinne,   10
Yet in those faithfull scales, where God throwes in
Mens workes, vanity weighs as much as sinne.

If our Soules have stain'd their first white, yet wee
May cloth them with faith, and deare honestie,
Which God imputes, as native puritie.   15

There is no Vertue, but Religion:
Wise, valiant, sober, just, are names, which none
Want, which want not Vice-covering discretion.

Seeke wee then our selves in our selves; for as
Men force the Sunne with much more force to passe,   20
By gathering his beames with a christall glasse;

So wee, If wee into our selves will turne,
Blowing our sparkes of vertue, may outburne
The straw, which doth about our hearts sojourne.

You know, Physitians, when they would infuse   25
Into any'oyle, the Soules of Simples, use
Places, where they may lie still warme, to chuse.

To Mr Rowland Woodward.   2 retirednesse, *1633–69 and some
MSS.:* a retirednesse, *other MSS.*   10 seeme,'and be light *1633
and most MSS.:* seem but light *1635–69 and some MSS.*   23
sparkes *1633–54 and most MSS.:* spark *1669 and some MSS.*

So

So workes retirednesse in us; To rome
Giddily, and be every where, but at home,
Such freedome doth a banishment become.   30

Wee are but farmers of our selves, yet may,
If we can stocke our selves, and thrive, uplay
Much, much deare treasure for the great rent day.

Manure thy selfe then, to thy selfe be'approv'd,
And with vaine outward things be no more mov'd,   35
But to know, that I love thee'and would be lov'd.

To Sr *Henry Wootton.*

HEre's no more newes, then vertue,'I may as well
Tell you *Cales*, or St *Michaels* tale for newes, as tell
That vice doth here habitually dwell.

Yet, as to'get stomachs, we walke up and downe,
And toyle to sweeten rest, so, may God frowne,   5
If, but to loth both, I haunt Court, or Towne.

For here no one is from the'extremitie
Of vice, by any other reason free,
But that the next to'him, still, is worse then hee.

In this worlds warfare, they whom rugged Fate,   10
(Gods Commissary,) doth so throughly hate,
As in'the Courts Squadron to marshall their state:

If they stand arm'd with seely honesty,
With wishing prayers, and neat integritie,
Like Indians 'gainst Spanish hosts they bee.   15

31 farmers *1635–69 and all MSS., but in MSS. it is generally spelt*
fermers: termers *1633*   33 deare *1633 and most MSS.:* good
1635–69 and some MSS.

To Sr Henry Wootton.   2 Cales] Calis *1633–69 and some MSS.:*
Calais *1719 and most modern editions*   tale *1633 and most MSS.:*
tales *1635–54 and some MSS.*   14 wishing prayers, *1633 and most*
MSS.: wishing, prayers, *1660 and one MS.:* wishes, prayers, *1635–54*
and some MSS.

                                        Suspitious

Suspitious boldnesse to this place belongs,
And to'have as many eares as all have tongues;
Tender to know, tough to acknowledge wrongs.

Beleeve mee Sir, in my youths giddiest dayes,
When to be like the Court, was a playes praise,   20
Playes were not so like Courts, as Courts'are like playes.

Then let us at these mimicke antiques jeast,
Whose deepest projects, and egregious gests
Are but dull Moralls of a game at Chests.

But now 'tis incongruity to smile,   25
Therefore I end; and bid farewell a while,
At Court; though *From Court*, were the better stile.

H: W: in Hiber: belligeranti.

WEnt you to conquer? and have so much lost
    Yourself, that what in you was best and most,
Respective friendship, should so quickly dye?
In publique gaine my share'is not such that I
Would lose your love for Ireland: better cheap   5
I pardon death (who though he do not reap
Yet gleanes hee many of our frends away)
Then that your waking mind should bee a prey
To lethargies. Lett shott, and boggs, and skeines
With bodies deale, as fate bids and restreynes;   10
Ere sicknesses attack, yong death is best,
Who payes before his death doth scape arrest.
Lett not your soule (at first with graces fill'd,
And since, and thorough crooked lymbecks, still'd
In many schools and courts, which quicken it,)   15
It self unto the Irish negligence submit.
I aske not labored letters which should weare

---

21 are like *1633 and most MSS.:* are om. (*metri causa*) *1635–69
and some MSS.*

Long

Long papers out: nor letters which should feare
Dishonest carriage: or a seers art:
Nor such as from the brayne come, but the hart.   20

To the Countesse of Bedford.

MADAME,

REason is our Soules left hand, Faith her right,
    By these wee reach divinity, that's you;
Their loves, who have the blessings of your light,
Grew from their reason, mine from faire faith grew.

But as, although a squint lefthandednesse   5
Be'ungracious, yet we cannot want that hand,
So would I, not to encrease, but to expresse
My faith, as I beleeve, so understand.

Therefore I study you first in your Saints,
Those friends, whom your election glorifies,   10
Then in your deeds, accesses, and restraints,
And what you reade, and what your selfe devize.

But soone, the reasons why you'are lov'd by all,
Grow infinite, and so passe reasons reach,
Then backe againe to'implicite faith I fall,   15
And rest on what the Catholique voice doth teach;

That you are good: and not one Heretique
Denies it: if he did, yet you are so.
For, rockes, which high top'd and deep rooted sticke,
Waves wash, not undermine, nor overthrow.   20

In every thing there naturally growes
A *Balsamum* to keepe it fresh, and new,
If 'twere not injur'd by extrinsique blowes;
Your birth and beauty are this Balme in you.

To the Countesse of Bedford. 3 blessings *1633 and some MSS.:*
blessing *1635–69 and most MSS.* light, *1633–69:* sight, *MSS.*   4
faire] farr *many MSS.*   16 voice *1635–69 and most MSS.:* faith *1633*
and some MSS.   19 high top'd and deep rooted *1633 and one MS.:*
high to sense deepe-rooted *1635–54 and so or similarly in many MSS.*

                                                     But

But you of learning and religion,   25
And vertue,'and such ingredients, have made
A methridate, whose operation
Keepes off, or cures what can be done or said.

Yet, this is not your physicke, but your food,
A dyet fit for you; for you are here   30
The first good Angell, since the worlds frame stood,
That ever did in womans shape appeare.

Since you are then Gods masterpeece, and so
His Factor for our loves; do as you doe,
Make your returne home gracious; and bestow   35
This life on that; so make one life of two.
    For so God helpe mee,'I would not misse you there
    For all the good which you can do me here.

To the Countesse of Bedford.

MADAME,

YOu have refin'd mee, and to worthyest things
    (Vertue, Art, Beauty, Fortune,) now I see
Rarenesse, or use, not nature value brings;
And such, as they are circumstanc'd, they bee.
    Two ills can ne're perplexe us, sinne to'excuse;   5
    But of two good things, we may leave and chuse.

Therefore at Court, which is not vertues clime,
(Where a transcendent height, (as, lownesse mee)
Makes her not be, or not show) all my rime
Your vertues challenge, which there rarest bee;   10
    For, as darke texts need notes: there some must bee
    To usher vertue, and say, *This is shee.*

So in the country'is beauty; to this place
You are the season (Madame) you the day,
'Tis but a grave of spices, till your face   15
Exhale them, and a thick close bud display.

36 This *1635–69 and MSS.:* Thy *1633*
                                                    Widow'd

Widow'd and reclus'd else, her sweets she'enshrines;
As China, when the Sunne at Brasill dines.

Out from your chariot, morning breaks at night,
And falsifies both computations so;   20
Since a new world doth rise here from your light,
We your new creatures, by new recknings goe.
    This showes that you from nature lothly stray,
    That suffer not an artificiall day.

In this you'have made the Court the Antipodes,   25
And will'd your Delegate, the vulgar Sunne,
To doe profane autumnall offices,
Whilst here to you, wee sacrificers runne;
    And whether Priests, or Organs, you wee'obey,
    We sound your influence, and your Dictates say.   30

Yet to that Deity which dwels in you,
Your vertuous Soule, I now not sacrifice;
These are *Petitions*, and not *Hymnes*; they sue
But that I may survay the edifice.
    In all Religions as much care hath bin   35
    Of Temples frames, and beauty,'as Rites within.

As all which goe to Rome, doe not thereby
Esteeme religions, and hold fast the best,
But serve discourse, and curiosity,
With that which doth religion but invest,   40
    And shunne th'entangling laborinths of Schooles,
    And make it wit, to thinke the wiser fooles:

So in this pilgrimage I would behold
You as you'are vertues temple, not as shee,
What walls of tender christall her enfold,   45
What eyes, hands, bosome, her pure Altars bee;
    And after this survay, oppose to all
    Bablers of Chappels, you th'Escuriall.

H

Yet

Yet not as consecrate, but merely'as faire,
On these I cast a lay and country eye. 50
Of past and future stories, which are rare,
I finde you all record, and prophecie.
   Purge but the booke of Fate, that it admit
   No sad nor guilty legends, you are it.

If good and lovely were not one, of both 55
You were the transcript, and originall,
The Elements, the Parent, and the Growth,
And every peece of you, is both their All:
   So'intire are all your deeds, and you, that you
   Must do the same thinge still; you cannot two. 60

But these (as nice thinne Schoole divinity
Serves heresie to furder or represse)
Tast of Poëtique rage, or flattery,
And need not, where all hearts one truth professe;
   Oft from new proofes, and new phrase, new doubts grow,
   As strange attire aliens the men wee know. 66

Leaving then busie praise, and all appeale
To higher Courts, senses decree is true,
The Mine, the Magazine, the Commonweale,
The story of beauty,'in Twicknam is, and you. 70
   Who hath seene one, would both; As, who had bin
   In Paradise, would seeke the Cherubin.

To Sʳ *Edward Herbert.* at *Julyers.*

MAn is a lumpe, where all beasts kneaded bee,
  Wisdome makes him an Arke where all agree;
The foole, in whom these beasts do live at jarre,
   Is sport to others, and a Theater,

To the Countesse of Bedford.   52 and prophecie] all prophecye
several MSS.   58 both *1633 and MSS.:* worth *1635–69 and one
MS.*   60 thinge *most MSS.:* things *1633–69 and one MS.*   66
aliens *1633, 1669, and MSS.:* alters *1635–54 and one MS.*

Nor

Nor scapes hee so, but is himselfe their prey;   5
  All which was man in him, is eate away,
And now his beasts on one another feed,
  Yet couple'in anger, and new monsters breed.
How happy'is hee, which hath due place assign'd
  To'his beasts, and disaforested his minde!   10
Empail'd himselfe to keepe them out, not in;
  Can sow, and dares trust corne, where they have bin;
Can use his horse, goate, wolfe, and every beast,
  And is not Asse himselfe to all the rest.
Else, man not onely is the heard of swine,   15
  But he's those devills too, which did incline
Them to a headlong rage, and made them worse:
  For man can adde weight to heavens heaviest curse.
As Soules (they say) by our first touch, take in
  The poysonous tincture of Originall sinne,   20
So, to the punishments which God doth fling,
  Our apprehension contributes the sting.
To us, as to his chickins, he doth cast
  Hemlocke, and wee as men, his hemlocke taste;
We do infuse to what he meant for meat,   25
  Corrosivenesse, or intense cold or heat.
For, God no such specifique poyson hath
  As kills we know not how; his fiercest wrath
Hath no antipathy, but may be good
  At least for physicke, if not for our food.   30
Thus man, that might be'his pleasure, is his rod,
  And is his devill, that might be his God.
Since then our businesse is, to rectifie
  Nature, to what she was, wee'are led awry
By them, who man to us in little show;   35
  Greater then due, no forme we can bestow
On him ; for Man into himselfe can draw
  All; All his faith can swallow,'or reason chaw.

To Sr Edward &c.   28 we know *1633 and MSS.:* men know
1635–69 and one MS.

All

All that is fill'd, and all that which doth fill,
   All the round world, to man is but a pill,   40
In all it workes not, but it is in all
   Poysonous, or purgative, or cordiall,
For, knowledge kindles Calentures in some,
   And is to others icy *Opium.*
As brave as true, is that profession than   45
   Which you doe use to make; that you know man.
This makes it credible; you have dwelt upon
   All worthy bookes, and now are such an one.
Actions are authors, and of those in you
   Your friends finde every day a mart of new.   50

To the Countesse of Bedford.

T'Have written then, when you writ, seem'd to mee
   Worst of spirituall vices, Simony,
And not t'have written then, seemes little lesse
   Then worst of civill vices, thanklessenesse.
In this, my debt I seem'd loath to confesse,   5
   In that, I seem'd to shunne beholdingnesse.
But 'tis not soe; *nothings,* as I am, may
   Pay all they have, and yet have all to pay.
Such borrow in their payments, and owe more
   By having leave to write so, then before.   10
Yet since rich mines in barren grounds are showne,
   May not I yeeld (not gold) but coale or stone?
Temples were not demolish'd, though prophane:
   Here *Peter Joves,* there *Paul* hath *Dian's* Fane.
So whether my hymnes you admit or chuse,   15
   In me you'have hallowed a Pagan Muse,
And denizend a stranger, who mistaught
   By blamers of the times they mard, hath sought

To the *&c.*   5 debt *1669 and MSS.:* doubt *1633–54*   7
nothings, 1635–54: nothing, *1633 and MS.:* Nothing *1669*

Vertues

Vertues in corners, which now bravely doe
    Shine in the worlds best part, or all It; You.   20
I have beene told, that vertue in Courtiers hearts
    Suffers an Ostracisme, and departs.
Profit, ease, fitnesse, plenty, bid it goe,
    But whither, only knowing you, I know;
Your (or you) vertue two vast uses serves,   25
    It ransomes one sex, and one Court preserves.
There's nothing but your worth, which being true,
    Is knowne to any other, not to you:
And you can never know it; To admit
    No knowledge of your worth, is some of it.   30
But since to you, your praises discords bee,
    Stoop, others ills to meditate with mee.
Oh! to confesse wee know not what we should,
    Is halfe excuse; wee know not what we would:
Lightnesse depresseth us, emptinesse fills,   35
    We sweat and faint, yet still goe downe the hills.
As new Philosophy arrests the Sunne,
    And bids the passive earth about it runne,
So wee have dull'd our minde, it hath no ends;
    Onely the bodie's busie, and pretends;   40
As dead low earth ecclipses and controules
    The quick high Moone: so doth the body, Soules.
In none but us, are such mixt engines found,
    As hands of double office: For, the ground
We till with them; and them to heav'n wee raise;   45
    Who prayer-lesse labours, or, without this, prayes,
Doth but one halfe, that's none; He which said, *Plough*
    And looke not back, to looke up doth allow.
Good seed degenerates, and oft obeyes
    The soyles disease, and into cockle strayes;   50
Let the minds thoughts be but transplanted so,
    Into the body,'and bastardly they grow.

20 or all It; You.] or all, in you. *1633*   25 Your (or you)
vertue *one MS.:* Your, or you vertue, *1633-54:* You, or you vertue *1669*
                                                  What

What hate could hurt our bodies like our love?
    Wee (but no forraine tyrants could) remove
These not ingrav'd, but inborne dignities,   55
    Caskets of soules; Temples, and Palaces:
For, bodies shall from death redeemed bee,
    Soules but preserv'd, not naturally free.
As men to'our prisons, new soules to us are sent,
    Which learne vice there, and come in innocent.   60
First seeds of every creature are in us,
    What ere the world hath bad, or pretious,
Mans body can produce, hence hath it beene
    That stones, wormes, frogges, and snakes in man are
        seene:
But who ere saw, though nature can worke soe,   65
    That pearle, or gold, or corne in man did grow?
We'have added to the world Virginia,'and sent
    Two new starres lately to the firmament;
Why grudge wee us (not heaven) the dignity
    T'increase with ours, those faire soules company.   70
But I must end this letter, though it doe
    Stand on two truths, neither is true to you.
Vertue hath some perversenesse; For she will
    Neither beleeve her good, nor others ill.
Even in you, vertues best paradise,   75
    Vertue hath some, but wise degrees of vice.
Too many vertues, or too much of one
    Begets in you unjust suspition;
And ignorance of vice, makes vertue lesse,
    Quenching compassion of our wrechednesse.   80

54 Wee (but no forraine tyrants could) remove *Ed:* Wee but no
forraine tyrants could, remove *one MS.:* Wee but no forraigne tyrants
could remove, *1633–54* (tyrans *1633*): We, but no forrain tyrants,
could remove *1669 and modern edd.*   58 not naturally free. *Ed:*
not naturally free; *1633 and one MS. group:* borne naturally free;
1635–69 and one MS.   59 prisons, new soules *1633:* prisons now,
soules *1635–69:* prisons, now soules *one MS.*   60 vice *1635–69:*
it *1633*

But

But these are riddles; Some aspersion
    Of vice becomes well some complexion.
Statesmen purge vice with vice, and may corrode
    The bad with bad, a spider with a toad:
For so, ill thralls not them, but they tame ill   85
    And make her do much good against her will,
But in your Commonwealth, or world in you,
    Vice hath no office, or good worke to doe.
Take then no vitious purge, but be content
    With cordiall vertue, your knowne nourishment.   90

To the Countesse of Bedford.

On New-yeares day.

THis twilight of two yeares, not past nor next,
    Some embleme is of mee, or I of this,
Who Meteor-like, of stuffe and forme perplext,
    Whose *what*, and *where*, in disputation is,
    If I should call mee *any thing*, should misse.   5

I summe the yeares, and mee, and finde mee not
    Debtor to th'old, nor Creditor to th'new,
That cannot say, My thankes I have forgot,
    Nor trust I this with hopes, and yet scarce true
    This bravery is, since these times shew'd mee you.   10

In recompence I would show future times
    What you were, and teach them to'urge towards such.
Verse embalmes vertue;'and Tombs, or Thrones of rimes,
    Preserve fraile transitory fame, as much
    As spice doth bodies from corrupt aires touch.   15

Mine are short-liv'd; the tincture of your name
    Creates in them, but dissipates as fast,
New spirits: for, strong agents with the same
    Force that doth warme and cherish, us doe wast;
    Kept hot with strong extracts, no bodies last: 20

        So,

So, my verse built of your just praise, might want
   Reason and likelihood, the firmest Base,
And made of miracle, now faith is scant,
   Will vanish soone, and so possesse no place,
   And you, and it, too much grace might disgrace.   25

When all (as truth commands assent) confesse
   All truth of you, yet they will doubt how I,
One corne of one low anthills dust, and lesse,
   Should name, know, or expresse a thing so high,
   And not an inch, measure infinity.   30

I cannot tell them, nor my selfe, nor you,
   But leave, lest truth b'endanger'd by my praise,
And turne to God, who knowes I thinke this true,
   And useth oft, when such a heart mis-sayes,
   To make it good, for, such a praiser prayes.   35

Hee will best teach you, how you should lay out
   His stock of *beauty, learning, favour, blood*;
He will perplex security with doubt,
   And cleare those doubts; hide from you,'and shew you
      good,
   And so increase your appetite and food;   40

Hee will teach you, that good and bad have not
   One latitude in cloysters, and in Court;
Indifferent there the greatest space hath got;
   Some pitty'is not good there, some vaine disport,
   On this side sinne, with that place may comport.   45

Yet he, as hee bounds seas, will fixe your houres,
   Which pleasure, and delight may not ingresse,
And though what none else lost, be truliest yours,
   Hee will make you, what you did not, possesse,
   By using others, not vice, but weakenesse.   50

   To the *&c.*   35 praiser prayes. *1635–69 and one MS.:* prayer
prayes. *1633:* prayer praise. *another MS.*

                                      He

He will make you speake truths, and credibly,
    And make you doubt, that others doe not so:
Hee will provide you keyes, and locks, to spie,
    And scape spies, to good ends, and hee will show
    What you may not acknowledge, what not know.   55

For your owne conscience, he gives innocence,
    But for your fame, a discreet warinesse,
And though to scape, then to revenge offence
    Be better, he showes both, and to represse
    Joy, when your state swells, *sadnesse* when'tis lesse.   60

From need of teares he will defend your soule,
    Or make a rebaptizing of one teare;
Hee cannot, (that's, he will not) dis-inroule
    Your name; and when with active joy we heare
    This private Ghospell, then'tis our New Yeare.   65

To the Countesse of Huntingdon.

MADAME,

MAn to Gods image; *Eve,* to mans was made,
    Nor finde wee that God breath'd a soule in her.
Canons will not Church functions you invade,
    Nor lawes to civill office you preferre.

Who vagrant transitory Comets sees,   5
    Wonders, because they'are rare; But a new starre
Whose motion with the firmament agrees,
    Is miracle; for, there no new things are;

In woman so perchance milde innocence
    A seldome comet is, but active good   10
A miracle, which reason scapes, and sense;
    For, Art and Nature this in them withstood.

As such a starre, the *Magi* led to view
    The manger-cradled infant, God below:

To the &c.   13 *Magi*] Magis *some MSS.: compare p.* 219 First
Anniversary, *l.* 390

                                             By

By vertues beames by fame deriv'd from you,   15
  May apt soules, and the worst may, vertue know.

If the worlds age, and death be argued well   '
  By the Sunnes fall, which now towards earth doth bend,
Then we might feare that vertue, since she fell
  So low as woman, should be neare her end.   20

But she's not stoop'd, but rais'd; exil'd by men
  She fled to heaven, that's heavenly things, that's you;
She was in all men, thinly scatter'd then,
  But now amass'd, contracted in a few.

She guilded us: But you are gold, and Shee;   25
  Us she inform'd, but transubstantiates you;
Soft dispositions which ductile bee,
  Elixarlike, she makes not cleane, but new.

Though you a wifes and mothers name retaine,
  'Tis not as woman, for all are not soe,   30
But vertue having made you vertue,'is faine
  T'adhere in these names, her and you to show,

Else, being alike pure, wee should neither see;
  As, water being into ayre rarify'd,
Neither appeare, till in one cloud they bee,   35
  So, for our sakes you do low names abide;

Taught by great constellations, which being fram'd,
  Of the most starres, take low names, *Crab*, and *Bull*,
When single planets by the *Gods* are nam'd,
  You covet not great names, of great things full.   40

So you, as woman, one doth comprehend,
  And in the vaile of kindred others see;
To some ye are reveal'd, as in a friend,
  And as a vertuous Prince farre off, to mee.

25–6 But you are gold, and Shee; . . . transubstantiates you; *Ed:*
But you are gold, and Shee, . . . transubstantiates you, *1633:*
    but you are gold; and she,
  Informed us, but transubstantiates you, *1635–69*

To

To whom, because from you all vertues flow,   45
   And 'tis not none, to dare contemplate you,
I, which doe so, as your true subject owe
   Some tribute for that, so these lines are due.

If you can thinke these flatteries, they are,
   For then your judgement is below my praise,   50
If they were so, oft, flatteries worke as farre,
   As Counsels, and as farre th'endeavour raise.

So my ill reaching you might there grow good,
   But I remaine a poyson'd fountaine still;
But not your beauty, vertue, knowledge, blood   55
   Are more above all flattery, then my will.

And if I flatter any,'tis not you
   But my owne judgement, who did long agoe
Pronounce, that all these praises should be true,
   And vertue should your beauty,'and birth outgrow. 60

Now that my prophesies are all fulfill'd,
   Rather then God should not be honour'd too,
And all these gifts confess'd, which hee instill'd,
   Your selfe were bound to say that which I doe.

So I, but your Recorder am in this,   65
   Or mouth, or Speaker of the universe,
A ministeriall Notary, for 'tis
   Not I, but you and fame, that make this verse;

I was your Prophet in your yonger dayes,
And now your Chaplaine, God in you to praise.   70

47 doe so, *1635–69 and one MS.:* doe *another MS.:* to you *1633*

To Mᵣ *T. W*.

ALl haile sweet Poët, more full of more strong fire,
  Then hath or shall enkindle any spirit,
   I lov'd what nature gave thee, but this merit
Of wit and Art I love not but admire;
Who have before or shall write after thee,   5
Their workes, though toughly laboured, will bee
   Like infancie or age to mans firme stay,
   Or earely and late twilights to mid-day.

Men say, and truly, that they better be
   Which be envyed then pittied: therefore I,   10
   Because I wish thee best, doe thee envie:
O wouldst thou, by like reason, pitty mee!
But care not for mee: I, that ever was
In Natures, and in Fortunes gifts, (alas,
   Before thy grace got in the Muses Schoole)   15
   A monster and a begger, am now a foole.

Oh how I grieve, that late borne modesty
   Hath got such root in easie waxen hearts,
   That men may not themselves, their owne good parts
Extoll, without suspect of surquedrie,   20

To Mᵣ *T. W. some good MSS.:* To M. *I. W. 1633–69 and one MS.*
group   2 any spirit, *1633 and most MSS.:* my dull spirit, *1635–69*
and some MSS.   3 this merit *1633 and most MSS.:* thy merit
1635–69 and some MSS.   12 mee! *Ed:* mee. *one MS.:* mee, *1633–69*
13 mee: *Ed:* mee, *1633–69*   ever was] never was *some MSS.*
14–16 In Natures, and in fortunes gifts, (alas,
     Before thy grace got in the Muses Schoole)
     A monster and a begger, *1633 (some copies: others read* 15
Before by thy grace *&c.) and most MSS.:*
     In Natures, and in fortunes gifts, alas,
     (But for thy grace got in the Muses Schoole)
     A Monster and a beggar, *1635–69*
16 am now a foole. *most MSS.:* am a foole. *1633–69 and some MSS.*

                                  For

For, but thy selfe, no subject can be found
Worthy thy quill, nor any quill resound
  Thy worth but thine: how good it were to see
  A Poëm in thy praise, and writ by thee.

Now if this song be too'harsh for rime, yet, as   25
  The Painters bad god made a good devill,
   'Twill be good prose, although the verse be evill,
If thou forget the rime as thou dost passe.
Then write, that I may follow, and so bee
Thy debter, thy'eccho, thy foyle, thy zanee.   30
  I shall be thought, if mine like thine I shape,
  All the worlds Lyon, though I be thy Ape.

To Mr *T. W.*

HAst thee harsh verse, as fast as thy lame measure
Will give thee leave, to him, my pain and pleasure.
I have given thee, and yet thou art too weake,
  Feete, and a reasoning soule and tongue to speake.
Plead for me, and so by thine and my labour   5
  I am thy Creator, thou my Saviour.
Tell him, all questions, which men have defended
  Both of the place and paines of hell, are ended;
And 'tis decreed our hell is but privation
  Of him, at least in this earths habitation: 10
And 'tis where I am, where in every street
  Infections follow, overtake, and meete:
Live I or die, by you my love is sent,
  And you'are my pawnes, or else my Testament.

23 worth *1669 and most MSS.:* worke *1633–54 and some MSS.* 27
evill, *one MS.:* evill. *1633–69* 28 passe. *one MS.:* passe, *1633–*
69 29 that I *1669 and most MSS.:* then I *1633–54 and one MS.*
  To Mr *T. W.* 5–6 *These lines only in one MS.* 9 our] *that*
one MS.

To

To Mr *T. W.*

PRegnant again with th'old twins Hope, and Feare,
　Oft have I askt for thee, both how and where
Thou wert, and what my hopes of letters were;

As in our streets sly beggers narrowly
Watch motions of the givers hand and eye,　　　　5
And evermore conceive some hope thereby.

And now thy Almes is given, thy letter'is read,
The body risen againe, the which was dead,
And thy poore starveling bountifully fed.

After this banquet my Soule doth say grace,　　　10
And praise thee for'it, and zealously imbrace
Thy love; though I thinke thy love in this case
　To be as gluttons, which say 'midst their meat,
　They love that best of which they most do eat.

To Mr *T. W.*

AT once, from hence, my lines and I depart,
　I to my soft still walks, they to my Heart;
I to the Nurse, they to the child of Art;

Yet as a firme house, though the Carpenter
Perish, doth stand: As an Embassadour　　　　5
Lyes safe, how e'r his king be in danger:

So, though I languish, prest with Melancholy,
My verse, the strict Map of my misery,
Shall live to see that, for whose want I dye.

To Mr *T. W.*　　5 Watch] Marke *one MS.* and eye, *MSS.:* or
eye, *1633–69*
　　To Mr *T. W. one MS: no heading, and following the preceding with-*
out any interval, 1633 and one MS. group: Incerto. *1635–69*

Therefore

Therefore I envie them, and doe repent,   10
That from unhappy mee, things happy'are sent;
Yet as a Picture, or bare Sacrament,
    Accept these lines, and if in them there be
    Merit of love, bestow that love on mee.

To Mr *R. W.*

Z Ealously my Muse doth salute all thee,
  Enquiring of that mistique trinitee
Whereof thou,'and all to whom heavens do infuse
Like fyer, are made; thy body, mind, and Muse.
Dost thou recover sicknes, or prevent?   5
Or is thy Mind travail'd with discontent?
Or art thou parted from the world and mee,
In a good skorn of the worlds vanitee?
Or is thy devout Muse retyr'd to sing
Vpon her tender Elegiaque string?   10
Our Minds part not, joyne then thy Muse with myne,
For myne is barren thus devorc'd from thyne.

To Mr *R. W.*

M Vse not that by thy mind thy body is led:
  For by thy mind, my mind's distempered.
So thy Care lives long, for I bearing part
It eates not only thyne, but my swolne heart.
And when it gives us intermission   5
We take new harts for it to feede upon.
But as a Lay Mans Genius doth controule
Body and mind; the Muse beeing the Soules Soule
Of Poets, that methinks should ease our anguish,
Although our bodyes wither and minds languish.   10
Write then, that my griefes which thine got may bee
Cur'd by thy charming soveraigne melodee.

   To Mr *R. W. two MSS.: first printed in Gosse's* Life and Letters of
John Donne, *&c.,* 1899   1 thee,] thee *one MS.*
   To Mr *R. W. two MSS.: printed* 1912 *for the first time*

To

To Mr C. B.

THy friend, whom thy deserts to thee enchaine,
    Urg'd by this unexcusable occasion,
  Thee and the Saint of his affection
Leaving behinde, doth of both wants complaine;
And let the love I beare to both sustaine   5
    No blott nor maime by this division,
  Strong is this love which ties our hearts in one,
And strong that love pursu'd with amorous paine;
But though besides thy selfe I leave behind
    Heavens liberall, and earths thrice-fairer Sunne,   10
  Going to where sterne winter aye doth wonne,
Yet, loves hot fires, which martyr my sad minde,
    Doe send forth scalding sighes, which have the Art
  To melt all Ice, but that which walls her heart.

To Mr E. G.

EVen as lame things thirst their perfection, so
    The slimy rimes bred in our vale below,
Bearing with them much of my love and hart,
Fly unto that Parnassus, where thou art.
There thou oreseest London: Here I have beene,   5
By staying in London, too much overseene.
Now pleasures dearth our City doth posses,
Our Theaters are fill'd with emptines;
As lancke and thin is every street and way
As a woman deliver'd yesterday.   10
Nothing whereat to laugh my spleen espyes
But bearbaitings or Law exercise.
Therefore I'le leave it, and in the Country strive
Pleasure, now fled from London, to retrive.

  To Mr C. B.   10 earths *1633, 1669, and MSS.:* the *1635-54*
thrice fairer *one MS.:* thrice-faire *1633-69 and one MS. group*   11
sterne *1633 and most MSS.:* sterv'd *1635-69 and one MS.*

Do thou so too: and fill not like a Bee   15
Thy thighs with hony, but as plenteously
As Russian Marchants, thy selfes whole vessell load,
And then at Winter retaile it here abroad.
Blesse us with Suffolks sweets; and as it is
Thy garden, make thy hive and warehouse this.   20

To Mr *R. W.*

IF, as mine is, thy life a slumber be,
    Seeme, when thou read'st these lines, to dreame of me,
Never did Morpheus nor his brother weare
    Shapes soe like those Shapes, whom they would appeare,
As this my letter is like me, for it   5
    Hath my name, words, hand, feet, heart, minde and wit;
It is my deed of gift of mee to thee,
    It is my Will, my selfe the Legacie.
So thy retyrings I love, yea envie,
    Bred in thee by a wise melancholy,   10
That I rejoyce, that unto where thou art,
    Though I stay here, I can thus send my heart,
As kindly'as any enamored Patient
    His Picture to his absent Love hath sent.

All newes I thinke sooner reach thee then mee;   15
    Havens are Heavens, and Ships wing'd Angels be,
The which both Gospell, and sterne threatnings bring;
    Guyanaes harvest is nip'd in the spring,
I feare; And with us (me thinkes) Fate deales so
    As with the Jewes guide God did; he did show   20
Him the rich land, but bar'd his entry in:
    Oh, slownes is our punishment and sinne.
Perchance, these Spanish businesse being done,
    Which as the Earth betweene the Moone and Sun

To Mr *R. W.*   3 brother *1633–69 and two MS. groups:*
brethren *one MS.*   22 Oh, *MSS.:* Our *1633–69*   23 businesse
1633 and one MS. group: busnesses *one MS.:* businesses *1635–69*

Eclipse

Eclipse the light which Guyana would give,   25
  Our discontinued hopes we shall retrive:
But if (as all th'All must) hopes smoake away,
  Is not Almightie Vertue'an India?

If men be worlds, there is in every one
  Some thing to answere in some proportion   30
All the worlds riches: And in good men, this,
  Vertue, our formes forme and our soules soule, is.

To Mr *R. W.*

K Indly I envy thy songs perfection
  Built of all th'elements as our bodyes are:
  That Litle of earth that is in it, is a faire
Delicious garden where all sweetes are sowne.
In it is cherishing fyer which dryes in mee   5
  Griefe which did drowne me: and halfe quench'd by it
  Are satirique fyres which urg'd me to have writt
In skorne of all: for now I admyre thee.
  And as Ayre doth fullfill the hollownes
  Of rotten walls; so it myne emptines,   10
Where tost and mov'd it did beget this sound
Which as a lame Eccho of thyne doth rebound.
  Oh, I was dead; but since thy song new Life did give,
  I recreated, even by thy creature, live.

To Mr *S. B.*

O Thou which to search out the secret parts
  Of the India, or rather Paradise
  Of knowledge, hast with courage and advise
Lately launch'd into the vast Sea of Arts,
Disdaine not in thy constant travailing   5
  To doe as other Voyagers, and make
  Some turnes into lesse Creekes, and wisely take

To Mr *R. W. one MS.: published* 1912 *for the first time*

Fresh

Fresh water at the Heliconian spring;
I sing not, Siren like, to tempt; for I
   Am harsh; nor as those Scismatiques with you,   10
   Which draw all wits of good hope to their crew;
But seeing in you bright sparkes of Poetry,
   I, though I brought no fuell, had desire
   With these Articulate blasts to blow the fire.

To Mr *I. L.*

OF that short Roll of friends writ in my heart
   Which with thy name begins, since their depart,
Whether in the English Provinces they be,
   Or drinke of Po, Sequan, or Danubie,
There's none that sometimes greets us not, and yet   5
   Your Trent is Lethe; that past, us you forget.
You doe not duties of Societies,
   If from the'embrace of a lov'd wife you rise,
View your fat Beasts, stretch'd Barnes, and labour'd fields,
   Eate, play, ryde, take all joyes which all day yeelds,   10
And then againe to your embracements goe:
   Some houres on us your frends, and some bestow
Upon your Muse, else both wee shall repent,
   I that my love, she that her guifts on you are spent.

To Mr *B. B.*

IS not thy sacred hunger of science
   Yet satisfy'd? Is not thy braines rich hive
Fulfil'd with hony which thou dost derive
   From the Arts spirits and their Quintessence?
Then weane thy selfe at last, and thee withdraw   5
   From Cambridge thy old nurse, and, as the rest,
   Here toughly chew, and sturdily digest
Th'immense vast volumes of our common law;

To Mr *I. L.*   13 your] thy *one MS.*   14 you] thee *one MS.*

                                      And

And begin soone, lest my griefe grieve thee too,
　　Which is, that that which I should have begun　　10
　　In my youthes morning, now late must be done;
And I as Giddy Travellers must doe,
　　Which stray or sleepe all day, and having lost
　　Light and strength, darke and tir'd must then ride post.

If thou unto thy Muse be marryed,　　　　　　　　15
　　Embrace her ever, ever multiply,
　　Be far from me that strange Adulterie
To tempt thee and procure her widowhed.
My Muse, (for I had one,) because I'am cold,
　　Divorc'd her selfe: the cause being in me,　　20
　　That I can take no new in Bigamye,
Not my will only but power doth withhold.
Hence comes it, that these Rymes which never had
　　Mother, want matter, and they only have
　　A little forme, the which their Father gave;　　25
They are prophane, imperfect, oh, too bad
　　To be counted Children of Poetry
　　Except confirm'd and Bishoped by thee.

To Mr *I. L.*

B Lest are your North parts, for all this long time
　　My Sun is with you, cold and darke'is our Clime;
Heavens Sun, which staid so long from us this yeare,
　　Staid in your North (I thinke) for she was there,
And hether by kinde nature drawne from thence,　　5
　　Here rages, chafes, and threatens pestilence;
Yet I, as long as shee from hence doth staie,
　　Thinke this no South, no Sommer, nor no day.

To Mr *B. B.*　　13 stray] stay *one MS.: compare* Sat. III. 78　　16
ever, ever multiply, *1633–69 and most MSS.:* still: encrease and
multiply; *one MS.*　　18 widowhed. *one MS.:* widdowhood, *1633-
39:* widdowhood; *1650–69*　　19 Muse, *MSS.:* nurse, *1633–69*
　　To Mr *I. L.*　　6 chafes,] burnes, *one MS.*

With

With thee my kinde and unkinde heart is run,
   There sacrifice it to that beauteous Sun: 10
And since thou art in Paradise and need'st crave
   No joyes addition, helpe thy friend to save.
So may thy pastures with their flowery feasts,
   As suddenly as Lard, fat thy leane beasts;
So may thy woods oft poll'd, yet ever weare   15
   A greene, and when thee list, a golden haire;
So may all thy sheepe bring forth Twins; and so
   In chace and race may thy horse all out goe;
So may thy love and courage ne'r be cold;
   Thy Sonne ne'r Ward; Thy lov'd wife ne'r seem old;
But maist thou wish great things, and them attaine,   21
   As thou telst her, and none but her, my paine.

To Sir *H. W.* at his going Ambassador to *Venice.*

AFter those reverend papers, whose soule is
   Our good and great Kings lov'd hand and fear'd name,
By which to you he derives much of his,
   And (how he may) makes you almost the same,

A Taper of his Torch, a copie writ   5
   From his Originall, and a faire beame
Of the same warme, and dazeling Sun, though it
   Must in another Sphere his vertue streame:

After those learned papers which your hand
   Hath stor'd with notes of use and pleasure too,   10
From which rich treasury you may command
   Fit matter whether you will write or doe:

11–12 *these lines from one MS.: they are not in old edd.*   16 when
thee list *1633 and one MS. group:* (when she list) *1635–69:* when thou
wilt *one MS.*   20 lov'd wife] fair wife *one MS.*

   To Sir *H. W.* at his *&c. 1633–54:* To Sir Henry Wotton, at his *&c.*
1669 and MSS.: printed in Walton's Life of Sir Henry Wotton, *1670,*
as a 'letter, sent by him to Sir *Henry Wotton,* the morning before he left
England', *i.e. July 13 (O. S.), 1604*   10 pleasure *1635–69, MSS.*
and Walton: pleasures *1633*

After

After those loving papers, where friends send
    With glad griefe, to your Sea-ward steps, farewel,
Which thicken on you now, as prayers ascend   15
    To heaven in troupes at'a good mans passing bell:

Admit this honest paper, and allow
    It such an audience as your selfe would aske;
What you must say at *Venice* this meanes now,
    And hath for nature, what you have for taske: 20

To sweare much love, not to be chang'd before
    Honour alone will to your fortune fit;
Nor shall I then honour your fortune, more
    Then I have done your honour wanting it.

But 'tis an easier load (though both oppresse)   25
    To want, then governe greatnesse, for wee are
In that, our owne and onely businesse,
    In this, wee must for others vices care;

'Tis therefore well your spirits now are plac'd
    In their last Furnace, in activity;   30
Which fits them (Schooles and Courts and Warres o'rpast)
    To touch and test in any best degree.

For mee, (if there be such a thing as I)
    Fortune (if there be such a thing as shee)
Spies that I beare so well her tyranny,   35
    That she thinks nothing else so fit for mee;

But though she part us, to heare my oft prayers
    For your increase, God is as neere mee here;
And to send you what I shall begge, his staires
    In length and ease are alike every where.   40

---

13 where *1633:* which *1635–69 and Walton*   19 must ... meanes]
would . . . sayes *Walton*   24 honour wanting it. *1633:* noble-
wanting-wit. *1635–69 and one MS.:* honour-wanting-wit. *Walton:*
noble wanting it. *one MS. group*   31 warres *1633–69:* tents *one MS.*
32 test] tast *1669 and Walton*   35 Spies] Finds *Walton*

To

To Mrs *M. H.*

MAd paper stay, and grudge not here to burne
　With all those sonnes whom my braine did create,
At lest lye hid with mee, till thou returne
　To rags againe, which is thy native state.

What though thou have enough unworthinesse　　　5
　To come unto great place as others doe,
That's much; emboldens, pulls, thrusts I confesse,
　But 'tis not all; Thou should'st be wicked too.

And, that thou canst not learne, or not of mee;
　Yet thou wilt goe? Goe, since thou goest to her　10
Who lacks but faults to be a Prince, for shee,
　Truth, whom they dare not pardon, dares preferre.

But when thou com'st to that perplexing eye
　Which equally claimes *love* and *reverence,*
Thou wilt not long dispute it, thou wilt die;　　　15
　And, having little now, have then no sense.

Yet when her warme redeeming hand, which is
　A miracle; and made such to worke more,
Doth touch thee (saples leafe) thou grow'st by this
　Her creature; glorify'd more then before.　　　20

Then as a mother which delights to heare
　Her early child mis-speake halfe uttered words,
Or, because majesty doth never feare
　Ill or bold speech, she Audience affords.

And then, cold speechlesse wretch, thou diest againe,　25
　And wisely; what discourse is left for thee?
For, speech of ill, and her, thou must abstaine,
　And is there any good which is not shee?

To Mrs *M. H.*　　2 sonnes] Sunnes *some MSS.*　　27 For, *1633:*
From *1635–69 and MSS.*

Yet

Yet maist thou praise her servants, though not her,
  And wit, and vertue,'and honour her attend,   30
And since they'are but her cloathes, thou shalt not erre,
  If thou her shape and beauty'and grace commend.

Who knowes thy destiny? when thou hast done,
  Perchance her Cabinet may harbour thee,
Whither all noble ambitious wits doe runne,   35
  A nest almost as full of Good as shee.

When thou art there, if any, whom wee know,
  Were sav'd before, and did that heaven partake,
When she revolves his papers, marke what show
  Of favour, she alone, to them doth make.   40

Marke, if to get them, she o'r skip the rest,
  Marke, if shee read them twice, or kisse the name;
Marke, if she doe the same that they protest,
  Marke, if she marke whether her woman came.

Marke, if slight things be'objected, and o'r blowne,   45
  Marke, if her oathes against him be not still
Reserv'd, and that shee grieves she's not her owne,
  And chides the doctrine that denies Freewill.

I bid thee not doe this to be my spie;
  Nor to make my selfe her familiar;   50
But so much I doe love her choyce, that I
  Would faine love him that shall be lov'd of her.

To the Countesse of Bedford.

HOnour is so sublime perfection,
  And so refinde; that when God was alone
And creaturelesse at first, himselfe had none;

But as of the elements, these which wee tread,
Produce all things with which wee'are joy'd or fed,   5
And, those are barren both above our head:

40 she alone, *1633:* she, alone, *1635–69*

So

So from low persons doth all honour flow;
Kings, whom they would have honoured, to us show,
And but *direct* our honour, not *bestow*.

For when from herbs the pure part must be wonne   10
From grosse, by Stilling, this is better done
By despis'd dung, then by the fire or Sunne.

Care not then, Madame,'how low your praysers lye;
In labourers balads oft more piety
God findes, then in *Te Deums* melodie.   15

And, ordinance rais'd on Towers, so many mile
Send not their voice, nor last so long a while
As fires from th'earths low vaults in *Sicil* Isle.

Should I say I liv'd darker then were true,
Your radiation can all clouds subdue;   20
But one,'tis best light to contemplate you.

You, for whose body God made better clay,
Or tooke Soules stuffe such as shall late decay,
Or such as needs small change at the last day.

This, as an Amber drop enwraps a Bee,   25
Covering discovers your quicke Soule; that we
May in your through-shine front your hearts thoughts see.

You teach (though wee learne not) a thing unknowne
To our late times, the use of specular stone,
Through which all things within without were shown. 30

Of such were Temples; so and of such you are;
Beeing and *seeming* is your equall care,
And *vertues* whole *summe* is but *know* and *dare*.

But as our Soules of growth and Soules of sense
Have birthright of our reasons Soule, yet hence   35
They fly not from that, nor seeke presidence:

To the Countesse of Bedford.   12 or Sunne] of Sunne *1635–54*
13 praysers *MSS. :* prayses *1633–69*   27 your hearts thoughts *MSS. :*
our hearts thoughts *1633–69*   31 so and of such *one MS. group:* so and
such *1633–69 and some MSS.*   33 is but to know and dare. *one MS.*

Natures

Natures first lesson, so, discretion,
Must not grudge zeale a place, nor yet keepe none,
Not banish it selfe, nor religion.

Discretion is a wisemans Soule, and so   40
Religion is a Christians, and you know
How these are one; her *yea*, is not her *no*.

Nor may we hope to sodder still and knit
These two, and dare to breake them; nor must wit
Be colleague to religion, but be it.   45

In those poor types of God (round circles) so
Religions tipes, the peecelesse centers flow,
And are in all the lines which all wayes goe.

If either ever wrought in you alone
Or principally, then religion   50
Wrought your ends, and your wayes discretion.

Goe thither still, goe the same way you went,
Who so would change, do covet or repent;
Neither can reach you, great and innocent.

To the Countesse of Huntington.

THat unripe side of earth, that heavy clime
    That gives us man up now, like *Adams* time
Before he ate; mans shape, that would yet bee
(Knew they not it, and fear'd beasts companie)
So naked at this day, as though man there   5
From Paradise so great a distance were,
As yet the newes could not arrived bee
Of *Adams* tasting the forbidden tree;
Depriv'd of that free state which they were in,
And wanting the reward, yet beare the sinne.   10
  But, as from extreme hights who downward looks,

40–2] *These lines precede* 34–9 *in* 1635–69 *and some MSS.*
48 alwayes *1633–69*

Sees

Sees men at childrens shapes, Rivers at brookes,
And loseth younger formes; so, to your eye,
These (Madame) that without your distance lie,
Must either mist, or nothing seeme to be,   15
Who are at home but wits mere *Atomi.*
But, I who can behold them move, and stay,
Have found my selfe to you, just their midway;
And now must pitty them; for, as they doe
Seeme sick to me, just so must I to you.   20
Yet neither will I vexe your eyes to see
A sighing Ode, nor crosse-arm'd Elegie.
I come not to call pitty from your heart,
Like some white-liver'd dotard that would part
Else from his slipperie soule with a faint groane,   25
And faithfully, (without you smil'd) were gone.
I cannot feele the tempest of a frowne,
I may be rais'd by love, but not throwne down.
Though I can pittie those sigh twice a day,
I hate that thing whispers it selfe away.   30
Yet since all love is fever, who to trees
Doth talke, doth yet in loves cold ague freeze.
'Tis love, but, with such fatall weaknesse made,
That it destroyes it selfe with its owne shade.
Who first look'd sad, griev'd, pin'd, and shew'd his paine, 35
Was he that first taught women, to disdaine.
  As all things were one nothing, dull and weake,
Vntill this raw disordered heape did breake,
And severall desires led parts away,
Water declin'd with earth, the ayre did stay,   40
Fire rose, and each from other but unty'd,
Themselves unprison'd were and purify'd:
So was love, first in vast confusion hid,
An unripe willingnesse which nothing did,

  To the Countesse of Huntington.   26 faithfully, *1635–69:*
finally *MSS.*   you smil'd *1635–54:* your smile *1669, MSS.*   30
whispers] vapours *one MS.*   31 fever] *feverish 1669*

                                        A thirst,

A thirst, an Appetite which had no ease,   45
That found a want, but knew not what would please.
What pretty innocence in those dayes mov'd?
Man ignorantly walk'd by her he lov'd;
Both sigh'd and enterchang'd a speaking eye,
Both trembled and were sick, both knew not why.   50
That naturall fearefulnesse that struck man dumbe,
Might well (those times consider'd) man become.
As all discoverers whose first assay
Findes but the place, after, the nearest way:
So passion is to womans love, about,   55
Nay, farther off, than when we first set out.
It is not love that sueth, or doth contend;
Love either conquers, or but meets a friend.
Man's better part consists of purer fire,
And findes it selfe allow'd, ere it desire.   60
Love is wise here, keepes home, gives reason sway,
And journeys not till it finde summer-way.
A weather-beaten Lover but once knowne,
Is sport for every girle to practise on.
Who strives through womans scornes, women to know,   65
Is lost, and seekes his shadow to outgoe;
It must bee sicknesse, after one disdaine,
Though he be call'd aloud, to looke againe.
Let others sigh, and grieve; one cunning sleight
Shall freeze my Love to Christall in a night.   70
I can love first, and (if I winne) love still;
And cannot be remov'd, unlesse she will.
It is her fault if I unsure remaine,
Shee onely can untie, and binde againe.
The honesties of love with ease I doe,   75
But am no porter for a tedious woo.
   But (madame) I now thinke on you; and here
Where we are at our hights, you but appeare,

50 both knew *1635–54:* but knew *MSS.:* yet, knew *1669*   67 It
must be] It is meer *1669*   74 and *one MS.:* I *1635–69, other MS.*

We

We are but clouds you rise from, our noone-ray
But a foule shadow, not your breake of day.   80
You are at first hand all that's faire and right,
And others good reflects but backe your light.
You are a perfectnesse, so curious hit,
That youngest flatteries doe scandall it.
For, what is more doth what you are restraine,   85
And though beyond, is downe the hill againe.
We'have no next way to you, we crosse to it:
You are the straight line, thing prais'd, attribute;
Each good in you's a light; so many a shade
You make, and in them are your motions made.   90
These are your pictures to the life. From farre
We see you move, and here your *Zani's* are:
So that no fountaine good there is, doth grow
In you, but our dimme actions faintly shew.

Then finde I, if mans noblest part be love,   95
Your purest luster must that shadow move.
The soule with body, is a heaven combin'd
With earth, and for mans ease, but nearer joyn'd.
Where thoughts the starres of soule we understand,
We guesse not their large natures, but command.   100
And love in you, that bountie is of light,
That gives to all, and yet hath infinite.
Whose heat doth force us thither to intend,
But soule we finde too earthly to ascend,
'Till slow accesse hath made it wholy pure,   105
Able immortall clearnesse to endure.
Who dare aspire this journey with a staine,
Hath waight will force him headlong backe againe.
No more can impure man retaine and move
In that pure region of a worthy love: 110

81 right] bright *one MS.* 84 youngest] quaintest *one MS.* flat-
teries] flatterers *MSS.*   86 though] what's *one MS.*   99 thoughts]
through *one MS.*   108 waight] weights *MSS.*   109 impure]
vapore *one MS.*

Then

Then earthly substance can unforc'd aspire,
And leave his nature to converse with fire:
Such may have eye, and hand; may sigh, may speak;
But like swoln bubles, when they are high'st they break.
   Though far removed Northerne fleets scarce finde 115
The Sunnes comfort; others thinke him too kinde.
There is an equall distance from her eye,
Men perish too farre off, and burne too nigh.
But as ayre takes the Sunne-beames equall bright
From the first Rayes, to his last opposite: 120
So able men, blest with a vertuous Love,
Remote or neare, or howsoe'r they move;
Their vertue breakes all clouds that might annoy,
There is no Emptinesse, but all is Ioy.
He much profanes whom violent heats do move 125
To stile his wandring rage of passion, *Love*:
Love that imparts in every thing delight,
Is fain'd, which only tempts mans appetite.
Why love among the vertues is not knowne
Is, that love is them all contract in one. 130

To the Countesse of Bedford.
Begun in France but never perfected.

THough I be *dead*, and buried, yet I have
   (Living in you,) Court enough in my grave,
As oft as there I thinke my selfe to bee,
   So many resurrections waken mee.

114 when they're highest break. *MSS.*   115 fleets] Isles *1669*
116 comfort; *1635–54:* sweet comfort, *1669*   others] yet some *1669*
119 But as the aire takes all sunbeams equall bright *one MS.*
121 able men *one MS.:* able man, *1635–54:* happy man, *1669:*
happy['s] man *Grosart and Chambers*   123 Their *1669, MSS.:*
There *1635–54, Chambers and Grolier*   125 violent *MSS.:* valiant
1635–69   127 imparts] imports *1669, one MS.*   128 Is fain'd, which
. . . appetite. *one MS.:* Is thought the mansion of sweet appetite. *one
MS.:* Is fancied *1635–39 (rest of line left blank):* Is fancied in the Soul,
not in the sight. *1650–54:* Is fancied by the Soul, not appetite. *1669*

That

That thankfullnesse your favours have begot   5
  In mee, embalmes mee, that I doe not rot.
This season as 'tis Easter, as 'tis spring,
  Must both to growth and to confession bring
My thoughts dispos'd unto your influence; so,
  These verses bud, so these confessions grow.   10
First I confesse I have to others lent
  Your stock, and over prodigally spent
Your treasure, for since I had never knowne
  Vertue or beautie, but as they are growne
In you, I should not thinke or say they shine,   15
  (So as I have) in any other Mine.
Next I confesse this my confession,
  For, 'tis some fault thus much to touch upon
Your praise to you, where half rights seeme too much,
  And make your minds sincere complexion blush.   20
Next I confesse my'impenitence, for I
  Can scarce repent my first fault, since thereby
Remote low Spirits, which shall ne'r read you,
  May in lesse lessons finde enough to doe,
By studying copies, not Originals,   25
       Desunt cætera.

A Letter to the Lady Carey, and Mrs Essex Riche, *From* Amyens.

MADAME,

Ere where by All All Saints invoked are,
  'Twere too much schisme to be singular,
And 'gainst a practise generall to warre.

Yet turning to Saincts, should my'humility
  To other Sainct then you directed bee,   5
That were to make my schisme, heresie.

Nor would I be a Convertite so cold,
  As not to tell it; If this be too bold,
Pardons are in this market cheaply sold.

                 Where,

Where, because Faith is in too low degree,   10
I thought it some Apostleship in mee
To speake things which by faith alone I see.

That is, of you, who are a firmament
Of virtues, where no one is growne, or spent,
They'are your materials, not your ornament.   15

Others whom wee call vertuous, are not so
In their whole substance, but, their vertues grow
But in their humours, and at seasons show.

For when through tastlesse flat humilitie
In dow bak'd men some harmelessenes we see,   20
'Tis but his *flegme* that's *Vertuous*, and not Hee:

Soe is the Blood sometimes; who ever ran
To danger unimportun'd, he was than
No better then a *sanguine* Vertuous man.

So cloysterall men, who, in pretence of feare   25
All contributions to this life forbeare,
Have Vertue in *Melancholy*, and only there.

Spirituall *Cholerique* Crytiques, which in all
Religions find faults, and forgive no fall,
Have, through this zeale, Vertue but in their Gall.   30

We'are thus but parcel guilt; to Gold we'are growne
When Vertue is our Soules complexion;
Who knowes his Vertues name or place, hath none.

Vertue'is but aguish, when 'tis severall,
By occasion wak'd, and circumstantiall.   35
True vertue is *Soule*, Alwaies in all deeds *All*.

This Vertue thinking to give dignitie
To your soule, found there no infirmitie,
For, your soule was as good Vertue, as shee;

A Letter to &c.   19 humility] humidity *1669*   30 this zeale,
1635–69 and most MSS.: their zeale, *1633 and one MS.*

Shee

Shee therefore wrought upon that part of you   40
Which is scarce lesse then soule, as she could do,
And so hath made your beauty, Vertue too.

Hence comes it, that your Beauty wounds not hearts,
As Others, with prophane and sensuall Darts,
But as an influence, vertuous thoughts imparts.   45

But if such friends by the honor of your sight
Grow capable of this so great a light,
As to partake your vertues, and their might,

What must I thinke that influence must doe,
Where it findes sympathie and matter too,   50
Vertue, and beauty of the same stuffe, as you?

Which is, your noble worthie sister, shee
Of whom, if what in this my Extasie
And revelation of you both I see,

I should write here, as in short Galleries   55
The Master at the end large glasses ties,
So to present the roome twice to our eyes,

So I should give this letter length, and say
That which I said of you; there is no way
From either, but by the other, not to stray.   60

May therefore this be enough to testifie
My true devotion, free from flattery;
He that beleeves himselfe, doth never lie.

To the Countesse of Salisbury. August. 1614.

FAire, great, and good, since seeing you, wee see
   What Heaven can doe, and what any Earth can be:
Since now your beauty shines, now when the Sunne
Growne stale, is to so low a value runne,

57 our eyes,] your eyes, *some MSS.*
   To the Countesse &c.   2 and what *1633, 1669, and one MS.
group:* what *1635–54, another MS. group*

I   That

That his disshevel'd beames and scattered fires   5
Serve but for Ladies Periwigs and Tyres
In lovers Sonnets: you come to repaire
Gods booke of creatures, teaching what is faire.
Since now, when all is withered, shrunke, and dri'd,
All Vertues ebb'd out to a dead low tyde,   10
All the worlds frame being crumbled into sand,
Where every man thinks by himselfe to stand,
Integritie, friendship, and confidence,
(Ciments of greatnes) being vapor'd hence,
And narrow man being fill'd with little shares,   15
Court, Citie, Church, are all shops of small-wares,
All having blowne to sparkes their noble fire,
And drawne their sound gold-ingot into wyre;
All trying by a love of littlenesse
To make abridgments, and to draw to lesse,   20
Even that nothing, which at first we were;
Since in these times, your greatnesse doth appeare,
And that we learne by it, that man to get
Towards him that's infinite, must first be great.
Since in an age so ill, as none is fit   25
So much as to accuse, must lesse mend it,
(For who can judge, or witnesse of those times
Where all alike are guiltie of the crimes?)
Where he that would be good, is thought by all
A monster, or at best fantasticall;   30
Since now you durst be good, and that I doe
Discerne, by daring to contemplate you,
That there may be degrees of faire, great, good,
Through your light, largenesse, vertue understood:
If in this sacrifice of mine, be showne   35
Any small sparke of these, call it your owne.
And if things like these, have been said by mee
Of others; call not that Idolatrie.
For had God made man first, and man had seene

38 Idolatrie.] Adulterie: *one MS. group*

The

The third daies fruits, and flowers, and various greene, 40
He might have said the best that he could say
Of those faire creatures, which were made that day;
And when next day he had admir'd the birth
Of Sun, Moone, Stars, fairer then late-prais'd earth,
Hee might have said the best that he could say,   45
And not be chid for praising yesterday;
So though some things are not together true,
As, that another is worthiest, and, that you:
Yet, to say so, doth not condemne a man,
If when he spoke them, they were both true than.   50
How faire a proofe of this, in our soule growes?
Wee first have soules of growth, and sense, and those,
When our last soule, our soule immortall came,
Were swallowed into it, and have no name.
Nor doth he injure those soules, which doth cast   55
The power and praise of both them, on the last;
No more doe I wrong any; I adore
The same things now, which I ador'd before,
The subject chang'd, and measure; the same thing
In a low constable, and in the King   60
I reverence; His power to work on mee:
So did I humbly reverence each degree
Of faire, great, good; but more, now I am come
From having found their *walkes,* to find their *home.*
And as I owe my first soules thankes, that they   65
For my last soule did fit and mould my clay,
So am I debtor unto them, whose worth,
Enabled me to profit, and take forth
This new great lesson, thus to study you;
Which none, not reading others, first, could doe.   70
Nor lacke I light to read this booke, though I
In a darke Cave, yea in a Grave doe lie;
For as your fellow Angells, so you doe
Illustrate them who come to study you.

57 any; I adore *1633 and MSS.:* any, if I adore *1635–69*

The

The first whom we in Histories doe finde   75
To have profest all Arts, was one borne blinde:
He lackt those eyes beasts have as well as wee,
Not those, by which Angels are seene and see;
So, though I'am borne without those eyes to live,
Which fortune, who hath none her selfe, doth give,   80
Which are, fit meanes to see bright courts and you,
Yet may I see you thus, as now I doe;
I shall by that, all goodnesse have discern'd,
And though I burne my librarie, be learn'd.

To the Lady Bedford.

YOu that are she and you, that's double shee,
   In her dead face, halfe of your selfe shall see;
Shee was the other part, for so they doe
   Which build them friendships, become one of two;
So two, that but themselves no third can fit,   5
   Which were to be so, when they were not yet;
Twinnes, though their birth *Cusco*, and *Musco* take,
   As divers starres one Constellation make;
Pair'd like two eyes, have equall motion, so
   Both but one meanes to see, one way to goe.   10
Had you dy'd first, a carcasse shee had beene;
   And wee your rich Tombe in her face had seene;
She like the Soule is gone, and you here stay,
   Not a live friend; but th'other halfe of clay.
And since you act that part, As men say, here   15
   Lies such a Prince, when but one part is there,
And do all honour and devotion due
   Unto the whole, so wee all reverence you;
For, such a friendship who would not adore
   In you, who are all what both were before,   20

To the &c. *1635–69:* Elegie to the Lady Bedford. *1633 and most
MSS. In 1633 it follows, in one MS. precedes, the Funerall Elegy
Death (p. 259), to which it is apparently a covering letter*

Not

Not all, as if some perished by this,
    But so, as all in you contracted is.
As of this all, though many parts decay,
    The pure which elemented them shall stay;
And though diffus'd, and spread in infinite,   25
    Shall recollect, and in one All unite:
So madame, as her Soule to heaven is fled,
    Her flesh rests in the earth, as in the bed;
Her vertues do, as to their proper spheare,
    Returne to dwell with you, of whom they were: 30
As perfect motions are all circular,
    So they to you, their sea, whence lesse streames are.
Shee was all spices, you all metalls; so
    In you two wee did both rich Indies know.
And as no fire, nor rust can spend or waste   35
    One dramme of gold, but what was first shall last,
Though it bee forc'd in water, earth, salt, aire,
    Expans'd in infinite, none will impaire;
So, to your selfe you may additions take,
    But nothing can you lesse, or changed make.   40
Seeke not in seeking new, to seeme to doubt,
    That you can match her, or not be without;
But let some faithfull booke in her roome be,
    Yet but of *Judith* no such booke as shee.

A N

A N

A N A T O M I E

OF THE WORLD.

Wherein,

By occasion of the untimely death of
Mistris ELIZABETH DRVRY,
the frailty and the decay of this
whole World is represented.

The first Anniversary.

To the praise of · the dead,

and the ANATOMIE.

WEll dy'd the World, that we might live to see
   This world of wit, in his Anatomie:
No evill wants his good; so wilder heires
Bedew their Fathers Tombes, with forced teares,
Whose state requites their losse: whiles thus we gain,   5
Well may wee walke in blacks, but not complaine.
Yet how can I consent the world is dead
While this Muse lives? which in his spirits stead
Seemes to informe a World; and bids it bee,
In spight of losse or fraile mortalitie?   10
And thou the subject of this welborne thought,
Thrice noble maid, couldst not have found nor sought

An Anatomie &c. *1611–33:* Anatomie &c. *1635–69*   The first
Anniversary. *1612–69: om. 1611*   To the praise of the dead &c.
1611–69 (Dead *1611*): *Jonson attributes the poem to Joseph Hall*

A fitter

A fitter time to yeeld to thy sad Fate,
Then whiles this spirit lives, that can relate
Thy worth so well to our last Nephews eyne,   15
That they shall wonder both at his and thine:
Admired match! where strives in mutuall grace
The cunning pencill, and the comely face:
A taske which thy faire goodnesse made too much
For the bold pride of vulgar pens to touch;   20
Enough is us to praise them that praise thee,
And say, that but enough those prayses bee,
Which hadst thou liv'd, had hid their fearfull head
From th'angry checkings of thy modest red:
Death barres reward and shame: when envy's gone,   25
And gaine, 'tis safe to give the dead their ovne
As then the wise Egyptians wont to lay
More on their Tombes, then houses: these of clay,
But those of brasse, or marble were: so wee
Give more unto thy Ghost, then unto thee.   30
Yet what wee give to thee, thou gav'st to us,
And may'st but thanke thy selfe, for being thus:
Yet what thou gav'st, and wert, O happy maid,
Thy grace profest all due, where 'tis repayd.
So these high songs that to thee suited bin   35
Serve but to sound thy Makers praise, in thine,
Which thy deare soule as sweetly sings to him
Amid the Quire of Saints, and Seraphim,
As any Angels tongue can sing of thee;
The subjects differ, though the skill agree: 40
For as by infant-yeares men judge of age,
Thy early love, thy vertues, did presage
What an high part thou bear'st in those best songs,
Whereto no burden, nor no end belongs.
Sing on thou virgin Soule, whose lossfull gaine   45
Thy lovesick parents have bewail'd in vaine;
Never may thy Name be in our songs forgot,
Till wee shall sing thy ditty and thy note.

An

An Anatomy of the World.
The first Anniversary.

*The entrie
into the
worke.*

WHen that rich Soule which to her heaven is gone,
    Whom all do celebrate, who know they have one,
(For who is sure he hath a Soule, unlesse
It see, and judge, and follow worthinesse,
And by Deedes praise it? hee who doth not this,   5
May lodge an In-mate soule, but 'tis not his.)
When that Queene ended here her progresse time,
And, as t'her standing house to heaven did climbe,
Where loath to make the Saints attend her long,
She's now a part both of the Quire, and Song,   10
This World, in that great earthquake languished;
For in a common bath of teares it bled,
Which drew the strongest vitall spirits out:
But succour'd then with a perplexed doubt,
Whether the world did lose, or gaine in this,   15
(Because since now no other way there is,
But goodnesse, to see her, whom all would see,
All must endeavour to be good as shee,)
This great consumption to a fever turn'd,
And so the world had fits; it joy'd, it mourn'd;   20
And, as men thinke, that Agues physick are,
And th'Ague being spent, give over care,
So thou sicke World, mistak'st thy selfe to bee
Well, when alas, thou'rt in a Lethargie.
Her death did wound and tame thee than, and than   25
Thou might'st have better spar'd the Sunne, or Man.
That wound was deep, but 'tis more misery,
That thou hast lost thy sense and memory.
'Twas heavy then to heare thy voyce of mone,
But this is worse, that thou art speechlesse growne.   30
Thou hast forgot thy name, thou hadst; thou wast

An Anatomy &c. *1611–69*   The first Anniversary. *1612–69*
(First *1612–25*): *om. 1611*   The entrie &c. *1612–21*: *om. 1625–33:
1611 and 1635–69 have no notes*

Nothing

Nothing but shee, and her thou hast o'rpast.
For as a child kept from the Font, untill
A prince, expected long, come to fulfill
The ceremonies, thou unnam'd had'st laid,   35
Had not her comming, thee her Palace made:
Her name defin'd thee, gave thee forme, and frame,
And thou forgett'st to celebrate thy name.
Some moneths she hath bcene dead (but being dead,
Measures of times are all determined)   40
But long she'ath beene away, long, long, yet none
Offers to tell us who it is that's gone.
But as in states doubtfull of future heires,
When sicknesse without remedie empaires
The present Prince, they're loth it should be said,   45
The Prince doth languish, or the Prince is dead:
So mankinde feeling now a generall thaw,
A strong example gone, equall to law,
The Cyment which did faithfully compact,
And glue all vertues, now resolv'd, and slack'd,   50
Thought it some blasphemy to say sh'was dead,
Or that our weaknesse was discovered
In that confession; therefore spoke no more
Then tongues, the Soule being gone, the losse deplore.
But though it be too late to succour thee,   55
Sicke World, yea, dead, yea putrified, since shee
Thy'intrinsique balme, and thy preservative,
Can never be renew'd, thou never live,
I (since no man can make thee live) will try,
What wee may gaine by thy Anatomy.   60
Her death hath taught us dearely, that thou art
Corrupt and mortall in thy purest part.
Let no man say, the world it selfe being dead,
'Tis labour lost to have discovered
The worlds infirmities, since there is none   65
Alive to study this dissection;

33 Font, *1611:* Fount, *1612–69*

For there's a kinde of World remaining still,
Though shee which did inanimate and fill
The world, be gone, yet in this last long night,
Her Ghost doth walke; that is, a glimmering light,   70
A faint weake love of vertue, and of good,
Reflects from her, on them which understood
Her worth; and though she have shut in all day,
The twilight of her memory doth stay;
Which, from the carcasse of the old world, free,   75
Creates a new world, and new creatures bee
Produc'd: the matter and the stuffe of this,
Her vertue, and the forme our practice is:
And though to be thus elemented, arme
These creatures, from home-borne intrinsique harme,   80
(For all assum'd unto this dignitie,
So many weedlesse Paradises bee,
Which of themselves produce no venemous sinne,
Except some forraine Serpent bring it in)
Yet, because outward stormes the strongest breake,   85
And strength it selfe by confidence growes weake,
This new world may be safer, being told

The dangers and diseases of the old:
For with due temper men doe then forgoe,
Or covet things, when they their true worth know.   90

There is no health; Physitians say that wee,
At best, enjoy but a neutralitie.
And can there bee worse sicknesse, then to know
That we are never well, nor can be so?
Wee are borne ruinous: poore mothers cry,   95
That children come not right, nor orderly;
Except they headlong come and fall upon
An ominous precipitation.
How witty's ruine! how importunate
Upon mankinde! it labour'd to frustrate   100
Even Gods purpose; and made woman, sent
For mans reliefe, cause of his languishment.

                                                    They

They were to good ends, and they are so still,
But accessory, and principall in ill;
For that first marriage was our funerall: 105
One woman at one blow, then kill'd us all,
And singly, one by one, they kill us now.
We doe delightfully our selves allow
To that consumption; and profusely blinde,
Wee kill our selves to propagate our kinde.   110
And yet we do not that; we are not men:
There is not now that mankinde, which was then,
When as the Sunne and man did seeme to strive,
(Joynt tenants of the world) who should survive;   *Shortnesse*
When, Stagge, and Raven, and the long-liv'd tree,   115 *of life.*
Compar'd with man, dy'd in minoritie;
When, if a slow pac'd starre had stolne away
From the observers marking, he might stay
Two or three hundred yeares to see't againe,
And then make up his observation plaine;   120
When, as the age was long, the sise was great;
Mans growth confess'd, and recompenc'd the meat;
So spacious and large, that every Soule
Did a faire Kingdome, and large Realme controule:
And when the very stature, thus erect,   125
Did that soule a good way towards heaven direct.
Where is this mankinde now? who lives to age,
Fit to be made *Methusalem* his page?
Alas, we scarce live long enough to try
Whether a true made clocke run right, or lie.   130
Old Grandsires talke of yesterday with sorrow,
And for our children wee reserve to morrow.
So short is life, that every peasant strives,
In a torne house, or field, to have three lives.
And as in lasting, so in length is man   135
Contracted to an inch, who was a spanne;   *Smalnesse*
                                                of stature.

114 survive; *1650–69:* survive. *1611, 1612–39*   116 minoritie;
1650–69: minoritee. *1611, 1621–25:* minoritie, *1633–39*

                                                              For

For had a man at first in forrests stray'd,
Or shipwrack'd in the Sea, one would have laid
A wager, that an Elephant, or Whale,
That met him, would not hastily assaile   140
A thing so equall to him: now alas,
The Fairies, and the Pigmies well may passe
As credible; mankinde decayes so soone,
We'are scarce our Fathers shadowes cast at noone:
Onely death addes t'our length: nor are wee growne 145
In stature to be men, till we are none.
But this were light, did our lesse volume hold
All the old Text; or had wee chang'd to gold
Their silver; or dispos'd into lesse glasse
Spirits of vertue, which then scatter'd was.   150
But 'tis not so: w'are not retir'd, but dampt;
And as our bodies, so our mindes are crampt:
'Tis shrinking, not close weaving that hath thus,
In minde, and body both bedwarfed us.
Wee seeme ambitious, Gods whole worke t'undoe;   155
Of nothing hee made us, and we strive too,
To bring our selves to nothing backe; and wee
Doe what wee can, to do't so soone as hee.
With new diseases on our selves we warre,
And with new Physicke, a worse Engin farre.   160
Thus man, this worlds Vice-Emperour, in whom
All faculties, all graces are at home;
And if in other creatures they appeare,
They're but mans Ministers, and Legats there,
To worke on their rebellions, and reduce   165
Them to Civility, and to mans use:
This man, whom God did wooe, and loth t'attend
Till man came up, did downe to man descend,
This man, so great, that all that is, is his,
Oh what a trifle, and poore thing he is!   170
If man were any thing, he's nothing now:

153 close weaving] close weaning *1611–25*

Helpe,

Helpe, or at least some time to wast, allow
T'his other wants, yet when he did depart
With her whom we lament, hee lost his heart.
She, of whom th'Ancients seem'd to prophesie,   175
When they call'd vertues by the name of *shee*;
Shee in whom vertue was so much refin'd,
That for Allay unto so pure a minde
Shee tooke the weaker Sex; shee that could drive
The poysonous tincture, and the staine of *Eve*,   180
Out of her thoughts, and deeds; and purifie
All, by a true religious Alchymie;
Shee, shee is dead; shee's dead: when thou knowest this,
Thou knowest how poore a trifling thing man is.
And learn'st thus much by our Anatomie,   185
The heart being perish'd, no part can be free.
And that except thou feed (not banquet) on
The supernaturall food, Religion,
Thy better Growth growes withered, and scant;
Be more then man, or thou'rt lesse then an Ant.   190
Then, as mankinde, so is the worlds whole frame
Quite out of joynt, almost created lame:
For, before God had made up all the rest,
Corruption entred, and deprav'd the best:
It seis'd the Angels, and then first of all   195
The world did in her cradle take a fall,
And turn'd her braines, and tooke a generall maime,
Wronging each joynt of th'universall frame.
The noblest part, man, felt it first; and than
Both beasts and plants, curst in the curse of man.   200   *Decay of*
So did the world from the first houre decay,   *nature in*
That evening was beginning of the day,   *other parts.*
And now the Springs and Sommers which we see,
Like sonnes of women after fiftie bee.
And new Philosophy calls all in doubt,   205
The Element of fire is quite put out;
The Sun is lost, and th'earth, and no mans wit

                                                    Can

Can well direct him where to looke for it.
And freely men confesse that this world's spent,
When in the Planets, and the Firmament   210
They seeke so many new; they see that this
Is crumbled out againe to his Atomies.
'Tis all in peeces, all cohaerence gone;
All just supply, and all Relation:
Prince, Subject, Father, Sonne, are things forgot,   215
For every man alone thinkes he hath got
To be a Phœnix, and that then can bee
None of that kinde, of which he is, but hee.
This is the worlds condition now, and now
She that should all parts to reunion bow,   220
She that had all Magnetique force alone,
To draw, and fasten sundred parts in one;
She whom wise nature had invented then
When she observ'd that every sort of men
Did in their voyage in this worlds Sea stray,   225
And needed a new compasse for their way;
She that was best, and first originall
Of all faire copies, and the generall
Steward to Fate; she whose rich eyes, and brest
Guilt the West Indies, and perfum'd the East;   230
Whose having breath'd in this world, did bestow
Spice on those Iles, and bad them still smell so,
And that rich Indie which doth gold interre,
Is but as single money, coyn'd from her:
She to whom this world must it selfe refer,   235
As Suburbs, or the Microcosme of her,
Shee, shee is dead; shee's dead: when thou knowst this,
Thou knowst how lame a cripple this world is.
And learn'st thus much by our Anatomy,
That this worlds generall sickenesse doth not lie   240
In any humour, or one certaine part;
But as thou sawest it rotten at the heart,
Thou seest a Hectique feaver hath got hold

                                          Of

Of the whole substance, not to be contrould,
And that thou hast but one way, not t'admit   245
The worlds infection, to be none of it.
For the worlds subtilst immateriall parts
Feele this consuming wound, and ages darts.
For the worlds beauty is decai'd, or gone,
Beauty, that's colour, and proportion.   250 *Disformity*
We thinke the heavens enjoy their Sphericall,   *of parts.*
Their round proportion embracing all.
But yet their various and perplexed course,
Observ'd in divers ages, doth enforce
Men to finde out so many Eccentrique parts,   255
Such divers downe-right lines, such overthwarts,
As disproportion that pure forme: It teares
The Firmament in eight and forty sheires,
And in these Constellations then arise
New starres, and old doe vanish from our eyes: 260
As though heav'n suffered earthquakes, peace or war,
When new Towers rise, and old demolish't are.
They have impal'd within a Zodiake
The free-borne Sun, and keepe twelve Signes awake
To watch his steps; the Goat and Crab controule,   265
And fright him backe, who else to either Pole
(Did not these Tropiques fetter him) might runne:
For his course is not round; nor can the Sunne
Perfit a Circle, or maintaine his way
One inch direct; but where he rose to-day   270
He comes no more, but with a couzening line,
Steales by that point, and so is Serpentine:
And seeming weary with his reeling thus,
He meanes to sleepe, being now falne nearer us.
So, of the Starres which boast that they doe runne   275
In Circle still, none ends where he begun.
All their proportion's lame, it sinkes, it swels.
For of Meridians, and Parallels,
Man hath weav'd out a net, and this net throwne

Upon

Upon the Heavens, and now they are his owne.   280
Loth to goe up the hill, or labour thus
To goe to heaven, we make heaven come to us.
We spur, we reine the starres, and in their race
They're diversly content t'obey our pace.
But keepes the earth her round proportion still?   285
Doth not a Tenarif, or higher Hill
Rise so high like a Rocke, that one might thinke
The floating Moone would shipwracke there, and sinke?
Seas are so deepe, that Whales being strooke to day,
Perchance to morrow, scarce at middle way   290
Of their wish'd journies end, the bottome, die.
And men, to sound depths, so much line untie,
As one might justly thinke, that there would rise
At end thereof, one of th'Antipodies:
If under all, a Vault infernall bee,   295
(Which sure is spacious, except that we
Invent another torment, that there must
Millions into a strait hot roome be thrust)
Then solidnesse, and roundnesse have no place.
Are these but warts, and pock-holes in the face   300
Of th'earth? Thinke so: but yet confesse, in this
The worlds proportion disfigured is;
Disorder in That those two legges whereon it doth rely,
the world.   Reward and punishment are bent awry.
And, Oh, it can no more be questioned,   305
That beauties best, proportion, is dead,
Since even griefe it selfe, which now alone
Is left us, is without proportion.
Shee by whose lines proportion should bee
Examin'd, measure of all Symmetree,   310
Whom had that Ancient seen, who thought soules made
Of Harmony, he would at next have said
That Harmony was shee, and thence infer,
That soules were but Resultances from her,

286 Tenarif, *1611, 1612–25:* Tenarus *1633–69*

And

And did from her into our bodies goe,   315
As to our eyes, the formes from objects flow:
Shee, who if those great Doctors truly said
That the Arke to mans proportions was made,
Had been a type for that, as that might be
A type of her in this, that contrary   320
Both Elements, and Passions liv'd at peace
In her, who caus'd all Civill war to cease.
Shee, after whom, what forme so'er we see,
Is discord, and rude incongruitie;
Shee, shee is dead, shee's dead; when thou knowst this 325
Thou knowst how ugly a monster this world is:
And learn'st thus much by our Anatomie,
That here is nothing to enamour thee:
And that, not only faults in inward parts,
Corruptions in our braines, or in our hearts,   330
Poysoning the fountaines, whence our actions spring,
Endanger us: but that if every thing
Be not done fitly'and in proportion,
To satisfie wise, and good lookers on,
(Since most men be such as most thinke they bee)   335
They're lothsome too, by this Deformitee.
For good, and well, must in our actions meete;
Wicked is not much worse than indiscreet.
But beauties other second Element,
Colour, and lustre now, is as neere spent.   340
And had the world his just proportion,
Were it a ring still, yet the stone is gone.
As a compassionate Turcoyse which doth tell
By looking pale, the wearer is not well,
As gold falls sicke being stung with Mercury,   345
All the worlds parts of such complexion bee.
When nature was most busie, the first weeke,
Swadling the new borne earth, God seem'd to like
That she should sport her selfe sometimes, and play,

318 proportions *1611-12:* proportion *1621-69*

To

To mingle, and vary colours every day: 350
And then, as though shee could not make inow,
Himselfe his various Rainbow did allow.
Sight is the noblest sense of any one,
Yet sight hath only colour to feed on,
And colour is decai'd: summers robe growes   355
Duskie, and like an oft dyed garment showes.
Our blushing red, which us'd in cheekes to spred,
Is inward sunke, and only our soules are red.
Perchance the world might have recovered,
If she whom we lament had not beene dead: 360
But shee, in whom all white, and red, and blew
(Beauties ingredients) voluntary grew,
As in an unvext Paradise; from whom
Did all things verdure, and their lustre come,
Whose composition was miraculous,   365
Being all colour, all Diaphanous,
(For Ayre, and Fire but thick grosse bodies were,
And liveliest stones but drowsie, and pale to her,)
Shee, shee, is dead: shee's dead: when thou know'st this,
Thou knowst how wan a Ghost this our world is: 370
And learn'st thus much by our Anatomie,
That it should more affright, then pleasure thee.
And that, since all faire colour then did sinke,
'Tis now but wicked vanitie, to thinke

Weaknesse To colour vicious deeds with good pretence,   375
in the want Or with bought colors to illude mens sense.
of corre-
spondence of Nor in ought more this worlds decay appeares,
heaven and Then that her influence the heav'n forbeares,
earth. Or that the Elements doe not feele this,
The father, or the mother barren is.   380
The cloudes conceive not raine, or doe not powre,
In the due birth time, downe the balmy showre;
Th'Ayre doth not motherly sit on the earth,

379–80 feele this, . . . barren is. *1611, 1612–69:* feele this. . . . barren
is; *Chambers.*

To

To hatch her seasons, and give all things birth;
Spring-times were common cradles, but are tombes;   385
And false-conceptions fill the generall wombes;
Th'Ayre showes such Meteors, as none can see,
Not only what they meane, but what they bee;
Earth such new wormes, as would have troubled much
Th'Ægyptian *Mages* to have made more such.   390
What Artist now dares boast that he can bring
Heaven hither, or constellate any thing,
So as the influence of those starres may bee
Imprison'd in an Hearbe, or Charme, or Tree,
And doe by touch, all which those stars could doe?   395
The art is lost, and correspondence too.
For heaven gives little, and the earth takes lesse,
And man least knowes their trade and purposes.
If this commerce twixt heaven and earth were not
Embarr'd, and all this traffique quite forgot,   400
She, for whose losse we have lamented thus,
Would worke more fully, and pow'rfully on us:
Since herbes, and roots, by dying lose not all,
But they, yea Ashes too, are medicinall,
Death could not quench her vertue so, but that   405
It would be (if not follow'd) wondred at:
And all the world would be one dying Swan,
To sing her funerall praise, and vanish than.
But as some Serpents poyson hurteth not,
Except it be from the live Serpent shot,   410
So doth her vertue need her here, to fit
That unto us; shee working more then it.
But shee, in whom to such maturity
Vertue was growne, past growth, that it must die;
She, from whose influence all Impressions came,   415
But, by Receivers impotencies, lame,
Who, though she could not transubstantiate
All states to gold, yet guilded every state,
So that some Princes have some temperance;

                                    Some

Some Counsellers some purpose to advance   420
The common profit; and some people have
Some stay, no more then Kings should give, to crave;
Some women have some taciturnity,
Some nunneries some graines of chastitie.
She that did thus much, and much more could doe,   425
But that our age was Iron, and rustie too,
Shee, shee is dead; shee's dead; when thou knowst this,
Thou knowst how drie a Cinder this world is.
And learn'st thus much by our Anatomy,
That 'tis in vaine to dew, or mollifie   430
It with thy teares, or sweat, or blood: nothing
Is worth our travaile, griefe, or perishing,
But those rich joyes, which did possesse her heart,
Of which she's now partaker, and a part.

Conclusion. But as in cutting up a man that's dead,   435
The body will not last out, to have read
On every part, and therefore men direct
Their speech to parts, that are of most effect;
So the worlds carcasse would not last, if I
Were punctuall in this Anatomy;   440
Nor smels it well to hearers, if one tell
Them their disease, who faine would think they're well.
Here therefore be the end: And, blessed maid,
Of whom is meant what ever hath been said,
Or shall be spoken well by any tongue,   445
Whose name refines course lines, and makes prose song,
Accept this tribute, and his first yeares rent,
Who till his darke short tapers end be spent,
As oft as thy feast sees this widowed earth,
Will yearely celebrate thy second birth,   450
That is, thy death; for though the soule of man
Be got when man is made, 'tis borne but than
When man doth die; our body's as the wombe,
And, as a Mid-wife, death directs it home.
And you her creatures, whom she workes upon,   455

                                                                  And

And have your last, and best concoction
From her example, and her vertue, if you
In reverence to her, do thinke it due,
That no one should her praises thus rehearse,
As matter fit for Chronicle, not verse; 460
Vouchsafe to call to minde that God did make
A last, and lasting'st peece, a song. He spake
To *Moses* to deliver unto all,
That song, because hee knew they would let fall
The Law, the Prophets, and the History, 465
But keepe the song still in their memory:
Such an opinion (in due measure) made
Me this great Office boldly to invade:
Nor could incomprehensiblenesse deterre
Mee, from thus trying to emprison her, 470
Which when I saw that a strict grave could doe,
I saw not why verse might not do so too.
Verse hath a middle nature: heaven keepes Soules,
The Grave keepes bodies, Verse the Fame enroules.

A Funerall ELEGIE.

'TIs lost, to trust a Tombe with such a guest,
Or to confine her in a marble chest.
Alas, what's Marble, Jeat, or Porphyrie,
Priz'd with the Chrysolite of either eye,
Or with those Pearles, and Rubies, which she was? 5
Joyne the two Indies in one Tombe, 'tis glasse;
And so is all to her materials,
Though every inch were ten Escurials,
Yet she's demolish'd: can wee keepe her then
In works of hands, or of the wits of men? 10
Can these memorials, ragges of paper, give
Life to that name, by which name they must live?

A Funerall ELEGIE.   1 lost, *1611, 1612–25:* lost *1633:* losse
1635–69

Sickly,

Sickly, alas, short-liv'd, aborted bee
Those carcasse verses, whose soule is not shee.
And can shee, who no longer would be shee,   15
Being such a Tabernacle, stoop to be
In paper wrapt; or, when shee would not lie
In such a house, dwell in an Elegie?
But 'tis no matter; wee may well allow
Verse to live so long as the world will now,   20
For her death wounded it. The world containes
Princes for armes, and Counsellors for braines,
Lawyers for tongues, Divines for hearts, and more,
The Rich for stomackes, and for backes, the Poore;
The Officers for hands, Merchants for feet,   25
By which, remote and distant Countries meet.
But those fine spirits which do tune, and set
This Organ, are those peeces which beget
Wonder and love; and these were shee; and shee
Being spent, the world must needs decrepit bee;   30
For since death will proceed to triumph still,
He can finde nothing, after her, to kill,
Except the world it selfe, so great as shee.
Thus brave and confident may Nature bee,
Death cannot give her such another blow,   35
Because shee cannot such another show.
But must wee say she's dead? may't not be said
That as a sundred clocke is peecemeale laid,
Not to be lost, but by the makers hand
Repollish'd, without errour then to stand,   40
Or as the Affrique Niger streame enwombs
It selfe into the earth, and after comes
(Having first made a naturall bridge, to passe
For many leagues) farre greater then it was,
May't not be said, that her grave shall restore   45
Her, greater, purer, firmer, then before?
Heaven may say this, and joy in't, but can wee

24 Poore] *spelt* Pore (*as pronounced*) *1611–12*

Who

Who live, and lacke her, here this vantage see?
What is't to us, alas, if there have beene
An Angell made a Throne, or Cherubin?   50
Wee lose by't: and as aged men are glad
Being tastlesse growne, to joy in joyes they had,
So now the sick starv'd world must feed upon
This joy, that we had her, who now is gone.
Rejoyce then Nature, and this World, that you,   55
Fearing the last fires hastning to subdue
Your force and vigour, ere it were neere gone,
Wisely bestow'd and laid it all on one.
One, whose cleare body was so pure and thinne,
Because it need disguise no thought within.   60
'Twas but a through-light scarfe, her minde t'inroule;
Or exhalation breath'd out from her Soule.
One, whom all men who durst no more, admir'd:
And whom, who ere had worth enough, desir'd;
As when a Temple's built, Saints emulate   65
To which of them, it shall be consecrate.
But, as when heaven lookes on us with new eyes,
Those new starres every Artist exercise,
What place they should assigne to them they doubt,
Argue,'and agree not, till those starres goe out: 70
So the world studied whose this peece should be,
Till shee can be no bodies else, nor shee:
But like a Lampe of Balsamum, desir'd
Rather t'adorne, then last, she soone expir'd,
Cloath'd in her virgin white integritie,   75
For marriage, though it doe not staine, doth dye.
To scape th'infirmities which wait upon
Woman, she went away, before sh'was one;

76 dye. *1611, 1612–69* (*spelt* die *1633–69*): *Chambers closes the
sentence at* 74 expir'd *and prints* 75–7 *thus*—
        Clothed in her virgin white integrity
        —For marriage, though it doth not stain, doth dye—
    To 'scape &c.

                                            And

And the worlds busie noyse to overcome,
Tooke so much death, as serv'd for *opium*;   80
For though she could not, nor could chuse to dye,
She'ath yeelded to too long an extasie:
Hee which not knowing her said History,
Should come to reade the booke of destiny,
How faire, and chast, humble, and high she'ad been,   85
Much promis'd, much perform'd, at not fifteene,
And measuring future things, by things before,
Should turne the leafe to reade, and reade no more,
Would thinke that either destiny mistooke,
Or that some leaves were torne out of the booke.   90
But 'tis not so; Fate did but usher her
To yeares of reasons use, and then inferre
Her destiny to her selfe, which liberty
She tooke but for thus much, thus much to die.
Her modestie not suffering her to bee   95
Fellow-Commissioner with Destinie,
She did no more but die; if after her
Any shall live, which dare true good prefer,
Every such person is her deligate,
T'accomplish that which should have beene her Fate. 100
They shall make up that Booke and shall have thanks
Of Fate, and her, for filling up their blankes.
For future vertuous deeds are Legacies,
Which from the gift of her example rise;
And 'tis in heav'n part of spirituall mirth,   105
To see how well the good play her, on earth.

83 said *1611, 1612–33:* sad *1635–69*

OF

OF THE
PROGRESSE
OF THE SOULE.

Wherein,

By occasion of the Religious death of
Mistris ELIZABETH DRVRY,
the incommodities of the Soule in
this life, and her exaltation in
the next, are contemplated.

The second Anniversary.

The Harbinger to the
PROGRESSE.

TWo soules move here, and mine (a third) must move
Paces of admiration, and of love;
Thy Soule (deare virgin) whose this tribute is,
Mov'd from this mortall Spheare to lively blisse;
And yet moves still, and still aspires to see   5
The worlds last day, thy glories full degree :
Like as those starres which thou o'r-lookest farre,
Are in their place, and yet still moved are:
No soule (whiles with the luggage of this clay
It clogged is) can follow thee halfe way;   10
Or see thy flight, which doth our thoughts outgoe
So fast, that now the lightning moves but slow:

But

But now thou art as high in heaven flowne
As heaven's from us; what soule besides thine owne
Can tell thy joyes, or say he can relate   15
Thy glorious Journals in that blessed state?
I envie thee (Rich soule) I envy thee,
Although I cannot yet thy glory see:
And thou (great spirit) which hers follow'd hast
So fast, as none can follow thine so fast;   20
So far, as none can follow thine so farre,
(And if this flesh did not the passage barre
Hadst caught her) let me wonder at thy flight
Which long agone hadst lost the vulgar sight,
And now mak'st proud the better eyes, that they   25
Can see thee less'ned in thine ayery way;
So while thou mak'st her soule by progresse knowne
Thou mak'st a noble progresse of thine owne,
From this worlds carkasse having mounted high
To that pure life of immortalitie.   30
Since thine aspiring thoughts themselves so raise
That more may not beseeme a creatures praise,
Yet still thou vow'st her more; and every yeare
Mak'st a new progresse, while thou wandrest here;
Still upward mount; and let thy Makers praise   35
Honor thy Laura, and adorne thy laies.
And since thy Muse her head in heaven shrouds,
Oh let her never stoope below the clouds:
And if those glorious sainted soules may know
Or what wee doe, or what wee sing below,   40
Those acts, those songs shall still content them best
Which praise those awfull Powers that make them blest.

The Harbinger &c.   28 owne, *1635–69:* owne. *1612–33*

OF

OF
THE PROGRESSE
OF THE SOULE.

The second Anniversarie.

Nothing could make me sooner to confesse   *The*
   That this world had an everlastingnesse,   *entrance.*[1]
Then to consider, that a yeare is runne,
Since both this lower world's, and the Sunnes Sunne,
The Lustre, and the vigor of this All,   5
Did set; 'twere blasphemie to say, did fall.
But as a ship which hath strooke saile, doth runne
By force of that force which before, it wonne:
Or as sometimes in a beheaded man,
Though at those two Red seas, which freely ranne,   10
One from the Trunke, another from the Head,
His soule be sail'd, to her eternall bed,
His eyes will twinckle, and his tongue will roll,
As though he beckned, and cal'd backe his soule,
He graspes his hands, and he pulls up his feet,   15
And seemes to reach, and to step forth to meet
His soule; when all these motions which we saw,
Are but as Ice, which crackles at a thaw:
Or as a Lute, which in moist weather, rings
Her knell alone, by cracking of her strings: 20
So struggles this dead world, now shee is gone;
For there is motion in corruption.
As some daies are at the Creation nam'd,
Before the Sunne, the which fram'd daies, was fram'd,

   [1] *The entrance. 1612–21: om. 1625–33: no notes, 1635–69*

                           So

So after this Sunne's set, some shew appeares,   25
And orderly vicissitude of yeares.
Yet a new Deluge, and of *Lethe* flood,
Hath drown'd us all, All have forgot all good,
Forgetting her, the maine reserve of all.
Yet in this deluge, grosse and generall,   30
Thou seest me strive for life; my life shall bee,
To be hereafter prais'd, for praysing thee;
Immortall Maid, who though thou would'st refuse
The name of Mother, be unto my Muse
A Father, since her chast Ambition is,   35
Yearely to bring forth such a child as this.
These Hymnes may worke on future wits, and so
May great Grand children of thy prayses grow.
And so, though not revive, embalme and spice
The world, which else would putrifie with vice.   40
For thus, Man may extend thy progeny,
Untill man doe but vanish, and not die.
These Hymnes thy issue, may encrease so long,
As till Gods great *Venite* change the song.

A just disestima-tion of this world. Thirst for that time, O my insatiate soule,   45
And serve thy thirst, with Gods safe-sealing Bowle.
Be thirstie still, and drinke still till thou goe
To th'only Health, to be Hydroptique so.
Forget this rotten world; And unto thee
Let thine owne times as an old storie bee.   50
Be not concern'd: studie not why, nor when;
Doe not so much as not beleeve a man.
For though to erre, be worst, to try truths forth,
Is far more businesse, then this world is worth.
The world is but a carkasse; thou art fed   55
By it, but as a worme, that carkasse bred;
And why should'st thou, poore worme, consider more,

43 issue, *1612–33:* issue *1635–69*   48 Health, *1612–33:* Health;
1635–69, Chambers and Grolier   so. *1612–21:* so, *1625–69, Chambers and Grolier*

When

When this world will grow better then before,
Then those thy fellow wormes doe thinke upon
That carkasses last resurrection.   60
Forget this world, and scarce thinke of it so,
As of old clothes, cast off a yeare agoe.
To be thus stupid is Alacritie;
Men thus Lethargique have best Memory.
Look upward; that's towards her, whose happy state   65
We now lament not, but congratulate.
Shee, to whom all this world was but a stage,
Where all sat harkning how her youthfull age
Should be emploi'd, because in all shee did,
Some Figure of the Golden times was hid.   70
Who could not lacke, what e'r this world could give,
Because shee was the forme, that made it live;
Nor could complaine, that this world was unfit
To be staid in, then when shee was in it;
Shee that first tried indifferent desires   75
By vertue, and vertue by religious fires,
Shee to whose person Paradise adher'd,
As Courts to Princes, shee whose eyes ensphear'd
Star-light enough, t'have made the South controule,
(Had shee beene there) the Star-full Northerne Pole,   80
Shee, shee is gone; she is gone; when thou knowest this,
What fragmentary rubbidge this world is
Thou knowest, and that it is not worth a thought;
He honors it too much that thinkes it nought.
Thinke then, my soule, that death is but a Groome,   85   *Contempla-*
Which brings a Taper to the outward roome,   *tion of our*
Whence thou spiest first a little glimmering light,   *state in our*
And after brings it nearer to thy sight: *death-bed.*
For such approaches doth heaven make in death.
Thinke thy selfe labouring now with broken breath,   90
And thinke those broken and soft Notes to bee
Division, and thy happyest Harmonie.
Thinke thee laid on thy death-bed, loose and slacke;

And

And thinke that, but unbinding of a packe,
To take one precious thing, thy soule from thence.   95
Thinke thy selfe parch'd with fevers violence,
Anger thine ague more, by calling it
Thy Physicke; chide the slacknesse of the fit.
Thinke that thou hear'st thy knell, and think no more,
But that, as Bels cal'd thee to Church before,   100
So this,.to the Triumphant Church, calls thee.
Thinke Satans Sergeants round about thee bee,
And thinke that but for Legacies they thrust;
Give one thy Pride, to'another give thy Lust:
Give them those sinnes which they gave thee before,   105
And trust th'immaculate blood to wash thy score.
Thinke thy friends weeping round, and thinke that they
Weepe but because they goe not yet thy way.
Thinke that they close thine eyes, and thinke in this,
That they confesse much in the world, amisse,   110
Who dare not trust a dead mans eye with that,
Which they from God, and Angels cover not.
Thinke that they shroud thee up, and think from thence
They reinvest thee in white innocence.
Thinke that thy body rots, and (if so low,   115
Thy soule exalted so, thy thoughts can goe,)
Think thee a Prince, who of themselves create
Wormes which insensibly devoure their State.
Thinke that they bury thee, and thinke that right
Laies thee to sleepe but a Saint Lucies night.   120
Thinke these things cheerefully: and if thou bee
Drowsie or slacke, remember then that shee,
Shee whose Complexion was so even made,
That which of her Ingredients should invade
The other three, no Feare, no Art could guesse: 125
So far were all remov'd from more or lesse.
But as in Mithridate, or just perfumes,
Where all good things being met, no one presumes
To governe, or to triumph on the rest,

Only

Only because all were, no part was best.   130
And as, though all doe know, that quantities
Are made of lines, and lines from Points arise,
None can these lines or quantities unjoynt,
And say this is a line, or this a point,
So though the Elements and Humors were   135
In her, one could not say, this governes there.
Whose even constitution might have wonne
Any disease to venter on the Sunne,
Rather then her: and make a spirit feare,
That hee to disuniting subject were.   140
To whose proportions if we would compare
Cubes, th'are unstable; Circles, Angular;
She who was such a chaine as Fate employes
To bring mankinde all Fortunes it enjoyes;
So fast, so even wrought, as one would thinke,   145
No Accident could threaten any linke;
Shee, shee embrac'd a sicknesse, gave it meat,
The purest blood, and breath, that e'r it eate;
And hath taught us, that though a good man hath
Title to heaven, and plead it by his Faith,   150
And though he may pretend a conquest, since
Heaven was content to suffer violence,
Yea though hee plead a long possession too,
(For they're in heaven on earth who heavens workes do)
Though hee had right and power and place, before,   155
Yet Death must usher, and unlocke the doore.
Thinke further on thy selfe, my Soule, and thinke   *Incommodi-*
How thou at first wast made but in a sinke;   *ties of the*
Thinke that it argued some infirmitie,   *Soule in the*
                                                              Body.
That those two soules, which then thou foundst in me, 160
Thou fedst upon, and drewst into thee, both
My second soule of sense, and first of growth.
Thinke but how poore thou wast, how obnoxious;
Whom a small lumpe of flesh could poyson thus.
This curded milke, this poore unlittered whelpe   165

My

My body, could, beyond escape or helpe,
Infect thee with Originall sinne, and thou
Couldst neither then refuse, nor leave it now.
Thinke that no stubborne sullen Anchorit,
Which fixt to a pillar, or a grave, doth sit   170
Bedded, and bath'd in all his ordures, dwels
So fowly as our Soules in their first-built Cels.
Thinke in how poore a prison thou didst lie
After, enabled but to suck, and crie.
Thinke, when'twas growne to most,'twas a poore Inne, 175
A Province pack'd up in two yards of skinne,
And that usurp'd or threatned with the rage
Of sicknesses, or their true mother, Age.
But thinke that Death hath now enfranchis'd thee,

Her liberty Thou hast thy'expansion now, and libertie;   180
by death. Thinke that a rustie Peece, discharg'd, is flowne
In peeces, and the bullet is his owne,
And freely flies: This to thy Soule allow,
Thinke thy shell broke, thinke thy Soule hatch'd but now.
And think this slow-pac'd soule, which late did cleave 185
To'a body, and went but by the bodies leave,
Twenty, perchance, or thirty mile a day,
Dispatches in a minute all the way
Twixt heaven, and earth; she stayes not in the ayre,
To looke what Meteors there themselves prepare;   190
She carries no desire to know, nor sense,
Whether th'ayres middle region be intense;
For th'Element of fire, she doth not know,
Whether she past by such a place or no;
She baits not at the Moone, nor cares to trie   195
Whether in that new world, men live, and die.
Venus retards her not, to'enquire, how shee
Can, (being one starre) *Hesper*, and *Vesper* bee;
Hee that charm'd *Argus* eyes, sweet *Mercury*,
Workes not on her, who now is growne all eye;   200
Who, if she meet the body of the Sunne,

Goes

Goes through, not staying till his course be runne;
Who findes in *Mars* his Campe no corps of Guard;
Nor is by *Jove*, nor by his father barr'd;
But ere she can consider how she went, 205
At once is at, and through the Firmament.
And as these starres were but so many beads
Strung on one string, speed undistinguish'd leads
Her through those Spheares, as through the beads, a string,
Whose quick succession makes it still one thing: 210
As doth the pith, which, lest our bodies slacke,
Strings fast the little bones of necke, and backe;
So by the Soule doth death string Heaven and Earth;
For when our Soule enjoyes this her third birth,
(Creation gave her one, a second, grace,) 215
Heaven is as neare, and present to her face,
As colours are, and objects, in a roome
Where darknesse was before, when Tapers come.
This must, my Soule, thy long-short Progresse bee;
To'advance these thoughts, remember then, that shee, 220
Shee, whose faire body no such prison was,
But that a Soule might well be pleas'd to passe
An age in her; she whose rich beauty lent
Mintage to other beauties, for they went
But for so much as they were like to her; 225
Shee, in whose body (if we dare preferre
This low world, to so high a marke as shee,)
The Westerne treasure, Easterne spicerie,
Europe, and Afrique, and the unknowne rest
Were easily found, or what in them was best; 230
And when w'have made this large discoverie
Of all, in her some one part then will bee
Twenty such parts, whose plenty and riches is

219–20 *text 1612–25:*
    This must, my Soule, thy long-short Progresse bee,
    To'advance these thoughts; Remember then that she,
           1633–69, Chambers and Grolier.

K   Enough

Enough to make twenty such worlds as this;
Shee, whom had they knowne who did first betroth   235
The Tutelar Angels, and assign'd one, both
To Nations, Cities, and to Companies,
To Functions, Offices, and Dignities,
And to each severall man, to him, and him,
They would have given her one for every limbe;   240
She, of whose soule, if wee may say, 'twas Gold,
Her body was th'Electrum, and did hold
Many degrees of that; wee understood
Her by her sight; her pure, and eloquent blood
Spoke in her cheekes, and so distinctly wrought,   245
That one might almost say, her body thought;
Shee, shee, thus richly and largely hous'd, is gone:
And chides us slow-pac'd snailes who crawle upon
Our prisons prison, earth, nor thinke us well,
Longer, then whil'st wee beare our brittle shell.   250

Her igno-
rance in
this life
and know-
ledge in
the next.

But 'twere but little to have chang'd our roome,
If, as we were in this our living Tombe
Oppress'd with ignorance, wee still were so.
Poore soule, in this thy flesh what dost thou know?
Thou know'st thy selfe so little, as thou know'st not,   255
How thou didst die, nor how thou wast begot.
Thou neither know'st, how thou at first cam'st in,
Nor how thou took'st the poyson of mans sinne.
Nor dost thou, (though thou know'st, that thou art so)
By what way thou art made immortall, know.   260
Thou art too narrow, wretch, to comprehend
Even thy selfe: yea though thou wouldst but bend
To know thy body. Have not all soules thought
For many ages, that our body'is wrought
Of Ayre, and Fire, and other Elements?   265
And now they thinke of new ingredients,
And one Soule thinkes one, and another way
Another thinkes, and 'tis an even lay.
Knowst thou but how the stone doth enter in

The

The bladders cave, and never breake the skinne? 270
Know'st thou how blood, which to the heart doth flow,
Doth from one ventricle to th'other goe?
And for the putrid stuffe, which thou dost spit,
Know'st thou how thy lungs have attracted it?
There are no passages, so that there is 275
(For ought thou know'st) piercing of substances.
And of those many opinions which men raise
Of Nailes and Haires, dost thou know which to praise?
What hope have wee to know our selves, when wee
Know not the least things, which for our use be? 280
Wee see in Authors, too stiffe to recant,
A hundred controversies of an Ant;
And yet one watches, starves, freeses, and sweats,
To know but Catechismes and Alphabets
Of unconcerning things, matters of fact; 285
How others on our stage their parts did Act;
What *Cæsar* did, yea, and what *Cicero* said.
Why grasse is greene, or why our blood is red,
Are mysteries which none have reach'd unto.
In this low forme, poore soule, what wilt thou doe? 290
When wilt thou shake off this Pedantery,
Of being taught by sense, and Fantasie?
Thou look'st through spectacles; small things seeme great
Below; But up unto the watch-towre get,
And see all things despoyl'd of fallacies: 295
Thou shalt not peepe through lattices of eyes,
Nor heare through Labyrinths of eares, nor learne
By circuit, or collections to discerne.
In heaven thou straight know'st all, concerning it,
And what concernes it not, shalt straight forget. 300
There thou (but in no other schoole) maist bee
Perchance, as learned, and as full, as shee,
Shee who all libraries had throughly read
At home in her owne thoughts, and practised

291 Pedantery] Pedantry *1650–54*

So

So much good as would make as many more: 305
Shee whose example they must all implore,
Who would or doe, or thinke well, and confesse
That all the vertuous Actions they expresse,
Are but a new, and worse edition
Of her some one thought, or one action: 310
She who in th'art of knowing Heaven, was growne
Here upon earth, to such perfection,
That she hath, ever since to Heaven she came,
(In a far fairer print,) but read the same:
Shee, shee not satisfied with all this waight,   315
(For so much knowledge, as would over-fraight
Another, did but ballast her) is gone
As well t'enjoy, as get perfection.
And cals us after her, in that shee tooke,

Of our com- (Taking her selfe) our best, and worthiest booke.   320
pany in this Returne not, my Soule, from this extasie,
life, and in And meditation of what thou shalt bee,
the next. To earthly thoughts, till it to thee appeare,
With whom thy conversation must be there.
With whom wilt thou converse? what station   325
Canst thou choose out, free from infection,
That will not give thee theirs, nor drinke in thine?
Shalt thou not finde a spungie slacke Divine
Drinke and sucke in th'instructions of Great men,
And for the word of God, vent them agen?   330
Are there not some Courts (and then, no things bee
So like as Courts) which, in this let us see,
That wits and tongues of Libellers are weake,
Because they do more ill, then these can speake?
The poyson's gone through all, poysons affect   335
Chiefly the chiefest parts, but some effect
In nailes, and haires, yea excrements, will show;
So lyes the poyson of sinne in the most low.
Up, up, my drowsie Soule, where thy new eare

327 will not] will nor *1612–25*

Shall

Shall in the Angels songs no discord heare;   340
Where thou shalt see the blessed Mother-maid
Joy in not being that, which men have said.
Where she is exalted more for being good,
Then for her interest of Mother-hood.
Up to those Patriarchs, which did longer sit   345
Expecting Christ, then they'have enjoy'd him yet.
Up to those Prophets, which now gladly see
Their Prophesies growne to be Historie.
Up to th'Apostles, who did bravely runne
All the Suns course, with more light then the Sunne.   350
Up to those Martyrs, who did calmly bleed
Oyle to th'Apostles Lamps, dew to their seed.
Up to those Virgins, who thought, that almost
They made joyntenants with the Holy Ghost,
If they to any should his Temple give.   355
Up, up, for in that squadron there doth live
She, who hath carried thither new degrees
(As to their number) to their dignities.
Shee, who being to her selfe a State, injoy'd
All royalties which any State employ'd;   360
For shee made warres, and triumph'd; reason still
Did not o'rthrow, but rectifie her will:
And she made peace, for no peace is like this,
That beauty, and chastity together kisse:
She did high justice, for she crucified   365
Every first motion of rebellious pride:
And she gave pardons, and was liberall,
For, onely her selfe except, she pardon'd all:
Shee coy'nd, in this, that her impressions gave
To all our actions all the worth they have: 370
She gave protections; the thoughts of her brest
Satans rude Officers could ne'r arrest.
As these prerogatives being met in one,
Made her a soveraigne State; religion
Made her a Church; and these two made her all.   375

She

She who was all this All, and could not fall
To worse, by company, (for she was still
More Antidote, then all the world was ill,)
Shee, shee doth leave it, and by Death, survive
All this, in Heaven; whither who doth not strive   380
The more, because shees there, he doth not know
That accidentall joyes in Heaven doe grow.
But pause, my soule; And study, ere thou fall
On accidentall joyes, th'essentiall.

Of essentiall
joy in this
life and in
the next.

Still before Accessories doe abide   385
A triall, must the principall be tride.
And what essentiall joy can'st thou expect
Here upon earth? what permanent effect
Of transitory causes? Dost thou love
Beauty? (And beauty worthy'st is to move)   390
Poore cousened cousenor, *that* she, and *that* thou,
Which did begin to love, are neither now;
You are both fluid, chang'd since yesterday;
Next day repaires, (but ill) last dayes decay.
Nor are, (although the river keepe the name)   395
Yesterdaies waters, and to daies the same.
So flowes her face, and thine eyes, neither now
That Saint, nor Pilgrime, which your loving vow
Concern'd, remaines; but whil'st you thinke you bee
Constant, you'are hourely in inconstancie.   400
Honour may have pretence unto our love,
Because that God did live so long above
Without this Honour, and then lov'd it so,
That he at last made Creatures to bestow
Honour on him; not that he needed it,   405
But that, to his hands, man might grow more fit.
But since all Honours from inferiours flow,
(For they doe give it; Princes doe but shew
Whom they would have so honor'd) and that this
On such opinions, and capacities   410
Is built, as rise and fall, to more and lesse:

Alas,

Alas, 'tis but a casuall happinesse.
Hath ever any man to'himselfe assign'd
This or that happinesse to'arrest his minde,
But that another man which takes a worse,   415
Thinks him a foole for having tane that course?
They who did labour Babels tower to'erect,
Might have considered, that for that effect,
All this whole solid Earth could not allow
Nor furnish forth materialls enow;   420
And that this Center, to raise such a place,
Was farre too little, to have beene the Base;
No more affords this world, foundation
To erect true joy, were all the meanes in one.
But as the Heathen made them severall gods,   425
Of all Gods Benefits, and all his Rods,
(For as the Wine, and Corne, and Onions are
Gods unto them, so Agues bee, and Warre)
And as by changing that whole precious Gold
To such small Copper coynes, they lost the old,   430
And lost their only God, who ever must
Be sought alone, and not in such a thrust:
So much mankinde true happinesse mistakes;
No Joy enjoyes that man, that many makes.
Then, Soule, to thy first pitch worke up againe;   435
Know that all lines which circles doe containe,
For once that they the Center touch, doe touch
Twice the circumference; and be thou such;
Double on heaven thy thoughts on earth emploid;
All will not serve; Only who have enjoy'd   440
The sight of God, in fulnesse, can thinke it;
For it is both the object, and the wit.
This is essentiall joy, where neither hee
Can suffer diminution, nor wee;
'Tis such a full, and such a filling good,   445
Had th'Angels once look'd on him, they had stood.
To fill the place of one of them, or more,

Shee

Shee whom wee celebrate, is gone before.
She, who had Here so much essentiall joy,
As no chance could distract, much lesse destroy;   450
Who with Gods presence was acquainted so,
(Hearing, and speaking to him) as to know
His face in any naturall Stone, or Tree,
Better then when in Images they bee:
Who kept by diligent devotion,   455
Gods Image, in such reparation,
Within her heart, that what decay was growne,
Was her first Parents fault, and not her owne:
Who being solicited to any act,
Still heard God pleading his safe precontract;   460
Who by a faithfull confidence, was here
Betroth'd to God, and now is married there;
Whose twilights were more cleare, then our mid-day;
Who dreamt devoutlier, then most use to pray;
Who being here fil'd with grace, yet strove to bee,   465
Both where more grace, and more capacitie
At once is given: she to Heaven is gone,
Who made this world in some proportion
A heaven, and here, became unto us all,
Joy, (as our joyes admit) essentiall.   470

Of acciden-
tall joys in
both places.
But could this low world joyes essentiall touch,
Heavens accidentall joyes would passe them much.
How poore and lame, must then our casuall bee?
If thy Prince will his subjects to call thee
My Lord, and this doe swell thee, thou art than,   475
By being greater, growne to bee lesse Man.
When no Physitian of redresse can speake,
A joyfull casuall violence may breake
A dangerous Apostem in thy breast;
And whil'st thou joyest in this, the dangerous rest,   480
The bag may rise up, and so strangle thee.
What e'r was casuall, may ever bee.
What should the nature change? Or make the same

Certaine,

Certaine, which was but casuall, when it came?
All casuall joy doth loud and plainly say,   485
Only by comming, that it can away.
Only in Heaven joyes strength is never spent;
And accidentall things are permanent.
Joy of a soules arrivall ne'r decaies;
For that soule ever joyes and ever staies.   490
Joy that their last great Consummation
Approaches in the resurrection;
When earthly bodies more celestiall
Shall be, then Angels were, for they could fall;
This kinde of joy doth every day admit   495
Degrees of growth, but none of losing it.
In this fresh joy, 'tis no small part, that shee,
Shee, in whose goodnesse, he that names degree,
Doth injure her; ('Tis losse to be cal'd best,
There where the stuffe is not such as the rest)   500
Shee, who left such a bodie, as even shee
Only in Heaven could learne, how it can bee
Made better; for shee rather was two soules,
Or like to full on both sides written Rols,
Where eyes might reade upon the outward skin,   505
As strong Records for God, as mindes within;
Shee, who by making full perfection grow,
Peeces a Circle, and still keepes it so,
Long'd for, and longing for it, to heaven is gone,
Where shee receives, and gives addition.   510
Here in a place, where mis-devotion frames   *Conclusion.*
A thousand Prayers to Saints, whose very names
The ancient Church knew not, Heaven knows not yet:
And where, what lawes of Poetry admit,
Lawes of Religion have at least the same,   515
Immortall Maide, I might invoke thy name.
Could any Saint provoke that appetite,
Thou here should'st make me a French convertite.
But thou would'st not; nor would'st thou be content,

                                        To

To take this, for my second yeares true Rent,   520
Did this Coine beare any other stampe, then his,
That gave thee power to doe, me, to say this.
Since his will is, that to posteritie,
Thou should'st for life, and death, a patterne bee,
And that the world should notice have of this,   525
The purpose, and th'Authoritie is his;
Thou art the Proclamation; and I am
The Trumpet, at whose voyce the people came.

EPICEDES

EPICEDES AND OBSEQVIES

Vpon

The deaths of sundry Personages.

Elegie upon the untimely death of the incomparable Prince Henry.

LOoke to mee faith, and looke to my faith, God;
For both my centers feele this period.
Of waight one center, one of greatnesse is;
And Reason is that center, Faith is this;
For into'our reason flow, and there do end   5
All, that this naturall world doth comprehend:
Quotidian things, and equidistant hence,
Shut in, for man, in one circumference.
But for th'enormous greatnesses, which are
So disproportion'd, and so angulare,   10
As is Gods essence, place and providence,
Where, how, when, what soules do, departed hence,
These things (eccentrique else) on faith do strike;
Yet neither all, nor upon all, alike.
For reason, put to'her best extension,   15
Almost meetes faith, and makes both centers one.
And nothing ever came so neare to this,
As contemplation of that Prince, wee misse.
For all that faith might credit mankinde could,
Reason still seconded, that this prince would.   20
If then least moving of the center, make
More, then if whole hell belch'd, the world to shake,

Epicedes &c. 1635-69: Elegie upon &c. 1613, *in the* Lachrymae
Lachrymarum &c. *of Joshua Sylvester.* Elegie on Prince Henry.
1633-54: An Elegie on the untimely &c. 1669   8 man 1633-69:
men 1613   18 that 1633-69: the 1613   19 might credit 1633-
69: could credit 1613   21 moving 1633-69: movings 1613

What

What must this do, centers distracted so,
That wee see not what to beleeve or know?
Was it not well beleev'd till now, that hee,   25
Whose reputation was an extasie
On neighbour States, which knew not why to wake,
Till hee discover'd what wayes he would take;
For whom, what Princes angled, when they tryed,
Met a *Torpedo*, and were stupified;   30
And others studies, how he would be bent;
Was his great fathers greatest instrument,
And activ'st spirit, to convey and tie
This soule of peace, through Christianity?
Was it not well beleev'd, that hee would make   35
This generall peace, th'Eternall overtake,
And that his times might have stretch'd out so farre,
As to touch those, of which they emblems are?
For to confirme this just beleefe, that now
The last dayes came, wee saw heav'n did allow,   40
That, but from his aspect and exercise,
In peacefull times, Rumors of war did rise.
But now this faith is heresie: we must
Still stay, and vexe our great-grand-mother, Dust.
Oh, is God prodigall? hath he spent his store   45
Of plagues, on us; and onely now, when more
Would ease us much, doth he grudge misery;
And will not let's enjoy our curse; to dy?
As, for the earth throwne lowest downe of all,
T'were an ambition to desire to fall,   50
So God, in our desire to dye, doth know
Our plot for ease, in being wretched so.
Therefore we live; though such a life wee have,
As but so many mandrakes on his grave.
What had his growth, and generation done,   55
When, what we are, his putrefaction

31 bent; *Ed:* bent, *1613, 1633–69*   42 did *1633:* should *1613, 1635–69*

Sustaines

Sustaines in us; Earth, which griefes animate?
Nor hath our world now, other Soule then that.
And could griefe get so high as heav'n, that Quire,
Forgetting this their new joy, would desire   60
(With griefe to see him) hee had staid below,
To rectifie our errours, They foreknow.
Is th'other center, Reason, faster then?
Where should we looke for that, now we'are not men?
For if our Reason be'our connexion   65
Of causes, now to us there can be none.
For, as, if all the substances were spent,
'Twere madnesse, to enquire of accident,
So is't to looke for reason, hee being gone,
The onely subject reason wrought upon.   70
If Fate have such a chaine, whose divers links
Industrious man discerneth, as hee thinks;
When miracle doth come, and so steale in
A new linke, man knowes not, where to begin:
At a much deader fault must reason bee,   75
Death having broke off such a linke as hee.
But now, for us, with busie proofe to come,
That we'have no reason, would prove wee had some.
So would just lamentations: Therefore wee
May safelyer say, that we are dead, then hee.   80
So, if our griefs wee do not well declare,
We'have double excuse; he'is not dead; and we are.
Yet I would not dy yet; for though I bee
Too narrow, to thinke him, as hee is hee,
(Our Soules best baiting, and midd-period,   85
In her long journey, of considering God)
Yet, (no dishonour) I can reach him thus,
As he embrac'd the fires of love, with us.

66 Of *1633–69:* With *1613*   71 Fate *1633–69:* Faith *1613*
73 come, *1633–69:* joine; *1613*   so steale in *1633–69:* to steal-in
1613   77 proofe *1633–69:* proofes *1613*   82 and we are.
1633–54: we are. *1613, 1669*

                                        Oh

Oh may I, (since I live) but see, or heare,
That she-Intelligence which mov'd this spheare,   90
I pardon Fate, my life: Who ere thou bee,
Which hast the noble conscience, thou art shee,
I conjure thee by all the charmes he spoke,
By th'oathes, which onely you two never broke,
By all the soules yee sigh'd, that if you see   95
These lines, you wish, I knew your history.
So much, as you two mutuall heav'ns were here,
I were an Angell, singing what you were.

To the Countesse of Bedford.

MADAME,

I Have learn'd by those lawes wherein I am a little conver-
sant, that hee which bestowes any cost upon the dead, obliges
him which is dead, but not the heire; I do not therefore send this
paper to your Ladyship, that you should thanke mee for it, or
thinke that I thanke you in it; your favours and benefits to mee
are so much above my merits, that they are even above my
gratitude, if that were to be judged by words which must expresse it: But, Madame, since your noble brothers fortune
being yours, the evidences also concerning it are yours, so his
vertue being yours, the evidences concerning it, belong also to
you, of which by your acceptance this may be one peece, in which
quality I humbly present it, and as a testimony how intirely
your familie possesseth

Your Ladiships most humble
and thankfull servant
JOHN DONNE.

97 So much, as you, *1633–69*

Obsequies to the Lord Harrington, brother to the Lady Lucy, Countesse of Bedford.

FAire soule, which wast, not onely, as all soules bee,
  Then when thou wast infused, harmony,
But did'st continue so; and now dost beare
A part in Gods great organ, this whole Spheare:
If looking up to God; or downe to us,   5
Thou finde that any way is pervious,
Twixt heav'n and earth, and that mans actions doe
Come to your knowledge, and affections too,
See, and with joy, mee to that good degree
Of goodnesse growne, that I can studie thee,   10
And, by these meditations refin'd,
Can unapparell and enlarge my minde,
And so can make by this soft extasie,
This place a map of heav'n, my selfe of thee.
Thou seest mee here at midnight, now all rest;   15
Times dead-low water; when all mindes devest
To morrows businesse, when the labourers have
Such rest in bed, that their last Church-yard grave,
Subject to change, will scarce be'a type of this,
Now when the clyent, whose last hearing is   20
To morrow, sleeps, when the condemned man,
(Who when hee opes his eyes, must shut them than
Againe by death,) although sad watch hee keepe,
Doth practice dying by a little sleepe,
Thou at this midnight seest mee, and as soone   25
As that Sunne rises to mee, midnight's noone,
All the world growes transparent, and I see
Through all, both Church and State, in seeing thee;
And I discerne by favour of this light,
My selfe, the hardest object of the sight.   30

Obsequies to &c.   7 mans *1633*, *one MS. group:* mens *1635–69 and most MSS.*

God

God is the glasse; as thou when thou dost see
Him who sees all, seest all concerning thee,
So, yet unglorified, I comprehend
All, in these mirrors of thy wayes, and end.
Though God be our true glasse, through which we see   35
All, since the beeing of all things is hee,
Yet are the trunkes which doe to us derive
Things, in proportion fit, by perspective,
Deeds of good men; for by their living here,
Vertues, indeed remote, seeme to be neare.   40
But where can I affirme, or where arrest
My thoughts on his deeds? which shall I call best?
For fluid vertue cannot be look'd on,
Nor can endure a contemplation.
As bodies change, and as I do not weare   45
Those Spirits, humors, blood I did last yeare,
And, as if on a streame I fixe mine eye,
That drop, which I looked on, is presently
Pusht with more waters from my sight, and gone,
So in this sea of vertues, can no one   50
Bee'insisted on; vertues, as rivers, passe,
Yet still remaines that vertuous man there was.
And as if man feed on mans flesh, and so
Part of his body to another owe,
Yet at the last two perfect bodies rise,   55
Because God knowes where every Atome lyes;
So, if one knowledge were made of all those,
Who knew his minutes well, hee might dispose
His vertues into names, and ranks; but I
Should injure Nature, Vertue, and Destinie,   60
Should I divide and discontinue so,
Vertue, which did in one intirenesse grow.
For as, hee that would say, spirits are fram'd
Of all the purest parts that can be nam'd,

35 our true glasse, *1633–69:* truly our glass *most MSS.*   53 feed
1635–69 and MSS.: feeds *1633*

Honours

Honours not spirits halfe so much, as hee 65
Which sayes, they have no parts, but simple bee;
So is't of vertue; for a point and one
Are much entirer then a million.
And had Fate meant to have his vertues told,
It would have let him live to have beene old; 70
So, then that vertue in season, and then this,
We might have seene, and said, that now he is
Witty, now wise, now temperate, now just:
In good short lives, vertues are faine to thrust,
And to be sure betimes to get a place, 75
When they would exercise, lacke time, and space.
So was it in this person, forc'd to bee
For lack of time, his owne epitome:
So to exhibit in few yeares as much,
As all the long breath'd Chronicles can touch. 80
As when an Angell down from heav'n doth flye,
Our quick thought cannot keepe him company,
Wee cannot thinke, now hee is at the Sunne,
Now through the Moon, now he through th'aire doth run,
Yet when he's come, we know he did repaire 85
To all twixt Heav'n and Earth, Sunne, Moon, and Aire;
And as this Angell in an instant knowes,
And yet wee know, this sodaine knowledge growes
By quick amassing severall formes of things,
Which he successively to order brings; 90
When they, whose slow-pac'd lame thoughts cannot goe
So fast as hee, thinke that he doth not so;
Just as a perfect reader doth not dwell,
On every syllable, nor stay to spell,
Yet without doubt, hee doth distinctly see 95
And lay together every A, and B;
So, in short liv'd good men, is'not understood
Each severall vertue, but the compound good;
For, they all vertues paths in that pace tread,
As Angells goe, and know, and as men read. 100

O why

O why should then these men, these lumps of Balme
Sent hither, this worlds tempests to becalme,
Before by deeds they are diffus'd and spred,
And so make us alive, themselves be dead?
O Soule, O circle, why so quickly bee   105
Thy ends, thy birth and death, clos'd up in thee?
Since one foot of thy compasse still was plac'd
In heav'n, the other might securely'have pac'd
In the most large extent, through every path,
Which the whole world, or man the abridgment hath.   110
Thou knowst, that though the tropique circles have
(Yea and those small ones which the Poles engrave,)
All the same roundnesse, evennesse, and all
The endlesnesse of the equinoctiall;
Yet, when we come to measure distances,   115
How here, how there, the Sunne affected is,
When he doth faintly worke, and when prevaile,
Onely great circles, then can be our scale:
So, though thy circle to thy selfe expresse
All, tending to thy endlesse happinesse,   120
And wee, by our good use of it may trye,
Both how to live well young, and how to die,
Yet, since we must be old, and age endures
His Torrid Zone at Court, and calentures
Of hot ambitions, irreligions ice,   125
Zeales agues, and hydroptique avarice,
Infirmities which need the scale of truth,
As well as lust, and ignorance of youth;
Why did'st thou not for these give medicines too,
And by thy doing tell us what to doe?   130
Though as small pocket-clocks, whose every wheele
Doth each mismotion and distemper feele,

102 this *MSS.:* the *1633–69*   tempests *most MSS.:* tempest
1633–69 and some MSS.   117 When . . . when *1633–69 and one
MS. group:* Where . . . where *most MSS.*   130 tell us *1633, 1669,
and most MSS.:* set us *1635–54 and some MSS.*

                                                        Whose

Whose *hand* gets shaking palsies, and whose *string*
(His sinewes) slackens, and whose *Soule*, the spring,
Expires, or languishes, whose pulse, the *flye*,   135
Either beates not, or beates unevenly,
Whose voice, the *Bell*, doth rattle, or grow dumbe,
Or idle,'as men, which to their last houres come,
If these clockes be not wound, or be wound still,
Or be not set, or set at every will;   140
So, youth is easiest to destruction,
If then wee follow all, or follow none.
Yet, as in great clocks, which in steeples chime,
Plac'd to informe whole towns, to'imploy their time,
An error doth more harme, being generall,   145
When, small clocks faults, only'on the wearer fall;
So worke the faults of age, on which the eye
Of children, servants, or the State relie.
Why wouldst not thou then, which hadst such a soule,
A clock so true, as might the Sunne controule,   150
And daily hadst from him, who gave it thee,
Instructions, such as it could never be
Disordered, stay here, as a generall
And great Sun-dyall, to have set us All?
O why wouldst thou be any instrument   155
To this unnaturall course, or why consent
To this, not miracle, but Prodigie,
That when the ebbs, longer then flowings be,
Vertue, whose flood did with thy youth begin,
Should so much faster ebb out, then flow in?   160
Though her flood was blowne in, by thy first breath,
All is at once sunke in the whirle-poole death.
Which word I would not name, but that I see
Death, else a desert, growne a Court by thee.
Now I grow sure, that if a man would have   165
Good companie, his entry is a grave.

133 *hand* gets MSS.: *hands* get 1633–54: *hands* gets 1669.   158
when 1633–69: *where* most MSS.: *whereas* one MS.

Mee

Mee thinkes all Cities, now, but Anthills bee,
Where, when the severall labourers I see,
For children, house, Provision, taking paine,
They'are all but Ants, carrying eggs, straw, and grain;   170
And Church-yards are our cities, unto which
The most repaire, that are in goodnesse rich.
There is the best concourse, and confluence,
There are the holy suburbs, and from thence
Begins Gods City, New Jerusalem,   175
Which doth extend her utmost gates to them.
At that gate then Triumphant soule, dost thou
Begin thy Triumph; But since lawes allow
That at the Triumph day, the people may,
All that they will, 'gainst the Triumpher say,   180
Let me here use that freedome, and expresse
My griefe, though not to make thy Triumph lesse.
By law, to Triumphs none admitted bee,
Till they as Magistrates get victorie;
Though then to thy force, all youthes foes did yield,   185
Yet till fit time had brought thee to that field,
To which thy ranke in this state destin'd thee,
That there thy counsailes might get victorie,
And so in that capacitie remove
All jealousies 'twixt Prince and subjects love,   190
Thou could'st no title, to this triumph have,
Thou didst intrude on death, usurp'dst a grave.
Then (though victoriously) thou hadst fought as yet
But with thine owne affections, with the heate
Of youths desires, and colds of ignorance,   195
But till thou should'st successefully advance
Thine armes 'gainst forraine enemies, which are
Both Envy, and acclamations popular,
(For, both these engines equally defeate,

192 usurp'dst *most MSS.*: usurp'st *1633 and some MSS.*: usurpe
1635–69 and some MSS.   198 acclamations *1669 and MSS.*: accla-
mation *1633–54*

Though

Though by a divers Mine, those which are great,) 200
Till then thy War was but a civill War,
For which to Triumph, none admitted are.
No more are they, who though with good successe,
In a defensive war, their power expresse;
Before men triumph, the dominion 205
Must be *enlarg'd*, and not *preserv'd* alone;
Why should'st thou then, whose battailes were to win
Thy selfe, from those straits nature put thee in,
And to deliver up to God that state,
Of which he gave thee the vicariate, 210
(Which is thy soule and body) as intire
As he, who takes endeavours, doth require,
But didst not stay, t'enlarge his kingdome too,
By making others, what thou didst, to doe;
Why shouldst thou Triumph now, when Heav'n no more
Hath got, by getting thee, then't had before? 216
For, Heav'n and thou, even when thou livedst here,
Of one another in possession were.
But this from Triumph most disables thee,
That, that place which is conquered, must bee 220
Left safe from present warre, and likely doubt
Of imminent commotions to breake out:
And hath he left us so? or can it bee
His territory was no more then Hee?
No, we were all his charge, the Diocis 225
Of ev'ry exemplar man, the whole world is,
And he was joyned in commission
With Tutelar Angels, sent to every one.
But though this freedome to upbraid, and chide
Him who Triumph'd, were lawfull, it was ty'd 230
With this, that it might never reference have
Unto the Senate, who this triumph gave;
Men might at Pompey jeast, but they might not
At that authoritie, by which he got
Leave to Triumph, before, by age, he might; 235

So,

So, though, triumphant soule, I dare to write,
Mov'd with a reverentiall anger, thus,
That thou so earely wouldst abandon us;
Yet I am farre from daring to dispute
With that great soveraigntie, whose absolute   240
Prerogative hath thus dispens'd with thee,
'Gainst natures lawes, which just impugners bee
Of early triumphs; And I (though with paine)
Lessen our losse, to magnifie thy gaine
Of triumph, when I say, It was more fit,   245
That all men should lacke thee, then thou lack it.
Though then in our time, be not suffered
That testimonie of love, unto the dead,
To die with them, and in their graves be hid,
As Saxon wives, and French soldurii did;   250
And though in no degree I can expresse
Griefe in great Alexanders great excesse,
Who at his friends death, made whole townes devest
Their walls and bullwarks which became them best:
Doe not, faire soule, this sacrifice refuse,   255
That in thy grave I doe interre my Muse,
Who, by my griefe, great as thy worth, being cast
Behind hand, yet hath spoke, and spoke her last.

Elegie on the Lady Marckham.

MAn is the World, and death th'Ocean,
    To which God gives the lower parts of man.
This Sea invirons all, and though as yet
    God hath set markes, and bounds, twixt us and it,
Yet doth it rore, and gnaw, and still pretend,   5
    And breaks our bankes, when ere it takes a friend.

241 with *1633–69, one MS.:* for *most MSS.*   247 time] times *1669
and many MSS.*   250 soldurii *one MS. group:* soldarii *1633–69*
    Elegie *&c.*   6 bankes *most MSS.:* bounds *some MSS.:* banke,
1633–69 and one MS. group

Then

Then our land waters (teares of passion) vent;
  Our waters, then, above our firmament,
(Teares which our Soule doth for her sins let fall)
  Take all a brackish tast, and Funerall,   10
And even these teares, which should wash sin, are sin.
  We, after Gods *Noe*, drowne our world againe.
Nothing but man of all invenom'd things
  Doth worke upon itselfe, with inborne stings.
Teares are false Spectacles, we cannot see   15
  Through passions mist, what wee are, or what shee.
In her this sea of death hath made no breach,
  But as the tide doth wash the slimie beach,
And leaves embroder'd workes upon the sand,
  So is her flesh refin'd by deaths cold hand.   20
As men of China,'after an ages stay,
  Do take up Porcelane, where they buried Clay;
So at this grave, her limbecke, which refines
  The Diamonds, Rubies, Saphires, Pearles, and Mines,
Of which this flesh was, her soule shall inspire   25
  Flesh of such stuffe, as God, when his last fire
Annuls this world, to recompence it, shall,
  Make and name then, th'Elixar of this All.
They say, the sea, when it gaines, loseth too;
  If carnall Death (the younger brother) doe   30
Usurpe the body,'our soule, which subject is
  To th'elder death, by sinne, is freed by this;
They perish both, when they attempt the just;
  For, graves our trophies are, and both deaths dust.
So, unobnoxious now, she'hath buried both;   35
  For, none to death sinnes, that to sinne is loth,
Nor doe they die, which are not loth to die;
  So hath she this, and that virginity.

11 these *one MS. group:* those *1633–69*   12 our world *1669 and most MSS.:* the world *1633–54 and some MSS.*   34 and both deaths dust. *Ed:* and both Deaths' dust. *Grolier:* and both, deaths dust. *1633:* and both death's dust. *1635–69 and Chambers:* and both dead dust. *most MSS.*

Grace

Grace was in her extremely diligent,
That kept her from sinne, yet made her repent.   40
Of what small spots pure white complaines! Alas,
How little poyson cracks a christall glasse!
She sinn'd, but just enough to let us see
That God's word must be true, All, sinners be.
Soe much did zeale her conscience rarefie,   45
That, extreme truth lack'd little of a lye,
Making omissions, acts; laying the touch
Of sinne, on things that sometimes may be such.
As *Moses* Cherubines, whose natures doe
Surpasse all speed, by him are winged too: 50
So would her soule, already'in heaven, seeme then,
To clyme by teares, the common staires of men.
How fit she was for God, I am content
To speake, that Death his vaine hast may repent.
How fit for us, how even and how sweet,   55
How good in all her titles, and how meet,
To have reform'd this forward heresie,
That women can no parts of friendship bee;
How Morall, how Divine shall not be told,
Lest they that heare her vertues, thinke her old: 60
And lest we take Deaths part, and make him glad
Of such a prey, and to his tryumph adde.

Elegie on M^ris Boulstred.

DEath I recant, and say, unsaid by mee
What ere hath slip'd, that might diminish thee.
Spirituall treason, atheisme 'tis, to say,
That any can thy Summons disobey.

---

42 cracks] breakes *most MSS.*   45 rarefie,] rectify, *most MSS.*
52 teares,] tears *Chambers*   the . . . men *in brackets one MS. group*
58 women *1635–69 and most MSS.:* woman *1633*   parts] parte *one
MS. group   This line written in large letters in several MSS.*   62
tryumph] triumphes *many MSS.*

                                        Th'earths

Th'earths face is but thy Table; there are set 5
   Plants, cattell, men, dishes for Death to eate.
In a rude hunger now hee millions drawes
   Into his bloody, or plaguy, or sterv'd jawes.
Now hee will seeme to spare, and doth more wast,
   Eating the best first, well preserv'd to last. 10
Now wantonly he spoiles, and eates us not,
   But breakes off friends, and lets us peecemeale rot.
Nor will this earth serve him; he sinkes the deepe
   Where harmelesse fish monastique silence keepe,
Who (were Death dead) by Roes of living sand, 15
   Might spunge that element, and make it land.
He rounds the aire, and breakes the hymnique notes
   In birds (Heavens choristers,) organique throats,
Which (if they did not dye) might seeme to bee
   A tenth ranke in the heavenly hierarchie. 20
O strong and long-liv'd death, how cam'st thou in?
   And how without Creation didst begin?
Thou hast, and shalt see dead, before thou dyest,
   All the foure Monarchies, and Antichrist.
How could I thinke thee nothing, that see now 25
   In all this All, nothing else is, but thou.
Our births and lives, vices, and vertues, bee
   Wastfull consumptions, and degrees of thee.
For, wee to live, our bellowes weare, and breath,
   Nor are wee mortall, dying, dead, but death. 30
And though thou beest, O mighty bird of prey,
   So much reclaim'd by God, that thou must lay
All that thou kill'st at his feet, yet doth hee
   Reserve but few, and leaves the most to thee.
And of those few, now thou hast overthrowne 35

Elegie on Mrs Boulstred. *In some MSS. this and the* Elegie, Death, be not proud (*p.* 386) *are given as one poem.* 5 there are set] and the meate *some MSS.* 6 dishes *1633, 1650–69:* dished *1635–39 and some MSS.* 10 first,] fruite *or* fruites *some MSS.* 27 lives, *1635–69 and some MSS.:* lifes, *one MS.:* life, *1633 and most MSS.*

One whom thy blow makes, not ours, nor thine own.
She was more stories high: hopelesse to come
   To her Soule, thou'hast offer'd at her lower roome.
Her Soule and body was a King and Court:
   But thou hast both of Captaine mist and fort.   40
As houses fall not, though the King remove,
   Bodies of Saints rest for their soules above.
Death gets 'twixt soules and bodies such a place
   As sinne insinuates 'twixt just men and grace,
Both worke a separation, no divorce.   45
   Her Soule is gone to usher up her corse,
Which shall be'almost another soule, for there
   Bodies are purer, then best Soules are here.
Because in her, her virtues did outgoe
   Her yeares, would'st thou, O emulous death, do so? 50
And kill her young to thy losse? must the cost
   Of beauty,'and wit, apt to doe harme, be lost?
What though thou found'st her proofe 'gainst sins of youth?
   Oh, every age a diverse sinne pursueth.
Thou should'st have stay'd, and taken better hold, 55
   Shortly, ambitious; covetous, when old,
She might have prov'd: and such devotion
   Might once have stray'd to superstition.
If all her vertues must have growne, yet might
   Abundant virtue'have bred a proud delight.   60
Had she persever'd just, there would have bin
   Some that would sinne, mis-thinking she did sinne.
Such as would call her friendship, love, and faine
   To sociablenesse, a name profane;
Or sinne, by tempting, or, not daring that,   65
   By wishing, though they never told her what.
Thus might'st thou'have slain more soules, had'st thou not
      crost
   Thy selfe, and to triumph, thine army lost.
Yet though these wayes be lost, thou hast left one,

41 King 1633 and MSS.: Kings 1635–69

Which

Which is, immoderate griefe that she is gone. 70
But we may scape that sinne, yet weepe as much,
  Our teares are due, because we are not such.
Some teares, that knot of friends, her death must cost,
  Because the chaine is broke, though no linke lost.

ELEGIE.

Death.

LAnguage thou art too narrow, and too weake
  To ease us now; great sorrow cannot speake;
If we could sigh out accents, and weepe words,
  Griefe weares, and lessens, that tears breath affords.
Sad hearts, the lesse they seeme the more they are, 5
  (So guiltiest men stand mutest at the barre)
Not that they know not, feele not their estate,
  But extreme sense hath made them desperate.
Sorrow, to whom we owe all that we bee;
  Tyrant, in the fift and greatest Monarchy, 10
Was't, that she did possesse all hearts before,
  Thou hast kil'd her, to make thy Empire more?
Knew'st thou some would, that knew her not, lament,
  As in a deluge perish th'innocent?
Was't not enough to have that palace wonne, 15
  But thou must raze it too, that was undone?
Had'st thou staid there, and look'd out at her eyes,
  All had ador'd thee that now from thee flies,
For they let out more light, then they tooke in,
  They told not when, but did the day beginne. 20

Here follow in 1635–54 By our first strange (*p.* 99), Madame, That
I (*p.* 265), *and* Death be not proud, (*p.* 386). *In 1669* My Fortune
and (*p.* 266) *precedes* Madame, That I
  Elegie. *1633:* Elegie XI. Death. *1635–54* (*being placed among the
Elegies*)*:* Elegie XI. *1669:* An Elegie upon the death of Mⁱˢ
Boulstred. *most MSS.* 2 sorrow *1633 and most MSS.:* sorrowes
1635–69 and some MSS.

                                        She

She was too Saphirine, and cleare for thee;
    Clay, flint, and jeat now thy fit dwellings be;
Alas, shee was too pure, but not too weake;
    Who e'r saw Christall Ordinance but would break?
And if wee be thy conquest, by her fall   25
    Th'hast lost thy end, for in her perish all;
Or if we live, we live but to rebell,
    They know her better now, that knew her well.
If we should vapour out, and pine, and die;
    Since, shee first went, that were not miserie.   30
Shee chang'd our world with hers; now she is gone,
    Mirth and prosperity is oppression;
For of all morall vertues she was all,
    The Ethicks speake of vertues Cardinall.
Her soule was Paradise; the Cherubin   35
    Set to keepe it was grace, that kept out sinne.
Shee had no more then let in death, for wee
    All reape consumption from one fruitfull tree.
God tooke her hence, lest some of us should love
    Her, like that plant, him and his lawes above,   40
And when wee teares, hee mercy shed in this,
    To raise our mindes to heaven where now she is;
Who if her vertues would have let her stay
    Wee'had had a Saint, have now a holiday.
Her heart was that strange bush, where, sacred fire,   45
    Religion, did not consume, but'inspire
Such piety, so chast use of Gods day,
    That what we turne to *feast*, she turn'd to *pray*,
And did prefigure here, in devout tast,
    The rest of her high Sabaoth, which shall last.   50

28 They . . . that . . . well; *1633 and most MSS.:* That know her
better now, who knew her well. *1635–69 and some MSS.*   34 The
Ethicks speake *1633 and most MSS.:* That Ethickes speake *1635–69
and some MSS.:* The ethenickes spake *one MS.*   48 That what
1633–69: That when *one MS.*   turne] turn'd *some MSS.*   to *feast*,
Ed: to feast, *1633–69*   to *pray, Ed:* to pray, *1633–69*

Angels

Angels did hand her up, who next God dwell,
  (For she was of that order whence most fell)
Her body left with us, lest some had said,
  Shee could not die, except they saw her dead;
For from lesse vertue, and lesse beautiousnesse,   55
  The Gentiles fram'd them Gods and Goddesses.
The ravenous earth that now wooes her to be
  Earth too, will be a *Lemnia*; and the tree
That wraps that christall in a wooden Tombe,
  Shall be tooke up spruce, fill'd with diamond;   60
And we her sad glad friends all beare a part
  Of griefe, for all would waste a Stoicks heart.

Elegie on the L. C.

SOrrow, who to this house scarce knew the way:
  Is, Oh, heire of it, our All is his prey.
This strange chance claimes strange wonder, and to us
Nothing can be so strange, as to weepe thus.
'Tis well his lifes loud speaking workes deserve,   5
And give praise too, our cold tongues could not serve:
'Tis well, hee kept teares from our eyes before,
That to fit this deepe ill, we might have store.
Oh, if a sweet briar, climbe up by'a tree,
If to a paradise that transplanted bee,   10
Or fell'd, and burnt for holy sacrifice,
Yet, that must wither, which by it did rise,
As we for him dead: though no familie
Ere rigg'd a soule for heavens discoverie
With whom more Venturers more boldly dare   15
Venture their states, with him in joy to share.
Wee lose what all friends lov'd, him; he gaines now
But life by death, which worst foes would allow,

58 *All the MSS. omit a before* Lemnia, *but one inserts*   62 waste
1633 and most MSS.: breake *1635–69 and some MSS.*
  Elegie *&c. 1635–69, following* Death be not proud. *Elegie VI.
(being placed among the* Elegies) *1633 and similarly in some MSS.*

If

If hee could have foes, in whose practise grew
All vertues, whose names subtile Schoolmen knew.   20
What ease, can hope that wee shall see'him, beget,
When wee must die first, and cannot dye yet?
His children are his pictures, Oh they bee
Pictures of him dead, senselesse, cold as he.
Here needs no marble Tombe, since hee is gone,   25
He, and about him, his, are turn'd to stone.

An hymne to the Saints, and to Marquesse Hamylton.

To Sir Robert Carr.

S I R,

I Presume you rather try what you can doe in me, then what I can doe in verse; you know my uttermost when it was best, and even then I did best when I had least truth for my subjects. In this present case there is so much truth as it defeats all Poetry. Call therefore this paper by what name you will, and, if it bee not worthy of him, nor of you, nor of mee, smother it, and bee that the sacrifice. If you had commanded mee to have waited on his body to Scotland and preached there, I would have embraced the obligation with more alacrity; But, I thanke you that you would command me that which I was loath to doe, for, even that hath given a tincture of merit to the obedience of

Your poore friend and
servant in Christ Jesus
J. D.

An hymne &c. 1633–69, in all of which it is classed with the Divine Poems, following Resurrection. In 1635–69 it is preceded by the letter To Sir Robert Carr.: in 1633 the letter follows, and has no heading: similarly in some MSS.   2 best] at the best one MS. 6–7 of him . . . sacrifice. 1635–69: of you nor of him, we will smother it, and be it your sacrifice. 1633: of him, nor of you, nor of anye; smother it, and bee that the sacrifice. one MS.   9 the 1635–69: your 1633 and one MS.   more] much 1633   11 loath] loather 1633

WHether

WHether that soule which now comes up to you
    Fill any former ranke or make a new;
Whether it take a name nam'd there before,
Or be a name it selfe, and *order* more
Then was in heaven till now; (for may not hee   5
Bee so, if every severall Angell bee
A *kind* alone?) What ever order grow
Greater by him in heaven, wee doe not so.
One of your orders growes by his accesse;
But, by his losse grow all our *orders* lesse;   10
The name of *Father*, *Master*, *Friend*, the name
Of *Subject* and of *Prince*, in one are lame;
Faire mirth is dampt, and conversation black,
The *household* widdow'd, and the *garter* slack;
The *Chappell* wants an eare, *Councell* a tongue;   15
Story, a theame; and *Musicke* lacks a song;
Blest *order* that hath him! the losse of him
Gangreend all *Orders* here; all lost a limbe.
Never made body such hast to confesse
What a soule was; All former comelinesse   20
Fled, in a minute, when the soule was gone,
And, having lost that beauty, would have none;
So fell our *Monasteries*, in one instant growne
Not to lesse houses, but, to heapes of stone;
So sent this body that faire forme it wore,   25
Unto the spheare of formes, and doth (before
His soule shall fill up his sepulchrall stone,)
Anticipate a Resurrection;
For, as in his fame, now, his soule is here,
So, in the forme thereof his bodie's there.   30
And if, faire soule, not with first *Innocents*
Thy station be, but with the *Pænitents*,
(And, who shall dare to aske then when I am
Dy'd scarlet in the blood of that pure Lambe,
Whether that colour, which is scarlet then,   35

Were

Were black or white before in eyes of men?)
When thou rememb'rest what sins thou didst finde
Amongst those many friends now left behinde,
And seest such sinners as they are, with thee
Got thither by repentance, Let it bee   40
Thy wish to wish all there, to wish them cleane;
Wish *him* a *David, her* a *Magdalen.*

36 in eyes] in the eyes *MSS.*

EPITAPHS.

EPITAPHS.

EPITAPH

ON HIMSELFE.

To the Countesse of Bedford.

MADAME,

THat I might make your Cabinet my tombe,
   And for my fame which I love next my soule,
Next to my soule provide the happiest roome,
   Admit to that place this last funerall Scrowle.
     Others by Wills give Legacies, but I   5
     Dying, of you doe beg a Legacie.

My fortune and my will this custome breake,
When we are senselesse grown to make stones speak,
Though no stone tell thee what I was, yet thou
In my graves inside see what thou art now: 10
Yet th'art not yet so good; till us death lay
To ripe and mellow there, w'are stubborne clay,
Parents make us earth, and soules dignifie
Vs to be glasse, here to grow gold we lie;
Whilst in our soules sinne bred and pampered is,   15
Our soules become worme-eaten Carkasses.

   Epitaph. *some MSS.*   On himselfe. *1635–69*   To the
Countesse of Bedford. *some MSS.*   *The introductory epistle, and the
first ten lines of the epitaph, the whole with heading* Elegie., *is printed
1635–54 among the* Funerall Elegies. *The full epitaph without epistle
and with heading* On himselfe. *is included among the* Divine Poems,
where it follows the Lamentations of Jeremy. *In 1669* On himselfe.
is transferred to the Funerall Elegies *and is followed immediately by the*
Elegie, *i. e. the epistle and incomplete epitaph. They are here given in a
separate group*   5 Wills *1635–69:* testaments *or* testament *MSS.*

Omnibus.

MY Fortune and my choice this custome break,
When we are speechlesse grown, to make stones speak,
Though no stone tell thee what I was, yet thou
In my graves inside seest what thou art now:
Yet thou'art not yet so good, till death us lay   5
To ripe and mellow here, we are stubborne Clay.
Parents make us earth, and soules dignifie
Vs to be glasse; heere to grow gold we lie.
Whilst in our soules sinne bred and pamper'd is,
Our soules become wormeaten carkases;   10
So we our selves miraculously destroy.
Here bodies with lesse miracle enjoy
Such priviledges, enabled here to scale
Heaven, when the Trumpets ayre shall them exhale.
Heare this, and mend thy selfe, and thou mendst me,   15
By making me being dead, doe good to thee,
   And thinke me well compos'd, that I could now
   A last-sicke houre to syllables allow.

Omnibus. one MS.: To all. *some MSS.:* Another on the same. *(i.e.*
Mrs Boulstred) one MS.: On himselfe. *1635–69: in MSS. this complete*
epitaph follows the epistle   4 seest] see *one MS.: compare incomplete*
version.   6 to thee, *MSS.:* for thee, *1635–69*

INFINITATI SACRUM,

16. *Augusti* 1601.

METEMPSYCHOSIS.

Poêma Satyricon.

Epistle.

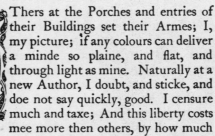

Thers at the Porches and entries of their Buildings set their Armes; I, my picture; if any colours can deliver a minde so plaine, and flat, and through light as mine. Naturally at a new Author, I doubt, and sticke, and doe not say quickly, good. I censure much and taxe; And this liberty costs mee more then others, by how much my owne things are worse then others. Yet I would not be so rebellious against my selfe, as not to doe it, since I love it; nor so unjust to others, to do it *sine talione*. As long as I give them as good hold upon mee, they must pardon mee my bitings. I forbid no reprehender, but him that like the Trent Councell forbids not bookes, but Authors, damning what ever such a name hath or shall write. None writes so ill, that he gives not some thing exemplary, to follow, or flie. Now when I beginne this booke, I have no purpose to come into any mans debt; how my stocke will hold out I know not; perchance waste, perchance increase in use; if

Infinitati *&c. 1633–69: and so in one MS. and another MS. group (in 1633 it is the first poem; in 1635–69 it follows the* Funerall Elegies, *from which it is separated by some prose letters, and precedes* Divine Poems *as here*) Metempsychosis. *1650–69:* Metempsycosis. *1633–39*

I doe

I doe borrow any thing of Antiquitie, besides that I make account that I pay it to posterity, with as much and as good: You shall still finde mee to acknowledge it, and to thanke not him onely that hath digg'd out treasure for mee, but that hath lighted mee a candle to the place. All which I will bid you remember, (for I will have no such Readers as I can teach) is, that the Pithagorian doctrine doth not onely carry one soule from man to man, nor man to beast, but indifferently to plants also: and therefore you must not grudge to finde the same soule in an Emperour, in a Post-horse, and in a Mucheron,[1] since no unreadinesse in the soule, but an indisposition in the organs workes this. And therefore though this soule could not move when it was a Melon, yet it may remember, and now tell mee,[2] at what lascivious banquet it was serv'd. And though it could not speake, when it was a spider, yet it can remember, and now tell me, who used it for poyson to attaine dignitie.   How ever the bodies have dull'd her other faculties, her memory hath ever been her owne, which makes me so seriously deliver you by her relation all her passages from her first making when shee was that apple which Eve eate, to this time when shee is hee,[3] whose life you shall finde in the end of this booke.

[1] Mucheron, *1633 and one MS. group:* Mushrome, *one MS.:* Maceron, *1635–69 and one MS.*   [2] and can now tell mee, *1635–69* [3] shee is hee, *1633 and MSS.:* shee is shee, *1635–69*

THE

THE
PROGRESSE
OF THE SOULE.

First Song.

I.

I Sing the progresse of a deathlesse soule,
Whom Fate, which God made, but doth not controule,
Plac'd in most shapes; all times before the law
Yoak'd us, and when, and since, in this I sing.
And the great world to his aged evening;   5
From infant morne, through manly noone I draw.
What the gold Chaldee, or silver Persian saw,
Greeke brasse, or Roman iron, is in this one;
A worke t'outweare *Seths* pillars, bricke and stone,
  And (holy writt excepted) made to yeeld to none.   10

II.

Thee, eye of heaven, this great Soule envies not,
By thy male force, is all wee have, begot.
In the first East, thou now beginst to shine,
Suck'st early balme, and Iland spices there,
And wilt anon in thy loose-rein'd careere   15
At Tagus, Po, Sene, Thames, and Danow dine,
And see at night thy Westerne land of Myne,
Yet hast thou not more nations seene then shee,
That before thee, one day beganne to bee,
  And thy fraile light being quench'd, shall long, long
    out live thee.   20

                                          III.

III.

Nor, holy *Janus*, in whose soveraigne boate
The Church, and all the Monarchies did floate;
That swimming Colledge, and free Hospitall
Of all mankinde, that cage and vivarie
Of fowles, and beasts, in whose wombe, Destinie   25
Us, and our latest nephewes did install
(From thence are all deriv'd, that fill this All,)
Did'st thou in that great stewardship embarke
So diverse shapes into that floating parke,
　　As have beene moved, and inform'd by this heavenly
　　　　sparke.   30

IV.

Great Destiny the Commissary of God,
That hast mark'd out a path and period
For every thing; who, where wee of-spring tooke,
Our wayes and ends seest at one instant; Thou
Knot of all causes, thou whose changelesse brow   35
Ne'r smiles nor frownes, O vouch thou safe to looke
And shew my story, in thy eternall booke:
That (if my prayer be fit) I may'understand
So much my selfe, as to know with what hand,
　　How scant, or liberall this my lifes race is spand.   40

V.

To my sixe lustres almost now outwore,
Except thy booke owe mee so many more,
Except my legend be free from the letts
Of steepe ambition, sleepie povertie,
Spirit-quenching sicknesse, dull captivitie,   45
Distracting businesse, and from beauties nets,
And all that calls from this, and to others whets,

27 From thence] For, thence *one MS.*   36 vouch thou safe *all MSS.:* vouch safe thou *1633–69*   45 Spirit-quenching] Spright-quenching *one MS.*

　　　　　　　　　　　　　　　　O let

O let me not launch out, but let mee save
Th'expense of braine and spirit; that my grave
   His right and due, a whole unwasted man may have.   50

VI.

But if my dayes be long, and good enough,
In vaine this sea shall enlarge, or enrough
It selfe; for I will through the wave, and fome,
And shall, in sad lone wayes a lively spright,
Make my darke heavy Poëm light, and light.   55
For though through many streights, and lands I roame,
I launch at paradise, and I saile towards home;
The course I there began, shall here be staid,
Sailes hoised there, stroke here, and anchors laid
   In Thames, which were at Tigrys, and Euphrates
     waide.   60

VII.

For the great soule which here amongst us now
Doth dwell, and moves that hand, and tongue, and brow,
Which, as the Moone the sea, moves us; to heare
Whose story, with long patience you will long;
(For 'tis the crowne, and last straine of my song)   65
This soule to whom *Luther*, and *Mahomet* were
Prisons of flesh; this soule which oft did teare,
And mend the wracks of th'Empire, and late Rome,
And liv'd when every great change did come,
   Had first in paradise, a low, but fatall roome.   70

VIII.

Yet no low roome, nor then the greatest, lesse,
If (as devout and sharpe men fitly guesse)
That Crosse, our joy, and griefe, where nailes did tye

59 hoised] hoisted *one MS.*   61 For the] For this *MSS.*: For
that *one MS.*   69 when] where *all MSS.*

                                       That

That All, which alwayes was all, every where;
Which could not sinne, and yet all sinnes did beare;   75
Which could not die, yet could not chuse but die;
Stood in the selfe same roome in Calvarie,
Where first grew the forbidden learned tree,
For on that tree hung in security
   This Soule, made by the Makers will from pulling
     free.   80

IX.

Prince of the orchard, faire as dawning morne,
Fenc'd with the law, and ripe as soone as borne
That apple grew, which this Soule did enlive,
Till the then climing serpent, that now creeps
For that offence, for which all mankinde weepes,   85
Tooke it, and t'her whom the first man did wive
(Whom and her race, only forbiddings drive)
He gave it, she t'her husband, both did eate;
So perished the eaters, and the meate:
   And wee (for treason taints the blood) thence die and
     sweat.   90

X.

Man all at once was there by woman slaine,
And one by one we'are here slaine o'er againe
By them. The mother poison'd the well-head,
The daughters here corrupt us, Rivolets;
No smalnesse scapes, no greatnesse breaks their nets;   95
She thrust us out, and by them we are led
Astray, from turning to whence we are fled.
Were prisoners Judges, 'twould seeme rigorous,
Shee sinn'd, we beare; part of our paine is, thus
   To love them, whose fault to this painfull love yoak'd
     us.   100

87 her] whose *one* MS.   94 corrupt us, *1635–69:* corrupts us,
1633

                                XI.

XI.

So fast in us doth this corruption grow,
That now wee dare aske why wee should be so.
Would God (disputes the curious Rebell) make
A law, and would not have it kept? Or can
His creatures will, crosse his? Of every man   105
For one, will God (and be just) vengeance take?
Who sinn'd? t'was not forbidden to the snake
Nor her, who was not then made; nor is't writ
That Adam cropt, or knew the apple; yet
     The worme and she, and he, and wee endure for it. 110

XII.

But snatch mee heavenly Spirit from this vaine
Reckoning their vanities, lesse is their gaine
Then hazard still, to meditate on ill,
Though with good minde; their reasons, like those toyes
Of glassie bubbles, which the gamesome boyes   115
Stretch to so nice a thinnes through a quill
That they themselves breake, doe themselves spill:
Arguing is heretiques game, and Exercise
As wrastlers, perfects them; Not liberties
     Of speech, but silence; hands, not tongues, end
     heresies.   120

XIII.

Just in that instant when the serpents gripe,
Broke the slight veines, and tender conduit-pipe,
Through which this soule from the trees root did draw
Life, and growth to this apple, fled away
This loose soule, old, one and another day.   125
As lightning, which one scarce dares say, he saw,
'Tis so soone gone, (and better proofe the law

117 breake, doe *1633 and MSS.:* breake, and doe *1635-69*
118 game] gaine *one MS.*   119 perfects] proffits *one MS.*
127 proofe] proofes *one MS.*

Of

Of sense, then faith requires) swiftly she flew
To a darke and foggie Plot; Her, her fates threw
 There through th'earths pores, and in a Plant hous'd
  her anew.   130

XIV.

The plant thus abled, to it selfe did force
A place, where no place was; by natures course
As aire from water, water fleets away
From thicker bodies, by this root throng'd so
His spungie confines gave him place to grow: 135
Just as in our streets, when the people stay
To see the Prince, and have so fill'd the way
That weesels scarce could passe, when she comes nere
They throng and cleave up, and a passage cleare,
 As if, for that time, their round bodies flatned were. 140

XV.

His right arme he thrust out towards the East,
West-ward his left; th'ends did themselves digest
Into ten lesser strings, these fingers were:
And as a slumberer stretching on his bed,
This way he this, and that way scattered 145
His other legge, which feet with toes upbeare.
Grew on his middle parts, the first day, haire,
To show, that in loves businesse hee should still
A dealer bee, and be us'd well, or ill:
 His apples kindle, his leaves, force of conception kill. 150

XVI.

A mouth, but dumbe, he hath; blinde eyes, deafe eares,
And to his shoulders dangle subtile haires;
A young *Colossus* there hee stands upright,

---

137 the Prince, and have so fill'd *one MS.:* the Princesse, and so
fill'd *1633 (but some copies read* the Prince, and so fill'd): the Prince,
and so fill up *1635–69:* the Prince, and so fill'd *one MS. group:* the
Prince, so filled is *one MS.*

             And

And as that ground by him were conquered
A leafie garland weares he on his head   155
Enchas'd with little fruits, so red and bright
That for them you would call your Loves lips white;
So, of a lone unhaunted place possest,
Did this soules second Inne, built by the guest,
  This living buried man, this quiet mandrake, rest.   16c

XVII.

No lustfull woman came this plant to grieve,
But 'twas because there was none yet but Eve:
And she (with other purpose) kill'd it quite;
Her sinne had now brought in infirmities,
And so her cradled child, the moist red eyes   165
Had never shut, nor slept since it saw light;
Poppie she knew, she knew the mandrakes might,
And tore up both, and so coold her childs blood;
Unvirtuous weeds might long unvex'd have stood;
  But hee's short liv'd, that with his death can doe most
      good.   170

XVIII.

To an unfetterd soules quick nimble hast
Are falling stars, and hearts thoughts, but slow pac'd:
Thinner then burnt aire flies this soule, and she
Whom foure new comming, and foure parting Suns
Had found, and left the Mandrakes tenant, runnes   175
Thoughtlesse of change, when her firme destiny
Confin'd, and enjayld her, that seem'd so free,
Into a small blew shell, the which a poore
Warme bird orespread, and sat still evermore,
  Till her inclos'd child kickt, and pick'd it selfe a
      dore.   180

180 inclos'd *1635–69 and two MSS.:* encloth'd *one MS. group:*
uncloath'd *1633* pick'd] peck'd *MSS.*

                                                  XIX.

XIX.

Outcrept a sparrow, this soules moving Inne,
On whose raw armes stiffe feathers now begin,
As childrens teeth through gummes, to breake with paine,
His flesh is jelly yet, and his bones threds,
All a new downy mantle overspreads,   185
A mouth he opes, which would as much containe
As his late house, and the first houre speaks plaine,
And chirps alowd for meat. Meat fit for men
His father steales for him, and so feeds then
    One, that within a moneth, will beate him from his hen. 190

XX.

In this worlds youth wise nature did make hast,
Things ripened sooner, and did longer last;
Already this hot cocke, in bush and tree,
In field and tent, oreflutters his next hen;
He asks her not, who did so last, nor when,   195
Nor if his sister, or his neece shee be;
Nor doth she pule for his inconstancie
If in her sight he change, nor doth refuse
The next that calls; both liberty doe use;
    Where store is of both kindes, both kindes may freely
        chuse.   200

XXI.

Men, till they tooke laws which made freedome lesse,
Their daughters, and their sisters did ingresse;
Till now unlawfull, therefore ill, 'twas not.
So jolly, that it can move, this soule is,
The body so free of his kindnesses,   205
That selfe-preserving it hath now forgot,
And slackneth so the soules, and bodies knot,
Which temperance streightens; freely on his she friends
He blood, and spirit, pith, and marrow spends,
    Ill steward of himself, himselfe in three yeares ends. 210

185 *a new downy 1635–69 and MSS.:* downy a new *1633*
195 last *Harl. 3998:* tast *Edd. and other MSS.*

XXII.

XXII.

Else might he long have liv'd; man did not know
Of gummie blood, which doth in holly grow,
How to make bird-lime, nor how to deceive
With faind calls, hid nets, or enwrapping snare,
The free inhabitants of the Plyant aire.   215
Man to beget, and woman to conceive
Askt not of rootes, nor of cock-sparrowes, leave:
Yet chuseth hee, though none of these he feares,
Pleasantly three, then streightned twenty yeares
    To live; and to encrease his race, himselfe outweares.220

XXIII.

This cole with overblowing quench'd and dead,
The Soule from her too active organs fled
T'a brooke. A female fishes sandie Roe
With the males jelly, newly lev'ned was,
For they had intertouch'd as they did passe,   225
And one of those small bodies, fitted so,
This soule inform'd, and abled it to rowe
It selfe with finnie oares, which she did fit:
Her scales seem'd yet of parchment, and as yet
    Perchance a fish, but by no name you could call it. 230

XXIV.

When goodly, like a ship in her full trim,
A swan, so white that you may unto him
Compare all whitenesse, but himselfe to none,
Glided along, and as he glided watch'd,
And with his arched necke this poore fish catch'd.   235
It mov'd with state, as if to looke upon
Low things it scorn'd, and yet before that one

214 hid *two MSS.:* his *1633–69 and one MS. group*   225 they
had intertouch'd *1635–69 and some MSS.:* they intertouched *1633:*
they intertouch'd *one MS. group*

                                                    Could

Could thinke he sought it, he had swallow'd cleare
This, and much such, and unblam'd devour'd there
    All, but who too swift, too great, or well armed were.240

XXV.

Now swome a prison in a prison put,
And now this Soule in double walls was shut,
Till melted with the Swans digestive fire,
She left her house the fish, and vapour'd forth;
Fate not affording bodies of more worth   265
For her as yet, bids her againe retire
T'another fish, to any new desire
Made a new prey; For, he that can to none
Resistance make, nor complaint, sure is gone.
    Weaknesse invites, but silence feasts oppression.   250

XXVI.

Pace with her native streame, this fish doth keepe,
And journeyes with her, towards the glassie deepe,
But oft retarded, once with a hidden net
Though with greate windowes, for when Need first taught
These tricks to catch food, then they were not wrought 255
As now, with curious greedinesse to let
None scape, but few, and fit for use, to get,
As, in this trap a ravenous pike was tane,
Who, though himselfe distrest, would faine have slain
    This wretch; So hardly are ill habits left again.   260

XXVII.

Here by her smallnesse shee two deaths orepast,
Once innocence scap'd, and left the oppressor fast.
The net through-swome, she keepes the liquid path,
And whether she leape up sometimes to breath
And suck in aire, or finde it underneath,   265

240 or] and *one MS.*   251 her *MSS.:* the *1633–69*

                                                     Or

Or working parts like mills or limbecks hath
To make the water thinne, and airelike faith
Cares not; but safe the Place she's come unto
Where fresh, with salt waves meet, and what to doe
   She knowes not, but betweene both makes a boord or
     two.   270

XXVIII.

So farre from hiding her guests, water is,
That she showes them in bigger quantities
Then they are. Thus doubtfull of her way,
For game and not for hunger a sea Pie
Spied through this traiterous spectacle, from high,   275
The seely fish where it disputing lay,
And t'end her doubts and her, beares her away:
Exalted she'is, but to the exalters good,
As are by great ones, men which lowly stood.
   It's rais'd, to be the Raisers instrument and food.   280

XXIX.

Is any kinde subject to rape like fish?
Ill unto man, they neither doe, nor wish:
Fishers they kill not, nor with noise awake,
They doe not hunt, nor strive to make a prey
Of beasts, nor their yong sonnes to beare away;   285
Foules they pursue not, nor do undertake
To spoile the nests industrious birds do make;
Yet them all these unkinde kinds feed upon,
To kill them is an occupation,   289
   And lawes make Fasts, and Lents for their destruction.

XXX.

A sudden stiffe land-winde in that selfe houre
To sea-ward forc'd this bird, that did devour
The fish; he cares not, for with ease he flies,
Fat gluttonies best orator: at last
So long hee hath flowen, and hath flowen so fast   295
                             That

That many leagues at sea, now tir'd hee lyes,
And with his prey, that till then languisht, dies:
The soules no longer foes, two wayes did erre,
The fish I follow, and keepe no calender
    Of the other; he lives yet in some great officer.   300

XXXI.

Into an embrion fish, our Soule is throwne,
And in due time throwne out againe, and growne
To such vastnesse as, if unmanacled
From Greece, Morea were, and that by some
Earthquake unrooted, loose Morea swome,   305
Or seas from Africks body had severed
And torne the hopefull Promontories head,
This fish would seeme these, and, when all hopes faile,
A great ship overset, or without saile
    Hulling, might (when this was a whelp) be like this
        whale.   310

XXXII.

At every stroake his brazen finnes do take,
More circles in the broken sea they make
Then cannons voices, when the aire they teare:
His ribs are pillars, and his high arch'd roofe
Of barke that blunts best steele, is thunder-proofe: 315
Swimme in him swallow'd Dolphins, without feare,
And feele no sides, as if his vast wombe were
Some Inland sea, and ever as hee went
Hee spouted rivers up, as if he ment
    To joyne our seas, with seas above the firmament.   320

XXXIII.

He hunts not fish, but as an officer,
Stayes in his court, at his owne net, and there
All suitors of all sorts themselves enthrall;

296 That many leagues at sea, *one MS.:* That leagues o'er-past at
sea, *1633–69:* That leagues at sea, *MSS.*   321 officer] favourite
one MS.   322–3 Lies still at Court, and is himself a nett where
one MS.   322 at] as *MSS.*

                                                    So

So on his backe lyes this whale wantoning,
And in his gulfe-like throat, sucks every thing   325
That passeth neare. Fish chaseth fish, and all,
Flyer and follower, in this whirlepoole fall;
O might not states of more equality
Consist? and is it of necessity
   That thousand guiltlesse smals, to make one great, must
      die?   330

XXXIV.

Now drinkes he up seas, and he cates up flocks,
He justles Ilands, and he shakes firme rockes.
Now in a roomefull house this Soule doth float,
And like a Prince she sends her faculties
To all her limbes, distant as Provinces.   335
The Sunne hath twenty times both crab and goate
Parched, since first lanch'd forth this living boate;
'Tis greatest now, and to destruction
Nearest; There's no pause at perfection;
   Greatnesse a period hath, but hath no station.   340

XXXV.

Two little fishes whom hee never harm'd,
Nor fed on their kinde, two not throughly arm'd
With hope that they could kill him, nor could doe
Good to themselves by his death (they did not eate
His flesh, nor suck those oyles, which thence outstreat) 345
Conspir'd against him, and it might undoe
The plot of all, that the plotters were two,
But that they fishes were, and could not speake.
How shall a Tyran wise strong projects breake,
   If wreches can on them the common anger wreake? 350

XXXVI.

The flaile-finn'd Thresher, and steel-beak'd Sword-fish
Onely attempt to doe, what all doe wish.

   344 did not eate] doe not eate *two MSS.*   345 outstreat] out
sweat *one MS.*

The

The Thresher backs him, and to beate begins;
The sluggard Whale yeelds to oppression,
And t'hide himselfe from shame and danger, downe   355
Begins to sinke; the Swordfish upward spins,
And gores him with his beake; his staffe-like finnes,
So well the one, his sword the other plyes,
That now a scoffe, and prey, this tyran dyes,   359
   And (his owne dole) feeds with himselfe all companies.

XXXVII.

Who will revenge his death? or who will call
Those to account, that thought, and wrought his fall?
The heires of slaine kings, wee see are often so
Transported with the joy of what they get,
That they, revenge and obsequies forget,   365
Nor will against such men the people goe,
Because h'is now dead, to whom they should show
Love in that act; Some kings by vice being growne
So needy of subjects love, that of their own
   They thinke they lose, if love be to the dead Prince
     shown.   370

XXXVIII.

This Soule, now free from prison, and passion,
Hath yet a little indignation
That so small hammers should so soone downe beat
So great a castle. And having for her house
Got the streight cloyster of a wreched mouse   375
(As basest men that have not what to eate,
Nor enjoy ought, doe farre more hate the great
Then they, who good repos'd estates possesse)
This Soule, late taught that great things might by lesse
   Be slain, to gallant mischiefe doth herselfe addresse.   380

XXXIX.

Natures great master-peece, an Elephant,
The onely harmlesse great thing; the giant

Of

Of beasts; who thought, no more had gone, to make one
    wise
But to be just, and thankfull, loth to offend,
(Yet nature hath given him no knees to bend)   385
Himselfe he up-props, on himselfe relies,
And foe to none, suspects no enemies,
Still sleeping stood; vex't not his fantasie
Blacke dreames; like an unbent bow, carelesly
    His sinewy Proboscis did remisly lie: 390

XL.

In which as in a gallery this mouse
Walk'd, and surveid the roomes of this vast house,
And to the braine, the soules bedchamber, went,
And gnaw'd the life cords there; Like a whole towne
Cleane undermin'd, the slaine beast tumbled downe;   395
With him the murtherer dies, whom envy sent
To kill, not scape, (for, only hee that ment
To die, did ever kill a man of better roome,)
And thus he made his foe, his prey, and tombe:
    Who cares not to turn back, may any whither come. 400

XLI.

Next, hous'd this Soule a Wolves yet unborne whelp,
Till the best midwife, Nature, gave it helpe,
To issue. It could kill, as soone as goe.
Abel, as white, and milde as his sheepe were,
(Who, in that trade, of Church, and kingdomes, there 405
Was the first type) was still infested soe,
With this wolfe, that it bred his losse and woe;
And yet his bitch, his sentinell attends
The flocke so neere, so well warnes and defends,
    That the wolfe, (hopelesse else) to corrupt her, in-
      tends.   410

383 who thought none had, to make him wise, *1635–69*

XLII.

XLII.

Hee tooke a course, which since, succesfully,
Great men have often taken, to espie
The counsels, or to breake the plots of foes.
To Abels tent he stealeth in the darke,
On whose skirts the bitch slept; ere she could barke,   415
Attach'd her with streight gripes, yet hee call'd those,
Embracements of love; to loves worke he goes,
Where deeds move more then words; nor doth she show,
Nor ⟨make⟩ resist, nor needs hee streighten so
   His prey, for, were shee loose, she would nor barke, nor
     goe.   420

XLIII.

Hee hath engag'd her; his, she wholy bides;
Who not her owne, none others secrets hides.
If to the flocke he come, and Abell there,
She faines hoarse barkings, but she biteth not,
Her faith is quite, but not her love forgot.   425
At last a trap, of which some every where
Abell had plac'd, ends all his losse, and feare,
By the Wolves death; and now just time it was
That a quicke soule should give life to that masse
   Of blood in Abels bitch, and thither this did passe. 430

XLIV.

Some have their wives, their sisters some begot,
But in the lives of Emperours you shall not
Reade of a lust the which may equall this;
This wolfe begot himselfe, and finished
What he began alive, when hee was dead;   435
Sonne to himselfe, and father too, hee is
A ridling lust, for which Schoolemen would misse

419 Nor ⟨make⟩ resist, *Ed:* Nor much resist, *1633–69:* Nowe must resist *one MS.:* Nowe much resist *some MSS.:* Resistance much *one MS.*   432 Emperours] Princes *one MS.*

A proper

A proper name. The whelpe of both these lay
In Abels tent, and with soft Moaba,
   His sister, being yong, it us'd to sport and play.   440

XLV.

Hee soone for her too harsh, and churlish grew,
And Abell (the dam dead) would use this new
For the field. Being of two kindes thus made,
He, as his dam, from sheepe drove wolves away,
And as his Sire, he made them his owne prey.   445
Five ycares he liv'd, and cosened with his trade,
Then hopelesse that his faults were hid, betraid
Himselfe by flight, and by all followed,
From dogges, a wolfe; from wolves, a dogge he fled;
   And, like a spie to both sides false, he perished.   450

XLVI.

It quicknned next a toyfull Ape, and so
Gamesome it was, that it might freely goe
From tent to tent, and with the children play.
His organs now so like theirs hee doth finde,
That why he cannot laugh, and speake his minde,   455
He wonders. Much with all, most he doth stay
With Adams fift daughter *Siphatecia*,
Doth gaze on her, and, where she passeth, passe,
Gathers her fruits, and tumbles on the grasse,
   And wisest of that kinde, the first true lover was.   460

XLVII.

He was the first that more desir'd to have
One then another; first that ere did crave
Love by mute signes, and had no power to speake;
First that could make love faces, or could doe
The valters sombersalts, or us'd to wooe   465
With hoiting gambolls, his owne bones to breake
To make his mistresse merry; or to wreake

                       Her

Her anger on himselfe. Sinnes against kinde
They easily doe, that can let feed their minde
   With outward beauty; beauty they in boyes and beasts
     do find.   470

XLVIII.

By this misled, too low things men have prov'd,
And too high; beasts and angels have beene lov'd.
This Ape, though else through-vaine, in this was wise,
He reach'd at things too high, but open way
There was, and he knew not she would say nay;   475
His toyes prevaile not, likelier meanes he tries,
He gazeth on her face with teare-shot eyes,
And up lifts subtly with his russet pawe
Her kidskinne apron without feare or awe
   Of nature; nature hath no gaole, though shee hath
     law.   480

XLIX.

First she was silly and knew not what he ment.
That vertue, by his touches, chaft and spent,
Succeeds an itchie warmth, that melts her quite;
She knew not first, nowe cares not what he doth,
And willing halfe and more, more then halfe loth,   485
She neither puls nor pushes, but outright
Now cries, and now repents; when *Tethlemite*
Her brother, entred, and a great stone threw
After the Ape, who, thus prevented, flew.   489
   This house thus batter'd downe, the Soule possest a new.

L.

And whether by this change she lose or win,
She comes out next, where the Ape would have gone in.
Adam and *Eve* had mingled bloods, and now
Like Chimiques equall fires, her temperate wombe
Had stew'd and form'd it: and part did become   495

---

485 loth *one MS.:* Tooth *1633, and one MS.: other MSS. leave a
blank space: in one a later hand has inserted* loath: wroth, *1635–69*

                      A spungie

A spungie liver, that did richly allow,
Like a free conduit, on a high hils brow,
Life-keeping moisture unto every part;
Part hardned it selfe to a thicker heart,
    Whose busie furnaces lifes spirits do impart.   500

LI.

Another part became the well of sense,
The tender well-arm'd feeling braine, from whence,
Those sinowie strings which do our bodies tie,
Are raveld out; and fast there by one end,
Did this Soule limbes, these limbes a soule attend;   505
And now they joyn'd: keeping some quality
Of every past shape, she knew treachery,
Rapine, deceit, and lust, and ills enow
To be a woman. *Themech* she is now,
    Sister and wife to *Caine*, *Caine* that first did plow.   510

LII.

Who ere thou beest that read'st this sullen Writ,
Which just so much courts thee, as thou dost it,
Let me arrest thy thoughts; wonder with mee,
Why plowing, building, ruling and the rest,
Or most of those arts, whence our lives are blest,   515
By cursed *Cains* race invented be,
And blest *Seth* vext us with Astronomie.
Ther's nothing simply good, nor ill alone,
Of every quality Comparison
    The onely measure is, and judge, Opinion.   520

The end of the Progresse of the Soule.

503 sinowie] sinewy *1639–54:* sinew *1669*

DIVINE

DIVINE POEMS.

To *E.* of *D.* with six holy Sonnets.

SEe Sir, how as the Suns hot Masculine flame
 Begets strange creatures on Niles durty slime,
 In me, your fatherly yet lusty Ryme
(For, these songs are their fruits) have wrought the same;
But though the ingendring force from whence they came 5
 Bee strong enough, and nature doe admit
 Seaven to be borne at once, I send as yet
But six; they say, the seaventh hath still some maime.
 I choose your judgement, which the same degree
 Doth with her sister, your invention, hold,   10
As fire these drossie Rymes to purifie,
 Or as Elixar, to change them to gold;
You are that Alchimist which alwaies had
Wit, whose one spark could make good things of bad.

To the Lady Magdalen Herbert : of St. Mary Magdalen.

HEr of your name, whose fair inheritance
 Bethina was, and jointure Magdalo:
An active faith so highly did advance,
 That she once knew, more than the Church did know,

Divine Poems. *one MS. group. In 1635–69 this is the title at head of each page, but the new section is headed* Holy Sonnets.   To E. of D. *&c. so headed 1633–69 but placed among* Letters *&c., and so in some MSS.: removed hither by Grosart.*   4 their fruits] the fruit *one MS.*
 To the Lady Magdalen Herbert: *&c. Ed:* To the Lady Magdalen Herbert, of *&c. Walton's* The Life of Mr George Herbert. (1670, *pp.* 25–6.)

The

The Resurrection; so much good there is   5
  Deliver'd of her, that some Fathers be
Loth to believe one Woman could do this;
  But, think these Magdalens were two or three.
Increase their number, Lady, and their fame:
  To their Devotion, add your Innocence;   10
Take so much of th'example, as of the name;
  The latter half; and in some recompence
That they did harbour Christ himself, a Guest,
  Harbour these Hymns, to his dear name addrest. J.D.

HOLY SONNETS.

La Corona.

1. D*Eigne at my hands this crown of prayer and praise,*
    Weav'd in my low devout melancholie,
Thou which of good, hast, yea art treasury,
All changing unchang'd Antient of dayes;
But doe not, with a vile crowne of fraile bayes,   5
Reward my muses white sincerity,
But what thy thorny crowne gain'd, that give mee,
A crowne of Glory, which doth flower alwayes;
The ends crowne our workes, but thou crown'st our ends,
For, at our end begins our endlesse rest;   10
The first last end, now zealously possest,
With a strong sober thirst, my soule attends.
'Tis time that heart and voice be lifted high,
Salvation to all that will is nigh.

HOLY SONNETS. *1633–69, being general title to the two groups:*
Holy Sonnets written 20 years since. *one MS.*
  La Corona. *1633–69:* The Crowne. *some MSS.*   2 low *1633
and most MSS.:* lone *1635–69 and some MSS.*   3 treasury, *1633–69*
a Treasurie, *some MSS.*

ANNUNCIATION.

ANNVNCIATION.

2. *Salvation to all that will is nigh;*
That All, which alwayes is All every where,
Which cannot sinne, and yet all sinnes must beare,
Which cannot die, yet cannot chuse but die,
Loe, faithfull Virgin, yeelds himselfe to lye   5
In prison, in thy wombe; and though he there
Can take no sinne, nor thou give, yet he'will weare
Taken from thence, flesh, which deaths force may trie.
Ere by the spheares time was created, thou
Wast in his minde, who is thy Sonne, and Brother;   10
Whom thou conceiv'st, conceiv'd; yea thou art now
Thy Makers maker, and thy Fathers mother;
Thou'hast light in darke; and shutst in little roome,
Immensity cloysterd in thy deare wombe.

NATIVITIE.

3. *Immensitie cloysterd in thy deare wombe,*
Now leaves his welbelov'd imprisonment,
There he hath made himselfe to his intent
Weake enough, now into our world to come;
But Oh, for thee, for him, hath th'Inne no roome?   5
Yet lay him in this stall, and from the Orient,
Starres, and wisemen will travell to prevent
Th'effect of *Herods* jealous generall doome.
Seest thou, my Soule, with thy faiths eyes, how he
Which fils all place, yet none holds him, doth lye?   10
Was not his pity towards thee wondrous high.
That would have need to be pittied by thee?
Kisse him, and with him into Egypt goe,
With his kinde mother, who partakes thy woe.

Annvnciation.   2–4 *Compare p. 272, ll. 74–6.*   9 created,]
begotten, *some MSS.*   11 conceiv'st,] conceiv'dst, *some MSS.*
   Nativitie.   7 will] shall *some MSS.*   8 effect *1669 and most
MSS.:* effects *1633–54 and one MS.*   jealous] dire and *most MSS.:*
zealous *one MS.*

TEMPLE.

4. *With his kinde mother who partakes thy woe,*
Joseph turne backe; see where your child doth sit,
Blowing, yea blowing out those sparks of wit,
Which himselfe on the Doctors did bestow;
The Word but lately could not speake, and loe,⁣   5
It sodenly speakes wonders, whence comes it,
That all which was, and all which should be writ,
A shallow seeming child, should deeply know?
His Godhead was not soule to his manhood,
Nor had time mellowed him to this ripenesse,⁣   10
But as for one which hath a long taske, 'tis good,
With the Sunne to beginne his businesse,
He in his ages morning thus began
By miracles exceeding power of man.

CRVCIFYING.

5. *By miracles exceeding power of man,*
Hee faith in some, envie in some begat,
For, what weake spirits admire, ambitious, hate;
In both affections many to him ran,
But Oh! the worst are most, they will and can,⁣   5
Alas, and do, unto the immaculate,
Whose creature Fate is, now prescribe a Fate,
Measuring selfe-lifes infinity to'a span,
Nay to an inch. Loe, where condemned hee
Beares his owne crosse, with paine, yet by and by⁣   10
When it beares him, he must beare more and die.
Now thou art lifted up, draw mee to thee,
And at thy death giving such liberall dole,
Moyst, with one drop of thy blood, my dry soule.

Temple.   11 a long taske, *1633–69 and one MS. group:* long
taskes *most MSS.*
    Crvcifying.   3 weake] meeke *most MSS.*   8 to'a span, *most MSS.:*
t*e* span, *1633–69 and some MSS.*

RESVRRECTION.

RESVRRECTION.

6. *Moyst with one drop of thy blood, my dry soule*
Shall (though she now be in extreme degree
Too stony hard, and yet too fleshly,) bee
Freed by that drop, from being starv'd, hard, or foule,
And life, by this death abled, shall controule   5
Death, whom thy death slue; nor shall to mee
Feare of first or last death, bring miserie,
If in thy little booke my name thou enroule,
Flesh in that long sleep is not putrified,
But made that there, of which, and for which 'twas;   10
Nor can by other meanes be glorified.
May then sinnes sleep, and deaths soone from me passe,
That wak't from both, I againe risen may
Salute the last, and everlasting day.

ASCENTION.

7. *Salute the last and everlasting day,*
Joy at the uprising of this Sunne, and Sonne,
Yee whose just teares, or tribulation
Have purely washt, or burnt your drossie clay;
Behold the Highest, parting hence away,   5
Lightens the darke clouds, which hee treads upon,
Nor doth hee by ascending, show alone,
But first hee, and hee first enters the way.
O strong Ramme, which hast batter'd heaven for mee,
Mild Lambe, which with thy blood, hast mark'd the path;
Bright Torch, which shin'st, that I the way may see,   11
Oh, with thy owne blood quench thy owne just wrath,
And if thy holy Spirit, my Muse did raise,
Deigne at my hands this crowne of prayer and praise.

Resvrrection.   5 this] thy *some MSS.*   8 little *1633 and some*
MSS.: life *1635–69 and some MSS.*   9 that long] that last long
some MSS.   11 glorified] purified *some MSS.*   12 deaths *some*
MSS.: death *1633–69*
   Ascention.   3 just *1633 and some MSS.:* true *1635–69 and some*
MSS.   11 the way] thy wayes *some MSS.*

Holy

Holy Sonnets.

I.

THou hast made me, And shall thy worke decay?
   Repaire me now, for now mine end doth haste,
I runne to death, and death meets me as fast,
And all my pleasures are like yesterday;
I dare not move my dimme eyes any way,   5
Despaire behind, and death before doth cast
Such terrour, and my feeble flesh doth waste
By sinne in it, which it t'wards hell doth weigh;
Onely thou art above, and when towards thee
By thy leave I can looke, I rise againe;   10
But our old subtle foe so tempteth me,
That not one houre my selfe I can sustaine;
Thy Grace may wing me to prevent his art,
And thou like Adamant draw mine iron heart.

II.

AS due by many titles I resigne
   My selfe to thee, O God, first I was made
By thee, and for thee, and when I was decay'd
Thy blood bought that, the which before was thine;
I am thy sonne, made with thy selfe to shine,   5
Thy servant, whose paines thou hast still repaid,
Thy sheepe, thine Image, and, till I betray'd
My selfe, a temple of thy Spirit divine;
Why doth the devill then usurpe on mee?
Why doth he steale, nay ravish that's thy right?   10
Except thou rise and for thine owne worke fight,
Oh I shall soone despaire, when I doe see
That thou lov'st mankind well, yet wilt'not chuse me.
And Satan hates mee, yet is loth to lose mee.

Holy Sonnets. *1633–69 (following* La Corona *as second group under the same general title)*   I. *1635–69 and some MSS.: omitted 1633 and some MSS.*   7 feeble *1635–69:* febled *some MSS.*

    II. *1635–69 and some MSS.*   I. *1633 and some MSS.*   9 on] in *some MSS.*   12 doe *1633 and most MSS.:* shall *1635–69 and some MSS.*

III.

III.

O Might those sighes and teares returne againe
Into my breast and eyes, which I have spent,
That I might in this holy discontent
Mourne with some fruit, as I have mourn'd in vaine;
In mine Idolatry what showres of raine   5
Mine eyes did waste? what griefs my heart did rent?
That sufferance was my sinne; now I repent;
'Cause I did suffer I must suffer paine.
Th'hydroptique drunkard, and night-scouting thiefe,
The itchy Lecher, and selfe tickling proud   10
Have the remembrance of past joyes, for reliefe
Of comming ills. To (poore) me is allow'd
No ease; for, long, yet vehement griefe hath beene
Th'effect and cause, the punishment and sinne.

IV.

OH my blacke Soule! now thou art summoned
By sicknesse, deaths herald, and champion;
Thou art like a pilgrim, which abroad hath done
Treason, and durst not turne to whence hee is fled,
Or like a thiefe, which till deaths doome be read,   5
Wisheth himselfe delivered from prison;
But damn'd and hal'd to execution,
Wisheth that still he might be imprisoned.
Yet grace, if thou repent, thou canst not lacke;
But who shall give thee that grace to beginne?   10
Oh make thy selfe with holy mourning blacke,
And red with blushing, as thou art with sinne;
Or wash thee in Christs blood, which hath this might
That being red, it dyes red soules to white.

III. *1635–69 and one MS. group: omitted 1633 and some MSS.*
7 sinne; now I *Ed:* sinne, now I *one MS.:* sinne I now *1635–69*
IV. *1635–69:* II. *1633 and some MSS.:* V. *other MSS.*

V.

V.

I Am a little world made cunningly
Of Elements, and an Angelike spright,
But black sinne hath betraid to endlesse night
My worlds both parts, and (oh) both parts must die.
You which beyond that heaven which was most high   5
Have found new sphears, and of new lands can write,
Powre new seas in mine eyes, that so I might
Drowne my world with my weeping earnestly,
Or wash it, if it must be drown'd no more:
But oh it must be burnt! alas the fire   10
Of lust and envie have burnt it heretofore,
And made it fouler; Let their flames retire,
And burne me ô Lord, with a fiery zeale
Of thee and thy house, which doth in eating heale.

VI.

THis is my playes last scene, here heavens appoint
My pilgrimages last mile; and my race
Idly, yet quickly runne, hath this last pace,
My spans last inch, my minutes latest point,
And gluttonous death, will instantly unjoynt   5
My body, and soule, and I shall sleepe a space,
But my'ever-waking part shall see that face,
Whose feare already shakes my every joynt:
Then, as my soule, to'heaven her first seate, takes flight,
And earth-borne body, in the earth shall dwell,   10
So, fall my sinnes, that all may have their right,
To where they'are bred, and would presse me, to hell.
Impute me righteous, thus purg'd of evill,
For thus I leave the world, the flesh, the devill.

V. *1635–69: omitted 1633 and some MSS.:* VII. *other MSS.*
6 lands *MSS.:* land *1635–69*   11 have *MSS.:* hath *one MS.:* om.
1635–69   12 their] those *one MS.*   13 Lord] God *one MS.*
VI. *1635–69 and some MSS.:* III. *1633 and other MSS.*   7 Or
presently, I know not, see that Face, *all MSS.*   14 the devill.] and
devill. *all MSS.*

VII.

VII.

AT the round earths imagin'd corners, blow
   Your trumpets, Angells, and arise, arise
From death, you numberlesse infinities
Of soules, and to your scattred bodies goe,
All whom the flood did, and fire shall o'erthrow,   5
All whom warre, dearth, age, agues, tyrannies,
Despaire, law, chance, hath slaine, and you whose eyes,
Shall behold God, and never tast deaths woe.
But let them sleepe, Lord, and mee mourne a space,
For, if above all these, my sinnes abound,   10
'Tis late to aske abundance of thy grace,
When wee are there; here on this lowly ground,
Teach mee how to repent; for that's as good
As if thou'hadst seal'd my pardon, with thy blood.

VIII.

IF faithfull soules be alike glorifi'd
   As Angels, then my fathers soule doth see,
And adds this even to full felicitie,.
That valiantly I hels wide mouth o'rstride:
But if our mindes to these soules be descry'd   5
By circumstances, and by signes that be
Apparent in us, not immediately,
How shall my mindes white truth by them be try'd?
They see idolatrous lovers weepe and mourne,
And vile blasphemous Conjurers to call   10
On Jesus name, and Pharisaicall
Dissemblers feigne devotion. Then turne
O pensive soule, to God, for he knowes best
Thy true griefe, for he put it in my breast.

VII. *1635–69:* IV. *1633 and some MSS.:* VIII. *other MSS.*
6 dearth, *one MS.:* death, *1633–69 and rest of MSS.*

VIII. *1635–69: omitted 1633 and some MSS.:* X. *other MSS.*
14 true *one MS.:* om. *1635–69*   in *one MS.:* into *1635–69 and some MSS.*

IX.

IX.

IF poysonous mineralls, and if that tree,
Whose fruit threw death on else immortall us,
If lecherous goats, if serpents envious
Cannot be damn'd; Alas; why should I bee?
Why should intent or reason, borne in mee,   5
Make sinnes, else equall, in mee more heinous?
And mercy being easie, and glorious
To God; in his sterne wrath, why threatens hee?
But who am I, that dare dispute with thee
O God? Oh! of thine onely worthy blood,   10
And my teares, make a heavenly Lethean flood,
And drowne in it my sinnes blacke memorie;
That thou remember them, some claime as debt,
I thinke it mercy, if thou wilt forget.

X.

DEath be not proud, though some have called thee
Mighty and dreadfull, for, thou art not soe,
For, those, whom thou think'st, thou dost overthrow,
Die not, poore death, nor yet canst thou kill mee.
From rest and sleepe, which but thy pictures bee,   5
Much pleasure, then from thee, much more must flow,
And soonest our best men with thee doe goe,
Rest of their bones, and soules deliverie.
Thou art slave to Fate, Chance, kings, and desperate men,
And dost with poyson, warre, and sicknesse dwell,   10
And poppie, or charmes can make us sleepe as well,
And better then thy stroake; why swell'st thou then?
One short sleepe past, wee wake eternally,
And death shall be no more; death, thou shalt die.

IX. *1635–69 and some MSS.:* V. *1633 and other MSS.*   9–10 thee
O God? *one MS.:* thee? O God, *1633–69*
X. *1635–69:* VI. *1633 and some MSS.:* XI. *other MSS.*   12
better] easier *some MSS.*   13 wake] live *some MSS.*

XI.

SPit in my face you Jewes, and pierce my side,
Buffet, and scoffe, scourge, and crucifie mee,
For I have sinn'd, and sinn'd, and onely hee,
Who could do no iniquitie, hath dyed:
But by my death can not be satisfied   5
My sinnes, which passe the Jewes impiety:
They kill'd once an inglorious man, but I
Crucifie him daily, being now glorified.
Oh let mee then, his strange love still admire:
Kings pardon, but he bore our punishment.   10
And *Jacob* came cloth'd in vile harsh attire
But to supplant, and with gainfull intent:
God cloth'd himselfe in vile mans flesh, that so
Hee might be weake enough to suffer woe.

XII.

WHy are wee by all creatures waited on?
Why doe the prodigall elements supply
Life and food to mee, being more pure then I,
Simple, and further from corruption?
Why brook'st thou, ignorant horse, subjection?   5
Why dost thou bull, and bore so seelily
Dissemble weaknesse, and by'one mans stroke die,
Whose whole kinde, you might swallow and feed upon?
Weaker I am, woe is mee, and worse then you,
You have not sinn'd, nor need be timorous.   10
But wonder at a greater wonder, for to us
Created nature doth these things subdue,
But their Creator, whom sin, nor nature tyed,
For us, his Creatures, and his foes, hath dyed.

XI. *1635–69:* VII. *1633 and most MSS.: omitted or added among*
Other Meditations. *some MSS.:* XIII. *one MS.* 3 onely] humbly *one MS.*
XII. *1635–69:* VIII. *1633 and most MSS.: omitted or added among*
Other Meditations. *some MSS.:* XIV. *one MS.* 1 are wee] ame I *one*
MS. 4 Simple, *1633 and some MSS.:* Simpler *1635–69 and other*
MSS 11 a greater wonder, *1633 and MSS.:* a greater, *1635–69*

XIII

XIII.

WHat if this present were the worlds last night?
 Marke in my heart, O Soule, where thou dost dwell,
The picture of Christ crucified, and tell
Whether that countenance can thee affright,
Teares in his eyes quench the amasing light,　　　　5
Blood fills his frownes, which from his pierc'd head fell.
And can that tongue adjudge thee unto hell,
Which pray'd forgivenesse for his foes fierce spight?
No, no; but as in my idolatrie
I said to all my profane mistresses,　　　　10
Beauty, of pitty, foulnesse onely is
A signe of rigour: so I say to thee,
To wicked spirits are horrid shapes assign'd,
This beauteous forme assures a pitious minde.

XIV.

BAtter my heart, three person'd God; for, you
 As yet but knocke, breathe, shine, and seeke to mend;
That I may rise, and stand, o'erthrow mee,'and bend
Your force, to breake, blowe, burn and make me new.
I, like an usurpt towne, to'another due,　　　　5
Labour to'admit you, but Oh, to no end,
Reason your viceroy in mee, mee should defend,
But is captiv'd, and proves weake or untrue.
Yet dearely'I love you,'and would be loved faine,
But am betroth'd unto your enemie:　　　　10
Divorce mee,'untie, or breake that knot againe,
Take mee to you, imprison mee, for I
Except you'enthrall mee, never shall be free,
Nor ever chast, except you ravish mee.

XIII. *1635–69:* IX. *1633 and some MSS.: om. or added among*
Other Meditations. *other MSS.:* XV. *one MS.* 4 that *most MSS.:*
his *1633–69 and one MS. group* 8 fierce] ranck *one MS.* 14
assures *all MSS.:* assumes *1633–69*
　XIV. *1635–69:* X. *1633 and some MSS.: om. other MSS.:* XVI.
one MS.

XV.

XV.

WIlt thou love God, as he thee! then digest,
My Soule, this wholsome meditation,
How God the Spirit, by Angels waited on
In heaven, doth make his Temple in thy brest.
The Father having begot a Sonne most blest,   5
And still begetting, (for he ne'r begonne)
Hath deign'd to chuse thee by adoption,
Coheire to'his glory,'and Sabbaths endlesse rest.
And as a robb'd man, which by search doth finde
His stolne stuffe sold, must lose or buy'it againe: 10
The Sonne of glory came downe, and was slaine,
Us whom he'had made, and Satan stolne, to unbinde.
'Twas much, that man was made like God before,
But, that God should be made like man, much more.

XVI.

FAther, part of his double interest
Unto thy kingdome, thy Sonne gives to mee,
His joynture in the knottie Trinitie
Hee keepes, and gives to me his deaths conquest.
This Lambe, whose death, with life the world hath blest, 5
Was from the worlds beginning slaine, and he
Hath made two Wills, which with the Legacie
Of his and thy kingdome, doe thy Sonnes invest.
Yet such are thy laws, that men argue yet
Whether a man those statutes can fulfill;   10
None doth; but all-healing grace and spirit
Revive againe what law and letter kill.
Thy lawes abridgement, and thy last command
Is all but love; Oh let this last Will stand!

XV. *1635–69:* XI. *1633 and some MSS.:* XII. *other MSS.* 11
sonne *1633:* Sunne *1635–69*   12 stolne, *1633 and some MSS.:* stole,
1635–69 and other MSS.

XVI. *1635–69:* XII. *1633 and some MSS.:* IV. *other MSS.* 8
doe *1633:* om. *1635–69:* doth *MSS.*   9 thy *some MSS.:* these

XVII.

XVII.

SInce she whom I lov'd hath payd her last debt
 To Nature, and to hers, and my good is dead,
And her Soule early into heaven ravished,
Wholly on heavenly things my mind is sett.
Here the admyring her my mind did whett   5
To seeke thee God; so streames do shew their head;
But though I have found thee, and thou my thirst hast fed,
A holy thirsty dropsy melts mee yett.
But why should I begg more Love, when as thou
Dost wooe my soule for hers; offring all thine: 10
And dost not only feare least I allow
My Love to Saints and Angels, things divine,
But in thy tender jealosy dost doubt
Least the World, Fleshe, yea Devill putt thee out.

XVIII.

SHow me deare Christ, thy spouse, so bright and clear.
 What! is it She, which on the other shore
Goes richly painted? or which rob'd and tore
Laments and mournes in Germany and here?
Sleepes she a thousand, then peepes up one yeare?   5
Is she selfe truth and errs? now new, now outwore?
Doth she, and did she, and shall she evermore
On one, on seaven, or on no hill appeare?
Dwells she with us, or like adventuring knights
First travaile we to seeke and then make Love?   10
Betray kind husband thy spouse to our sights,
And let myne amorous soule court thy mild Dove,
Who is most trew, and pleasing to thee, then
When she'is embrac'd and open to most men.

1633–69: those *other MS.*   11 but all-healing *all MSS.:* but thy
all-healing *1633–69*   12 Revive againe] Revive and quicken *some
MSS.*   14 this *1633–69:* that *some MSS.:* thy *some MSS.*
   XVII. *from one MS.: first printed in Gosse's* The Jacobean Poets,
1894, with the two that follow

XIX.

XIX.

OH, to vex me, contraryes meet in one:
Inconstancy unnaturally hath begott
A constant habit; that when I would not
I change in vowes, and in devotione.
As humorous is my contritione   5
As my prophane Love, and as soone forgott:
As ridlingly distemper'd, cold and hott,
As praying, as mute; as infinite, as none.
I durst not view heaven yesterday; and to day
In prayers, and flattering speaches I court God: 10
To morrow I quake with true feare of his rod.
So my devout fitts come and go away
Like a fantastique Ague: save that here
Those are my best dayes, when I shake with feare.

The Crosse.

SInce Christ embrac'd the Crosse it selfe, dare I
His image, th'image of his Crosse deny?
Would I have profit by the sacrifice,
And dare the chosen Altar to despise?
It bore all other sinnes, but is it fit   5
That it should beare the sinne of scorning it?
Who from the picture would avert his eye,
How would he flye his paines, who there did dye?
From mee, no Pulpit, nor misgrounded law,
Nor scandall taken, shall this Crosse withdraw,   10
It shall not, for it cannot; for, the losse
Of this Crosse, were to mee another Crosse;
Better were worse, for, no affliction,
No Crosse is so extreme, as to have none.
Who can blot out the Crosse, which th'instrument   15
Of God, dew'd on mee in the Sacrament?

The Crosse.   8 paines] pangs *one MS.*

Who

Who can deny mee power, and liberty
To stretch mine armes, and mine owne Crosse to be?
Swimme, and at every stroake, thou art thy Crosse;
The Mast and yard make one, where seas do tosse;　20
Looke downe, thou spiest out Crosses in small things;
Looke up, thou seest birds rais'd on crossed wings;
All the Globes frame, and spheares, is nothing else
But the Meridians crossing Parallels.
Materiall Crosses then, good physicke bee,　25
But yet spirituall have chiefe dignity.
These for extracted chimique medicine serve,
And cure much better, and as well preserve;
Then are you your own physicke, or need none,
When Still'd, or purg'd by tribulation.　30
For when that Crosse ungrudg'd, unto you stickes,
Then are you to your selfe, a Crucifixe.
As perchance, Carvers do not faces make,
But that away, which hid them there, do take;
Let Crosses, soe, take what hid Christ in thee,　35
And be his image, or not his, but hee.
But, as oft Alchimists doe coyners prove,
So may a selfe-dispising, get selfe-love,
And then as worst surfets, of best meates bee,
Soe is pride, issued from humility,　40
For, 'tis no child, but monster; therefore Crosse
Your joy in crosses, else, 'tis double losse.
And crosse thy senses, else, both they, and thou
Must perish soone, and to destruction bowe.
For if the'eye seeke good objects, and will take　45
No crosse from bad, wee cannot scape a snake.
So with harsh, hard, sowre, stinking, crosse the rest,
Make them indifferent all; call nothing best.
But most the eye needs crossing, that can rome,
And move; To th'other th'objects must come home.　50

48 indifferent all; call nothing best. *Ed:* indifferent; call nothing
best. *1633 and MSS.:* indifferent; all, nothing best. *1635–69*

And

And crosse thy heart: for that in man alone
Points downewards, and hath palpitation.
Crosse those dejections, when it downeward tends,
And when it to forbidden heights pretends.
And as the braine through bony walls doth vent   55
By sutures, which a Crosses forme present,
So when thy braine workes, ere thou utter it,
Crosse and correct concupiscence of witt.
Be covetous of Crosses, let none fall.
Crosse no man else, but crosse thy selfe in all.   60
Then doth the Crosse of Christ worke fruitfully
Within our hearts, when wee love harmlessly
That Crosses pictures much, and with more care
That Crosses children, which our Crosses are.

Resurrection, imperfect.

SLeep sleep old Sun, thou canst not have repast
As yet, the wound thou took'st on friday last;
Sleepe then, and rest; The world may beare thy stay,
A better Sun rose before thee to day,
Who, not content to'enlighten all that dwell   5
On the earths face, as thou, enlightned hell,
And made the darke fires languish in that vale,
As, at thy presence here, our fires grow pale.
Whose body having walk'd on earth, and now
Hasting to Heaven, would, that he might allow   10
Himselfe unto all stations, and fill all,
For these three daies become a minerall;
Hee was all gold when he lay downe, but rose
All tincture, and doth not alone dispose
Leaden and iron wills to good, but is   15

52 Points *some MSS.:* Pants *1633–69 and other MSS.*   53 dejections *1633:* detorsions *1635–69*   61 fruitfully *all MSS.:* faithfully *1633–69*   63 That *all MSS.:* The *1633–69*

Resurrection, imperfect.   15 good, *1633–69 and MSS.: Chambers
suggests* gold

Of

Of power to make even sinfull flesh like his.
Had one of those, whose credulous pietie
Thought, that a Soule one might discerne and see
Goe from a body,'at this sepulcher been,
And, issuing from the sheet, this body seen,   20
He would have justly thought this body a soule,
If not of any man, yet of the whole.
                    Desunt cætera.

The Annuntiation and Passion.

TAmely, fraile body,'abstaine to day; to day
      My soule eates twice, Christ hither and away.
Shee sees him man, so like God made in this,
That of them both a circle embleme is,
Whose first and last concurre; this doubtfull day   5
Of feast or fast, Christ came, and went away.
Shee sees him nothing twice at once, who'is all;
Shee sees a Cedar plant it selfe, and fall,
Her Maker put to making, and the head
Of life, at once, not yet alive, yet dead.   10
She sees at once the virgin mother stay
Reclus'd at home, Publique at Golgotha;
Sad and rejoyc'd shee's seen at once, and seen
At almost fiftie, and at scarce fifteene.
At once a Sonne is promis'd her, and gone,   15
Gabriell gives Christ to her, He her to John;
Not fully a mother, Shee's in Orbitie,
At once receiver and the legacie.
All this, and all betweene, this day hath showne,
Th'Abridgement of Christs story, which makes one   20
(As in plaine Maps, the furthest West is East)
Of the'Angels *Ave,*'and *Consummatum est.*

The Annuntiation and Passion. *1633–69:* Upon the Annuntiation and Passion falling upon one day. Anno Dñi 1608. *some MSS.*
10 yet dead. *Ed:* yet dead; *1633:* and dead; *1635–69 and (with full
stop) most MSS.*   13 Sad and rejoyc'd] Rejoyc'd and sad *some MSS.*

How

How well the Church, Gods Court of faculties
Deales, in some times, and seldome joyning these!
As by the selfe-fix'd Pole wee never doe   25
Direct our course, but the next starre thereto,
Which showes where the'other is, and which we say
(Because it strayes not farre) doth never stray;
So God by his Church, neerest to him, wee know,
And stand firme, if wee by her motion goe;   30
His Spirit, as his fiery Pillar doth
Leade, and his Church, as cloud; to one end both.
This Church, by letting these daies joyne, hath shown
Death and conception in mankinde is one;
Or 'twas in him the same humility,   35
That he would be a man, and leave to be:
Or as creation he hath made, as God,
With the last judgement, but one period,
His imitating Spouse would joyne in one
Manhoods extremes: He shall come, he is gone: 40
Or as though one blood drop, which thence did fall,
Accepted, would have serv'd, he yet shed all;
So though the least of his paines, deeds, or words,
Would busie a life, she all this day affords;
This treasure then, in grosse, my Soule uplay,   45
And in my life retaile it every day.

Goodfriday, 1613.   *Riding Westward.*

Let mans Soule be a Spheare, and then, in this,
The intelligence that moves, devotion is,
And as the other Spheares, by being growne
Subject to forraigne motions, lose their owne,

33 these *all MSS.:* those *1633–69*   daies *1633 and best MSS..*
feasts *1635–69 and some MSS.*   34 is one. *1633:* are one. *1635–69*
   Goodfriday, *&c. 1633–69:* Good Friday. 1613.   Riding towards Wales. *some MSS.:* Good Friday. 1613. Riding to Sʳ Edward
Harbert in Wales. *one MS.:* Mʳ J. Duñ goeing from Sir H. G. on
good friday sent him back this meditation on the way. *one MS.*   4
motions *all MSS.:* motion, *1633–69*

And

And being by others hurried every day, 5
Scarce in a yeare their naturall forme obey:
Pleasure or businesse, so, our Soules admit
For their first mover, and are whirld by it.
Hence is't, that I am carryed towards the West
This day, when my Soules forme bends toward the East. 10
There I should see a Sunne, by rising set,
And by that setting endlesse day beget;
But that Christ on this Crosse, did rise and fall,
Sinne had eternally benighted all.
Yet dare I'almost be glad, I do not see 15
That spectacle of too much weight for mee.
Who sees Gods face, that is selfe life, must dye;
What a death were it then to see God dye?
It made his owne Lieutenant Nature shrinke,
It made his footstoole crack, and the Sunne winke. 20
Could I behold those hands which span the Poles,
And turne all spheares at once, peirc'd with those holes?
Could I behold that endlesse height which is
Zenith to us, and our Antipodes,
Humbled below us? or that blood which is 25
The seat of all our Soules, if not of his,
Made durt of dust, or that flesh which was worne
By God, for his apparell, rag'd, and torne?
If on these things I durst not looke, durst I
Upon his miserable mother cast mine eye, 30
Who was Gods partner here, and furnish'd thus
Halfe of that Sacrifice, which ransom'd us?
Though these things, as I ride, be from mine eye,
They'are present yet unto my memory,
For that looks towards them; and thou look'st towards mee,
O Saviour, as thou hang'st upon the tree; 36
I turne my backe to thee, but to receive

13 this Crosse, *1633 and most MSS.*: his Crosse, *1635–69 and some*
MSS. 22 turne *some MSS.*: tune *1633–69 and some MSS.* 30
Upon his miserable *1633 and MSS.*: On his distressed *1635–69*

Corrections,

Corrections, till thy mercies bid thee leave.
O thinke mee worth thine anger, punish mee,
Burne off my rusts, and my deformity,   40
Restore thine Image, so much, by thy grace,
That thou may'st know mee, and I'll turne my face.

THE LITANIE.

I.

The FATHER.

FAther of Heaven, and him, by whom
It, and us for it, and all else, for us
  Thou madest, and govern'st ever, come
And re-create mee, now growne ruinous:
      My heart is by dejection, clay,   5
      And by selfe-murder, red.
From this red earth, O Father, purge away
All vicious tinctures, that new fashioned
I may rise up from death, before I'am dead.

II.

The SONNE.

O Sonne of God, who seeing two things,   10
Sinne, and death crept in, which were never made,
  By bearing one, tryed'st with what stings
The other could thine heritage invade;
      O be thou nail'd unto my heart,
      And crucified againe,   15
Part not from it, though it from thee would part,
But let it be, by applying so thy paine,
Drown'd in thy blood, and in thy passion slaine.

40 rusts, *1633 and most MSS.:* rust, *1635-69 and some MSS.*
The Litanie. *1633-69:* A Letanie. *MSS.*

III.

III.

The HOLY GHOST.

O Holy Ghost, whose temple I
Am, but of mudde walls, and condensed dust,   20
   And being sacrilegiously
Halfe wasted with youths fires, of pride and lust,
     Must with new stormes be weatherbeat;
     Double in my heart thy flame,
Which let devout sad teares intend; and let   25
(Though this glasse lanthorne, flesh, do suffer maime)
Fire, Sacrifice, Priest, Altar be the same.

IV.

The TRINITY.

O Blessed glorious Trinity,
Bones to Philosophy, but milke to faith,
   Which, as wise serpents, diversly   30
Most slipperinesse, yet most entanglings hath.
     As you distinguish'd undistinct
     By power, love, knowledge bee,
Give mee a such selfe different instinct
Of these; let all mee elemented bee,   35
Of power, to love, to know, you unnumbered three.

V.

The Virgin MARY.

For that faire blessed Mother-maid,
Whose flesh redeem'd us; That she-Cherubin,
   Which unlock'd Paradise, and made
One claime for innocence, and disseiz'd sinne,   40

34 a such *1633:* such *1635–69:* such a *MSS.*

Whose

Whose wombe was a strange heav'n, for there
God cloath'd himselfe, and grew,
Our zealous thankes wee poure. As her deeds were
Our helpes, so are her prayers; nor can she sue
In vaine, who hath such titles unto you. 45

VI.

The Angels.

And since this life our nonage is,
And wee in Wardship to thine Angels be,
Native in heavens faire Palaces,
Where we shall be but denizen'd by thee,
As th'earth conceiving by the Sunne, 50
Yeelds faire diversitie,
Yet never knowes which course that light doth run,
So let mee study, that mine actions bee
Worthy their sight, though blinde in how they see.

VII.

The Patriarches.

And let thy Patriarches Desire 55
(Those great Grandfathers of thy Church, which saw
More in the cloud, then wee in fire,
Whom Nature clear'd more, then us Grace and Law,
And now in Heaven still pray, that wee
May use our new helpes right,) 60
Be satisfy'd, and fructifie in mee;
Let not my minde be blinder by more light
Nor Faith, by Reason added, lose her sight.

48 Native] Natives *some MSS.*   61 satisfy'd, *1635-69 and most*
MSS.: sanctified, *1633*

VIII.

VIII.
The Prophets.

Thy Eagle-sighted Prophets too,
Which were thy Churches Organs, and did sound   65
    That harmony, which made of two
One law, and did unite, but not confound;
      Those heavenly Poëts which did see
      Thy will, and it expresse
In rythmique feet, in common pray for mee,   70
That I by them excuse not my excesse
In seeking secrets, or Poëtiquenesse.

IX.
The Apostles.

And thy illustrious Zodiacke
Of twelve Apostles, which ingirt this All,
    (From whom whosoever do not take   75
Their light, to darke deep pits, throw downe, and fall,)
      As through their prayers, thou'hast let mee know
      That their bookes are divine;
May they pray still, and be heard, that I goe
Th'old broad way in applying; O decline   80
Mee, when my comment would make thy word mine.

X.
The Martyrs.

And since thou so desirously
Did'st long to die, that long before thou could'st,
    And long since thou no more couldst dye,
Thou in thy scatter'd mystique body wouldst   85
      In Abel dye, and ever since
      In thine; let their blood come

75 whosoever] whoever *most MSS.*   76 throw downe, and fall,)
1633 and MSS.: thrown down do fall) *1635–69*

To

To begge for us, a discreet patience
Of death, or of worse life: for Oh, to some
Not to be Martyrs, is a martyrdome.   90

XI.
The Confessors.

Therefore with thee triumpheth there
A Virgin Squadron of white Confessors,
  Whose bloods betroth'd, not marryed were,
Tender'd, not taken by those Ravishers:
      They know, and pray, that wee may know,   95
        In every Christian
Hourly tempestuous persecutions grow;
Tentations martyr us alive; A man
Is to himselfe a Dioclesian.

XII.
The Virgins.

The cold white snowie Nunnery,   100
Which, as thy mother, their high Abbesse, sent
  Their bodies backe againe to thee,
As thou hadst lent them, cleane and innocent,
      Though they have not obtain'd of thee,
      That or thy Church, or I,   105
Should keep, as they, our first integrity;
Divorce thou sinne in us, or bid it die,
And call chast widowhead Virginitie.

XIII.
The Doctors.

Thy sacred Academie above
Of Doctors, whose paines have unclasp'd, and taught 110
  Both bookes of life to us (for love
To know thy Scriptures tells us, we are wrote

100 The] Thy *some MSS.*   109 Academie *1633 and one MS.
group:* Academ *1635–69:* Academe *some MSS.*

                                                       In

In thy other booke) pray for us there
  That what they have misdone
Or mis-said, wee to that may not adhere;   115
Their zeale may be our sinne. Lord let us runne
Meane waies, and call them stars, but not the Sunne.

XIV.

And whil'st this universall Quire,
That Church in triumph, this in warfare here,
  Warm'd with one all-partaking fire   120
Of love, that none be lost, which cost thee deare,
   Prayes ceaslesly,'and thou hearken too,
   (Since to be gratious
Our taske is treble, to pray, beare, and doe)
Heare this prayer Lord: O Lord deliver us 125
From trusting in those prayers, though powr'd out thus.

XV.

From being anxious, or secure,
Dead clods of sadnesse, or light squibs of mirth,
  From thinking, that great courts immure
All, or no happinesse, or that this earth   130
   Is only for our prison fram'd,
   Or that thou art covetous
To them whom thou lovest, or that they are maim'd
From reaching this worlds sweet, who seek thee thus,
With all their might, Good Lord deliver us. 135

XVI.

From needing danger, to bee good,
From owing thee yesterdaies teares to day,
  From trusting so much to thy blood,
That in that hope, wee wound our soule away,

134 sweet, *1633 and some MSS.:* sweets, *1635–69 and other MSS.*

         From

From bribing thee with Almes, to excuse   140
Some sinne more burdenous,
From light affecting, in religion, newes,
From thinking us all soule, neglecting thus
Our mutuall duties, Lord deliver us.

XVII.

From tempting Satan to tempt us,   145
By our connivence, or slack companie,
From measuring ill by vitious,
Neglecting to choake sins spawne, Vanitie,
From indiscreet humilitie,
Which might be scandalous,   150
And cast reproach on Christianitie,
From being spies, or to spies pervious,
From thirst, or scorne of fame, deliver us.

XVIII.

Deliver us for thy descent
Into the Virgin, whose wombe was a place   155
Of middle kind; and thou being sent
To'ungratious us, staid'st at her full of grace;
And through thy poore birth, where first thou
Glorifiedst Povertie,
And yet soone after riches didst allow,   160
By accepting Kings gifts in the Epiphanie,
Deliver, and make us, to both waies free.

XIX.

And through that bitter agonie,
Which is still the agonie of pious wits,
Disputing what distorted thee,   165
And interrupted evennesse, with fits;

154 for *1633 and most MSS.:* through *1635–69 and some MSS.*
163 that] thy *some MSS.*

And

And through thy free confession
Though thereby they were then
Made blind, so that thou might'st from them have gone,
Good Lord deliver us, and teach us when   170
Wee may not, and we may blinde unjust men.

XX.

Through thy submitting all, to blowes
Thy face, thy clothes to spoile; thy fame to scorne,
   All waies, which rage, or Justice knowes,
And by which thou could'st shew, that thou wast born; 175
     And through thy gallant humblenesse
     Which thou in death did'st shew,
Dying before thy soule they could expresse,
Deliver us from death, by dying so,
To this world, ere this world doe bid us goe.   180

XXI.

When senses, which thy souldiers are,
Wee arme against thee, and they fight for sinne,
   When want, sent but to tame, doth warre
And worke despaire a breach to enter in,
     When plenty, Gods image, and seale   185
     Makes us Idolatrous,
And love it, not him, whom it should reveale,
When wee are mov'd to seeme religious
Only to vent wit, Lord deliver us.

XXII.

In Churches, when the'infirmitie   190
Of him which speakes, diminishes the Word,
   When Magistrates doe mis-apply
To us, as we judge, lay or ghostly sword,

173 clothes *1633 and most MSS.:* robes *1635–69 and some MSS.*

When

When plague, which is thine Angell, raignes,
    Or wars, thy Champions, swaie,   195
When Heresie, thy second deluge, gaines;
In th'houre of death, the'Eve of last judgement day,
Deliver us from the sinister way.

XXIII.

Heare us, O heare us Lord; to thee
A sinner is more musique, when he prayes,   200
    Then spheares, or Angels praises bee,
In Panegyrique Allelujaes;
        Heare us, for till thou heare us, Lord
        We know not what to say;
Thine eare to'our sighes, teares, thoughts gives voice and
        word.   205
O Thou who Satan heard'st in Jobs sicke day,
Heare thy selfe now, for thou in us dost pray.

XXIV.

That wee may change to evennesse
This intermitting aguish Pietie;
    That snatching cramps of wickednesse   210
And Apoplexies of fast sin, may die;
        That musique of thy promises,
        Not threats in Thunder may
Awaken us to our just offices;
What in thy booke, thou dost, or creatures say,   215
That we may heare, Lord heare us, when wee pray.

XXV.

That our eares sicknesse wee may cure,
And rectifie those Labyrinths aright;
    That wee, by harkning, not procure
Our praise, nor others dispraise so invite;   220
        That wee get not a slipperinesse
        And senslesly decline,

197 last judgement] the last *one MS.*: Gods judgement *one MS.*

From

From hearing bold wits jeast at Kings excesse,
To'admit the like of majestie divine;
That we may locke our eares, Lord open thine.   225

XXVI.

That living law, the Magistrate,
Which to give us, and make us physicke, doth
   Our vices often aggravate,
That Preachers taxing sinne, before her growth,
     That Satan, and invenom'd men   230
     Which well, if we staive, dine,
When they doe most accuse us, may see then
Us, to amendment, heare them; thee decline:
That we may open our eares, Lord lock thine.

XXVII.

That learning, thine Ambassador,   235
From thine allegeance wee never tempt,
   That beauty, paradises flower
For physicke made, from poyson be exempt,
     That wit, borne apt high good to doe,
     By dwelling lazily   240
On Natures nothing, be not nothing too,
That our affections kill us not, nor dye,
Heare us, weake ecchoes, O thou eare, and cry.

XXVIII.

Sonne of God heare us, and since thou
By taking our blood, owest it us againe,   245
   Gaine to thy self, or us allow;
And let not both us and thy selfe be slaine;
     O Lambe of God, which took'st our sinne
     Which could not stick to thee,

231 well, *1633 and most MSS.*: will, *1635–69, one MS., Chambers and Grolier*   243 weake ecchoes, O thou eare, and cry. *1633–69 and most MSS.*: weake wretches, O thou eare and eye. *some MSS. and Chambers*   246 or us *1633 and most MSS.*: and us *1635–69 and some MSS.*

                        O let

O let it not returne to us againe,   250
But Patient and Physition being free,
As sinne is nothing, let it no where be.

Vpon the translation of the Psalmes by Sir Philip Sydney, *and the Countesse of Pembroke
his Sister.*

ETernall God, (for whom who ever dare
   Seeke new expressions, doe the Circle square,
And thrust into strait corners of poore wit
Thee, who art cornerlesse and infinite)
I would but blesse thy Name, not name thee now;   5
(And thy gifts are as infinite as thou:)
Fixe we our prayses therefore on this one,
That, as thy blessed Spirit fell upon
These Psalmes first Author in a cloven tongue;
(For 'twas a double power by which he sung   10
The highest matter in the noblest forme;)
So thou hast cleft that spirit, to performe
That worke againe, and shed it, here, upon
Two, by their bloods, and by thy Spirit one;
A Brother and a Sister, made by thee   15
The Organ, where thou art the Harmony.
Two that make one *John Baptists* holy voyce,
And who that Psalme, *Now let the Iles rejoyce,*
Have both translated, and apply'd it too,
Both told us what, and taught us how to doe.   20
They shew us Ilanders our joy, our King,
They tell us *why,* and teach us *how* to sing;
Make all this All, three Quires, heaven, earth, and sphears;
The first, Heaven, hath a song, but no man heares,
The Spheares have Musick, but they have no tongue,   25
Their harmony is rather danc'd than sung;
But our third Quire, to which the first gives eare,

Vpon the *&c. 1635–69: no extant MSS.*

(For,

(For, Angels learne by what the Church does here)
This Quire hath all. The Organist is hee
Who hath tun'd God and Man, the Organ we: 30
The songs are these, which heavens high holy Muse
Whisper'd to *David*, *David* to the Jewes:
And *Davids* Successors, in holy zeale,
In formes of joy and art doe re-reveale
To us so sweetly and sincerely too,   35
That I must not rejoyce as I would doe
When I behold that these Psalmes are become
So well attyr'd abroad, so ill at home,
So well in Chambers, in thy Church so ill,
As I can scarce call that reform'd untill   40
This be reform'd; Would a whole State present
A lesser gift than some one man hath sent?
And shall our Church, unto our Spouse and King
More hoarse, more harsh than any other, sing?
For *that* we pray, we praise thy name for *this*,   45
Which, by ⟨this⟩ *Moses* and this *Miriam*, is
Already done; and as those Psalmes we call
(Though some have other Authors) *Davids* all:
So though some have, some may some Psalmes translate,
We thy Sydnean Psalmes shall celebrate,   50
And, till we come th'Extemporall song to sing,
(Learn'd the first hower, that we see the King,
Who hath translated those translators) may
These their sweet learned labours, all the way
Be as our tuning; that, when hence we part,   55
We may fall in with them, and sing our part.

To Mr Tilman *after he had taken orders.*

THou, whose diviner soule hath caus'd thee now
    To put thy hand unto the holy Plough,
Making Lay-scornings of the Ministry,
Not an impediment, but victory;

46 this Moses *Grosart:* thy *Moses* 1635–69

What

What bringst thou home with thee? how is thy mind   5
Affected since the vintage? Dost thou finde
New thoughts and stirrings in thee? and as Steele
Toucht with a Loadstone, dost new motions feele?
Or, as a Ship after much paine and care,
For Iron and Cloth brings home rich Indian ware,   10
Hast thou thus traffiqu'd, but with farre more gaine
Of noble goods, and with lesse time and paine?
Thou art the same materials, as before,
Onely the stampe is changed; but no more.
And as new crowned Kings alter the face,   15
But not the monies substance; so hath grace
Chang'd onely Gods old Image by Creation,
To Christs new stampe, at this thy Coronation;
Or, as we paint Angels with wings, because
They beare Gods message, and proclaime his lawes,   20
Since thou must doe the like, and so must move,
Art thou new feather'd with cœlestiall love?
Deare, tell me where thy purchase lies, and shew
What thy advantage is above, below.
But if thy gainings doe surmount expression,   25
Why doth the foolish world scorne that profession,
Whose joyes passe speech? Why do they think unfit
That Gentry should joyne families with it?
As if their day were onely to be spent
In dressing, Mistressing and complement;   30
Alas poore joyes, but poorer men, whose trust
Seemes richly placed in sublimed dust;
(For, such are cloathes and beauty, which though gay,
Are, at the best, but of sublimed clay.)
Let then the world thy calling disrespect,   35
But goe thou on, and pitty their neglect.
What function is so noble, as to bee
Embassadour to God and destinie?
To open life, to give kingdomes to more
Than Kings give dignities; to keepe heavens doore?   40

Maries

Maries prerogative was to beare Christ, so
'Tis preachers to convey him, for they doe
As Angels out of clouds, from Pulpits speake;
And blesse the poore beneath, the lame, the weake.
If then th'Astronomers, whereas they spie   45
A new-found Starre, their Opticks magnifie,
How brave are those, who with their Engine, can
Bring man to heaven, and heaven againe to man?
These are thy titles and preheminences,
In whom must meet Gods graces, mens offences,   50
And so the heavens which beget all things here,
And the earth our mother, which these things doth beare,
Both these in thee, are in thy Calling knit,
And make thee now a blest Hermaphrodite.

A Hymne to Christ, at the Authors last going into Germany.

IN what torne ship soever I embarke,
That ship shall be my embleme of thy Arke;
What sea soever swallow mee, that flood
Shall be to mee an embleme of thy blood;
Though thou with clouds of anger do disguise   5
Thy face; yet through that maske I know those eyes,
    Which, though they turne away sometimes,
        They never will despise.

I sacrifice this Iland unto thee,
And all whom I lov'd there, and who lov'd mee;   10
When I have put our seas twixt them and mee,
Put thou thy sea betwixt my sinnes and thee.

A Hymne &c. *1633–69:* A Hymne to Christ. *one MS. group:*
At his going with my Lord of Doncaster 1619. *(or similarly) some
MSS.: in MSS. last two lines of each stanza given as one*   10
I lov'd there, *1633, MSS.:* I love here, *1635–69*   who lov'd
mee; *1633, one MS. group:* who love mee; *1635–69 and other MSS.*
11 our seas *1633, one MS. group:* this flood *1635–69:* these (or those)
seas *some MSS.*   12 sea *MSS.:* seas *1633:* blood *1635–69*

As

As the trees sap doth seeke the root below
In winter, in my winter now I goe,
   Where none but thee, th'Eternall root   15
    Of true Love I may know.

Nor thou nor thy religion dost controule,
The amorousnesse of an harmonious Soule,
But thou would'st have that love thy selfe: As thou
Art jealous, Lord, so I am jealous now,   20
Thou lov'st not, till from loving more, thou free
My soule: Who ever gives, takes libertie:
   O, if thou car'st not whom I love
    Alas, thou lov'st not mee.

Seale then this bill of my Divorce to All,   25
On whom those fainter beames of love did fall;
Marry those loves, which in youth scattered bee
On Fame, Wit, Hopes (false mistresses) to thee.
Churches are best for Prayer, that have least light:
To see God only, I goe out of sight: 30
   And to scape stormy dayes, I chuse
    An Everlasting night.

The Lamentations of Jeremy, *for the most part according to* Tremelius.

CHAP. I.

1 HOw sits this citie, late most populous,
   Thus solitary, and like a widdow thus!
Amplest of Nations, Queene of Provinces
   She was, who now thus tributary is!

2 Still in the night shee weepes, and her teares fall   5
   Downe by her cheekes along, and none of all
Her lovers comfort her; Perfidiously
   Her friends have dealt, and now are enemie.

28 Fame, *1633, one MS. group:* Face, *1635–69 and other MSS.*
   The Lamentations *&c. 1633–69* (Tremellius *1639–69*), *three MSS.: Tr in the notes stands for* Tremellius, *Vulg for* Vulgate

3 Unto

3 Unto great bondage, and afflictions
  Juda is captive led; Those nations   10
With whom shee dwells, no place of rest afford,
  In streights shee meets her Persecutors sword.

4 Emptie are the gates of Sion, and her waies
  Mourne, because none come to her solemne dayes.
Her Priests doe groane, her maides are comfortlesse, 15
  And shee's unto her selfe a bitternesse.

5 Her foes are growne her head, and live at Peace,
  Because when her transgressions did increase,
The Lord strooke her with sadnesse: Th'enemie
  Doth drive her children to captivitie.   20

6 From Sions daughter is all beauty gone,
  Like Harts, which seeke for Pasture, and find none,
Her Princes are, and now before the foe
  Which still pursues them, without strength they go.

7 Now in her daies of Teares, Jerusalem   25
  (Her men slaine by the foe, none succouring them)
Remembers what of old, shee esteemed most,
  Whilest her foes laugh at her, for what she hath lost.

8 Jerusalem hath sinn'd, therefore is shee
  Remov'd, as women in uncleannesse bee;   30
Who honor'd, scorne her, for her foulnesse they
  Have seene; her selfe doth groane, and turne away.

9 Her foulnesse in her skirts was seene, yet she
  Remembred not her end; Miraculously
Therefore shee fell, none comforting: Behold   35
  O Lord my affliction, for the Foe growes bold.

25 her *one MS.:* their *1633-69 and other MSS.:* the *one MS.:*
diebus afflictionis suae et ploratuum suorum *Tr*

10 Upon all things where her delight hath beene,
 The foe hath stretch'd his hand, for shee hath seene
Heathen, whom thou command'st, should not doe so,
 Into her holy Sanctuary goe.   40

11 And all her people groane, and seeke for bread;
 And they have given, only to be fed,
All precious things, wherein their pleasure lay:
 How cheape I'am growne, O Lord, behold, and weigh.

12 All this concernes not you, who passe by mee,   45
 O see, and marke if any sorrow bee
Like to my sorrow, which Jehova hath
 Done to mee in the day of his fierce wrath?

13 That fire, which by himselfe is governed
 He hath cast from heaven on my bones, and spred 50
A net before my feet, and mee o'rthrowne,
 And made me languish all the day alone.

14 His hand hath of my sinnes framed a yoake
 Which wreath'd, and cast upon my neck, hath broke
My strength. The Lord unto those enemies   55
 Hath given mee, from whom I cannot rise.

15 He under foot hath troden in my sight
 My strong men; He did company invite
To breake my young men; he the winepresse hath
 Trod upon Juda's daughter in his wrath.   60

16 For these things doe I weepe, mine eye, mine eye
 Casts water out; For he which should be nigh
To comfort mee, is now departed farre;
 The foe prevailes, forlorne my children are.

---

53 hand] hands *1650–69:* manu ejus *Tr*   56 from whom *1635–
69 and MSS.:* from whence *1633*   58 invite *1633, one MS.:* accite
1635–69 and other MSS.

17 There's

17 There's none, though *Sion* do stretch out her hand,   65
    To comfort her, it is the Lords command
That *Jacobs* foes girt him. *Jerusalem*
    Is as an uncleane woman amongst them.

18 But yet the Lord is just, and righteous still,
    I have rebell'd against his holy will;   70
O heare all people, and my sorrow see,
    My maides, my young men in captivitie.

19 I called for my *lovers* then, but they
    Deceiv'd mee, and my Priests, and Elders lay
Dead in the citie; for they sought for meat   75
    Which should refresh their soules, they could not get.

20 Because I am in streights, *Jehova* see
    My heart o'rturn'd, my bowells muddy bee,
Because I have rebell'd so much, as fast
    The sword without, as death within, doth wast.   80

21 Of all which heare I mourne, none comforts mee,
    My foes have heard my griefe, and glad they be,
That thou hast done it; But thy promis'd day
    Will come, when, as I suffer, so shall they.

22 Let all their wickednesse appeare to thee,   85
    Doe unto them, as thou hast done to mee,
For all my sinnes: The sighs which I have had
    Are very many, and my heart is sad.

Chap. II.

1 HOw over Sions daughter hath God hung
    His wraths thicke cloud! and from heaven hath
        flung   90
To earth the beauty of *Israel*, and hath
    Forgot his foot-stoole in the day of wrath!

76 they could not get. *1633:* and none could get. *1635–69: Grolier
conjectures that in* 75 *we should read* the sought-for meat   81 heare
I mourne, *1633–35 and some MSS.:* heare me mourn, *one MS.:* here
I mourn, *1639–69 and mod. edd.:* Audientium me in gemitu esse
nemo consolatur me. *Tr*

2 The

2 The Lord unsparingly hath swallowed
  All Jacobs dwellings, and demolished
To ground the strengths of *Juda*, and prophan'd   95
  The Princes of the Kingdome, and the land.

3 In heat of wrath, the horne of *Israel* hee
  Hath cleane cut off, and lest the enemie
Be hindred, his right hand he doth retire,
  But is towards *Jacob*, All-devouring fire.   100

4 Like to an enemie he bent his bow,
  His right hand was in posture of a foe,
To kill what *Sions* daughter did desire,
  'Gainst whom his wrath, he poured forth, like fire.

5 For like an enemie *Jehova* is,   105
  Devouring *Israel*, and his Palaces,
Destroying holds, giving additions
  To *Juda's* daughters lamentations.

6 Like to a garden hedge he hath cast downe
  The place where was his congregation,   110
And *Sions* feasts and sabbaths are forgot;
  Her King, her Priest, his wrath regardeth not.

7 The Lord forsakes his Altar, and detests
  His Sanctuary, and in the foes hand rests
His Palace, and the walls, in which their cries   115
  Are heard, as in the true solemnities.

8 The Lord hath cast a line, so to confound
  And levell *Sions* walls unto the ground;
He drawes not back his hand, which doth oreturne
  The wall, and Rampart, which together mourne.   120

  95 strengths *1633, one MS.:* strength *1635–69 and other MSS.:*
munitiones *Tr and Vulg*   114 hand *MSS.:* hands *1633–69:* tradit
in manum inimici muros, palatia illius *Tr*

9 Their gates are sunke into the ground, and hee
  Hath broke the barres; their King and Princes bee
Amongst the heathen, without law, nor there
  Unto their Prophets doth the Lord appeare.

10 There *Sions Elders* on the ground are plac'd,   125
  And silence keepe; Dust on their heads they cast,
In sackcloth have they girt themselves, and low
  The Virgins towards ground, their heads do throw.

11 My bowells are growne muddy, and mine eyes
  Are faint with weeping: and my liver lies   130
Pour'd out upon the ground, for miserie
  That sucking children in the streets doe die.

12 When they had cryed unto their Mothers, where
  Shall we have bread, and drinke? they fainted there,
And in the streets like wounded persons lay   135
  Till 'twixt their mothers breasts they went away.

13 *Daughter Jerusalem*, Oh what may bee
  A witnesse, or comparison for thee?
Sion, to ease thee, what shall I name like thee?
  Thy breach is like the sea, what help can bee?   140

14 For thee vaine foolish things thy Prophets sought,
  Thee, thine iniquities they have not taught,
Which might disturne thy bondage: but for thee
  False burthens, and false causes they would see.

15 The passengers doe clap their hands, and hisse,   145
  And wag their head at thee, and say, Is this
That citie, which so many men did call
  Joy of the earth, and perfectest of all?

122 barres; *some MSS.:* barre; *1633–69, one MS. group:* vectes ejus
Tr   135 streets *some MSS.:* street *1633–69, one MS. group:* in plateis
civitatis *Tr*   143 disturne *1633–54 and MSS.:* dis-urn *1669:*
disturb *Chambers:* ad avertendum captivitatem tuam *Tr*

16 Thy

16 Thy foes doe gape upon thee, and they hisse,
  And gnash their teeth, and say, Devoure wee this, 150
For this is certainly the day which wee
  Expected, and which now we finde, and see.

17 The Lord hath done that which he purposed,
  Fulfill'd his word of old determined;
He hath throwne downe, and not spar'd, and thy foe 155
  Made glad above thee, and advanc'd him so.

18 But now, their hearts against the Lord do call,
  Therefore, O walls of *Sion*, let teares fall
Downe like a river, day and night; take thee
  No rest, but let thine eye incessant be. 160

19 Arise, cry in the night, poure, for thy sinnes,
  Thy heart, like water, when the watch begins;
Lift up thy hands to God, lest children dye,
  Which, faint for hunger, in the streets doe lye.

20 Behold O Lord, consider unto whom 165
  Thou hast done this; what, shall the women come
To eate their children of a spanne? shall thy
  Prophet and Priest be slaine in Sanctuary?

21 On ground in streets, the yong and old do lye,
  My virgins and yong men by sword do dye; 170
Them in the day of thy wrath thou hast slaine,
  Nothing did thee from killing them containe.

22 As to a solemne feast, all whom I fear'd
  Thou call'st about mee; when thy wrath appear'd,
None did remaine or scape, for those which I 175
  Brought up, did perish by mine enemie.

157 against *1633:* unto *1635–69 and MSS.:* clamat cor istorum
contra Dominum *Tr:* ad Dominum *Vulg* 174 thy] his *1633*

CHAP. III.

Chap. III.

1 I Am the man which have affliction seene,
  Under the rod of Gods wrath having beene,
2 He hath led mee to darknesse, not to light,
  3 And against mee all day, his hand doth fight. 180

4 Hee hath broke my bones, worne out my flesh and skinne,
  5 Built up against mee; and hath girt mee in
With hemlocke, and with labour; 6 and set mee
  In darke, as they who dead for ever bee.

7 Hee hath hedg'd me lest I scape, and added more 185
  To my steele fetters, heavier then before.
8 When I crie out, he out shuts my prayer: 9 And hath
  Stop'd with hewn stone my way, and turn'd my path.

10 And like a Lion hid in secrecie,
  Or Beare which lyes in wait, he was to mee. 190
11 He stops my way, teares me, made desolate,
  12 And hee makes mee the marke he shooteth at.

13 Hee made the children of his quiver passe
  Into my reines, 14 I with my people was
All the day long, a song and mockery. 195
  15 Hee hath fill'd mee with bitternesse, and he

Hath made me drunke with wormewood. 16 He hath burst
  My teeth with stones, and covered mee with dust;
17 And thus my Soule farre off from peace was set,
  And my prosperity I did forget. 200

18 My strength, my hope (unto my selfe I said)
  Which from the Lord should come, is perished.
19 But when my mournings I do thinke upon,
  My wormwood, hemlocke, and affliction,

20 My Soule is humbled in remembring this; 205
  21 My heart considers, therefore, hope there is.
22 'Tis Gods great mercy we'are not utterly
  Consum'd, for his compassions do not die;

182 girt] hemde *some MSS.*

N 23 For

23 For every morning they renewed bee,
 For great, O Lord, is thy fidelity.   210
24 The Lord is, saith my Soule, my portion,
 And therefore in him will I hope alone.

25 The Lord is good to them, who on him relie,
 And to the Soule that seeks him earnestly.
26 It is both good to trust, and to attend 215
 (The Lords salvation) unto the end:

27 'Tis good for one his yoake in youth to beare;
 28 He sits alone, and doth all speech forbeare,
Because he hath borne it. 29 And his mouth he layes
 Deepe in the dust, yet then in hope he stayes. 220

30 He gives his cheekes to whosoever will
 Strike him, and so he is reproched still.
31 For, not for ever doth the Lord forsake,
 32 But when he'hath strucke with sadnes, hee doth take

Compassion, as his mercy'is infinite;   225
 33 Nor is it with his heart, that he doth smite;
34 That underfoot the prisoners stamped bee,
 35 That a mans right the Judge himselfe doth see

To be wrung from him, 36 That he subverted is
 In his just cause; the Lord allowes not this. 230
37 Who then will say, that ought doth come to passe,
 But that which by the Lord commanded was?

38 Both good and evill from his mouth proceeds;
 39 Why then grieves any man for his misdeeds?
40 Turne wee to God, by trying out our wayes; 235
 41 To him in heaven, our hands with hearts upraise.

42 Wee have rebell'd, and falne away from thee,
 Thou pardon'st not; 43 Usest no clemencie;
Pursuest us, kill'st us, coverest us with wrath,
 44 Cover'st thy selfe with clouds, that our prayer hath

 239 coverest us with wrath] coverest with thy wrath *some MSS.*

No

No power to passe. 45 And thou hast made us fall   241
As refuse, and off-scouring to them all.
46 All our foes gape at us. 47 Feare and a snare
With ruine, and with waste, upon us are.

48 With watry rivers doth mine eye oreflow   245
For ruine of my peoples daughter so;
49 Mine eye doth drop downe teares incessantly,
50 Untill the Lord looke downe from heaven to see.

51 And for my citys daughters sake, mine eye
Doth breake mine heart. 52 Causles mine enemy, 250
Like a bird chac'd me. 53 In a dungeon
They have shut my life, and cast on me a stone.

54 Waters flow'd o'r my head, then thought I, I am
Destroy'd; 55 I called Lord, upon thy name
Out of the pit. 56 And thou my voice didst heare;   255
Oh from my sigh, and crye, stop not thine eare.

57 Then when I call'd upon thee, thou drew'st nere
Unto mee, and said'st unto mee, do not feare.
58 Thou Lord my Soules cause handled hast, and thou
Rescud'st my life. 59 O Lord do thou judge now, 260
Thou heardst my wrong. 60 Their vengeance all they
    have wrought;
    61 How they reproach'd, thou hast heard, and what
    they thought,
62 What their lips uttered, which against me rose,
And what was ever whisper'd by my foes.

63 I am their song, whether they rise or sit,   265
    64 Give them rewards Lord, for their working fit,
65 Sorrow of heart, thy curse. 66 And with thy might
Follow, and from under heaven destroy them quite.

246 daughter *MSS.:* daughters *1633–69:* propter contritionem filiae
populi mei *Tr*   249 citys *one MS.:* city *1633–69:* propter omnes
filias civitatis meae *Tr*   252 on me *MSS.:* me on *1633–69:* pro-
jiciunt lapides in me. *Tr:* posuerunt lapidem super me. *Vulg*   260
Rescud'st *two MSS.:* Rescuest *1633–69, one MS. group:* vindicabas *Tr*

CHAP. IV.

CHAP. IV.

1 HOw is the gold become so dimme? How is
    Purest and finest gold thus chang'd to this?   270
The stones which were stones of the Sanctuary,
    Scattered in corners of each street do lye.

2 The pretious sonnes of Sion, which should bee
    Valued at purest gold, how do wee see
Low rated now, as earthen Pitchers, stand,   275
    Which are the worke of a poore Potters hand.

3 Even the Sea-calfes draw their brests, and give
    Sucke to their young; my peoples daughters live,
By reason of the foes great cruelnesse,
    As do the Owles in the vast Wildernesse.   280

4 And when the sucking child doth strive to draw,
    His tongue for thirst cleaves to his upper jaw.
And when for bread the little children crye,
    There is no man that doth them satisfie.

5 They which before were delicately fed,   285
    Now in the streets forlorne have perished,
And they which ever were in scarlet cloath'd,
    Sit and embrace the dunghills which they loath'd.

6 The daughters of my people have sinned more,
    Then did the towne of *Sodome* sinne before;   290
Which being at once destroy'd, there did remaine
    No hands amongst them, to vexe them againe.

7 But heretofore purer her Nazarite
    Was then the snow, and milke was not so white;
As carbuncles did their pure bodies shine,   295
    And all their polish'dnesse was Saphirine.

274 at *1633-39:* as *1650-69*, *MSS.:* qui taxandi erant auro
purgatissimo *Tr*   296 Saphirine. *1635-69:* Seraphine. *1633:*
Sapphirina polities eorum *Tr*

8 They

8 They are darker now then blacknes, none can know
　　Them by the face, as through the streets they goe,
For now their skin doth cleave unto the bone,
　　And withered, is like to dry wood growne.　　300

9 Better by sword then famine 'tis to dye;
　　And better through pierc'd, then through penury.
10 Women by nature pitifull, have eate
　　Their children drest with their owne hands for meat.

11 *Jehova* here fully accomplish'd hath　　305
　　His indignation, and powr'd forth his wrath,
Kindled a fire in *Sion*, which hath power
　　To eate, and her foundations to devour.

12 Nor would the Kings of the earth, nor all which live
　　In the inhabitable world beleeve,　　310
That any adversary, any foe
　　Into *Jerusalem* should enter so.

13 For the Priests sins, and Prophets, which have shed
　　Blood in the streets, and the just murthered:
14 Which when those men, whom they made blinde, did
　　　　stray　　315
　　Thorough the streets, defiled by the way

With blood, the which impossible it was
　　Their garments should scape touching, as they passe,
15 Would cry aloud, depart defiled men,
　　Depart, depart, and touch us not; and then　　320

They fled, and strayd, and with the *Gentiles* were,
　　Yet told their friends, they should not long dwell there;
16 For this they are scattered by Jehovahs face
　　Who never will regard them more; No grace

298 streets *two MSS.:* street *1633–69, one MS. group:* in vicis *Tr:*
in plateis *Vulg*　　299 the *two MSS.:* their *1633–69*　　302 through
penury.] by penury, *1633 and one MS. group:* confossi gladio quam
confossi fame. *Tr*　　304 hands *two MSS.:* hand *1633–69*　　318
garments *1633:* garment *1635–69:* quem non possunt quin tangant
vestimentis suis *Tr*

Unto

Unto their old men shall the foe afford,　　325
　　Nor, that they are Priests, redeeme them from the sword.
17　And wee as yet, for all these miseries
　　Desiring our vaine helpe, consume our eyes:

And such a nation as cannot save,
　　We in desire and speculation have.　　330
18　They hunt our steps, that in the streets wee feare
　　To goe: our end is now approached neere,

Our dayes accomplish'd are, this the last day.
　19　Eagles of heaven are not so swift as they
Which follow us, o'r mountaine tops they flye　　335
　　At us, and for us in the desart lye.

20　The annointed Lord, breath of our nostrils, hee
　　Of whom we said, under his shadow, wee
Shall with more ease under the Heathen dwell,
　　Into the pit which these men digged, fell.　　340

21　Rejoyce O *Edoms daughter*, joyfull bee
　　Thou which inhabitst *Huz*, for unto thee
This cup shall passe, and thou with drunkennesse
　　Shalt fill thy selfe, and shew thy nakednesse.

22　And then thy sinnes O *Sion*, shall be spent,　　345
　　The Lord will not leave thee in banishment.
Thy sinnes O *Edoms daughter*, hee will see,
　　And for them, pay thee with captivitie.

Chap. V.

1　REmember, O Lord, what is fallen on us;
　　See, and marke how we are reproached thus,　　350
2　For unto strangers our possession
　　Is turn'd, our houses unto Aliens gone,

342 Huz *or* Hus *MSS.:* her, *1633:* Uz, *1635–69:* in terra Hutzi *Tr*

3 Our

3 Our mothers are become as widowes, wee
  As Orphans all, and without father be;
4 Waters which are our owne, wee drunke, and pay, 355
  And upon our owne wood a price they lay.

5 Our persecutors on our necks do sit,
  They make us travaile, and not intermit,
6 We stretch our hands unto th'*Egyptians*
  To get us bread; and to the *Assyrians.* 360

7 Our Fathers did these sinnes, and are no more,
  But wee do beare the sinnes they did before.
8 They are but servants, which do rule us thus,
  Yet from their hands none would deliver us.

9 With danger of our life our bread wee gat; 365
  For in the wildernesse, the sword did wait.
10 The tempests of this famine wee liv'd in,
  Black as an Oven colour'd had our skinne:

11 In *Judaes* cities they the maids abus'd
  By force, and so women in *Sion* us'd. 370
12 The Princes with their hands they hung; no grace
  Nor honour gave they to the Elders face.

13 Unto the mill our yong men carried are,
  And children fell under the wood they bare.
14 Elders, the-gates; youth did their songs forbeare, 375
15   Gone was our joy; our dancings, mournings were.

16 Now is the crowne falne from our head; and woe
  Be unto us, because we'have sinned so.
17 For this our hearts do languish, and for this
  Over our eyes a cloudy dimnesse is. 380

354 ather *two MSS.*: fathers *1633–69:* Pupilli sumus ac nullo patre *Tr:* absque patre *Vulg*　355 drunke, *1633 and one MS. group:* drinke *1635–69 and two MSS.*　368 Oven *1635–69:* Ocean *1633:* Pelles nostrae ut furnus atratae sunt *Tr*　376 15 Gone *&c.*] *Old edd. transfer* 15 *to next line, wrongly. In consequence, the remaining verses are all a number short, but the complete number of* 22 *is made up by breaking the last verse,* 'For oughtest thou *&c.*,' *into two. I have corrected throughout.*

18 Because

18 Because mount *Sion* desolate doth lye,
    And foxes there do goe at libertie:
19 But thou O Lord art ever, and thy throne
    From generation, to generation.

20 Why should'st thou forget us eternally?   385
    Or leave us thus long in this misery?
21 Restore us Lord to thee, that so we may
    Returne, and as of old, renew our day.

22 For oughtest thou, O Lord, despise us thus,
    And to be utterly enrag'd at us?   390

Hymne to God my God, in my sicknesse.

SInce I am comming to that Holy roome,
    Where, with thy Quire of Saints for evermore,
I shall be made thy Musique; As I come
    I tune the Instrument here at the dore,
    And what I must doe then, thinke here before.   5

Whilst my Physitians by their love are growne
    Cosmographers, and I their Mapp, who lie
Flat on this bed, that by them may be showne
    That this is my South-west discoverie
    Per fretum febris, by these streights to die,   10

I joy, that in these straits, I see my West;
    For, though theire currants yeeld returne to none,
What shall my West hurt me? As West and East
    In all flatt Maps (and I am one) are one,
    So death doth touch the Resurrection.   15

Hymn to God &c. *1635–69, one MS., and in part Walton* (Life
of Dᴿ John Donne. 1670), *who adds* March 23, 1630, *but Sir
Julius Caesar's copy (Addl. MSS. 34, 324) gives date* December 1623
4 the Instrument *1635–69:* my instrument *Walton*   6 Whilst . . .
love] Since . . . loves *Walton*   12 theire *MS.:* those *1635–69*

                                                              Is

Is the Pacifique Sea my home? Or are
  The Easterne riches? Is *Jerusalem*?
Anyan, and *Magellan,* and *Gibraltare,*
  All streights, and none but streights, are wayes to them,
  Whether where *Japhet* dwelt, or *Cham,* or *Sem.*   20

We thinke that *Paradise* and *Calvarie,*
  Christs Crosse, and *Adams* tree, stood in one place;
Looke Lord, and finde both *Adams* met in me;
  As the first *Adams* sweat surrounds my face,
  May the last *Adams* blood my soule embrace.   25

So, in his purple wrapp'd receive mee Lord,
  By these his thornes give me his other Crowne;
And as to others soules I preach'd thy word,
  Be this my Text, my Sermon to mine owne,
  Therfore that he may raise the Lord throws down.   30

A Hymne to God the Father:

I.

WIlt thou forgive that sinne where I begunne,
  Which was my sin, though it were done before?
Wilt thou forgive that sinne; through which I runne,
  And do run still: though still I do deplore?
    When thou hast done, thou hast not done,   5
      For, I have more.

II.

Wilt thou forgive that sinne which I have wonne
  Others to sinne? and, made my sinne their doore?
Wilt thou forgive that sinne which I did shunne
  A yeare, or two: but wallowed in, a score?   10
    When thou hast done, thou hast not done,
      For I have more.

28 othe**r**s soules] other souls *Walton and one MS.*   30 That, he may
raise; therefore, *Walton*
  A Hymne &c. 1633–69: To Christ. *some MSS.:* Christo Salvatori.
other MSS.: for the text of the MSS. see next page   8 my sinne] my
sins *1639–69*

                                       III.

III.

I have a sinne of feare, that when I have spunne
  My last thred, I shall perish on the shore;
But sweare by thy selfe, that at my death thy sonne   15
  Shall shine as he shines now, and heretofore;
    And, having done that, Thou hast done,
      I feare no more.

To Christ.

Wilt thou forgive that sinn, where I begunn,
  W^ch is my sinn, though it were done before?
Wilt thou forgive those sinns through wch I runn
  And doe them still, though still I doe deplore?
    When thou hast done, thou hast not done,   5
      for I have more.

Wilt thou forgive that sinn, by wch I'have wonne
  Others to sinn, & made my sinn their dore?
Wilt thou forgive that sinn wch I did shunne
  A yeare or twoe, but wallowed in a score?   10
    When thou hast done, thou hast not done,
      for I have more.

I have a sinn of feare y^t when I have spunn
  My last thred, I shall perish on the shore;
Sweare by thy self that at my Death, thy Sunn   15
  Shall shine as it shines nowe, & heretofore;
    And having done that, thou hast done,
      I have noe more.

To Christ. *or* Christo Salvatori. *MSS.*   4 them *one MS. group:*
runne *other MSS.*   15 thy Sunne *some MSS.:* this Sunn *one MS.*
group

ELEGIES

TO THE MEMORIE OF
MY EVER DESIRED FRIEND
Dʳ. Donne.

TO have liv'd eminent, in a degree
    Beyond our lofty'st flights, that is, like Thee,
Or t'have had too much merit, is not safe;
For, such excesses finde no Epitaph.
At common graves we have Poetique eyes   5
Can melt themselves in easie Elegies,
Each quill can drop his tributary verse,
And pin it, like the Hatchments, to the Hearse:
But at Thine, Poeme, or Inscription
(Rich soule of wit, and language) we have none.   10
Indeed a silence does that tombe befit,
Where is no Herald left to blazon it.
Widow'd invention justly doth forbeare
To come abroad, knowing Thou art not here,
Late her great Patron; Whose Prerogative   15
Maintain'd, and cloth'd her so, as none alive
Must now presume, to keepe her at thy rate,
Though he the Indies for her dowre estate.
Or else that awfull fire, which once did burne
In thy cleare Braine, now falne into thy Urne   20
Lives there, to fright rude Empiricks from thence,
Which might prophane thee by their Ignorance.
Who ever writes of Thee, and in a stile
Unworthy such a Theme, does but revile
Thy precious Dust, and wake a learned Spirit   25
Which may revenge his Rapes upon thy Merit.
For, all a low pitch't phansie can devise,
Will prove, at best, but Hallow'd Injuries.
    Thou, like the dying Swanne, didst lately sing
Thy Mournfull Dirge, in audience of the King;   30

To the &c. *Also in* Deaths Duell. *1632, Walton's* Lives *1670,*
King's Poems. *1657, 1664, 1700*   14 here] there *1632*

When

When pale lookes, and faint accents of thy breath,
Presented so, to life, that peece of death,
That it was fear'd, and prophesi'd by all,
Thou thither cam'st to preach thy Funerall.
O! had'st Thou in an Elegiacke Knell   35
Rung out unto the world thine owne farewell,
And in thy High Victorious Numbers beate
The solemne measure of thy griev'd Retreat;
Thou might'st the Poets service now have mist
As well, as then thou did'st prevent the Priest;   40
And never to the world beholding bee
So much, as for an Epitaph for thee.
   I doe not like the office. Nor is 't fit
Thou, who did'st lend our Age such summes of wit,
Should'st now re-borrow from her bankrupt Mine,   45
That Ore to Bury Thee, which once was Thine,
Rather still leave us in thy debt; And know
(Exalted Soule) more glory 't is to owe
Unto thy Hearse, what we can never pay,
Then, with embased Coine those Rites defray.   50
   Commit we then Thee to Thy selfe: Nor blame
Our drooping loves, which thus to thy owne Fame
Leave Thee Executour. Since, but thine owne,
No pen could doe Thee Justice, nor Bayes Crowne
Thy vast desert; Save that, wee nothing can   55
Depute, to be thy Ashes Guardian.
   So Jewellers no Art, or Metall trust
   To forme the Diamond, but the Diamonds dust.
                      H. K.

To the deceased Author,

U)on the *Promiscuous* printing of his Poems, the *Looser sort*, with the *Religious.*

WHen thy *Loose* raptures, *Donne*, shall meet with Those
        That doe confine
  Tuning, unto the Duller line,
  And sing not, but in *Sanctified Prose*;

     31 faint] weak 1632   57 or] nor *1632*

                                How

How will they, with sharper eyes,   5
    The *Fore-skinne* of thy phansie circumcise?
And feare, thy *wantonnesse* should now, begin
Example, that hath ceased to be *Sin?*

And that *Feare* fannes their *Heat*; whilst knowing eyes
    Will not admire   10
      At this *Strange Fire*,
    That here is *mingled with thy Sacrifice*:
      But dare reade even thy *Wanton Story*,
    As thy *Confession*, not thy *Glory*.
And will so envie *Both* to future times,   15
That they would buy thy *Goodnesse*, with thy *Crimes*.
              Tho: Browne.

On the death of Dr Donne.

I Cannot blame those men, that knew thee well,
  Yet dare not helpe the world, to ring thy knell
In tunefull *Elegies*; there's not language knowne
Fit for thy mention, but 'twas first thy owne;
The *Epitaphs* thou writst, have so bereft   5
Our tongue of wit, there is not phansie left
Enough to weepe thee; what henceforth we see
Of Art or Nature, must result from thee.
There may perchance some busie gathering friend
Steale from thy owne workes, and that, varied, lend,   10
Which thou bestow'st on others, to thy Hearse,
And so thou shalt live still in thine owne verse;
Hee that shall venture farther, may commit
A pitied errour, shew his zeale, not wit.
Fate hath done mankinde wrong; vertue may aime   15
Reward of conscience, never can, of fame,
Since her great trumpet's broke, could onely give
Faith to the world, command it to beleeve;
    Hee then must write, that would define thy parts:
    Here lyes the best Divinitie, All the Arts.   20
              Edw. Hyde.

On the &c. *Also in* Deaths Duell. *1632*   4 thy] thine *1632*
6 tongue] pens *1632*

                     On

On *Doctor* Donne,
By *Dʳ* C. B. *of* O.

HEe that would write an Epitaph for thee,
 And do it well, must first beginne to be
Such as thou wert; for, none can truly know
Thy worth, thy life, but he that hath liv'd so;
He must have wit to spare and to hurle downe: 5
Enough, to keepe the gallants of the towne.
He must have learning plenty; both the Lawes,
Civill, and Common, to judge any cause;
Divinity great store, above the rest;
Not of the last Edition, but the best.   10
Hee must have language, travaile, all the Arts;
Judgement to use; or else he wants thy parts.
He must have friends the highest, able to do;
Such as *Mecœnas*, and *Augustus* too.
He must have such a sicknesse, such a death;   15
Or else his vaine descriptions come beneath;
  Who then shall write an Epitaph for thee,
  He must be dead first, let'it alone for mee.

An *Elegie upon the incomparable*
Dʳ DONNE.

ALl is not well when such a one as I
 Dare peepe abroad, and write an *Elegie*;
When smaller *Starres* appeare, and give their light,
Phœbus is gone to bed: Were it not night,
And the world witlesse now that DONNE is dead,   5
You sooner should have broke, then seene my head.
Dead did I say? Forgive this *Injury*
I doe him, and his worthes *Infinity*,
To say he is but dead; I dare averre
It better may be term'd a *Massacre*,   10

By Dʳ &c. *i.e. Dʳ Corbet, Bishop of Oxford: also in Corbet's
Poems 1647*

Then

Then *Sleepe* or *Death*; See how the *Muses* mourne
Upon their oaten *Reeds*, and from his *Vrne*
Threaten the World with this *Calamity*,
    They shall have *Ballads*, but no *Poetry*.

Language lyes speechlesse; and *Divinity*,   15
Lost such a *Trump* as even to *Extasie*
Could charme the Soule, and had an *Influence*
To teach best *judgements*, and please dullest *Sense*.
The *Court*, the *Church*, the *Vniversitie*,
Lost *Chaplaine*, *Deane*, and *Doctor*, All these, Three.   20
    It was his *Merit*, that his *Funerall*
    Could cause a losse so *great* and *generall*.

If there be any Spirit can answer give
Of such as hence depart, to such as live:
Speake, Doth his body there vermiculate,   25
Crumble to dust, and feele the lawes of Fate?
Me thinkes, *Corruption*, *Wormes*, what else is foule
Should spare the *Temple* of so faire a *Soule*.
I could beleeve they doe; but that I know
What inconvenience might hereafter grow: 30
    Succeeding ages would *Idolatrize*,
    And as his *Numbers*, so his *Reliques* prize.

If that Philosopher, which did avow
The world to be but Motes, was living now:
He would affirme that th'*Atomes* of his mould   35
Were they in severall bodies blended, would
Produce new worlds of *Travellers*, *Divines*,
Of *Linguists*, *Poets*: sith these severall *lines*
In him concentred were, and flowing thence
Might fill againe the worlds *Circumference*.   40
I could beleeve this too; and yet my faith
Not want a *President*: The *Phœnix* hath
(And such was He) a power to animate
Her ashes, and herselfe perpetuate.
But, busie Soule, thou dost not well to pry   45
Into these Secrets; *Griefe*, and *Jealousie*,
The more they know, the further still advance,
And finde no way so safe as *Ignorance*.

                                                        Let

Let this suffice thee, that his *Soule* which flew
A pitch of all admir'd, known but of few,⠀⠀⠀⠀⠀⠀⠀⠀50
(Save those of purer mould) is now translated
From Earth to Heavên, and there *Constellated.*
⠀⠀For, if each *Priest* of God shine as a *Starre,*
⠀⠀His *Glory* is as his *Gifts,* 'bove others farre.
⠀⠀⠀⠀⠀⠀⠀⠀⠀⠀⠀⠀HEN. VALENTINE.

An Elegie upon Dr Donne.

IS *Donne,* great *Donne* deceas'd? then England say
⠀Thou'hast lost a man where language chose to stay
And shew it's gracefull power. I would not praise
That and his vast wit (which in these vaine dayes
Make many proud) but as they serv'd to unlock⠀⠀⠀5
That Cabinet, his minde: where such a stock
Of knowledge was repos'd, as all lament
(Or should) this generall cause of discontent.
⠀⠀And I rejoyce I am not so severe,
But (as I write a line) to weepe a teare⠀⠀⠀⠀⠀10
For his decease; Such sad extremities
May make such men as I write *Elegies.*
⠀⠀And wonder not; for, when a generall losse
Falls on a nation, and they slight the crosse,
God hath rais'd *Prophets* to awaken them⠀⠀⠀⠀15
From stupifaction; witnesse my milde pen,
Not us'd to upbraid the world, though now it must
Freely and boldly, for, the cause is just.
⠀⠀Dull age, Oh I would spare thee, but th'art worse,
Thou art not onely dull, but hast a curse⠀⠀⠀⠀20
Of black ingratitude; if not, couldst thou
Part with *miraculous Donne,* and make no vow
For thee and thine, successively to pay
A sad remembrance to his dying day?

⠀⠀An Elegie *&c. Also, with variants, in Walton's* Life of Donne
1658, 1670.
1-3⠀⠀Our Donne is dead; England should mourne, may say
⠀⠀⠀⠀We had a man where language chose to stay
⠀⠀⠀⠀And shew her gracefull power *1635-69*

⠀⠀⠀⠀⠀⠀⠀⠀⠀⠀⠀⠀⠀⠀⠀⠀⠀⠀⠀⠀Did

Did his youth scatter *Poetrie*, wherein   25
Was all Philosophie? Was every sinne,
Character'd in his *Satyres*? made so foule
That some have fear'd their shapes, and kept their soule
Freer by reading verse? Did he give *dayes*
Past marble monuments, to those, whose praise   30
He would perpetuate? Did hee (I feare
The dull will doubt:) these at his twentieth yeare?
    But, more matur'd: Did his full soule conceive,
And in harmonious-holy-numbers weave
A *Crowne of sacred sonets*, fit to adorne   *La Corona.* 35
A dying Martyrs brow: or, to be worne
On that blest head of *Mary Magdalen:*
After she wip'd Christs feet, but not till then?
Did hee (fit for such penitents as shee
And hee to use) leave us a *Litany*?   40
Which all devout men love, and sure, it shall,
As times grow better, grow more classicall.
Did he write *Hymnes*, for piety and wit
Equall to those great grave *Prudentius* writ?
Spake he all *Languages*? knew he all *Lawes*?   45
The grounds and use of *Physicke*; but because
'Twas mercenary wav'd it? Went to see
That blessed place of *Christs nativity*?
Did he returne and preach him? preach him so
As none but hee did, or could do? They know   50
(Such as were blest to heare him know) 'tis truth.
Did he confirme thy age? convert thy youth?
Did he these wonders? And is this deare losse
Mourn'd by so few? (few for so great a crosse.)
    But sure the silent are ambitious all   55
To be *Close Mourners* at his Funerall;
If not; In common pitty they forbare
By repetitions to renew our care;
Or, knowing, griefe conceiv'd, conceal'd, consumes
Man irreparably, (as poyson'd fumes   60
Do waste the braine) make silence a safe way
To'inlarge the Soule from these walls, mud and clay,

      26 Was all] Lay Loves *1658, 1670*

                  (Materialls

(Materialls of this body) to remaine
With *Donne* in heaven, where no promiscuous paine
Lessens the joy wee have, for, with *him*, all   65
Are satisfyed with *joyes essentiall.*

My thoughts, Dwell on this *Ioy*, and do not call
Griefe backe, by thinking of his Funerall;
Forget he lov'd mee; Waste not my sad yeares;
(Which haste to *Davids* seventy, fill'd with feares   70
And sorrow for his death;) Forget his parts,
Which finde a living grave in good mens hearts;
And, (for, my first is daily paid for sinne)
Forget to pay my second sigh for him:
Forget his powerfull preaching; and forget   75
I am his *Convert.* Oh my frailtie! let
My flesh be no more heard, it will obtrude
This lethargie: so should my gratitude,
My vowes of gratitude should so be broke;
Which can no more be, then *Donnes* vertues spoke   80
By any but himselfe; for which cause, I
    Write no *Encomium*, but an *Elegie.*

                        Iz. Wᴀ.

An Elegie upon the death of the
Deane of Pauls, Dʳ. John Donne:
By *Mʳ. Tho: Carie.*

CAn we not force from widdowed Poetry,
  Now thou art dead (Great Dᴏɴɴᴇ) one Elegie
To crowne thy Hearse? Why yet dare we not trust
Though with unkneaded dowe-bak't prose thy dust,
Such as the uncisor'd Churchman from the flower   5
Of fading Rhetorique, short liv'd as his houre,
Dry as the sand that measures it, should lay
Upon thy Ashes, on the funerall day?
Have we no voice, no tune? Did'st thou dispense
Through all our language, both the words and sense?   10
'Tis a sad truth; The Pulpit may her plaine,

    An Elegie &c.   *Also, with variants, in Carew's* Poems *1640.*

                                    And

And sober Christian precepts still retaine,
Doctrines it may, and wholesome Uses frame,
Grave Homilies, and Lectures, But the flame
Of thy brave Soule, that shot such heat and light,   15
As burnt our earth, and made our darknesse bright,
Committed holy Rapes upon our Will,
Did through the eye the melting heart distill;
And the deepe knowledge of darke truths so teach,
As sense might judge, what phansie could not reach;   20
Must be desir'd for ever. So the fire,
That fills with spirit and heat the Delphique quire,
Which kindled first by thy Promethean breath,
Glow'd here a while, lies quench't now in thy death;
The Muses garden with Pedantique weedes   25
O'rspred, was purg'd by thee; The lazie seeds
Of servile imitation throwne away;
And fresh invention planted, Thou didst pay
The debts of our penurious bankrupt age;
Licentious thefts, that make poëtique rage   30
A Mimique fury, when our soules must bee
Possest, or with Anacreons Extasie,
Or Pindars, not their owne; The subtle cheat
Of slie Exchanges, and the jugling feat
Of two-edg'd words, or whatsoever wrong   35
By ours was done the Greeke, or Latine tongue,
Thou hast redeem'd, and open'd Us a Mine
Of rich and pregnant phansie, drawne a line
Of masculine expression, which had good
Old Orpheus seene, Or all the ancient Brood   40
Our superstitious fooles admire, and hold
Their lead more precious, then thy burnish't Gold,
Thou hadst beene their Exchequer, and no more
They each in others dust, had rak'd for Ore.
Thou shalt yield no precedence, but of time,   45
And the blinde fate of language, whose tun'd chime
More charmes the outward sense; Yet thou maist claime
From so great disadvantage greater fame,
Since to the awe of thy imperious wit
Our stubborne language bends, made only fit   50

With

With her tough-thick-rib'd hoopes to gird about
Thy Giant phansie, which had prov'd too stout
For their soft melting Phrases. As in time
They had the start, so did they cull the prime
Buds of invention many a hundred yeare,   55
And left the rifled fields, besides the feare
To touch their Harvest, yet from those bare lands
Of what is purely thine, thy only hands
(And that thy smallest worke) have gleaned more
Then all those times, and tongues could reape before;   60
But thou art gone, and thy strict lawes will be
Too hard for Libertines in Poetrie.
They will repeale the goodly exil'd traine
Of gods and goddesses, which in thy just raigne
Were banish'd nobler Poems, now, with these   65
The silenc'd tales o'th'Metamorphoses
Shall stuffe their lines, and swell the windy Page,
Till Verse refin'd by thee, in this last Age,
Turne ballad rime, Or those old Idolls bee
Ador'd againe, with new apostasie;   70
Oh, pardon mee, that breake with untun'd verse
The reverend silence that attends thy herse,
Whose awfull solemne murmures were to thee
More then these faint lines, A loud Elegie,
That did proclaime in a dumbe eloquence   75
The death of all the Arts, whose influence
Growne feeble, in these panting numbers lies
Gasping short winded Accents, and so dies:
So doth the swiftly turning wheele not stand
In th'instant we withdraw the moving hand,   80
But some small time maintaine a faint weake course
By vertue of the first impulsive force:
And so whil'st I cast on thy funerall pile
Thy crowne of Bayes, Oh, let it crack a while,
And spit disdaine, till the devouring flashes   85
Suck all the moysture up, then turne to ashes.
I will not draw the envy to engrosse
All thy perfections, or weepe all our losse;

87 the] *i.e. probably* thee

Those

Those are too numerous for an Elegie,
And this too great, to be express'd by mee.
Though every pen should share a distinct part, 90
Yet art thou Theme enough to tyre all Art;
Let others carve the rest, it shall suffice
I on thy Tombe this Epitaph incise.

> *Here lies a King, that rul'd as hee thought fit*
> *The universall Monarchy of wit;* 95
> *Here lie two Flamens, and both those, the best,*
> *Apollo's first, at last, the true Gods Priest.*

An Elegie on D^r. DONNE: *By Sir Lucius Carie.*

POets attend, the Elegie I sing
Both of a doubly-named Priest, and King:
In stead of Coates, and Pennons, bring your Verse,
For you must bee chiefe mourners at his Hearse,
A Tombe your Muse must to his Fame supply, 5
No other Monuments can never die;
And as he was a two-fold Priest; in youth,
Apollo's; afterwards, the voice of Truth,
Gods Conduit-pipe for grace, who chose him for
His extraordinary Embassador, 10
So let his Liegiers with the Poets joyne,
Both having shares, both must in griefe combine:
Whil'st Johnson forceth with his Elegie
Teares from a griefe-unknowing Scythians eye,
(Like Moses at whose stroke the waters gusht 15
From forth the Rock, and like a Torrent rusht.)
Let Lawd his funerall Sermon preach, and shew
Those vertues, dull eyes were not apt to know,
Nor leave that Piercing Theme, till it appeares
To be goodfriday, by the Churches Teares; 20
Yet make not griefe too long oppresse our Powers,
Least that his funerall Sermon should prove ours.
Nor yet forget that heavenly Eloquence,
With which he did the bread of life dispense,
Preacher and Orator discharg'd both parts 25
With pleasure for our sense, health for our hearts,

And

And the first such (Though a long studied Art
Tell us our soule is all in every part,)
None was so marble, but whil'st him he heares,
His Soule so long dwelt only in his eares.   30
And from thence (with the fiercenesse of a flood
Bearing downe vice) victual'd with that blest food
Their hearts; His seed in none could faile to grow,
Fertile he found them all, or made them so:
No Druggist of the Soule bestow'd on all   35
So Catholiquely a curing Cordiall.
Nor only in the Pulpit dwelt his store,
His words work'd much, but his example more,
That preach't on worky dayes, His Poetrie
It selfe was oftentimes divinity,   40
Those Anthemes (almost second Psalmes) he writ
To make us know the Crosse, and value it,
(Although we owe that reverence to that name
Wee should not need warmth from an under flame.)
Creates a fire in us, so neare extreme   45
That we would die, for, and upon this theme.
Next, his so pious Litany, which none can
But count Divine, except a Puritan,
And that but for the name, nor this, nor those
Want any thing of Sermons, but the prose.   50
Experience makes us see, that many a one
Owes to his Countrey his Religion;
And in another, would as strongly grow,
Had but his Nurse and Mother taught him so.
Not hee the ballast on his Judgement hung;   55
Nor did his preconceit doe either wrong.
He labour'd to exclude what ever sinne
By time or carelessenesse had entred in;
Winnow'd the chaffe from wheat, but yet was loath
A too hot zeale should force him burne them both;   60
Nor would allow of that so ignorant gall,
Which to save blotting often would blot all;
Nor did those barbarous opinions owne,
To thinke the Organs sinne, and faction, none;
Nor was there expectation to gaine grace   65

From

From forth his Sermons only, but his face;
So Primitive a looke, such gravitie
With humblenesse, and both with Pietie;
So milde was Moses countenance, when he prai'd
For them whose Satanisme his power gainsaid;   70
And such his gravitie, when all Gods band
Receiv'd his word (through him) at second hand,
Which joyn'd, did flames of more devotion move
Then ever Argive Hellens could of love.
Now to conclude, I must my reason bring,   75
Wherefore I call'd him in his title King;
That Kingdome the Philosophers beleev'd
To excell Alexanders, nor were griev'd
By feare of losse (that being such a Prey
No stronger then ones selfe can force away)   80
The Kingdome of ones selfe, this he enjoy'd,
And his authoritie so well employ'd,
That never any could before become
So Great a Monarch, in so small a roome;
He conquer'd rebell passions, rul'd them so,   85
As under-spheares by the first Mover goe,
Banish't so farre their working, that we can
But know he had some, for we knew him man.
Then let his last excuse his first extremes,
His age saw visions, though his youth dream'd dreams.   90

On D^r. DONNES *death:*
By M^r. Mayne *of Christ-Church in Oxford.*

WHo shall presume to mourn thee, *Donne,* unlesse
    He could his teares in thy expressions dresse,
And teach his griefe that reverence of thy Hearse,
To weepe lines, learned, as thy Anniverse,
A Poëme of that worth, whose every teare   5
Deserves the title of a severall yeare.
Indeed so farre above its Reader, good,
That wee are thought wits, when 'tis understood.

            An Elegie &c. 72 Receiv'd] Receiv' *1633*

                                                    There

There that blest maid to die, who now should grieve?
After thy sorrow, 'twere her losse to live;   10
And her faire vertues in anothers line,
Would faintly dawn, which are made Saints in thine.
Hadst thou beene shallower, and not writ so high,
Or left some new way for our pennes, or eye,
To shed a funerall teare, perchance thy Tombe   15
Had not beene speechlesse, or our Muses dumbe;
But now wee dare not write, but must conceale
Thy Epitaph, lest we be thought to steale,
For, who hath read thee, and discernes thy worth,
That will not say, thy carelesse houres brought forth   20
Fancies beyond our studies, and thy play
Was happier, then our serious time of day?
So learned was thy chance; thy haste had wit,
And matter from thy pen flow'd rashly fit,
What was thy recreation turnes our braine,   25
Our rack and palenesse, is thy weakest straine.
And when we most come neere thee, 'tis our blisse
To imitate thee, where thou dost amisse.
Here light your muse, you that do onely thinke,
And write, and are just Poëts, as you drinke,   3
In whose weake fancies wit doth ebbe and flow,
Just as your recknings rise, that wee may know
In your whole carriage of your worke, that here
This flash you wrote in Wine, and this in Beere,
This is to tap your Muse, which running long   35
Writes flat, and takes our eare not halfe so strong;
Poore Suburbe wits, who, if you want your cup,
Or if a Lord recover, are blowne up.
Could you but reach this height, you should not need
To make, each meale, a project ere you feed,   40
Nor walke in reliques, clothes so old and bare,
As if left off to you from *Ennius* were,
Nor should your love, in verse, call Mistresse, those,
Who are mine hostesse, or your whores in prose;
From this Muse learne to Court, whose power could move 45
A Cloystred coldnesse, or a Vestall love,
And would convey such errands to their eare,

That

That Ladies knew no oddes to grant and heare;
But I do wrong thee, *Donne*, and this low praise
Is written onely for thy yonger dayes.   50
I am not growne up, for thy riper parts,
Then should I praise thee, through the Tongues, and Arts,
And have that deepe Divinity, to know,
What mysteries did from thy preaching flow,
Who with thy words could charme thy audience,   55
That at thy sermons, eare was all our sense;
Yet have I seene thee in the pulpit stand,
Where wee might take notes, from thy looke, and hand;
And from thy speaking action beare away
More Sermon, then some teachers use to say.   60
Such was thy carriage, and thy gesture such,
As could divide the heart, and conscience touch.
Thy motion did confute, and wee might see
An errour vanquish'd by delivery.
Not like our Sonnes of Zeale, who to reforme   65
Their hearers, fiercely at the Pulpit storme,
And beate the cushion into worse estate,
Then if they did conclude it reprobate,
Who can out pray the glasse, then lay about
Till all Predestination be runne out.   70
And from the point such tedious uses draw,
Their repetitions would make Gospell, Law.
No, In such temper would thy Sermons flow,
So well did Doctrine, and thy language show,
And had that holy feare, as, hearing thee,   75
The Court would mend, and a good Christian bee.
And Ladies though unhansome, out of grace,
Would heare thee, in their unbought lookes, and face.
More I could write, but let this crowne thine Urne,
Wee cannot hope the like, till thou returne.   80

Upon

Upon Mr J. Donne, *and his* Poems.

WHo dares say thou art dead, when he doth see
   (Unburied yet) this living part of thee?
This part that to thy beeing gives fresh flame,
   And though th'art *Donne,* yet will preserve thy name.
Thy flesh (whose channels left their crimsen hew,   5
   And whey-like ranne at last in a pale blew)
May shew thee mortall, a dead palsie may
   Seise on't, and quickly turne it into clay;
Which like the Indian earth, shall rise refin'd:
   But this great Spirit thou hast left behinde,   10
This Soule of Verse (in it's first pure estate)
   Shall live, for all the World to imitate,
But not come neer, for in thy Fancies flight
   Thou dost not stoope unto the vulgar sight,
But, hovering highly in the aire of Wit,   15
   Hold'st such a pitch, that few can follow it;
Admire they may. Each object that the Spring
   (Or a more piercing influence) doth bring
T'adorne Earths face, thou sweetly did'st contrive
   To beauties elements, and thence derive   20
Unspotted Lillies white; which thou did'st set
   Hand in hand, with the veine-like Violet,
Making them soft, and warme, and by thy power,
   Could'st give both life, and sense, unto a flower.
The Cheries thou hast made to speake, will bee   25
   Sweeter unto the taste, then from the tree.
And (spight of winter stormes) amidst the snow
   Thou oft hast made the blushing Rose to grow.
The Sea-nimphs, that the watry cavernes keepe,
   Have sent their Pearles and Rubies from the deepe   30
To deck thy love, and plac'd by thee, they drew
   More lustre to them, then where first they grew.
All minerals (that Earths full wombe doth hold
   Promiscuously) thou couldst convert to gold,
And with thy flaming raptures so refine,   35
   That it was much more pure then in the Mine.

The

The lights that guild the night, if thou did'st say,
   They looke like eyes, those did out-shine the day;
For there would be more vertue in such spells,
   Then in Meridians, or crosse Parallels: 40
What ever was of worth in this great Frame,
   That Art could comprehend, or Wit could name,
It was thy theme for Beauty; thou didst see,
   Woman, was this faire Worlds Epitomie.
Thy nimble *Satyres* too, and every straine   45
   (With nervy strength) that issued from thy brain,
Will lose the glory of their owne cleare bayes,
   If they admit of any others praise.
But thy diviner Poëms (whose cleare fire
   Purges all drosse away) shall by a Quire   50
Of Cherubims, with heavenly Notes be set
   (Where flesh and blood could ne'r attaine to yet)
There purest Spirits sing such sacred Layes,
   In Panegyrique Alleluiaes.

                                Arth. Wilson.

In memory of Doctor Donne:
By Mr R. B.

DOnne dead? 'Tis here reported true, though I
   Ne'r yet so much desir'd to heare a lye,
'Tis too too true, for so wee finde it still,
Good newes are often false, but seldome, ill:
But must poore fame tell us his fatall day,   5
And shall we know his death, the common way,
Mee thinkes some Comet bright should have foretold
The death of such a man, for though of old
'Tis held, that Comets Princes death foretell,
Why should not his, have needed one as well?   10
Who was the Prince of wits, 'mongst whom he reign'd,
High as a Prince, and as great State maintain'd?
Yet wants he not his signe, for wee have seene
A dearth, the like to which hath never beene,
Treading on harvests heeles, which doth presage   15
The death of wit and learning, which this age

                                  Shall

Shall finde, now he is gone; for though there bee
Much graine in shew, none brought it forth as he,
Or men are misers; or if true want raises
The dearth, then more that dearth *Donnes* plenty praises.   20
Of learning, languages, of eloquence,
And Poësie, (past rauishing of sense,)
He had a magazine, wherein such store
Was laid up, as might hundreds serve of poore.
  But he is gone, O how will his desire   25
Torture all those that warm'd them by his fire?
Mee thinkes I see him in the pulpit standing,
Not eares, or eyes, but all mens hearts commanding,
Where wee that heard him, to our selves did faine
Golden Chrysostome was alive againe;   30
And never were we weari'd, till we saw
His houre (and but an houre) to end did draw.
How did he shame the doctrine-men, and use,
With helps to boot, for men to beare th'abuse
Of their tir'd patience, and endure th'expence   35
Of time, O spent in hearkning to non-sense,
With markes also, enough whereby to know,
The speaker is a zealous dunce, or so.
'Tis true, they quitted him, to their poore power,
They humm'd against him; And with face most sowre   40
Call'd him a strong lin'd man, a Macaroon,
And no way fit to speake to clouted shoone,
As fine words [truly] as you would desire,
But [verily,] but a bad edifier.
Thus did these beetles slight in him that good,   45
They could not see, and much lesse understood.
But we may say, when we compare the stuffe
Both brought; He was a candle, they the snuffe.
Well, Wisedome's of her children justifi'd,
Let therefore these poore fellowes stand aside;   50
Nor, though of learning he deserv'd so highly,
Would I his booke should save him; Rather slily
I should advise his Clergie not to pray,
Though of the learn'dst sort; Me thinkes that they
Of the same trade, are Judges not so fit,   55

There's

There's no such emulation as of wit.
Of such, the Envy might as much perchance
Wrong him, and more, then th'others ignorance.
It was his Fate (I know't) to be envy'd
As much by Clerkes, as lay men magnifi'd;   60
And why? but 'cause he came late in the day,
And yet his Penny earn'd, and had as they.
No more of this, least some should say, that I
Am strai'd to Satyre, meaning Elegie.
No, no, had DONNE need to be judg'd or try'd,   65
A Jury I would summon on his side,
That had no sides, nor factions, past the touch
Of all exceptions, freed from Passion, such
As nor to feare nor flatter, e'r were bred,
These would I bring, though called from the dead: 70
Southampton, Hambleton, Pembrooke, Dorsets Earles,
Huntingdon, Bedfords Countesses (the Pearles
Once of each sexe.) If these suffice not, I
Ten *decem tales* have of Standers by:
All which, for DONNE, would such a verdict give,   75
As can belong to none, that now doth live.
    But what doe I? A diminution 'tis
To speake of him in verse, so short of his,
Whereof he was the master; All indeed
Compar'd with him, pip'd on an Oaten reed.   80
O that you had but one 'mongst all your brothers
Could write for him, as he hath done for others:
(Poets I speake to) When I see't, I'll say,
My eye-sight betters, as my yeares decay,
Meane time a quarrell I shall ever have   85
Against these doughty keepers from the grave,
Who use, it seemes their old Authoritie,
When (Verses men immortall make) they cry:
Which had it been a Recipe true tri'd,
Probatum esset, DONNE had never dy'd.   90
    For mee, if e'r I had least sparke at all
Of that which they Poetique fire doe call,
Here I confesse it fetched from his hearth,
Which is gone out, now he is gone to earth.

                                          This

This only a poore flash, a lightning is   95
Before my Muses death, as after his.
Farewell (faire soule) and deigne receive from mee
This Type of that devotion I owe thee,
From whom (while living) as by voice and penne
I learned more, then from a thousand men: 100
So by thy death, am of one doubt releas'd,
And now beleeve that miracles are ceas'd.

Epitaph.

HEere lies Deane Donne; Enough; Those words alone
Shew him as fully, as if all the stone
His Church of Pauls contains, were through inscrib'd
Or all the walkers there, to speake him, brib'd.
None can mistake him, for one such as Hee   5
DONNE, Deane, or Man, more none shall ever see.
Not man? No, though unto a Sunne each eye
Were turn'd, the whole earth so to overspie.
A bold brave word; Yet such brave Spirits as knew
His Spirit, will say, it is lesse bold then true.   10

Epitaph upon Dr. DONNE,
By *Endy: Porter.*

THis decent Urne a sad inscription weares,
Of *Donnes* departure from us, to the spheares;
And the dumbe stone with silence seemes to tell
The changes of this life, wherein is well
Exprest, A cause to make all joy to cease,   5
And never let our sorrowes more take ease;
For now it is impossible to finde
One fraught with vertues, to inrich a minde;
But why should death, with a promiscuous hand
At one rude stroke impoverish a land?   10
Thou strict Attorney, unto stricter Fate,
Didst thou confiscate his life out of hate
To his rare Parts? Or didst thou throw thy dart,
With envious hand, at some Plebeyan heart;

And

And he with pious vertue stept betweene 15
To save that stroke, and so was kill'd unseene
By thee? O 'twas his goodnesse so to doe,
Which humane kindnesse never reacht unto.
Thus the hard lawes of death were satisfi'd,
And he left us like Orphan friends, and di'de. 20
Now from the Pulpit to the peoples eares,
Whose speech shall send repentant sighes, and teares?
Or tell mee, if a purer Virgin die,
Who shall hereafter write her Elegie?
Poets be silent, let your numbers sleepe, 25
For he is gone that did all phansie keepe;
Time hath no Soule, but his exalted verse;
Which with amazements, we may now reherse.

In obitum venerabilis viri *Iohannis Donne*, sacræ
Theologiæ Doctoris, Ecclesiæ Cathedralis Divi *Pauli*, nu-
per Decani; Illi honoris, tibi (multum mihi colende
Vir) observantiæ ergo Hæc ego.

COnquerar? ignavoq̃ sequar tua funera planctu?
Sed lachrimæ clausistis iter: nec muta querelas
Lingua potest proferre pias: ignoscite manes
Defuncti, & tacito sinite indulgere dolori.
    Sed scelus est tacuisse: cadant in mœsta lituræ 5
Verba. Tuis (docta umbra) tuis hæc accipe jussis
Cæpta, nec officii contemnens pignora nostri
Aversare tuâ non dignum laude Poëtam.
    O si Pythagoræ non vanum dogma fuisset:
Inq̃ meum â vestro migraret pectore pectus 10
Musa, repentinos tua nosceret urna furores.
Sed frustra, heu frustra hæc votis puerilibus opto:
Tecum abiit, summoq̃ sedens jam monte Thalia
Ridet anhelantes, Parnassi & culmina vates
Desperare jubet. Verum hâc nolente coactos 15

In obitum &c. *1635–69, taking the place of the lines by* Tho: Browne.
10 pectore] pectore, *1635*

Scribimus

Scribimus audaces numeros, & flebile carmen
Scribimus (ô soli qui te dilexit) habendum.
  Siccine perpetuus liventia lumina somnus
Clausit? & immerito merguntur funere virtus?
Et pietas? & quæ poterant fecisse beatum,   20
Cætera, sed nec te poterant servare beatum.
  Quo mihi doctrinam? quorsum impallescere chartis
Nocturnis juvat? & totidem olfecisse lucernas?
Decolor & longos studiis deperdere Soles
Vt prius aggredior, longamque arcessere famam.   25
Omnia sed frustra: mihi dum cunctisque minatur
Exitium crudele & inexorabile fatum.
  Nam post te sperare nihil decet: hoc mihi restat
Vt moriar, tenues fugiatque obscurus in auras
Spiritus: ô doctis saltem si cognitus umbris.   30
Illic te (venerande) iterum, (venerande) videbo.
Et dulces audire sonôs, & verba diserti
Oris, & æternas dabitur mihi carpere voces.
Quêis ferus infernæ tacuisset Ianitor aulæ
Auditis: Nilusq̃ minus strepuisset: Arion   35
Cederet, & sylvas qui post se traxerat Orpheus.
Eloquio sic ille viros, sic ille movere
Voce feros potuit: quis enim tam barbarus? aut tam
Facundis nimis infestus non motus ut illo
Hortante, & blando victus sermone sileret?   40
  Sic oculos, sic ille manus, sic ora ferebat,
Singula sic decuere senem, sic omnia. Vidi,
Audivi & stupui quoties orator in Æde
Paulina stetit, & mira gravitate levantes
Corda, oculosq̃ viros tenuit: dum Nestoris ille   45
Fudit verba (omni quanto mage dulcia melle?)
Nunc habet attonitos, pandit mysteria plebi
Non concessa prius nondum intellecta: revolvunt
Mirantes, tacitique arrectis auribus astant.

21 beatum.] beatum *1635*   23 olfecisse] olfecissë *1635*   25
prius aggredior, *1635–69:* prius, aggredior, *1719*   arcessere *Ed:*
accessere *1635–69*   26–7 mihi dum ... Exitium *1719:* mihi, dum
... Exitium, *1635–39:* mihi dum, ... Exitium, *1650–69*   38 Voce
feros] Voceferos *1635, 1669*

                                                          Mutatis

Mutatis mox ille modo, formáq̃ loquendi 50
Tristia pertractat: fatúmq̃ & flebile mortis
Tempus, & in cineres redeunt quod corpora primos
Tunc gemitum cunctos dare, tunc lugere videres,
Forsitan à lachrymis aliquis non temperat, atque
Ex oculis largum stillat rorem; ætheris illo 55
Sic pater audito voluit succumbere turbam,
Affectúsq̃ ciere suos, & ponere notæ
Vocis ad arbitrium, divinæ oracula mentis
Dum narrat, rostrisque potens dominatur in altis.

   Quo feror? audaci & forsan pietate nocenti 60
In nimia ignoscas vati, qui vatibus olim
Egregium decus, et tanto excellentior unus
Omnibus; inferior quanto est, et pessimus, impar
Laudibus hisce, tibi qui nunc facit ista Poëta.
Et quo nos canimus? cur hæc tibi sacra? Poëtæ 65
Desinite: en fati certus, sibi voce canorâ
Inferias præmisit olor, cum Carolus Albâ
(Vltima volventem et Cycnæâ voce loquentem)
Nuper eum, turba & magnatum audiret in Aulâ.

   Tunc Rex, tunc Proceres, Clerus, tunc astitit illi 70
Aula frequens. Solâ nunc in tellure recumbit,
Vermibus esca, pio malint nisi parcere: quidni
Incipiant & amare famem? Metuere Leones
Sic olim, sacrosque artus violare Prophetæ
Bellua non ausa est quàmquam jejuna, sitímq̃, 75
Optaret nimis humano satiare cruore.

   At non hæc de te sperabimus; omnia carpit
Prædator vermis: nec talis contigit illi
Præda diu; forsan metrico pede serpet ab inde:
Vescere, & exhausto satia te sanguine. Iam nos 80
Adsumus; et post te cupiet quis vivere? Post te
Quis volet, aut poterit? nam post te vivere mors est.

   Et tamen ingratas ignavi ducimus auras:
Sustinet & tibi lingua vale, vale dicere: parce
Non festinanti æternum requiescere turbæ. 85
Ipsa satis properat quæ nescit Parca morari,

79 inde:] inde *1635–39*   86 Parca] parca *1635–69* morari,]
morari *1635*

O   *Nunc*

Nunc urgere colum, trahére atq̃ occare videmus.
Quin rursus (Venerande) Vale, vale: ordine nos te
Quo Deus, & quo dura volet natura sequemur.
  Depositum interea lapides servate fideles.   90
Fœlices illâ quêis Ædis parte locari
Quâ jacet iste datur. Forsan lapis inde loquetur,
Parturietq̃ viro plenus testantia luctus
Verba: & carminibus quæ Donni suggeret illi
Spiritus, insolitos testari voce calores   95
Incipiet: (non sic Pyrrhâ jactante calebat.)
  Mole sub hâc tegitur quicquid mortale relictum est
  De tanto mortale viro. Qui præfuit Ædi huic,
  Formosi pecoris pastor, formosior ipse.
  Ite igitur, dignisq̃ illum celebrate loquelis,   100
  Et quæ demuntur vitæ date tempora famæ,
        Indignus tantorum meritorum Præco, virtutum
        tuarum cultor religiosissimus,
                                DANIEL DARNELLY.

Elegie on D. D.

NOw, by one yeare, time and our frailtie have
  Lessened our first confusion, since the Grave
Clos'd thy deare Ashes, and the teares which flow
In these, have no springs, but of solid woe:
Or they are drops, which cold amazement froze   5
At thy decease, and will not thaw in Prose:
All streames of Verse which shall lament that day,
Doe truly to the Ocean tribute pay;
But they have lost their saltnesse, which the eye
In recompence of wit, strives to supply: 10
Passions excesse for thee wee need not feare,
Since first by thee our passions hallowed were;
Thou mad'st our sorrowes, which before had bin
Onely for the Successe, sorrowes for sinne,

  88 rursus *1719:* rusus *1635:* nusus *1639–69*   96 Incipiet: ..
calebat. *1719: no stops, 1635–69*
  Elegie on D. D. *1635–69: it follows Walton's elegy.*

                                                      We

We owe thee all those teares, now thou art dead, 15
Which we shed not, which for our selves we shed.
Nor didst thou onely consecrate our teares,
Give a religious tincture to our feares;
But even our joyes had learn'd an innocence,
Thou didst from gladnesse separate offence: 20
All mindes at once suckt grace from thee, as where
(The curse revok'd) the Nations had one eare.
Pious dissector: thy one houre did treate
The thousand mazes of the hearts deceipt;
Thou didst pursue our lov'd and subtill sinne, 25
Through all the foldings wee had wrapt it in,
And in thine owne large minde finding the way
By which our selves we from our selves convey,
Didst in us, narrow models, know the same
Angles, though darker, in our meaner frame. 30
How short of praise is this? My Muse, alas,
Climbes weakly to that truth which none can passe,
Hee that writes best, may onely hope to leave
A Character of all he could conceive
But none of thee, and with mee must confesse, 35
That fansie findes some checke, from an excesse
Of merit; most, of nothing, it hath spun,
And truth, as reasons task and theame, doth shunne.
She makes a fairer flight in emptinesse,
Than when a bodied truth doth her oppresse. 40
Reason againe denies her scales, because
Hers are but scales, shee judges by the lawes
Of weake comparison, thy vertue sleights
Her feeble Beame, and her unequall Weights.
What prodigie of wit and pietie 45
Hath she else knowne, by which to measure thee?
Great soule: we can no more the worthinesse
Of what you were, then what you are, expresse.

                    Sidney Godolphin.

On

On Dr John Donne, *late Deane of S.* Paules,
London.

LOng since this taske of teares from you was due,
  Long since, ô Poëts, he did die to you,
Or left you dead, when wit and he tooke flight
On divine wings, and soard out of your sight.
Preachers, 'tis you must weep; The wit he taught   5
You doe enjoy; the Rebels which he brought
From ancient discord, Giants faculties,
And now no more religions enemies;
Honest to knowing, unto vertuous sweet,
Witty to good, and learned to discreet,   10
He reconcil'd, and bid the Vsurper goe;
Dulnesse to vice, religion ought to flow;
He kept his loves, but not his objects; wit
Hee did not banish, but transplanted it,
Taught it his place and use, and brought it home   15
To Pietie, which it doth best become;
He shew'd us how for sinnes we ought to sigh,
And how to sing Christs Epithalamy:
The Altars had his fires, and there hee spoke
Incense of loves, and fansies holy smoake: 20
Religion thus enrich'd, the people train'd,
And God from dull vice had the fashion gain'd.
The first effects sprung in the giddy minde
Of flashy youth, and thirst of woman-kinde,
By colours lead, and drawne to a pursuit,   25
Now once againe by beautie of the fruit,
As if their longings too must set us free,
And tempt us now to the commanded tree.
Tell me, had ever pleasure such a dresse,
Have you knowne crimes so shap'd? or lovelinesse   30
Such as his lips did cloth religion in?
Had not reproofe a beauty passing sinne?
Corrupted nature sorrow'd when she stood

On Dr John Donne &c. *1635–69, where it follows Godolphin's
Elegie*

So

So neare the danger of becomming good,
And wish'd our so inconstant eares exempt   35
From piety that had such power to tempt:
Did not his sacred flattery beguile
Man to amendment? The law, taught to smile,
Pension'd our vanitie, and man grew well
Through the same frailtie by which he fell.   40
O the sick state of man, health does not please
Our tasts, but in the shape of the disease.
Thriftlesse is charitie, coward patience,
Justice is cruell, mercy want of sense.
What meanes our Nature to barre vertue place,   45
If shee doe come in her owne cloathes and face?
Is good a pill, we dare not chaw to know?
Sense the soules servant, doth it keep us so
As we might starve for good, unlesse it first
Doe leave a pawne of relish in the gust?   50
Or have we to salvation no tie
At all, but that of our infirmitie?
Who treats with us must our affections move
To th' good we flie by those sweets which we love,
Must seeke our palats, and with their delight   55
To gaine our deeds, must bribe our appetite.
These traines he knew, and laying nets to save,
Temptingly sugred all the health hee gave.
But, where is now that chime? that harmony
Hath left the world, now the loud organ may   60
Appeare, the better voyce is fled to have
A thousand times the sweetnesse which it gave.
I cannot say how many thousand spirits
The single happinesse this soule inherits,
Damnes in the other world, soules whom no crosse   65
O'th sense afflicts, but onely of the losse,
Whom ignorance would halfe save, all whose paine
Is not in what they feele, but others gaine,
Selfe executing wretched spirits, who
Carrying their guilt, transport their envy too: 70
But those high joyes which his wits youngest flame
Would hurt to chuse, shall not we hurt to name?

Verse

Verse statues are all robbers, all we make
Of monument, thus doth not give but take
As Sailes which Seamen to a forewinde fit,　　　75
By a resistance, goe along with it,
So pens grow while they lessen fame so left;
A weake assistance is a kinde of theft.
Who hath not love to ground his teares upon,
Must weep here if he have ambition.　　　80

I. Chudleigh

FINIS.

DE LIBRO CVM MVTV-
aretur Impresso ; Domi à pueris fru-
statim lacerato ; et post reddito
Manuscripto.
Doctissimo Amicissimoque v.
D. D. Andrews.

P*Arturiunt madidu quae nixu praela, recepta,*
Sed quae scripta manu, sunt veneranda magis.
Qui liber in pluteos, blattis cinerique relictos,
Si modo sit praeli sanguine tinctus, abit;
Accedat calamo scriptus, reverenter habetur, 5
Involat et veterum scrinia summa Patrum.
Dicat Apollo modum; Pueros infundere libro
Nempe vetustatem canitiemque novo.
Nil mirum, medico pueros de semine natos,
Haec nova fata libro posse dedisse novo. 10
Si veterem faciunt pueri, qui nuperus, Annon
Ipse Pater Iuvenem me dabit arte senem?
Hei miseris senibus! nos vertit dura senectus
Omnes in pueros, neminem at in Iuvenem.
Hoc tibi servasti praestandum, Antique Dierum, 15
Quo viso, et vivit, et juvenescit Adam.
Interea, infirmae fallamus taedia vitae,
Libris, et Coelorum aemulâ amicitiâ.
Hos inter, qui a te mihi redditus iste libellus,
Non mihi tam charus, tam meus, ante fuit. 20

⟨Epigramma⟩
Transiit in Sequanam Moenus; Victoris in aedes;
Et Francofurtum, te revehente, meat.

DE LIBRO &c. *1635–69 among certain prose letters in Latin and*
English Title:—mutuaretur Impresso;] mutuaretur, Impresso,
1635–69 frustatim] frustratim *1635–69*
⟨Epigramma⟩ *Ed: in old edd. these lines are 3 and 4 of above poem.*

Amicissimo,

Amicissimo, & meritissimo BEN. JONSON.
In Vulponem.

QVod arte ausus es hic tuâ, Poeta,
  Si auderent hominum Deique juris
Consulti, veteres sequi aemularierque,
O omnes saperemus ad salutem.
His sed sunt veteres araneosi;   5
Tam nemo veterum est sequutor, ut tu
Illos quod sequeris novator audis.
Fac tamen quod agis; tuique primâ
Libri canitie induantur horâ:
Nam chartis pueritia est neganda,   10
Nascanturque senes, oportet, illi
Libri, queis dare vis perennitatem.
Priscis, ingenium facit, laborque
Te parem; hos superes, ut et futuros,
Ex nostrâ vitiositate sumas,   15
Quâ priscos superamus, et futuros.

To Mr *George Herbert,* with one of my
Seal⟨s⟩, of the Anchor and Christ.

QVi prius assuetus Serpentum fasce Tabellas
  Signare, (haec nostrae symbola parva Domus)
Adscitus domui Domini, patrioque relicto
  Stemmate, nanciscor stemmata jure nova.
Hinc mihi Crux primo quae fronti impressa lavacro,   5
  Finibus extensis, anchora facta patet.

Amicissimo &c. in sheets added 1650: prefixed originally to Quarto edition of *Jonson's* Volpone. 1607, later to Folio edition of The Workes of Beniamin Jonson. 1616., when In Vulponem was added: in both signed I. D.   11 Nascanturque 1607: Nascanturque 1616, 1650–69
   To Mr George Herbert &c. 1650–69, in sheets added 1650: two and a half lines in Walton's Life of Donne (1658)   Title:—sent him with one Walton (1670)   Seal, 1650–69: Seales Walton 1 fasce] falce Walton   5 fronti] fronte 1650–69

Anchorae

Anchorae in effigiem Crux tandem desinit ipsam,
  Anchora fit tandem Crux tolerata diu.
Hoc tamen ut fiat, Christo vegetatur ab ipso
  Crux, et ab Affixo, est Anchora facta, Iesu.   10
Nec Natalitiis penitus serpentibus orbor,
  Non ita dat Deus, ut auferat ante data.
Quâ sapiens, Dos est; Quâ terram lambit et ambit,
  Pestis; At in nostra fit Medicina Cruce,
Serpens; fixa Cruci si sit Natura; Crucique   15
  A fixo, nobis, Gratia tota fluat.
Omnia cum Crux sint, Crux Anchora facta, sigillum
  Non tam dicendum hoc quam Catechismus erit.
Mitto nec exigua, exiguâ sub imagine, dona,
  Pignora amicitiae, et munera; Vota, preces.   20
Plura tibi accumulet, sanctus cognominis, Ille
  Regia qui flavo Dona sigillat Equo.

A Sheafe of Snakes used heretofore to be
  My Seal, The Crest of our poore Family.
Adopted in Gods Family, and so
Our old Coat lost, unto new armes I go.
The Crosse (my seal at Baptism) spred below,   5
Does, by that form, into an Anchor grow.
Crosses grow Anchors; Bear, as thou shouldst do
Thy Crosse, and that Crosse grows an Anchor too.
But he that makes our Crosses Anchors thus,
Is Christ, who there is crucifi'd for us.   10
Yet may I, with this, my first Serpents hold,
God gives new blessings, and yet leaves the old;

17 *facta*,] *fixa, 1650–69*
A sheafe &c.] *1650–69 and in Walton's Life of Donne (1658), in all
of which and in all subsequent editions except Grolier the first two lines
are printed as a title, Walton bracketing them:—*
          A sheafe of Snakes used heretofore to be
            my Seal, The Crest of our poore Family.
4 Our . . . unto] My . . . into *Walton*   5 at] in *Walton*   11 with
this I may *Walton*

                                                    The

The Serpent, may, as wise, my pattern be;
My poison, as he feeds on dust, that's me.
And as he rounds the Earth to murder sure,   15
My death he is, but on the Crosse, my cure.
Crucifie nature then, and then implore
All Grace from him, crucified there before;
When all is Crosse, and that Crosse Anchor grown,
This Seal's a Catechism, not a Seal alone.   20
Under that little Seal great gifts I send,
⟨Wishes,⟩ and prayers, pawns, and fruits of a friend.
And may that Saint which rides in our great Seal,
To you, who bear his name, great bounties deal.

Translated out of *Gazæus, Vota Amico*
facta. fol. 160.

GOd grant thee thine own wish, and grant thee mine,
Thou, who dost, best friend, in best things outshine;
May thy soul, ever chearfull, nere know cares,
Nor thy life, ever lively, know gray haires.
Nor thy hand, ever open, know base holds,   5
Nor thy purse, ever plump, know pleits, or folds.
Nor thy tongue, ever true, know a false thing,
Nor thy word, ever mild, know quarrelling.
Nor thy works, ever equall, know disguise,
Nor thy fame, ever pure, know contumelies.   10
Nor thy prayers, know low objects, still Divine;
God grant thee thine own wish, and grant thee mine.

---

15 to murder sure,] to murder, sure *Walton*   16 He is my death;
Walton   22 Wishes, *Ed:* Works, *1650–69:* Both works *Walton:* Lat.
vota   23–4 Oh may that Saint that rides on our great Seal,
　　　　　To you that bear his name large bounty deal.   *Walton.*

APPENDIX

APPENDIX B.

POEMS WHICH HAVE BEEN ATTRIBUTED
TO JOHN DONNE IN THE OLD EDITIONS
AND THE PRINCIPAL MS. COLLECTIONS,
ARRANGED ACCORDING TO THEIR PRO-
BABLE AUTHORS.

I.

POEMS

PROBABLY BY SIR JOHN ROE, KNT.

To Sr Nicholas Smyth.

SLeep, next Society and true friendship,
  Mans best contentment, doth securely slip
His passions and the worlds troubles. Rock me
O sleep, wean'd from my dear friends company,
In a cradle free from dreams or thoughts, there   5
Where poor men ly, for Kings asleep do fear.
Here sleeps House by famous Ariosto,
By silver-tongu'd Ovid, and many moe,
Perhaps by golden-mouth'd Spencer too pardie,
(Which builded was some dozen Stories high)   10
I had repair'd, but that it was so rotten,
As sleep awak'd by Ratts from thence was gotten:
And I will build no new, for by my Will,
Thy fathers house shall be the fairest still
In Excester. Yet, methinks, for all their Wit,   15
Those wits that say nothing, best describe it.
Without it there is no Sense, only in this
Sleep is unlike a long Parenthesis.

To Sr Nicholas Smyth. *Ed:* A Satire: to Sr Nicholas Smith. *1602*
or A Satyricall Letter to Sr Nich: Smith. *and similarly or no title MSS.:*
Satyre VI. *1669 (on which the present text is based)*   2 slip *1669:*
skipp *MSS.*   4 my *MSS.:* thy *1669*

Not

Not to save charges, but would I had slept
The time I spent in London, when I kept   20
Fighting and untrust gallants Company,
In which Natta, the new Knight, seiz'd on me,
And offered me the experience he had bought
With great Expence. I found him throughly taught
In curing Burnes. His thing hath had more scars   25
Then Things himselfe; like Epps it often wars,
And still is hurt. For his Body and State
The Physick and Counsel which came too late,
'Gainst Whores and Dice, hee nowe on mee bestowes
Most superficially: hee speaks of those   30
(I found by him) least soundly who most knows:
He swears well, speakes ill, but best of Clothes,
What fits Summer, what Winter, what the Spring.
He had Living, but now these waies come in
His whole Revenues. Where each Whore now dwells, 35
And hath dwelt, since his fathers death, he tells.
Yea he tells most cunningly each hid cause
Why Whores forsake their Bawds. To these some Laws
He knows of the Duello, and touch his Skill
The least Jot in that or those he quarrell will,   40
Though sober; but so never fought. I know
What made his Valour, undubb'd, Windmill go,

25 hath had *most MSS.:* had had *1669:* had *one MS.*   26 Things
MSS.: T   *1669*   . 28–31 *text from MSS., which bracket* which
. . . late:
  The Physick and Councel (which came too late
  'Gainst Whores and Dice) he now on me bestows:
  Most superficially he speaks of those.
  I found, by him, least sound him who most knows. *1669*
35 each *MSS.:* his *1669*   37 cunningly *1669 and some MSS.:*
perfectly *some MSS.*   39 Duello, *MSS.:* Duel, *1669*   41 but so
never fought. *MSS.:* but nere fought. *1669*   42 Valour, undubb'd,
Windmill go, *Ed:* Valour undubd Windmill go. *1669:* valours undubb'd Wine-mill go. *some MSS.:* his undouted valour windmill goe.
or his undaunted valour windmill goe. *some MSS.*

             Within

Within a Pint at most: yet for all this
(Which is most strange) Natta thinks no man is
More honest than himself. Thus men may want   45
Conscience, whilst being brought up ignorant,
They use themselves to vice. And besides those
Illiberal Arts forenam'd, no Vicar knows,
Nor other Captain less then he; His Schools
Are Ordinaries, where civil men seem fools,   50
Or are for being there; His best bookes, Plaies,
Where, meeting godly Scenes, perhaps he praies.
His first set prayer was for his father, ill
And sick, that he might dye: That had, until
The Lands were gone, he troubled God no more: 55
And then ask'd him but his Right, That the whore
Whom he had kept, might now keep him: She spent,
They left each other on even terms; she went
To Bridewel, he unto the Wars, where want
Hath made him valiant, and a Lieutenant   60
He is become: Where, as they pass apace,
He steps aside, and for his Captains place
He praies again: Tells God, he will confess
His sins, swear, drink, dice and whore thenceforth less,
On this Condition, that his Captain dye   65
And he succeed; But his Prayer did not; They
Both cashir'd came home, and he is braver now
Than'his captain: all men wonder, few know how.
Can he rob? No. Cheat? No. Or doth he spend
His own? No. Fidus, he is thy dear friend,   70
That keeps him up. I would thou wert thine own,
Or thou'hadst as good a friend as thou art one.
No present Want nor future hope made me,
Desire (as once I did) thy friend to be:
But he had cruelly possest thee then,   75
And as our Neighbours the Low-Country men,
Being (whilst they were Loyal, with Tyranny
Opprest) broke loose, have since refus'd to be

Subject

Subject to good Kings, I found even so,
Wer't thou well rid of him, thou't have no moe.   80
Could'st thou but chuse as well as love, to none
Thou should'st be second: Turtle and Damon
Should give thee place in songs, and Lovers sick
Should make thee only Loves Hieroglyphick:
Thy Impress should be the löving Elm and Vine,   85
Where now an ancient Oak, with Ivy twine
Destroy'd, thy Symbol is. O dire Mischance!
And, Ó vile verse! And yet your Abraham France
Writes thus, and jests not. Good Fidus for this
Must pardon me, Satyres bite when they kiss.   90
But as for Natta, we have since faln out:
Here on his knees he pray'd, else we had fought.
And because God would not he should be winner,
Nor yet would have the Death of such a sinner,
At his seeking, our Quarrel is deferr'd,   95
I'll leave him at his Prayers, and (as I heard)
His last; Fidus, and you, and I do know,
I was his friend, and durst have been his foe,
And would be either yet; But he dares be
Neither; Sleep blots him out and takes in thee.   100
"The mind, you know is like a Table-book,
"Which, th'old unwipt, new writing never took.
Hear how the Huishers Checques, Cupbord and Fire
I pass'd; by which Degrees young men aspire
In Court; And how that idle and she-state,   105
Whenas my judgment cleer'd, my soul did hate;
How I found there (if that my trifling Pen
Durst take so hard a Task) Kings were but men,
And by their Place more noted, if they erre;
How they and their Lords unworthy men prefer;   110

88 your *MSS.:* our *1669*   97 Fidus, and you, and I *one MS.:*
and Fidus, you and I *1669;* Fidus, and you, and he *some MSS.*
100 Neither; *MSS.:* Neither yet. *1669*   102 Which, th'old unwipt, *MSS.:* "The old unwipt *1669*

                                                      And,

And, as unthrifts had rather give away
Great Summs to flatterers, than small debts pay,
So they their weakness hide, and greatness show,
By giving them that which to worth they owe:
What Treason is, and what did Essex kill,   115
Not true Treason, but Treason handled ill;
And which of them stood for their Countries good,
Or what might be the Cause of so much Blood.
He said she stunck, and men might not have said
That she was old before that she was dead.   120
His Case was hard, to do or suffer; loth
To do, he made it harder, and did both.
Too much preparing lost them all their Lives,
Like some in Plagues kill'd with preservatives.
Friends, like land-souldiers in a storm at Sea,   125
Not knowing what to do, for him did pray.
They told it all the world; where was their wit?
Cuffs putting on a sword, might have told it.
And Princes must fear Favorites more then Foes,
For still beyond Revenge Ambition goes.   130
How since Her death, with Sumpter-horse that Scot
Hath rid, who, at his coming up, had not
A Sumpter-dog. But till that I can write
Things worth thy Tenth reading (dear Nick) goodnight.

Satyre.

MEn write that love and reason disagree,
   But I ne'r saw't exprest as 'tis in thee.
Well, I may lead thee, God must make thee see,
But, thine eyes blinde too, there's no hope for thee.
Thou say'st shee's wise and witty, faire and free,   5

113 weakness *some MSS.:* greatness *1669, one MS. group*   132
Hath rid,] Doth ryde, *one MS.*
   Satyre. *or* A Satire: upon one who was his Rivall in a widdowes
Love. *MSS.:* Satyre VI. *1635–54:* Satyre. VII. *1669 (where* Satyre
VI. *is* Sleep, next Society *&c.*)

All

All these are reasons why she should scorne thee.
Thou dost protest thy love, and wouldst it shew
By matching her as she would match her foe:
And wouldst perswade her to a worse offence,
Then that whereof thou didst accuse her wench.　　10
Reason there's none for thee, but thou may'st vexe
Hér with example. Say, for feare her sexe
Shunne her, she needs must change; I doe not see
How reason e'r can bring that *must* to thee.
Thou art a match a Justice to rejoyce,　　15
Fit to be his, and not his daughters choyce.
Urg'd with his threats shee'd scarcely stay with thee,
And wouldst th'have this to chuse thee, being free?
Goe then and punish some soone-gotten stuffe,
For her dead husband this hath mourn'd enough,　　20
In hating thee. Thou maist one like this meet;
For spight take her, prove kinde, make thy breath sweet,
Let her see she hath cause, and to bring to thee
Honest children, let her dishonest bee.
If shee be a widow, I'll warrant her　　25
Shee'll thee before her first husband preferre,
And will wish thou hadst had her maidenhead,
(Shee'll love thee so) for then thou hadst bin dead.
But thou such strong love, and weake reasons hast,
Thou must thrive there, or ever live disgrac'd.　　30
Yet pause a while; and thou maist live to see
A time to come, wherein she may beg thee;
If thou'lt not pause nor change, she'll beg thee now.
Doe what she can, love for nothing shee'll allow.
Besides, her⟨s⟩ were too much gaine and merchandise, 35
And when thou art rewarded, desert dies.
Now thou hast odds ·of him she loves, he may doubt
Her constancy, but none can put thee out.
Againe, be thy love true, shee'll prove divine,

17 Urg'd *MSS.:* Dry'd *1635–69*　　35 Besides, hers *Ed:* Besides,
here *1635–69:* But hers *one MS.:* Besides her *one MS.*

And

And in the end the good on't will be thine: 40
For thou must never think on other love,
And so wilt advance her as high above
Vertue as cause above effect can bee:
'Tis vertue to be chast, which shee'll make thee.

AN ELEGIE.

Reflecting on his passion for his mistrisse.

COme, Fates; I feare you not. All whom I owe
Are paid, but you. Then 'rest me ere I goe.
But, Chance from you all soveraignty hath got,
Love woundeth none but those whom death dares not;
Else, if you were, and just, in equitie 5
I should have vanquish'd her, as you did me.
Else Lovers should not brave death's pains, and live,
But 'tis a rule, *Death comes not to relieve.*
Or, pale and wan deaths terrours, are they lay'd
So deepe in Lovers, they make death afraid? 10
Or (the least comfort) have I company?
Orecame she Fates, Love, Death, as well as mee?
   Yes, Fates doe silke unto her distaffe pay,
For their ransome, which taxe on us they laye.
Love gives her youth, which is the reason why 15
Youths, for her sake, some wither and some die.
Poore Death can nothing give; yet, for her sake,
Still in her turne, he doth a Lover take:

41 For thou must never think on *or* And thou must never think
on *MSS.:* For though thou must ne'r thinke of *1635–69*
   An Elegie. Reflecting on *&c. or* An Elegie. *MSS.:* Eleg. XIII.
1635–69 5 Else, if you were, and just, in equitie *MS.:* Else, if
you were, and just in equitie, *1635–54:* True, if you were, and just in
equitie, *1669* 12 Orecame she Fates, Love, Death, *MSS.:* Or can
the Fates love death, *1635–69* 13 distaffe *1635–69 and some MSS.:*
distaves *other MSS.* 14 For their . . . on us they laye. *MSS.:* For
ransome, which taxe they on us doe lay. *1635–69:* For Ransome, but
a taxe on us they lay: *one MS.*

P   **And**

And if Death should prove false, she feares him not;
Our Muses, to redeeme her she hath got. 20
That fatall night wee last kiss'd, I thus pray'd,
Or rather, thus despair'd; I should have said:
Kisses, and yet despaire? The forbid tree
Did promise (and deceive) no more then shee.
Like Lambs that see their teats, and must eat Hay, 25
A food, whose tast hath made me pine away.
Dives, when thou saw'st blisse, and crav'dst to touch
A drop of water, thy great paines were such.
Here griefe wants a fresh wit, for mine being spent,
And my sighes weary, groanes are all my rent; 30
Vnable longer to indure the paine,
They breake like thunder, and doe bring down rain.
Thus, till dry teares soulder mine eyes, I weepe;
And then, I dreame, how you securely sleepe,
And in your dreames doe laugh at me. I hate, 35
And pray Love, All may: He pitties my state,
But sayes, I therein no revenge should finde;
The Sunne would shine, though all the world were blind.
Yet, to trie my hate, Love shew'd me your teare;
And I had dy'd, had not your smile beene there. 40
Your frowne undoes me; your smile is my wealth;
And as you please to looke, I have my health.
Me thought, Love pittying me, when he saw this,
Gave me your hands, the backs and palmes to kisse.
That cur'd me not, but to beare paine gave strength, 45
And what it lost in force, it tooke in length.
I call'd on Love againe, who fear'd you so,
That his compassion still prov'd greater woe;
For, then I dream'd I was in bed with you,
But durst not feele, for feare't should not prove true. 50

21 That fatall night we last kiss'd *1635–69:* That last fatall night
wee kiss'd *MSS.*　　37 should *most MSS.:* shall *1635–69 and some
MSS.*　　44 the *1635–69:* their *MSS.*　　46 it . . . it *all MSS.:*
is . . . is *1635–69*

This

This merits not your anger, had it beene:
The Queene of Chastitie was naked seene,
And in bed, not to feele, the paine I tooke,
Was more then for *Actæon* not to looke.
And that brest which lay ope, I did not know,   55
But for the clearnesse, from a lump of snowe,
Nor that sweet teat which on the top it bore
From the rose-bud, which for my sake you wore.
These griefs to issue forth, by verse, I prove,
Or turne their course, by travaile, or new love: 60
All would not doe. The best at last I tryde:
Vnable longer to hould out I dyed.
And then I found I lost life, death by flying:
Who hundreds live are but soe long a dying.
Charon did let me passe: I'le him requite.   65
To marke the groves or shades wrongs my delight.
I'le speake but of those ghosts I found alone,
Those thousand ghosts, whereof myself made one,
All images of thee. I ask'd them, why?
The Judge told me, all they for thee did dye,   70
And therefore had for their Elisian blisse,
In one another their owne Loves to kisse.
O here I miss'd not blisse, but being dead;
For loe, I dream'd, I dream'd; and waking said,
Heaven, if who are in thee there must dwell,   75
How is't, I now was there, and now I fell.

An Elegie to M^{ris} Boulstred: 1602.

SHall I goe force an Elegie? abuse
My witt? and breake the Hymen of my muse
For one poore houres love? Deserves it such

56 snowe,] snowe. *1635–69 and some MSS., which end here: text
of rest from other MSS.*
An Elegie &c. *or* Elegie *or* Elegie to his M. promising to love him
                                                                 Which

Which serves not me, to doe on her as much?
Or if it could, I would that fortune shunn:　　5
Who would be rich, to be soe soone undone?
The beggars best is, wealth he doth not know;
And but to shew it him, encreases woe.
But we two may enjoye an hour? When never
It returnes, who would have a losse for ever?　　10
Nor can so short a love, if true, but bring
A halfe howres feare, with the thought of losing:
Before it, all howres were hope; and all are
(That shall come after it,) yeares of dispaire.
This joye brings this doubt, whether it were more　　15
To have enjoy'd it, or have died before?
T'is a lost paradise, a fall from grace,
Which I thinke, Adam felt more then his race.
Nor need those angells any other Hell;
It is enough for them, from Heaven they fell.　　20
Besides, Conquest in love is all in all;
That when I liste, shee under me may fall:
And for this turne, both for delight and view.
I'le have a Succuba, as good as you.
But when these toyes are past, and hott blood ends,　　25
The best enjoying is, we still are frends.
Love can but be frendshipps outside; their two
Beauties differ, as myndes and bodies do.
Thus, I this great Good still would be to take,
Vnless one houre, another happy make:　　30
Or, that I might forgett it instantlie;
Or in that blest estate, that I might die.
But why doe I thus travaile in the skill
Of despis'd poetrie, and perchance spill

an hour. *one MS.: several MSS. add initials* J. R.: An Elegy 1602.
To Mrs Boulstrede. *Le Prince d'Amour. &c.* 1660　　*7 text from
Hawthornden MS.:* The beggers best is, that wealth he doth ⟨not⟩
know, *MS.:* The beggar's best, his *&c. most MSS.*　　32 *Poem
closes, some MSS.*

My

My fortune? or undoe myself in sport 35
By having but that dangerous name in Court?
I'le leave, and since I doe your poet prove,
Keep you my lines as secret as my Love.

An Elegie.

TRue Love findes witt, but he whose witt doth move
Him to love, confesses he doth not love:
And from his witt, passions and true desire
Are forc'd as hard, as from the flint is fire.
My love's all fire whose flames my soule do nurse, 5
Whose smokes are sighes; whose every sparke's a verse.
Doth measure women win? Then I know why
Most of our Ladies with the Scotts doe lie.
A Scott is measur'd in each syllable, terse
And smooth as a verse: and like that smooth verse 10
Is shallow, and wants matter, but in his handes,
And they are rugged; Her state better standes
Whom dauncing measures tempted, not the Scott:
In brief she's out of measure, lost, soe gott.
Greene-sickness wenches, (not needes must but) may 15
Looke pale, breathe short; at Court none so long stay.
Good witt ne're despair'd there, or *Ay me* said:
For never Wench at Court was ravished.
And shee but cheates on Heaven, whom you so winne,
Thinking to share the sport, but not the sinne. 20

Song.

DEare Love, continue nice and chaste,
For, if you yeeld you doe me wrong,
Let duller wits to loves end haste,
I have enough to wooe thee long.

An Elegie. *first printed by Grosart*

All

All paine and joy is in their way;   5
The things we feare bring lesse annoy
Then feare; and hope brings greater joy;
But in themselves they cannot stay.

Small favours will my prayers increase;
Granting my suit you give me all,   10
And then my prayers must needs surcease,
For, I have made your Godhead fall.

Beasts cannot witt nor beauty see,
They mans affections onely move;
Beasts other sports of love doe prove,   15
With better feeling farre than we.

Then Love prolong my suite, for thus
By losing sport, I sport doe win;
And that may vertue prove in us,
Which ever yet hath beene a sinne.   20

My comming neare may spie some ill,
And now the world is given to scoffe;
To keepe my Love, (then) keepe me off,
And so I shall admire thee still.

Say I have made a perfect choyce,   25
Satietie our Love may kill;
Then give me but thy face and voyce,
Mine eye and eare thou canst not fill.

To make me rich (oh) be not poore,
Give me not all, yet something lend,   30
So I shall still my suite commend,
And you at will doe lesse or more.
    But, if to all you condescend,
    My love, our sport, your Godhead end.

Song.   13 witt] will, *1635–54*   14 They, *1635–69:* Those
one MS.   26 Love *MSS.:* selves *1635–69*

To

To Ben. Johnson, 6 Jan. 1603.

THe State and mens affaires are the best playes
   Next yours; 'Tis nor more nor lesse than due praise.
Write, but touch not the much descending race
Of Lords houses, so settled in worths place,
As but themselves none thinke them usurpers.   5
It is no fault in thee to suffer theirs.
If the Queene Masque, or King a hunting goe,
Though all the Court follow, Let them. We know
Like them in goodnesse that Court ne'r will be,
For that were vertue, and not flatterie.   10
Forget we were thrust out; It is but thus,
God threatens Kings, Kings Lords, as Lords doe us.
Judge of strangers, Trust and believe your friend,
And so me; And when I true friendship end,
With guilty conscience let me be worse stonge,   15
Then with *Pophams* sentence theeves, or *Cookes* tongue
Traitors are. Friends are our selves. This I thee tell
As to my friend, and to my selfe as Counsell;
Let for a while the times unthrifty rout
Contemne learning, and all your studies flout.   20
Let them scorne Hell, they will a Sergeant feare,
More then wee *that*; ere long God may forbeare,
But Creditors will not. Let them increase
In riot and excesse as their meanes cease;
Let them scorne him that made them, and still shun   25
His Grace, but love the whore who hath undone
Them and their soules. But; that they that allow
But one God, should have religions enow
For the Queens Masque, and their husbands, far more

To Ben. Johnson, 6 Ian. 1603.   22 More then wee *that*; *Ed:*
More then wee that *MSS.:* More then wee them; that, *1635–69*
(them *in ital. 1635–54*)   28 enow *MSS.:* enough *1635–69*   29
far *one MS.:* for *1635–69 and one MS.*

Then

Then all the Gentiles knew, or *Atlas* bore! 30
Well, let all passe, and trust him who nor cracks
The bruised Reed, nor quencheth smoking flaxe.

To Ben. Johnson, 9. Novembris, 1603.

IF great men wrong me, I will spare my selfe;
If meane, I will spare them. I know that pelf
Which is ill got the Owner doth upbraid.
It may corrupt a Judge, make me afraid
And a Jury; But 'twill revenge in this, 5
That, though himselfe be judge, hee guilty is.
What care I though of weaknesse men taxe me,
I had rather sufferer than doer be.
That I did trust, it was my Natures praise,
For breach of word I knew but as a phrase. 10
That judgement is, that surely can comprise
The world in precepts, most happy and most wise.
What though? Though lesse, yet some of both have we,
Who have learn'd it by use and misery.
Poore I, whom every pety crosse doth trouble, 15
Who apprehend each hurt thats done me, double,
Am of this (though it should sinke me) carelesse,
It would but force me to a stricter goodnesse.
They have great odds of me, who gaine doe winne,
(If such gaine be not losse) from every sinne. 20
The standing of great mens lives would afford
A pretty summe, if God would sell his Word.
He cannot; they can theirs, and breake them too.
How unlike they are that they are likened to?
Yet I conclude, they are amidst my evils, 25
If good, like Gods, the naught are so like devils.

> To Ben Johnson, 9. Novembris, 1603   2 that *MSS.:* the
> *1635–69*   19 odds *MSS.*   gaine *1635–69*

To

To Sr Tho. Rowe. 1603.

Deare Thom:

TEll her if she to hired servants shew
   Dislike, before they take their leave they goe;
When nobler spirits start at no disgrace,
For who hath but one minde, hath but one face:
If then why I tooke not my leave she aske,   5
Aske her againe why she did not unmaske?
Was she or proud or cruell, or knew shee
'Twould make my losse more felt, and pittyed me?
Or did she feare one kisse might stay for moe?
Or else was she unwilling I should goe?   10
I thinke the best, and love so faithfully
I cannot chuse but thinke that she loves mee.
If this prove not my faith, then let her trie
How in her service I would fructifie.
Ladies have boldly lov'd; bid her renew   15
That decay'd worth, and prove the times past true.
Then he whose wit and verse goes now so lame,
With songs to her will the wild Irish tame.
Howe'r, I'll weare the black and white ribband,
White for her fortunes, blacke for mine shall stand.   20
I doe esteeme her favours, not their stuffe;
If what I have was given, I have enough:
And all's well; for had she lov'd, I had had
All my friends hate; for now, departing sad
I feele not that; Yet as the Rack the Gout   25
Cures, so hath *this* worse griefe *that* quite put out:
My first disease nought but that worse cureth,
Which (which I dare foresee) nought cures but death.

To Sir Tho. Rowe. 1603. *1635–69:* An Elegie, complayning a
want of complement in his mistrisse, at his leave-taking. *one MS.*
5 tooke *MSS.:* take *1635–69*   14 I would *1635–69:* it will *some
MSS.*   21 favours, not their *MSS.:* favour, not the *1635–69*   23 had
had *MSS.:* had not had *1635–69 and one MS.*   28 Which (which I
dare foresee) nought *MSS.:* Which (I dare foresay) nothing *1635–69*

Tell her all this before I am forgot,
That not too late shee grieve shee lov'd me not.   30
    Burden'd with this, I was to depart lesse
    Willing, then those which die, and not confesse.

II.

Elegie.

DEath be not proud, thy hand gave not this blow,
    Sinne was her captive, whence thy power doth flow;
The executioner of wrath thou art,
But to destroy the just is not thy part.
Thy comming, terrour, anguish, griefe denounce;   5
Her happy state, courage, ease, joy pronounce.
From out the Christall palace of her breast,
The clearer soule was call'd to endlesse rest,
(Not by the thundering voyce, wherewith God threats,
But, as with crowned Saints in heaven he treats,)   10
And, waited on by Angels, home was brought,
To joy that it through many dangers sought;
The key of mercy gently did unlocke
The doores 'twixt heaven and it, when life did knock.
    Nor boast, the fairest frame was made thy prey,   15
Because to mortall eyes it did decay;
A better witnesse than thou art, assures,
That though dissolv'd, it yet a space endures;
No dramme thereof shall want or losse sustaine,
When her best soule inhabits it again.   20
Goe then to people curst before they were,
Their spoyles in Triumph of thy conquest weare.
Glory not thou thy selfe in these hot teares
Which our face, not for hers, but our harme weares,

Elegie. *Ed:* Elegye on the Lady Markham. By L. C. of B. *one MS.: do.* By C. L. of B. *another MS.:* Elegie on Mistris Boulstred. *1635–69: given as continuation of* Death I recant &c. *some MSS.*   22
spoyles ... of ... weare. *MSS.:* soules ... to ... beare, *1635–69*

The

The mourning livery given by Grace, not thee,　　　25
Which wils our soules in these streams washt should be,
And on our hearts, her memories best tombe,
In this her Epitaph doth write thy doome.
Blinde were those eyes, saw not how bright did shine
Through fleshes misty vaile the beames divine.　　　30
Dcafe were the eares, not charm'd with that sweet sound
Which did i'th spirit-instructed voice abound.
Of flint the conscience, did not yeeld and melt,
At what in her last Act it saw, heard, felt.

Weep not, nor grudge then, to have lost her sight,　35
Taught thus, our after stay's but a short night:
But by all soules not by corruption choaked
Let in high rais'd notes that power be invoked.
Calme the rough seas, by which she sayles to rest,
From sorrowes here, to a kingdome ever blest;　　　40
And teach this hymne of her with joy, and sing,
　　The grave no conquest gets, Death hath no sting.

III.

Absence.

That time and absence proves
Rather helps than hurts to loves.

Probably by John Hoskins.

ABsence heare my protestation
　　　Against thy strengthe
　　　Distance and lengthe,
Doe what thou canst for alteration:

34 saw, heard, felt. *MSS.* : saw and felt. *1635–69*　　39 she sayles
1635–69: shee's sayl'd *some MSS.* : shee's fled *other MSS.*　　41 And
preach this Hymn which hers (*or* she) with joy did sing, *some MSS.*
　　Absence. *The Grove (1721): do. or no title, several MSS.* : *also
in* Davison's Poetical Rhapsody (*PR*) *1602 and (a maimed and altered
version) in* Wit Restored (*WR*) *1658*　　1 heare *some MSS. and Grove:*
heare thou *most MSS.*　　3 Distance] Disdayne *one MS.*　　4 you
can *PR:* yee dare *one MS.*

　　　　　　　　　　　　　　　　　　　For

For harts of truest mettall   5
Absence doth joyne, and time doth settle.

Who loves a Mistris of right quality,
His mind hath founde
Affections grounde
Beyond time, place, and all mortality: 10
To harts that cannot vary
Absence is present, time doth tary:

My Sences want their outward motion
Which now within
Reason doth win,   15
Redoubled by her secret notion:
Like rich men that take pleasure
In hidinge more then handling treasure.

By absence this good means I gaine
That I can catch her   20
Where none can watch her
In some close corner of my braine:
There I embrace and there kiss her,
And so enjoye her, and so misse her.

5 For hearts where love's refined *WR*   6 Are absent joyned,
by tyme combined. *WR*   7 right *one MS. :* such *Grove and some
MSS.*   8 He soon hath found *PR*   12 present] presence *one MS.*
13 motion] motions *PR*   16 by . . . notion:] in . . . notions: *PR.·* in
. . . notion *MS.*   18 hidinge] finding *Grove*   23 There I embrace
and there kiss her, *one MS. :* There I embrace her, and *&c. one MS. :*
There I embrace and there I kiss her, *several MSS. :* There I embrace
and kiss her, *Grove and some MSS.*   24 and so misse her *all MSS. :*
while none misse her. *Grove:* I both enjoy and miss her. *PR*

IV.

IV.

Song.

Probably by the Earl of Pembroke.

SOules joy, now I am gone,
  And you alone,
   (Which cannot be,
Since I must leave my selfe with thee,
  And carry thee with me)   5
  Yet when unto our eyes
   Absence denyes
   Each others sight,
And makes to us a constant night,
  When others change to light;   10
   O give no way to griefe,
   But let beliefe
    Of mutuall love,
   This wonder to the vulgar prove
    Our Bodyes, not wee move.   15

Let not thy wit beweepe
  Wounds but sense-deepe,
   For when we misse
By distance our lipp-joyning blisse,
  Even then our soules shall kisse.   20
  Fooles have no meanes to meet,
   But by their feet.
   Why should our clay,
Over our spirits so much sway,
  To tie us to that way?   25
   O give no way to griefe, &c.

Song. *1635–69: also in the* Poems &c. *(1660) of the Earle of Pembroke and Sr Benjamin Ruddier, and the Lansdowne MS.* 777, *where it is signed* E. of Pembroke.   1 now] *when 1660, Lansd. MS.* 19 lipp-joyning *one MS.:* hopes joyning *1635–69*

            A Dialogue.

A Dialogue.

EARLE OF PEMBROKE.

IF her disdaine least change in you can move,
>> you doe not love,
For whilst your hopes give fuell to the fire,
>> you sell desire.
>>> Love is not love, but given free, 5
>>> And so is mine, so should yours bee.

Her heart that melts at others moane,
>> to mine is stone.
Her eyes that weepe a strangers hurt to see,
>> joy to wound mee: 10
>>> Yet I so much affect each part,
>>> As (caus'd by them) I love my smart.

Say her disdaynings justly must be grac't
>> with name of chaste.
And that shee frownes least longing should exceed, 15
>> and raging breed;
>>> Soe can her rigor ne'er offend
>>> Unlesse selfe-love seeke private end.

A Dialogue. *Ed:* A Dialogue betweene Sᵣ Henry Wotton and Mᵣ
Donne. *1635–69 among* Letters to Severall Personages: *no heading but
divided between* Earle of Pembroke *and* Ben: Ruddier *some MSS.:
and so between* P *and* R *in the* Poems &c. (1660) *of Pembroke and
Ruddier: in one MS. the first part is given to* Earl of Pembroke *and*
Sᵣ Henry Wotton, *the second to* Sᵣ Ben. Ruddier *and* Dᵣ John Donne
3 whilst your hopes give *MSS.:* when the hope gives *1635–54:* when
that hope gives *1669* 7 melts at *MSS.:* melts to hear of *1635–69*
9 hurt *MSS.:* eyes *1635–69 and mod. edd.* 11 much *MSS.:* well
1635–69 17–18 *text MSS.:*
>> So her disdaines can ne'er offend;
>> Vnlesse selfe-love take private end. *1635–69*

BEN:

BEN: RUDDIER

'Tis love breeds love in mee, and cold disdaine
                                    kils that againe,   20
As water causeth fire to fret and fume,
                                    till all consume.
        Who can of love more free gift make,
        Then to loves self, for loves own sake.

I'll never dig in Quarry of an heart   25
                                    to have no part,
Nor roast in fiery eyes, which alwayes are
                                    Canicular.
        Who this way would a Lover prove,
        May shew his patience, not his love.   30

A frowne may be sometimes for physick good,
                                    But not for food;
And for that raging humour there is sure
                                    A gentler Cure.
        Why barre you love of private end,   35
        Which never should to publique tend?

V.
Break of Daye.
Perhaps by John Dowland.

STay, O sweet, and do not rise,
    The light that shines comes from thine eyes;
The day breaks not, it is my heart,
Because that you and I must part.
        Stay, or else my joys will die,   5
        And perish in their infancie.

27 roast 1669, one MS.: rest 1635–54: waste *some MSS.*
    Break of &c.] *Prefixed to Donne's poem (p. 22) in 1669 and one MS.:
given as a separate poem in some MSS.: printed in John Dowland's* A
Pilgrim's Solace (1612)   1 Stay, O sweet] Lie still my dear *MSS.*

APPENDIX C.

APPENDIX C.

A SELECTION OF POEMS WHICH FREQUENTLY ACCOMPANY POEMS BY JOHN DONNE IN MANUSCRIPT COLLECTIONS OR HAVE BEEN ASCRIBED TO DONNE BY MODERN EDITORS.

POEMS FROM ADDITIONAL MSS. 25707.

A Letter written by S H: G: and J: D: alternis*
vicibus.

Since ev'ry Tree begins to blossome now,
Perfuminge and enamelinge each bow,
Hartes should as well as they, some fruits allow.

For since one old poore sunn serves all the rest,
You sev'rall sunns that warme, and light each brest   5
Doe by that influence all your thoughts digest.

And that you two may soe your vertues move,
On better matter then beames from above,
Thus our twin'd souls send forth these buds of love.

As in devotions men Joyne both their hands,   10
Wee make ours doe one Act to seale the bands,
By which we enthrall ourselves to your commands,

And each for others faith and zeale stand bound:
As safe as spirits are from any wound,
Soe free from impure thoughts they shal be found.   15

Admit our magique then by which wee doe
Make you appeere to us, and us to you,
Supplying all the Muses in you twoe.

Wee doe consider noe flower that is sweet,
But wee your breath in that exhaling meet,   20
And as true types of you, them humbly greet.

Heere

Heere in our Nightingales we heere you singe
Who soe doe make the whole yeare through a springe,
And save us from the feare of Autumns stinge.

In Anchors calme face wee your smoothnes see,   25
Your mindes unmingled, and as cleare as shee
That keepes untoucht her first virginitie.

Did all St. Edith nunns descend againe
To honor Polesworth with their cloystred traine,
Compar'd with you each would confesse some stayne. 30

Or should wee more bleed out our thoughts in inke,
Noe paper (though it woulde be glad to drinke
Those drops) could comprehend what wee doe thinke.

For t'were in us ambition to write
Soe, that because wee two, you two unite,   35
Our letter should as you, bee infinite.

O Frutefull Garden.

O Frutefull garden, and yet never tilde,
  Box full of Treasure yet by noe man filde.
O thou which hast made him that first made thee;
O neare of kinne to all the Trinetie;
O Pallace where the kinge of all, and more,   5
Went in, and out, yet never opened doore;
Whose flesh is purer, than an others sperrit,
Reache him our Prayers, and reach us down his merrit;
O bread of lyfe which sweld'ste up without Leaven;
O bridge which joynst togeather earth and heaven; 10
Whose eyes see me through these walles, and throughe
    glasse,
And through this fleshe as thorowe Cipres passe.

25 Anchors *Chambers:* Anchos *MS.*
  O Frutefull Garden. *MS.:* [TO THE BLESSED VIRGIN
MARY.] *Chambers*

Behould

Behould a little harte made greate by thee,
Swellinge, yet shrinkinge at thy majestie.
O dwell in it, for where soe ere thou go'ste   15
There is the Temple of the Holy Ghoste.

To my Lord of Pembroke.

FYe, Fye you sonnes of Pallas what madd rage
    Makes you contend that Love's, or God, or page?
Hee that admires, his weaknes doth confess;
For as Love greater growes; soe hee growes less.
Hee that disdaines, what honor wynns thereby,   5
That he feeles not, or triumphes on a fly?
If love with queasie paine thy stomack move,
Soe will a slutt whome none dare touch; or love.
If it with sacred straines doe thee inspire
Of Poetrie; soe wee maye want admire.   10
If it thee valiant make, his ryvall hate
Can out doe that and make men desperate.
Yealdinge to us, all woemen conquer us,
By gentlenes we are betrayed thus.
We will not strive with Love that's a shee beaste;   15
But playinge wee are bounde, and yeald in Jest;
As in a Cobwebb toyle, a flye hath beene
Undone; so have I some fainte lover seene.
Love cannot take away our strength, but tame,
And wee less feele the thinge then feare the name;   20
Love is a temperate bath; hee that feeles more
Heate or could there, was hott, or could before.
But as Suñ beames which would but norishe, burne,
Drawne into hollow Christall, soe we turne
To fire her bewties Lustre willingly,   25
By gatheringe it in our false treacherous eye.
Love is nor you, nor you; but I a balme,

To my lord &c. 27 I a balme, *MS.:* Aye a calm, *Chambers
conjectures*

Sword

Sword to the stiff, unto the wounded balme.
Prayes noe thinge adds, if it be infinite,
If it be nothing, who can lessen it?　　　　　30

Of a Lady in the Black Masque.

WHy chose shee black; was it that in whitenes
　　Shee did Leda equal? whose brightnes
Must suffer loss to put a bewtie on
Which hath no grace but from proportion.
It is but Coullor, which to loose is gayne,　　　5
For shee in black doth th'Æthiopian staine,
Beinge the forme that beautifies the creature
Her rareness not in Coullor is; but feature.
Black on her receaves soe strong a grace
It seemes the fittest beautie for the face.　　　10
Coullor is not, but in æstimation
Faire, or foule, as it is stild by fashion.
Kinges wearing sackcloath it doth royall make;
Soe black⟨ne⟩s from her face doth beautie take.
It not in Coullor but in her, inheres,　　　15
For what she is, is faire, not what she weares;
The Moore shalle envye her, as much, or more,
As did the Ladies of our Court before.
The Sunn shall mourne that hee had westwarde beene,
To seeke his Love; whilst shee i'th North was seene.　20
Her blacknes lends like lustre to her eyes,
As in the night pale Phoebe glorifyes.
Hell, synne, and vice their attributes shall loose
Of black, for it wan, and pale whitenes choose,
As like themselves, Common, and most in use:　　25
Sad of that Coulor is the late abuse.

Of a Lady &c. MS., *Chambers*　　10 face. *Ed:* face *MS.*　　13
make; *Ed:* make *MS.*　　14 black[ne]s *Chambers:* blacks *MS.*
16 weares; *Ed:* weares, *MS.*

⟨*Farewel,*

⟨*Farewel, ye guilded follies.*⟩

FArewel ye guilded follies, pleasing troubles,
   Farewel ye honour'd rags, ye glorious bubbles;
Fame's but a hollow echo, gold pure clay,
Honour the darling but of one short day.
Beauty (th'eyes idol) but a damasked skin,   5
State but a golden prison, to keepe in
And torture free-born minds; imbroidered trains
Meerly but Pageants, proudly swelling vains,
And blood ally'd to greatness, is a loane
Inherited, not purchased, not our own.   10
   Fame, honor, beauty, state, train, blood and birth,
   Are but the fading blossomes of the earth.

I would be great, but that the Sun doth still
Level his rayes against the rising hill:
I would be high, but see the proudest Oak   15
Most subject to the rending Thunder-stroke;
I would be rich, but see men too unkind
Dig in the bowels of the richest mine;
I would be wise, but that I often see
The Fox suspected whilst the Ass goes free;   20
I would be fair, but see the fair and proud
Like the bright sun, oft setting in a cloud;
I would be poor, but know the humble grass
Still trampled on by each unworthy Asse;
Rich, hated; wise, suspected; scorn'd, if poor;   25
Great, fear'd; fair, tempted; high, stil envied more:
   I have wish'd all, but now I wish for neither,
   Great, high, rich, wise, nor fair, poor I'l be rather.

Would the world now adopt me for her heir,
Would beauties Queen entitle me the Fair,   30
Fame speak me fortune's Minion, could I vie
Angels with India, with a speaking eye

                                            Command

Command bare heads, bow'd knees, strike Justice dumb
As wel as blind and lame, or give a tongue
To stones, by Epitaphs, be called great Master 35
In the loose rhimes of every Poetaster;
Could I be more then any man that lives,
Great, fair, rich, wise in all Superlatives;
Yet I more freely would these gifts resign
Then ever fortune would have made them mine, 40
    And hold one minute of this holy leasure,
    Beyond the riches of this empty pleasure.

Welcom pure thoughts, welcom ye silent groves,
These guests, these Courts, my soul most dearly loves,
Now the wing'd people of the Skie shall sing 45
My cheerful Anthems to the gladsome Spring;
A Pray'r book now shall be my looking-glasse,
Wherein I will adore sweet vertues face.
Here dwell no hateful looks, no Pallace cares,
No broken vows dwell here, nor pale-faced fears, 50
Then here I'l sit and sigh my hot loves folly,
And learn t'affect an holy melancholy.
    And if contentment be a stranger, then
    I'l nere look for it, but in heaven again.

INDEX OF FIRST LINES

The poems marked * *are contained in Appendixes B and C of doubtful or unauthentic poems. Those marked* † *are poems to or on Donne.*

OXFORD

MORE OXFORD PAPERBACKS

Details of a selection of other Oxford Paperbacks follow. A complete list of Oxford Paperbacks, including The World's Classics, Twentieth-Century Classics, OPUS, Past Masters, Oxford Authors, Oxford Shakespeare, and Oxford Paperback Reference, is available in the UK from the General Publicity Department, Oxford University Press (RS), Walton Street, Oxford, OX2 6DP.

In the USA, complete lists are available from the Paperbacks Marketing Manager, Oxford University Press, 200 Madison Avenue, New York, NY 10016.

Oxford Paperbacks are available from all good bookshops. In case of difficulty, customers in the UK can order direct from Oxford University Press Bookshop, 116 High Street, Oxford, Freepost, OX1 4BR, enclosing full payment. Please add 10 per cent of the published price for postage and packing.

THE CONCISE OXFORD DICTIONARY OF ENGLISH LITERATURE

Second Edition

Revised by Dorothy Eagle

This handy and authoritative reference book is essential for anyone who reads and enjoys English literature. It contains concise yet informative entries on English writers from the *Beowulf* poet to Samuel Beckett and W. H. Auden, defines literary movements and genres, and refers the reader to sources for more than a thousand characters from books and plays. It also includes a host of sources of influence on English literary achievement, such as foreign books and writers, art, and major historical events.

The Concise Oxford Dictionary of English Literature is an abridgement of Paul Harvey's classic *Oxford Companion to English Literature*.

Oxford Reference

JACOBEAN TRAGEDIES

The Malcontent; The Revenger's Tragedy; The Atheist's Tragedy; The Changeling; Women Beware Women

Edited by A. H. Gomme

The five plays in this volume date from the reign of James I, the most prolific period of English dramatic writing. They all share an obsession with death, with moral and physical decay, and with sexual passion—combined with a strong sense of sin—which gives them an impressive and sombre force.

METAPHYSICAL LYRICS AND POEMS OF THE SEVENTEENTH CENTURY

Edited by H. J. C. Grierson

This classic anthology, first published in 1921, has been instrumental in reviving interest in the seventeenth-century metaphysical poets and in securing for them the high reputation they now enjoy. Included in this representative selection are love poems, divine poems, elegies, satires, epistles, and meditations by over twenty-five poets. The poems range from Suckling's impish love songs to Donne's holy sonnets, from Marvell's 'The Garden' to George Herbert's 'Easter Wings'. They exemplify the intellectual wit, the learned imagery, the ability to articulate experience, and above all the peculiar blend of passion and thought which characterize metaphysical poetry.

The brilliant essay by Sir Herbert Grierson, who made this selection, serves as an illuminating introduction to this group of poets, and has become a classic piece of criticism.

THIS STAGE-PLAY WORLD

English Literature and its Background, 1580–1625

Julia Briggs

The later years of Elizabeth and the reign of James I produced a dazzling array of literary talent: Shakespeare, Sidney, Spenser, Donne, Marlowe, Jonson, Webster, Bacon, and Burton. Aware that students are often unfamiliar with the social, ideological, religious, and political background to the period, Julia Briggs has drawn on the most up-to-date historical scholarship to set these writers in context.

'lucid and up-to-date . . . particularly sensitive to the problems of relating literature to its background' *Times Literary Supplement*

An OPUS book

THE FORCE OF POETRY

Christopher Ricks

Each of these scintillating essays asks how a poet's words reveal 'the force of poetry', that force—in Dr Johnson's words—'which calls new powers into being, which embodies sentiment, and animates matter'. The poets range from John Gower to Geoffrey Hill, and among them are Marvell, Milton, Johnson, Wordsworth, Beddoes, Housman, Empson, Stevie Smith, Lowell, and Larkin. Concluding the book are four wider essays: on clichés; on lies; on misquotations; and on American English in its relation to the transitory.

'These essays show Christopher Ricks as the closest of close readers, conducting a series of master classes in how to read a poem—a work of enormous brilliance.' Bernard Bergonzi, *Encounter*

'The richness and variety of these essays is truly remarkable.' John Bayley, *Listener*

'Reading Professor Ricks's comments and observations convinces me that he is exactly the kind of critic every poet dreams of finding.' W. H. Auden

THE LIFE OF JOHN MILTON

A. N. Wilson

'the best short life there is' *Standard*

'warmly recommended for its intelligence and readability' *The Times*

'a very wide range of readers will find this book enormously entertaining' *Evening Standard*

Oxford Lives